# THE L.M. MONTGOMERY READER

*Volume 3: A Legacy in Review*

Advertisement for *Rilla of Ingleside*, by L.M. Montgomery,
*The Bookseller and Stationer* (New York, NY),
1 September 1921, inside front cover

# THE
# L.M. MONTGOMERY
# READER

## Volume 3: A Legacy in Review

Edited by Benjamin Lefebvre

UNIVERSITY OF TORONTO PRESS
Toronto Buffalo London

© University of Toronto Press 2015
Toronto  Buffalo  London
www.utppublishing.com
Printed in the U.S.A.

ISBN 978-1-4426-4493-9 (cloth)

Printed on acid-free, 100% post-consumer recycled paper
with vegetable-based inks.

---

**Library and Archives Canada Cataloguing in Publication**

The L.M. Montgomery reader / edited by Benjamin Lefebvre.

Includes bibliographical references and indexes.
Contents: Volume three. A critical heritage.
ISBN 978-1-4426-4493-9 (v. 3 : bound)

1. Montgomery, L.M. (Lucy Maud), 1874–1942 – Criticism and interpretation.
I. Lefebvre, Benjamin, 1977–, editor of compilation.
II. Title: Legacy in review.

PS8526.O55Z63538 2015    C813'.52    C2013-905295-X

---

University of Toronto Press acknowledges the financial assistance to its publishing
program of the Canada Council for the Arts and the Ontario Arts Council,
an agency of the Government of Ontario.

Canada Council    Conseil des Arts
for the Arts      du Canada

**ONTARIO ARTS COUNCIL**
**CONSEIL DES ARTS DE L'ONTARIO**
an Ontario government agency
un organisme du gouvernement de l'Ontario

This book has been published with the help of a grant from the
Canadian Federation for the Humanities and Social Sciences, through the
Awards to Scholarly Publications Program, using funds provided by the
Social Sciences and Humanities Research Council of Canada.

University of Toronto Press acknowledges the financial support of the
Government of Canada through the Canada Book Fund for its publishing activities.

# Contents

Contents

# Acknowledgments

Like the two volumes that precede it, this third and final volume of *The L.M. Montgomery Reader* is indebted to a number of friends and colleagues whose assistance and encouragement over several years of research are greatly appreciated. I am grateful to Vanessa Brown, Mary Beth Cavert, Carolyn Strom Collins, Cecily Devereux, Kelly Norah Drukker, Elizabeth Rollins Epperly, Melanie Fishbane, Carole Gerson, Vappu Kannas, Jennifer H. Litster, Andrea McKenzie, Laura M. Robinson, Mary Henley Rubio, Cynthia Soulliere, Kate Sutherland, Elizabeth Hillman Waterston, Emily Woster, and Lorraine York, as well as to two anonymous referees for their feedback on an earlier draft of the manuscript. Thanks as well to Sarina Annis and Joshua Ginter for their help in tracking down some of these items, and especially to Christy Woster for her generosity in sharing numerous reviews and ads from her own collection.

My thanks as well to several colleagues: Siobhan McMenemy, Frances Mundy, and Ani Deyirmenjian at University of Toronto Press; Kathryn Harvey and Darlene Wiltsie, Archival and Special Collections, University of Guelph Library; Smaro Kamboureli and Karen Bygden, formerly of the TransCanada Institute, University of Guelph; Mark Leggott and Simon Lloyd, University of Prince Edward Island Library; and the staff at the University of Guelph Storage Annex. I gratefully acknowledge the Macdonald Stewart Foundation for supporting the Visiting Scholar position at the L.M. Montgomery Institute, University of Prince Edward Island, which I held between 2009 and 2011, and the 2013

## Acknowledgments

Marie Tremaine Fellowship awarded by the Bibliographical Society of Canada / La Société bibliographique du Canada.

My special thanks are for my partner, Jacob Letkemann, and for my mother, Claire Pelland Lefebvre. I dedicate this volume to the rest of my supportive family: my siblings, Melanie Lefebvre and Jeremy Lefebvre; my siblings-in-law, Éric Lemay and Julie Trépanier; as well as my five nieces and my nephew.

# Abbreviations

The following abbreviations refer to sources attributed to L.M. Montgomery:

AA        *Anne of Avonlea.* 1909. Toronto: Seal Books, 1996.

AfGG      *After Green Gables: L.M. Montgomery's Letters to Ephraim Weber, 1916–1941.* Edited by Hildi Froese Tiessen and Paul Gerard Tiessen. Toronto: University of Toronto Press, 2006.

AGG       *Anne of Green Gables.* 1908. Toronto: Seal Books, 1996.

AHD       *Anne's House of Dreams.* 1917. Toronto: Seal Books, 1996.

AIn       *Anne of Ingleside.* 1939. Toronto: Seal Books, 1996.

AIs       *Anne of the Island.* 1915. Toronto: Seal Books, 1996.

AP        *The Alpine Path: The Story of My Career.* 1917. N.p.: Fitzhenry and Whiteside, n.d.

AWP       *Anne of Windy Poplars.* 1936. Toronto: Seal Books, 1996.

BC        *The Blue Castle.* 1926. Toronto: Seal Books, 1988.

BQ        *The Blythes Are Quoted.* Edited by Benjamin Lefebvre. Toronto: Viking Canada, 2009.

CA        *Chronicles of Avonlea.* 1912. Toronto: Seal Books, 1993.

DSOS      *The Doctor's Sweetheart and Other Stories.* Selected by Catherine McLay. Toronto: McGraw–Hill Ryerson, 1979.

# Abbreviations

| | |
|---|---|
| *EC* | *Emily Climbs*. 1925. Toronto: Seal Books, 1998. |
| *ENM* | *Emily of New Moon*. 1923. Toronto: Seal Books, 1998. |
| *EQ* | *Emily's Quest*. 1927. Toronto: Seal Books, 1998. |
| *GGL* | *The Green Gables Letters from L.M. Montgomery to Ephraim Weber, 1905–1909*. Edited by Wilfrid Eggleston. Toronto: The Ryerson Press, 1960. |
| *GR* | *The Golden Road*. 1913. Toronto: Seal Books, 1987. |
| *JLH* | *Jane of Lantern Hill*. 1937. Toronto: Seal Books, 1993. |
| *KO* | *Kilmeny of the Orchard*. 1910. Toronto: Seal Books, 1987. |
| *MDMM* | *My Dear Mr. M: Letters to G.B. MacMillan from L.M. Montgomery*. Edited by Francis W.P. Bolger and Elizabeth R. Epperly. Toronto: McGraw–Hill Ryerson, 1980. |
| *MM* | *Magic for Marigold*. 1929. Toronto: Seal Books, 1988. |
| *MP* | *Mistress Pat*. 1935. Toronto: Seal Books, 1988. |
| *RI* | *Rilla of Ingleside*. 1921. Edited by Benjamin Lefebvre and Andrea McKenzie. Toronto: Viking Canada, 2010. |
| *RV* | *Rainbow Valley*. 1919. Toronto: Seal Books, 1996. |
| *RY* | *The Road to Yesterday*. Toronto: McGraw–Hill Ryerson, 1974. |
| *SG* | *The Story Girl*. 1911. Toronto: Seal Books, 1987. |
| *SJLMM* | *The Selected Journals of L.M. Montgomery*, Volume 1: *1889–1910*; Volume 2: *1910–1921*; Volume 3: *1921–1929*; Volume 4: *1929–1935*; Volume 5: *1935–1942*. Edited by Mary Rubio and Elizabeth Waterston. Toronto: Oxford University Press, 1985, 1987, 1992, 1998, 2004. |
| *SR* | "Scrapbook of Reviews from Around the World Which L.M. Montgomery's Clipping Service Sent to Her, 1910–1935." L.M. Montgomery Collection, University of Guelph archives. |
| *TW* | *A Tangled Web*. 1931. Toronto: Seal Books, 1989. |
| *WOP* | *The Watchman and Other Poems*. Toronto: McClelland, Goodchild, and Stewart, 1916. |

# THE L.M. MONTGOMERY READER

*Volume 3: A Legacy in Review*

# Introduction: A Legacy in Review

BENJAMIN LEFEBVRE

In a journal entry dated 1 March 1930, L.M. Montgomery (1874–1942) culled from her scrapbook of newspaper clippings extracts from reviews of her books in the popular press. Her list of contradictory quotations was so extensive – as Montgomery biographer Mary Henley Rubio notes, the project of assembling them "must have taken days" – that only selections are included in the corresponding volume of *The Selected Journals of L.M. Montgomery*, published in 1998. Montgomery did not identify the source of any of these quotations, but the act of compiling these "slaps and caresses" offered the journal's posthumous readers a rare glimpse at the ways in which reviewers had responded to her books throughout her career. Moreover, although she had been publishing numerous short stories, serials, and poems in North American periodicals as early as 1890, it was only after the publication of *Anne of Green Gables* in 1908 that she began to experience this form of critical attention toward her work – or, as she phrased it in this 1930 journal entry, "*Green Gables* of course began it."[1]

By 1930, Montgomery was in a position to take stock of her career retroactively, secure in her position as an author whose books had remained popular with readers for over two decades; she had even discovered a year and a half earlier that the market for her more recent books was being undercut not by new trends and fads but by the continued high sales of her early work. But in 1908, upon the publication of her first book, she confided in her correspondent Ephraim Weber that she doubted it would receive much attention from reviewers at all, assuming that they "don't often take account of such small fry as juvenile books." In a later letter to him, she revealed that she had received sixty reviews from her clipping service within three months of the book's publication, most of which were overwhelmingly positive.[2] She pasted these reviews in scrapbooks along with news items, copies of numerous essays and interviews, and coverage of stage and screen adaptations of her work as a personal record (one that would benefit future researchers and readers), but except for fewer than a dozen reviews reprinted in critical editions of *Anne of Green Gables* as evidence of the novel's critical reception, they have remained a neglected part of the conversation about Montgomery's work and how it was received in mainstream print media. As this volume shows, these reviews are a treasure trove of questions and insights about genre, setting, character, audience, and nationalism that anticipate the scholarly debates that continue in the twenty-first century.

The first two volumes of *The L.M. Montgomery Reader* offer an exhaustive account of Montgomery's evolving critical reception and literary reputation from the publication of *Anne of Green Gables* to the present day, including not only trends and turning points in Montgomery's publishing history and the construction of a canon of Canadian literature but also the evolution of Canadian literary criticism and the emergence of the international and interdisciplinary field of L.M. Montgomery Studies. Volume 1, *A Life in Print*, collects eighty-one items from the popular press and elsewhere, including Montgomery's own attempts to participate in the dissemination of information about her life and career in the form of essays, interviews, and letters, as well as commentary on her work, ending two years after her death. Volume 2, *A Critical Heritage*, picks up these threads by placing twenty samples from the field of Montgomery Studies, originally published between 1966 and 2012, in the context of L.M. Montgomery's posthumous life. This third volume, subtitled *A Legacy in Review*, looks at the coverage Montgomery's books have received in these reviews in the context of ads, notices, and bestseller lists appearing in print media dedicated to supporting the book industry.

As a concise evaluation of a book's strengths and weaknesses, a book review can offer a spontaneous response to a work (one that is less easily influenced by the opinion of past critics or readers) and also give a sense of the periodical and the time in which it was published. While book reviews are undervalued as a form of literary criticism, they are designed to engage and influence the larger reading public in ways that more sustained scholarship, addressing a much smaller readership, does not.

Moreover, because the reviews collected here hail not only from Canada and the United States but also the United Kingdom, Cuba, India, South Africa, Australia, and New Zealand, this volume offers a unique account of Montgomery's international reception in the English-speaking world since the publication of *Anne of Green Gables*. Montgomery expressed ambivalence about the "series of contradictions" inherent in these reviews, stating in a 1939 letter to Weber that "I gave up trying to fathom the mentality of reviewers years ago. My literary scrapbooks of thirty years make very amusing reading now."[3] On occasion she also recorded in these scrapbooks moments of resistance in ink, determined to have the last word in this unique record of her career.

The materials included here were collected by means of three streams of research. First, I attempted to obtain copies of the previously known reviews of the books published in Montgomery's lifetime, including the 104 English-language reviews listed in Russell, Russell, and Wilmshurst's *Lucy Maud Montgomery: A Preliminary Bibliography* (1986) and the eleven reviews reprinted in critical editions of *Anne of Green Gables*, including *The Annotated Anne of Green Gables* (1997), edited by Wendy E. Barry, Margaret Anne Doody, and Mary E. Doody Jones; a Broadview edition (2004), edited by Cecily Devereux; and a Norton edition (2007), edited by Mary Henley Rubio and Elizabeth Waterston. From there, I consulted print indexes of old magazines and, on many occasions, sat in libraries combing through back issues of newspapers and magazines in hard copy or on microfilm. Second, I searched for all of Montgomery's book titles on digital and text-searchable repositories such as Google News, ProQuest, Archive.org, HathiTrust, the Library of Congress, Newspaper Archive, and Genealogy Bank, which yielded hundreds of PDFs that had to be downloaded, sorted, catalogued, and transcribed. And third, I read through and transcribed what the University of Guelph Library has catalogued as Montgomery's "Scrapbook of Reviews from Around the World Which L.M. Montgomery's Clipping Service Sent to Her, 1910–1935." Doing so generated leads for even more reviews: for instance, a single review in *Vogue* in Montgomery's scrapbook led me to that magazine's online archive, where I found reviews of four more of her books. As well, colleagues who have also been tracking down periodical pieces related to Montgomery have sent me many of their findings as well as additional leads. I have lost track of how many reviews I have located in total, but this volume includes a representative sample of 370 of them. Needless to say, there is no limit to the number of reviews and ads that were published during Montgomery's lifetime.

Indeed, even more so than Volume 1 of *The L.M. Montgomery Reader*, this third volume is much indebted to Montgomery's "Scrapbook of Reviews." This hardcover book, signed "L.M. Montgomery Macdonald" above the date 10 January 1912, consists of six hundred unlined pages, of which 473 are filled with the most comprehensive available account of Montgomery's reception as a novelist. Most of the items were sent to her by a number of clipping services, including Henry Romeike of New York ("The First Established and Most Complete Newspaper Cutting Bureau in the World"), the International Press-Cutting Bureau of London, and the Woolgar and Roberts' Press Cutting, Printing, and Advertising Agency of London, which typically included with each clipping a card identifying the periodical name and publication date (but not the page number). Several clippings, particularly the earliest ones, apparently originated elsewhere; sometimes these are identified in Montgomery's hand with incomplete bibliographical information, and sometimes they have no identifying information at all. The 1912 date inscribed in her hand on the flyleaf indicates that Montgomery began this scrapbook three months after arriving in Leaskdale, Ontario, as a Presbyterian minister's wife, but the first reviews pasted into the scrapbook are of her third novel, *Kilmeny of the Orchard*, released in April 1910. The last clippings pasted onto scrapbook pages are from 1935, but tucked inside the scrapbook were two dozen or so additional clippings of reviews of her final three books, which she evidently had not had a chance to paste inside. Montgomery mentioned earlier clippings in her journal entry dated 1930, but these seem to have been collected in a different scrapbook that has gone astray.

What do these reviews reveal about past assessments of Montgomery's career and legacy? Plenty. An unidentified clipping from around 1923 states that "every critic in the English-speaking world heaps abuse on L.M. Montgomery, Gene Stratton-Porter, Harold Bell Wright and Ethel M. Dell, and 'everybody' reads these authors," but as this volume shows, only the second of the two statements is true.[4] Most of the reviews of all twenty-four of her books published in her lifetime, from *Anne of Green Gables* to *Anne of Ingleside*, were overwhelmingly positive, and most – though certainly not all – reviewers either took for granted that Montgomery's fiction was intended for adults or actively wrote against any impression that it might be otherwise. A second clipping from this period argued that "though L.M. Montgomery's books happen to make excellent fiction for girls, we believe it is a mistake to treat them as juveniles, or to place copies on the young people's shelves only. They are written for adults and as far as our own experience shows have had their greatest popularity as adult fiction." A 1929 clipping in the *New York Tribune* extended that argument, confessing that "whether they are to be classed as juvenile or adult, new or old style, we have an incurable weakness for the books of L.M. Montgomery."[5] This recurring question about target audience and genre is not particularly surprising – it appeared throughout the materials collected in Volumes 1 and 2 of *The L.M. Montgomery Reader* – but the continued blurring of the boundary between adult fiction and children's literature demonstrates that Montgomery's fictional worlds have always been interpreted as appropriate for readers of all ages and circumstances. An unidentified clipping from around 1914, for instance, reveals the response from an adult reader living in Prince Edward Island: "I like *Anne of Green Gables*, by L.M. Montgomery, because of the vivid way she tells of the beauties of our Island. I am an invalid, and when reading her word pictures of fields and woods, I forget for a while that I am a shut-in. I love children, and find the children in Miss Montgomery's books very charming."[6]

Such a perspective may be surprising, given that Montgomery's books are now assumed to be part of children's literature exclusively – at least according to where they are shelved in most bookstores and libraries, as opposed to the focus of much of the recent scholarship. But although Montgomery famously downplayed *Anne of Green Gables* as "a simple little tale, written ... with a juvenile audience in view" as a way to cope with the runaway success of the book and the early pressures of literary celebrity, such a perception did not occur to most of the earliest reviewers. Beginning with the first known review of *Anne of Green Gables* in the *New York Times Saturday Review* (included in full in this volume), the impression that Anne was a role model for actual girls to emulate was not found in most of these earliest contributions to the conversation. Indeed, when these reviews made any mention of a target audience, it was to celebrate the fact that these examples of adult fiction could be made accessible to children – or as the *New York Observer* claimed of *Anne of Green Gables* in December 1908, "Boys and girls will enjoy this book as much as their elders, for Anne appeals to all ages."[7] Only in the 1920s did this general pattern begin to shift, from adult books that could also be enjoyed by children to children's books that could also be enjoyed by adults. This shift is important, because the distinction between "adult fiction" and "children's literature" pertains not only to perceived audience but also to the conventions of genre: after all, Anne as a character reads entirely differently if she is assumed to be a role model for actual girls than if she is an embodiment of childhood exuberance for the entertainment of adults. Moreover, the fact that these reviews were inconsistent about this distinction throughout Montgomery's career indicates that the matter was far from settled in her lifetime – just as it continues to be debated today.

Indeed, the most unexpected revelation in these reviews has to do with Montgomery's popularity: although the sales figures of her books clearly indicate that they have always been popular with readers, reviewers took a different tack in terms of Montgomery's relationship with the popular fiction of her day. As the *Whit Weekly* of Kingston, Ontario, noted in its review of *Anne of the Island* (1915), "In these days when so many books deal with the sex problem, or drag their impossible characters through unseemly adventures 'in search of their souls,' it is a relief and a delight to find such a book as this – simple, wholesome and altogether beautiful." To this the *Philadelphia Record* added, in a review of *Anne's House of Dreams*, "The book is so far above the modern love story that one scarcely knows what not to say, lest the reader be defrauded when she possesses the treasure ... By such stories as Miss Montgomery's the world's faith in humanity is relighted, for without an occasional book of this sort one is too apt to drift into the open Sea of Doubt." An unidentified clipping entitled "What Do 'Flappers' Read?" claimed that "there are few adequate books supplied for the flapper age, but L.M. Montgomery provides a novel that succeeds in being at once wholesome and to the flapper taste in *Rilla of Ingleside* ... a novel of young people who are up to the times but a delightful contrast to the over-slangy, rebellious type we are getting tired of."[8]

And so, although the continually strong sales of her books have indicated their ongoing appeal to readers of all ages, Montgomery's work was celebrated by reviewers during her lifetime for its ability to appeal differently yet simultaneously to adults and to children and for providing refreshing alternatives to the trends and tropes that were then in vogue: instead of writing about flappers, modernity, "sex problems," high society, changes in technology, and the fast pace of urban life, Montgomery's fiction was seen not as mainstream but as going against the grain of popular fiction. Moreover, a good many of these reviewers predicted – rightly, as time has shown – that her books would last far longer than those of most of her contemporaries. In August 1911, in the *Greensboro Daily News* of North Carolina, an ad for the Wills Book and Stationer Company declared that "these books, by Miss L.M. Montgomery, have taken a place as books of permanent value and not fiction of a day."[9]

This praise was not only unqualified but also international, as revealed in a review of *Rainbow Valley* in the John O'Groats *Journal* in Scotland:

> There are few writers who get such a hold on their readers. The spontaneous humour and sunshiny philosophy of her books banish care for the moment, and, lightly written as her books seem to be, there is marked ability in always maintaining the interest of the story at its highest pitch. After all, it is difficult to write a story about young people which will appeal to the mature tastes of grown-ups. How this is done is Miss Montgomery's secret. *Anne of Green Gables* was, on its first appearance, regarded with suspicion as being merely a girl's book, but before two months had passed it was the treasured possession of countless grandfathers and grandmothers ... [*Rainbow Valley*] is a book that can be read with pleasure by young and old alike. Its mingling of pathos and humour, and its healthy contempt for undue sentimentality, mark it out from its fellows as something quite out of the common.[10]

As this review makes clear, the comments about Montgomery's particular brand of storytelling began with *Anne of Green Gables*, the book that established her popularity, her literary reputation, and the benchmark against which all her subsequent work would be measured. Moreover, reviewers' perceptions about her work did not always mesh with Montgomery's private opinions or with her own creative process.

### "A Story of Character": *Anne of Green Gables*, 1908

Although Montgomery initially claimed to know "absolutely nothing" about her first publisher, L.C. Page and Company of Boston, she revealed to Weber three months after the publication of *Anne of Green Gables* that Page and his staff "seem[ed] to be pushing the advertising well."[11] What she was perhaps unaware of was that Page's marketing strategy had actually begun several months before the publication of the novel on 13 June 1908. The earliest mention of the book I have found to date is in the 29 February 1908 issue of the New York periodical *The Publishers' Weekly* – at the time subtitled *The American Book Trade Journal* – announcing the forthcoming publication by Page of "a story of character by L.M. Montgomery, another new writer of promise, to be called *Anne of Green Gables*." In another notice in mid-March, the same periodical referred to the novel – at the time with publication planned for April – as one that "promises to have as a heroine one of the most delightful and original girl characters in fiction since Mrs. Wiggin's charming Rebecca made her bow to the reading world" – the first of numerous comparisons with *Rebecca of Sunnybrook Farm* (1903), a novel by American author and educator Kate Douglas Wiggin (1856–1923). In the next week's issue, an ad announcing Page's spring publications promised that "every one, young or old, who reads the story of 'Anne of Green Gables' will fall in love with her, and tell their friends of her irresistible charm. In her creation of the young heroine of this delightful tale Miss Montgomery will receive praise for her fine sympathy with and delicate appreciation of sensitive and imaginative girlhood" – claims that would be repeated in two more ads in the weeks to come. And finally, on the day of its publication on 13 June 1908, the lead notice in the "Notes in Season" column claimed the novel was "said to be delightful in a way that is different from the usual ways in which we experience that emotion," and an ad for the novel took up the entire front cover:

In *Anne of Green Gables* we believe that we have discovered another "Rebecca."

Anne is one of the most original heroines in recent fiction, and every one, young or old, who reads her story will fall in love with her, and tell their friends of her irresistible charm. The quaint sayings of Anne are the sort one person repeats to another until they become household words.

Several impartial critics who read advance proofs have prophesied that *Anne* is to be the "leading lady" of the book world of 1908. One of these, Mr. Temple Scott, says:

"*Anne of Green Gables* is one of the most delightful books we have read since many a day. It is delightful in a way that is different from the usual ways in which we experience that emotion ... As for Anne herself, she is a gem, even with her red hair and freckles. We should dearly have enjoyed Anne Shirley in the flesh."

*Instead of the question "How Old is Anne?" you can with perfect propriety ask your customer, "Have you read Anne – Anne of Green Gables?"*[12]

As evidence of Page's skill and determination as a publisher, consider that all of these ads and notices appeared before the book was even published and in the pages of a single periodical that catered to the book industry. Montgomery's initial contract may have been for "ANNE OF GREEN GABLES A JUVENILE STORY," but Page seemed uninterested in marketing the book as a juvenile title. Many more notices appeared elsewhere: in mid-March, the *New York Times* announced the book as one that "will be read both by children and parents," claiming that its title heroine "is as voluble as Rebecca, but less startling in her projects, although quite as amazing in her misfortunes"; a month later, this periodical referred to the novel as Montgomery's "delightful romance of young girlhood." In its lists of books about to be published by the Page Company, the Chicago magazine *The Dial* listed *Anne of Green Gables* under "Fiction" rather than under "Books for the Young," whereas *The Bookseller, Newsdealer and Stationer* described it as follows: "Farm life is the background for 'Anne,' who is adopted by a farmer and his crabbed spinster sister." In mid-June, as part of its "Items of Interest" column, this periodical explained that the novel "has been delayed over a month beyond the date originally announced, due to the difficulty the publishers found in securing an attractive cover design. On the cover finally selected appears a charming girl's head by George Gibbs, reproduced in colors." Also commenting on the cover art, the *New York Times* added that Gibbs's portrait "really resembles the pleasing girl of the text, and does not look like all the other pretty girls on the book covers of 1908." Coverage for this novel persisted even after the book's release. Two weeks after its publication, the *Boston Herald* listed "Mrs. Montgomery's 'Anne of Green Gables'" as one of two recent novels "in demand for second editions," and of Montgomery's, "the Messrs. Page found themselves bereft 10 days after the first issue." In the August 1908 issue of the New York *Bookman*, a new ad for *Anne of Green Gables* repeated the earlier statement promising that all readers would fall in love with the title protagonist and added a second paragraph, as though to increase the appeal of adult readers, drawing from an ad that appeared at the back of the first edition of the book: "The story would take rank for the character of Anne alone; but in the delineation of the characters of the old farmer and his crabbed, dried-up spinster sister, who adopt her, the author has shown an insight and descriptive power which add much to the fascination of the book." Finally, later that month the Toronto *Globe* published an ad proclaiming the novel to be "The Brightest Book of the Year," a week after its own glowing review (reproduced in its entirety in this volume), adding, "Once more a Canadian scores a great success in the world of letters. [The novel] entered the world of fiction unheralded less than two months ago. The critics and the reading public, however, were not slow to discover ANNE's ability to amuse and entertain, and already two large editions have been exhausted."[13]

In the months that followed, Page's marketing machine ensured continuous coverage of every reprinting, and as shown in Volume 1 of *The L.M. Montgomery Reader*, later ads included celebrity endorsements by Mark Twain, Bliss Carman, and several others. As well, the novel remained visible to the public every time it appeared on a list of best sellers: in mid-March 1909, an ad in the *Boston Herald* boasted of the novel's positioning "among the six best sellers in Boston for sixteen successive weeks" and "among the best sellers in the United States for the past six months," asking its target reader the daring question: "Have You Read It?" In June 1909, the New York *Bookman* noted that while the novel had appeared infrequently on lists of the top six best sellers in cities across the United States in the year since its publication, it "has attracted attention by the persistence with which it has been knocking at the door. It is the only book still a contender in the race for popularity that dates back to the end of last summer. One secret of this success is that it has an appeal both as fiction for adults and as a juvenile."[14] But such a statement provides only a partial account of the placement of *Anne of Green Gables* in the monthly best-seller lists included in the pages of the *Bookman*, which tracked the six top sellers in forty or so American cities (as well as a single Canadian city, Toronto). It is accurate to state that, during its first year of publication, *Anne of Green Gables* was listed sporadically yet persistently as a best-seller in a number of places – mid-sized cities such as Cincinnati, Pittsburgh, Baltimore, and Cleveland much more frequently than a metropolis such as New York or Boston. But while the novel appeared in these monthly lists twenty-five times over its first seven months of publication, by February 1909 the addition of a separate category for juvenile books led to an unusual trend, in that *Anne of Green Gables* was tracked on the best-seller lists for adult fiction in some cities but as a juvenile book in others. By June 1909, it was appearing exclusively on a list of juvenile best-sellers: in first place in Baltimore, Indianapolis, Kansas City (Missouri), New Orleans, Philadelphia, Portland (Oregon), St. Paul, Toronto, and Worcester (Massachusetts), and in second place in New York City (Uptown), Minneapolis, and Toledo.[15] This confusion about whether *Anne of Green Gables* was for adults or for children was noticed by the *New York Times* and persisted elsewhere as well, including in two ads in the same issue of the *Los Angeles Sunday Times* in mid-December 1908: in a "Departmentized Index of Desirable Holiday

Books Obtainable in Los Angeles," *Anne of Green Gables* is listed under "Fiction" rather than "Juveniles," yet in an ad for Bullock's department store, the novel appears under "Books that always have been and always will be ideal gifts for girls."[16]

A similar response greeted the novel's publication in Great Britain. Although Russell, Russell, and Wilmshurst's bibliography notes that the original British edition, published by Sir Isaac Pitman and Sons, bore a copyright date of 1908, a notice in the London *Bookman* suggests that it actually released in January 1909 – although this notice does refer to the novel as "Nune of Green Gables." As the *New York Times* stated in mid-February of that year, noting that a third printing had already been ordered, "Perhaps the book may owe a little of the favor which it has found in Great Britain to its Colonial scene and authorship, but were it not for the mention of Queen's College the story might be taken for an American tale." As a notice in the *Boston Herald* added, the novel "is winning as many lovers in England as in the land of her birth ... The English critics have welcomed the novel with an enthusiasm fully equal to that shown by reviewers in this country." *The Athenaeum*, which had already described the novel as "a story of misunderstanding between a clever, imaginative girl and her homely relatives and friends" and as "the story of an imaginative, talkative, and perplexing child," included an ad that quoted from two reviews, including one from the *Daily Telegraph*: "We feel we have added another real friend to those we have made in fiction ... A piece of work which is quite uncommonly good, as well as thoroughly interesting from the first page to the last." And according to the London *Bookman*, the *World* had given the novel a stunning review:

> It is given to very few writers to be able to tell so simple a tale as this history of the imaginative, precocious, but wholly lovable little Anne in such a thoroughly human and entrancing fashion. It is a book full of laughter and tears, and one ventures to say that it is destined to live as long as "Alice in Wonderland" and "Little Women" and one or two other delightful studies of girlhood ... A book that no one will read and fail to recommend to others. Its charm is of a nature that will endure. It is better to have written one such book as this than to have produced a dozen novels of the ordinary type.[17]

This aggressive amount of coverage would taper off somewhat with Montgomery's subsequent books, at which point advertisers and reviewers would rely more and more on an additional source: Montgomery's own reputation as a novelist, established with this blockbuster first volume, which created what I have called the "Anne brand."[18]

## After *Anne*: 1909–1915

Given how extensively Montgomery's first novel was advertised prior to and immediately after its publication in June 1908, it seems especially curious that there are so few mentions of the novel's planning, composition, progress, and revision in the author's life writing. As the materials collected in Volume 1 of *The L.M. Montgomery Reader* show, Montgomery did, in published essays and letters as well as in interviews, reveal details after the fact about the creative process that remain largely absent in her more private life writing, but as far as the big questions are concerned – such as *when*, *how*, and *why* – she stayed silent. As Cecily Devereux has noted concerning Montgomery's journals, "Montgomery simply did not write about writing *Anne*, prior to its acceptance at any rate." She also waited until after its acceptance before mentioning it to her correspondents – as she explained to Weber, "I didn't squeak a word to anyone about it because I feared desperately I wouldn't find a publisher for it." Given that the few clues given tend to contradict one another, critics have been able only to speculate about the timing of the writing, revision, and submission processes of *Anne of Green Gables*.[19]

Montgomery had been living with her grandmother in Cavendish and writing full-time almost without interruption since 1898, and had been earning a considerable living writing fiction and poetry for North American magazines. As she phrased it in several of the essays included in Volume 1 of *The L.M. Montgomery Reader*, the acceptance of her first novel by L.C. Page and Company meant that her "struggle" as an author had ended; perhaps for that reason, she felt more secure in sharing details of the progress of later books in her journals and letters. Many critics have assumed that the runaway success of *Anne of Green Gables* prompted her to write a sequel, when in fact, according to her journal, Page had requested a sequel with his acceptance of the first book.[20] Moreover, she had apparently brainstormed and outlined her first sequel to *Anne of Green Gables* in the summer of 1907 and had begun drafting it that October. She found the actual writing more difficult, and even the euphoria over the runaway success of *Green Gables* did not dissuade her from her opinion of its sequel. "It is not nearly so good as *Green Gables*," she wrote upon completing the manuscript early in August

1908. To Weber, she related another problem that would continue to dog her in the years to come: "Anne, grown-up, couldn't be made as quaint and unexpected as the child Anne." In March 1909, she mentioned to him that the publication of her new book – which she had wanted to call *The Later Adventures of Anne* but which Page insisted on calling *Anne of Avonlea* – would be delayed until September 1909, in order to avoid undercutting the continued strong sales of its predecessor. And so, although the Toronto *Globe* mentioned on 21 August 1909 that Montgomery had stated in a letter that she "ha[d] been busy in the quiet of her Prince Edward Island home upon her second 'Anne' book," she had in fact, according to a letter to MacMillan, corrected the novel's proofs in May.[21]

Because *Anne of Green Gables* remained a top seller by September 1909, many of the ads for *Anne of Avonlea* ended up promoting both books, some of them with the enticing question "Have You Met Her Yet?" An ad in the *Boston Herald* quoted a review that had appeared in the *Philadelphia Press*: "She's a winsome maid – just 'half-past sixteen,' with red hair and a quick temper. But she is delightful whether she is treading the highways of our workaday world or wandering along an enchanted path into the realm of fancy where even her dearest friends might not follow. Hers is the happy gift of make-believe." An ad in the *Boston Globe* even referred to Anne Shirley – less than fifteen months after her June 1908 debut – as "The Immortal Girl of Fiction." Later ads in the New York *Bookman* verged on the aggressive in their enthusiasm for the character: "'*Get better acquainted with that "ANNE GIRL"*' has been the advice of the entire reading world ever since the charming 'keep-you-a-guessing' *Anne Shirley* came to live at *Green Gables*," raved an ad appearing in the February 1910 issue; in its August 1910 issue, noting that *Anne of Green Gables* was in its eighteenth printing and *Anne of Avonlea* in its eighth, an ad commanded, "If YOU haven't met ANNE yet – get acquainted."[22]

In spite of the incredibly strong reception of the first two Anne books, Montgomery did not contemplate writing a third at this time. She had begun work on *The Story Girl* in June 1909, soon after correcting the proofs for *Anne of Avonlea,* and she evidently intended it to be her next offering to the book-buying public. But its progress was not swift enough for Page, who persuaded her to expand and revise a 23,000-word serial, "Una of the Garden" – which had been published in five instalments in the Minneapolis magazine *The Housekeeper* the preceding winter – into what would become the 40,000-word novel *Kilmeny of the Orchard.* As she explained to MacMillan, she changed the protagonist's name at her publisher's request and substituted an orchard for a garden due to the similarity with Hester Gray's garden in *Anne of Avonlea* (this in spite of the fact that an orchard would figure prominently in *The Story Girl*). In her journal, Montgomery called it "a love story with a psychological interest – very different from my other books and so a rather doubtful experiment with a public who expects a certain style from an author and rather resents having anything else offered it." At the same time, she disliked the process of rewriting the story several times to double its length and expressed indifference when she received her author's copies; writing about it a year later, she noted that it "reflects very little out of my own experience."[23]

At this point in Montgomery's career, the expectations for her third novel were sky-high: as the *Boston Globe* reported in mid-January 1910, "With 16 large editions of *Anne of Green Gables* and seven editions of her later book, *Anne of Avonlea*, already demanded, Miss L.M. Montgomery, that modest Prince Edward Island author, who sprang into prominence in the book world a year and a half ago, is now completing a new story with a new heroine for publication in the summer."[24] Whereas the publication of *Anne of Avonlea* had been delayed because of a fear that it would undercut the continued strong sales of *Anne of Green Gables*, this third novel was published only seven months after the second, in April 1910, with the opposite effect: an ad for the Page Company in *The Bookman* in October 1910 claimed that "the *delightful* and *irresistible* ANNE Books" were "in GREATER DEMAND than ever." Indeed, ads for *Kilmeny* did much to capitalize on the continued sales frenzy of the two Anne books: an ad in the *Boston Globe* called Kilmeny "another unusual heroine who is bound to rival even 'that ANNE girl' in the affections of thousands of readers," whereas one in the *Toronto Daily Star* called the novel "equal, if not better, than the previous books of this celebrated author." Four months after its publication, the *Charlotte Daily Observer* of North Carolina proclaimed that the book was "selling everywhere," adding that "if you have read the other two books by this author you will want to read this one, too. If you have read none of them you have missed a world of pleasant reading matter." Ads in the *Boston Herald* in late September and in the New York edition of *The Bookman* in February 1911 called it "one of the best selling books in the country. Have *you* read it yet?"[25]

After sending off the manuscript of the book to her publisher around New Year's Day in 1910, Montgomery resumed work on the novel whose progress *Kilmeny* had interrupted – an idyll focusing on a group of eight children, aged eleven to fourteen, led by Sara Stanley, known in the PEI community of Carlisle as the Story Girl. At the time, however, she reported that she had made "very poor progress" on the project. "The hours are rare when I am in a mood for creative work and I do not wish to spoil it by working at it when I cannot do my conception of it justice." Nevertheless, when the manuscript was completed in November 1910, she pronounced it "the best piece of work I have yet done. It may not be as popular as *Anne* – somehow I don't fancy it will. But from a literary point of view it is far ahead of it." Yet completing the novel was bittersweet, given her worries about her increasingly frail grandmother.[26]

Whether or not she shared with her publisher her opinion about the high literary quality of this fourth novel, Page certainly used it as a hook for his advertising campaign, which included an ad that appeared in several of his books during this period: "To quote from one of our editor's reports on the new Montgomery book – 'Miss Montgomery has decidedly *arrived* in this story!' The remarkable success of her delightful ANNE books and of the charming *Kilmeny of the Orchard* has established her as one of America's leading authors – a writer of books which touch the heart, uplift the spirit, and leave an imprint of lasting sweetness on the memory. But in *The Story Girl*, everywhere the touch of the *finished* artist is evident – a smoothness and polish which heightens the unusual style of a gifted author."[27] Even prior to the publication of this novel, Montgomery's stature as an enormously successful author was a regular part of the conversation. In Toronto, *The Canadian Courier* declared that Montgomery "is making as much money as any of the women fictionists of the continent." As for intended audience, the *Boston Herald* described it in its announcement as "a plotless story, and, although its principal character is a young girl, it is not a juvenile book. The thought of making it a juvenile book never occurred to the author." In fact, an ad for the Page Company that appeared in the *New York Observer*, the *Boston Globe*, the *Boston Herald*, and the New York *Sun* made no mention of the age of the protagonist, describing her simply as "a heroine to whom has come a rare gift – that of weaving the bright thread of romance out of what the world might call 'commonplaces.'" And in July, an ad in the *Times–Dispatch* of Richmond, Virginia, declared that "*it may be 110 degrees in the shade to-morrow*, but you won't notice it so if you have a copy of that delightful new book ... by the author of *Anne of Green Gables*, and every bit as good a story." Moreover, according to the *Boston*

*Herald*, the publication of the novel in May 1911 had been delayed by "the exigencies of an unusually large first edition, to be simultaneously published in the United States, Canada, Great Britain and Australia."[28]

In March 1911, two months before the publication of *The Story Girl*, Montgomery's grandmother died of pneumonia at the age of eighty-seven. Her grandmother's death freed her to marry Ewan Macdonald, to whom she had been secretly engaged since prior to the acceptance of *Anne of Green Gables* by L.C. Page. That marriage would mean some major changes, including a move to rural Ontario and added responsibilities as the wife of a Presbyterian minister. Within a year of her marriage, she would add to her busy schedule the responsibilities of motherhood. Juggling all these responsibilities as well as her writing would prove to be a challenge, but on one point she was absolutely clear: she would continue to use her maiden name in relation to her writing.[29]

When she understandably could not produce her sequel to *The Story Girl* quickly enough during this year of major life changes, Page asked her to rewrite some of her best short stories for inclusion in a volume that would be called *Chronicles of Avonlea* – a title Montgomery found "somewhat delusive."[30] She later claimed in a letter to MacMillan that she had sent Page far more stories than could be included in a single volume. Indeed, the title page in the first edition of the text announces the volume as "Chronicles of Avonlea / In which Anne Shirley of Green Gables and Avonlea plays some part, and which have to do with other personalities and events, including The Hurrying of Ludovic, Old Lady Lloyd, The Training of Felix, Little Joscelyn, The Winning of Lucinda, Old Man Shaw's Girl, Aunt Olivia's Beau, The Quarantine at Alexander Abraham's, Pa Sloane's Purchase, The Courting of Prissy Strong, The Miracle at Carmody, and finally The End of a Quarrel. / All related by L.M. Montgomery." With the exception of "The Training of Felix," which appears in the book itself as "Each in His Own Tongue" (the title under which this story was published prior to its revision for this volume), this list corresponds perfectly to the contents of the book in terms of both titles and order. Yet an ad for the book in the endmatter of the first edition includes an alternative list that mentions stories not included in the text: "other personalities and events, including The Purchase of Sloane, The Baby Which Came to Jane, The Mystery of Her Father's Daughter and of Tannis of the Flats, The Promise of Lucy Ellen, The Beau and Aunt Olivia, The Deferment of Hester, and finally of The Hurrying of Ludovic." It is unclear why this list was not updated prior to publication or to what extent Montgomery was involved in the final selection, order, and titles of the contents of this volume.

*The Publishers' Weekly* announced the book in its 24 February 1912 issue as "the leading fiction title" for L.C. Page and Company. As the *Boston Herald* added in its own announcement at the beginning of May, "It is, indeed, welcome news to hear that the delightful Anne Shirley of Green Gables fame plays some part in the 'Chronicles,' which have to do also with other interesting personalities and events of Avonlea." A notice in the *New York Times* the following week listed it as a "new novel" rather than a collection of linked stories, adding that "Anne Shirley is promised for reappearance." An ad in the *Boston Herald* quoted a review in the *Chicago Daily Tribune*, which called *Chronicles of Avonlea* "a book so thoroughly pleasing and sentimentally wholesome that one wants to pass it on to all one's friends and then to the whole cityful and countryside." But while some of the reviews included in this volume revealed a dissatisfaction with the collection due to the infrequent appearance of Anne, this did not have a negative impact on sales: a list in *The Publishers' Weekly* for 1912 best-sellers placed *Chronicles of Avonlea* in fourth place and *The Story Girl* tied for twentieth place on the list of best-selling juvenile books. Moreover, the book was celebrated for its literary quality: as Marjory MacMurchy noted in a "Retrospect of a Year's Books" in *The Canadian Courier,* "They are sweet, straightforward, wholesome and full of laughter. This is Miss Montgomery's best work." Montgomery was relieved once the book was done, telling MacMillan she was looking forward to attempting "work more after my own heart" – a sequel to *The Story Girl*.[31]

In the 21 June 1913 issue of *The Publishers' Weekly*, its "Literary and Trade Notes" section mentioned a letter from Montgomery to her publisher indicating that work on her next novel, *The Golden Road*, was "progressing merrily" – a report that followed this periodical's announcement of the book the preceding February and that also appeared in *The Dial*.[32] In spite of this reassurance to her publisher, behind the scenes Montgomery was having difficulty learning to write amid the new pressures and constraints of her life in Leaskdale. By the time she began work on this volume in April 1912, she was still getting used to the responsibilities of a minister's wife, which were made worse by the discomforts of her first pregnancy. When she finished the volume in May 1913, she noted that the writing process had not been enjoyable due to the constant interruptions and pressures. To MacMillan she added that "the whole book was written in odds and ends of time and so left a disagreeable impression of 'unfinishedness' on my mind."[33]

Once again, Page placed additional ads in *The Publishers' Weekly* in the months leading up to the publication of this sequel to *The Story Girl*: "Don't forget the author's previous books ... sold about one half a million copies and still in big demand," one ad declared on 5 July; three weeks later, another proclaimed that Montgomery's books were "in wide demand in educational circles for supplementary reading purposes." A later ad in mid-September proclaimed that "the expected has happened! Miss Montgomery's new book is hailed everywhere as 'a volume of delight'" – although it is worth noting that an ad in the same periodical two weeks earlier had called it "a new novel of delight." The mid-September ad continued: "The advance orders exhausted the first large edition long before publication day. The second large edition is now ready to meet your requirements." An ad in the New York edition of *The Bookman* that same month added that "more than half a million copies of Miss Montgomery's books have been sold," a figure amended the following month: "Nearly half a million copies of this author's previous books have been sold." This later notice added that "Miss Montgomery again proves that she is a distinct acquisition to American literature." This high praise extended to Britain as well, where *The Athenaeum* referred to it, shortly before its publication early in 1914, as "a joyous volume telling of the golden road of youth, its buoyant optimism, its problems and pleasures."[34]

In her journal early in September 1913, the same day she received her copies of *The Golden Road*, and more than three years after she had told George Boyd MacMillan about her lack of interest in such a project ("The freshness has gone out of the *Anne* idea"), Montgomery announced that she had finally begun work on a third novel about Anne. She found the prospect "hopeless" due to the way she perceived her strengths and weaknesses as a writer: "My forte is in writing humor. Only childhood and elderly people can be treated humorously in books. Young women in the bloom of youth and romance should be sacred from humor. It is the time of sentiment and I am not good at depicting sentiment – I can't do it well. Yet there *must* be sentiment in this book. I must at least engage Anne for I'll never be given any rest until I do." She continued to have misgivings about the novel – which depicts Anne and her friends at university in Nova Scotia and ends with Anne's engagement to Gilbert Blythe – and was relieved to finish it in November 1914, not only because of her doubts about its quality but also because the drafting was interrupted by the stillbirth of her second son, Hugh, in August 1914, just eight days after England declared war on Germany. She was also disgruntled that Page had vetoed her chosen title, "Anne of Redmond," and insisted on publishing the book as *Anne of the Island*.[35] In spite of her resentment toward the public clamour for the novel, she dedicated it "to all the girls all over the world who have 'wanted more' about Anne."

When this book appeared late in July 1915, it contained a change on the frontispiece: whereas her previous books had simply listed "Works by L.M. Montgomery" in order of their publication, this book listed "The Four Avonlea Books" first, with *Chronicles of Avonlea* appearing before *Anne of the Island*, followed by her three non-Anne volumes, even though many of the book's notices, ads, and reviews announced the novel as "the last book of the 'Anne of Green Gables' trilogy."[36] The production of this supposedly final Anne book was not without mishap, however; a note in *The Publishers' Weekly* explained that its publication had been delayed for two weeks because of "difficulty in the color printing of the jacket," whereas a column in the *Los Angeles Times* provided further details about why Page had decided to "throw away the entire first two printings of the color work on the slip-jacket. The printer was unable to secure the special inks imported from Germany, and the experiments were unsatisfactory." But public demand led to the book going through three printings even before the book was actually published, at which point Page published an ad in the New York *Sun* proudly stating the sales figures for all of "Miss Montgomery's Previous Successes" up to that point: 310,000 copies of *Anne of Green Gables*, 109,000 copies of *Anne of Avonlea*, 33,000 copies of *Chronicles of Avonlea*, 45,000 copies of *The Story Girl*, 27,000 copies of *The Golden Road*, and 45,000 copies of *Kilmeny of the Orchard*.[37]

Additional notices were crystal clear in declaring their excitement for this highly anticipated volume. These included a notice of its upcoming publication in the New York magazine *The Independent* in mid-April: "Another story, just announced, about that fascinating maiden Anne of Green Gables, makes one again wonder why, while the conventional young man, the man you would not find noticeably odd did you meet him at a dinner, still serves acceptably as hero, the maidens who make 'best sellers' have the spiritual nature of fireworks and keep the reader sitting up every instant to see how they will 'go off' next. There is a philosophical reason for this, tho not space to work it out." A notice in *The Publishers' Weekly* a week after the book's publication could barely resist spoiling the mystery of Anne's engagement: "Anne and her friends of [the] author's earlier books reappear a little more grown-up. There are merry doings at Redmond, where the young folks are studying for their A B's and finding time for lovemaking as well. Anne is popular as ever and has a new admirer in Roy Gardner, a young man of means; but when it comes to deciding for life, Anne knows that old friends are best." Moreover, the announcement of the forthcoming publication of the novel in the *Saint John Globe* of New Brunswick revealed the limits of one reviewer's expectations of a novel about a young woman: "Just what Anne will do in this story, unless she gets married, it is difficult to surmise. It would be too cruel to kill her, both for her own sake and for the very practical reason that she occupies the utilitarian position of a domestic bird whose eggs were golden – so the legend runs." Meanwhile, a column on "Canadian Notes" in *The Publishers' Weekly* complained that the novel "is a Page publication and has not even the distinction of having a Canadian edition."[38] This was about to change, although not purely for reasons of nationalistic fervour.

## The Great War and Other Conflicts, 1916–1921

When L.M. Montgomery first announced the acceptance of *Anne of Green Gables* in her journal, she noted that the terms of her royalty were "not generous even for a new writer, and they have bound me to give them all my books on the same terms for five years." Wary of rocking the boat after four other publishers had rejected the manuscript, she reluctantly agreed to these terms but soon found herself in a complicated relationship with her aggressive publisher, which Carole Gerson notes "suggest[s] a dynamic that we now associate with battered wife syndrome": "her gratitude to him for having launched her career conflicts with her anger at the knowledge that his royalty arrangements have paid her less than half of what she should have received." Montgomery was dismayed in 1910 to discover that a trip to Boston to meet her publisher and be celebrated by the literati had been a ruse to manipulate her into extending the binding clause for another five years after she had expressly stated she would not do so. She managed to have that clause removed from her contract for *Chronicles of Avonlea*, which Page agreed to do "with a very bad grace" – and, although Montgomery would have gladly continued publishing with Page had he offered a more standard royalty rate, he did not do so and she assumed it would be pointless to ask for an increase.[39]

She considered herself free to make new arrangements for her subsequent books once *Anne of the Island* had been published, and by spring 1916 she had decided to give the Canadian rights to her next book to the Toronto firm of McClelland, Goodchild and Stewart and to appoint this firm as her literary agent, still with the intention of offering the Page Company the American rights. What helped her agree to this arrangement was the McClelland firm's interest in bringing out a volume of her poems, a project that Page, thinking more of the bottom line than of keeping his authors happy, had long refused to consider. Rather than negotiate with McClelland for the American rights to her subsequent books as she directed Page to do, he responded by threatening to take her to court. Inundated with offers from other firms for the American rights to her next book, Montgomery and her Canadian publishers eventually settled on the Frederick A. Stokes Company of New York, which would publish all her subsequent books (with the exception of *Courageous Women*) in tandem with identical Canadian editions by McClelland, Goodchild and Stewart (which became McClelland and Stewart in 1918). Although Montgomery was elated to receive a much higher royalty rate, she found these new terms daunting. "Can I continue to write up to them? I am always haunted by the fear that I shall find myself 'written out.'" When Montgomery announced the news about Stokes in her journal entry dated 16 December 1916, she left out a crucial detail. According to George L. Parker, the Stokes contract for *Anne's House of Dreams* was signed on 9 December 1916, and on 13 December 1916, a second Stokes contract was signed, this time for *The Watchman and Other Poems*, which the firm would reissue the following year.[40]

Five weeks before these contracts were signed, however, Montgomery recorded in her journal that she had received her copy of *The Watchman and Other Poems* from McClelland. "It is very nicely gotten up. I expect no great things of it." Dedicated "to the memory of the gallant Canadian soldiers who have laid down their lives for their country and their empire," the book consists of ninety-five poems originally published between 1899 and 1916. It has three parts – "Songs of Sea," "Songs of the Hills and Woods," and "Miscellaneous" – which are preceded by the title poem, first published in *Everybody's Magazine* in 1910. An ad for the book in the Toronto *Globe* declared it "one of the choicest books of the year, 108 pages of beautiful poems of rare quality, delicate, lilting and full of music ... a Canadian book through and through." The notice in *The Bookseller, Newsdealer and Stationer* in April 1917, announcing the American edition, was much more tepid: "Those who have read *Anne of Green Gables* and other of Miss Montgomery's novels, will not be surprised that she has written a volume of poetry."[41] And although Montgomery's poetry has been largely overlooked by more recent scholars, the book did receive high praise from reviewers of the era.

By the time *The Watchman* was released in November 1916, Montgomery was putting the finishing touches on the manuscript of her next novel, *Anne's House of Dreams* – a book she called "the best I have ever written not even excepting *Green Gables* or my own favorite 'The Story Girl.' But will the dear public think so?" Montgomery's decision to write further Anne books is curious in many ways, especially given her reluctance to write *Anne of the Island*. Once again, in her journals and letters, she remained mostly silent about her plans and ambitions as an author. It seems understandable that she would want to start off her new publishing arrangement with projects that would be almost guaranteed to do well. Yet in her journals she mentioned in passing, when discussing the breakdown of her professional relationship with Lewis Page, that the two had had "some correspondence about the literary contents of my next book," and while she did not provide details or indicate whether the plan for another Anne book was her idea or his, it seems that she had planned to write another Anne book even before leaving Page's firm. Only in a letter to Ephraim Weber, dated November 1917 and published in 2006, did she indicate the likelihood that she had planned all along to use the Anne characters as the basis for a novel set during the Great War: "I am now at work on a book in which Anne's children figure and then I plan to write one in which her sons go to the front." She referred to these future books disingenuously as "harmless pot-boilers" designed to "occupy these busy hurried years," but thankfully most critics would not agree with this private assessment.[42]

Indeed, expectations for this new Anne novel were remarkably high. A notice in the 11 August 1917 issue of *The Publishers' Weekly* stated that it would be published on 24 August, "just in time for every girl to take a copy away with her for train reading on the way to boarding school." But an ad that appeared in the same issue of *The Publishers' Weekly* and four days later in *The Bookseller, Newsdealer and Stationer* revealed that the market for the novel was much broader. "Those who have read *Anne of Green Gables* will want this new novel in which Anne's 'dream' comes true," with a note added "*to the bookseller*:– Run over in your mind the four or five American Novelists whose sales run into six figures. Will there be a new book by any one of them this Autumn except L.M. Montgomery? This means an enormous demand for her *Anne's House of Dreams*." While more recent scholarship has tended to focus on the novel's subplot about a neighbour trapped in a nightmarish marriage, later ads and notices kept the focus on the positive. "Red-haired Anne Shirley, the heroine of Green Gables and Avonlea, now Mrs. Gilbert Blythe, makes her little house at Four Winds Harbor just what she always dreamed a home should be," stated the notice in *The Publishers' Weekly*. "To it come her neighbors: Miss Cornelia; Captain Jim, the lighthouse keeper; aristocratic Marshall Elliott; and Leslie Moore with her mysterious love-story which unfolds itself and comes to a happy ending along with Anne's own simpler romance." An ad that appeared in both the *New York Tribune* and the *New York Times* called it "a wholesome novel of a seacoast community, with romance, pathos and humor happily blended … All romance lovers will enjoy it whether they have read the author's previous works or not." And in England, where the novel was scheduled initially for fall 1917 but then delayed till spring 1918, *The Athenaeum* called it "a cheery story which shows us Anne of Green Gables in her married life, and some of her friends and neighbours," whereas an ad in the London *Bookman* quoted a review in the *British Weekly*: "This is the hour for sunshiny books."[43]

For her next book, a sequel set thirteen years after *Anne's House of Dreams*, Montgomery shifted the focus from Anne to her children and their playmates, the four children of the widowed minister nearby. As she noted in her journal upon completing the manuscript of *Rainbow Valley* late in December 1918, it "still averages up pretty well of its kind. But I'm tired of the kind … My publishers keep me at this sort of stuff because it sells and because they claim that the public, having become used to this from my pen, would not tolerate a change."[44] Although the novel is set in the first decade of the twentieth century, echoes of the war are everywhere, beginning in Montgomery's dedication of the book "to the memory of Goldwin Lapp, Robert Brookes and Morley Shier," young men in her congregation "who made the supreme sacrifice that the happy valleys of their home land might be kept sacred from the ravage of the invader."

Yet an ad in *The Publishers' Weekly* called it "a simple, wholesome love story [that] overflows with real humor and pure romance. It solves no problems, there is no hint of the war in it – it is just a simple love story chronicling the everyday events in a community of kindly people whose lives are the counterpart of other lives the country over." A similar ad in

*The Bookseller, Newsdealer and Stationer* called it "the simple, whole-some sort of novel that will satisfy those of your customers who want 'pure romance' and 'a good story well told' ... Its appeal isn't limited to grown-ups – you are perfectly safe in suggesting it for girls of any age." Indeed, an ad in the *New York Times* declared that the novel was fit for "any one who likes a wholesome, human novel full of humor and peopled by kindly, likable characters," and a later ad in that newspaper quoted a review in the *Oakland Tribune* of California: "One of the old-fashioned, homely, cheerful romances that tend to restore faith in the world about us." Moreover, ads appearing in both the Toronto *Globe* and the *Manitoba Free Press* closer to the holiday season declared that "this well-known writer grips your attention from the first page." An ad-ditional ad appearing in Montgomery's scrapbook also praised her depic-tion of rural community life: "The light deftness of literary touch which is the gift of L.M. Montgomery is something that even a Jane Austen might almost envy, for she has the power of setting before us the events and people of everyday life in a typical Canadian community, and of showing us with a fine sympathetic insight, the humor, the beauty, and the pathos of what we might have passed by as commonplace or unwor-thy of our attention."[45]

Montgomery may have been planning a second Anne trilogy as early as 1917, but the publication of the final volume was once again inter-rupted for largely the same reason as in the case of *Anne of the Island*, albeit with a twist. Since her break from the L.C. Page Company in 1916, she had become fed up with Page's shady business practices, such as his invention of bookkeeping "errors." Suing him for unpaid royal-ties, she travelled to Boston for a hearing early in 1919. In the end, Page offered to buy all remaining rights – including claims to all future royal-ties – to the seven books published by his firm. Eager to sever ties with him, Montgomery agreed to this, and they eventually settled on a fee of $17,800. This led to two unexpected complications: the first, that Page then turned right around and sold the film rights to the four Anne books for $40,000, cheating Montgomery out of her 50 per cent share; the second, that Page manipulated her into agreeing to the publication of a volume of *Further Chronicles of Avonlea*, initially proposing to use the leftover stories from *Chronicles*, then admitting that he did not actually have copies of those stories in his possession, prompting Montgomery, who claimed she had destroyed these leftovers after they were returned to her in 1912, to revise them from scratch. Montgomery consented in order to retain some control over the project, on two conditions: that he not release the book in a year when she had another new volume out, and that the book include no mention of Anne Shirley. In the end, after Montgomery had already rewritten the stories again to fit the setting of Avonlea, Page revealed that his firm *did* have copies of the original 1912 leftovers and published them with a cover design and frontispiece that matched the earlier books, prompting another lawsuit that would not be settled until eight years later.[46]

Yet for all of Lewis Page's apparent ruthlessness, a series of ads in the semi-monthly periodical *The Bookseller, Newsdealer and Stationer* reveal that this project was delayed repeatedly. "READY IN FEBRUARY!" declared the front cover of the 15 January issue, in spite of the report inside the same issue that the book would be published "this month." "COMING THIS MONTH!" promised an ad on the back cover of the 1 February issue, and two weeks later, the book was "To be published in March!" By the time the book was actually published in April 1920, an ad on the back cover of the 1 April issue was quick to declare that "2nd Printing Being Rushed!" – and a month later, "2nd Large Edition Selling – 3rd Being Rushed!" In an ad for "The Five Avonlea Books" in the *Syracuse Herald* in mid-April 1920, the book was included in a list of "Books that Particular Mothers Will Be Pleased to Have Their Daughters Read AND Books That DAUGHTERS will find very interesting."[47] As with the first volume of *Chronicles*, this volume was published with a chapter-by-chapter description on the title page, but with numerous discrepancies between the description and the contents in terms of titles and chronology: "Further Chronicles of Avonlea / Which have to do with many personalities and events in and about Avonlea, the Home of the Heroine of Green Gables, including tales of Aunt Cynthia, The Materializing of Cecil, David Spencer's Daughter, Jane's Baby, The Failure of Robert Monroe, The Return of Hester, The Little Brown Book of Miss Emily, Sara's Way, The Son of Thyra Carewe, The Education of Betty, The Selflessness of Eunice Carr, The Dream-Child, The Conscience Case of David Bell, Only a Common Fellow, and finally the story of Tannis of the Flats." This volume was illustrated by John Goss – indeed, it was the only Montgomery book besides *Anne of Green Gables* and *Kilmeny of the Orchard* to have interior illustrations beyond a frontispiece image – and contains a glowing introduction by Nathan Haskell Dole (which appears in Volume 1 of *The L.M. Montgomery Reader*). Montgomery succeeded in having the book pulled from Page's list in 1928, after several years of lawsuits and countersuits, but in an odd twist, a revised version of the text resurfaced in the mid-1950s and remains in print today.

In the midst of these legal battles and other worries at home, Montgomery continued with what she intended would be the last volume about Anne Shirley Blythe. In *Rilla of Ingleside*, she continued to shift away from Anne and Gilbert and toward their children, particularly their youngest daughter, Rilla, who is fifteen at the beginning of the First World War, and their twenty-year-old son Walter, the romantic poet whose death on the battlefields of France is depicted as a necessary sacrifice for future peace. Montgomery did not like the title her publishers had chosen – she had wanted to call it "Rilla-My-Rilla" or "Rilla Blythe" – and had some misgivings about its sales potential given its publication almost three years after the war's end: "The public are said to be sick of anything connected with the war. But at least I did my best to reflect the life we lived in Canada during those four years."[48] In public statements about the ideological work of the book, however, she left no room for any doubt, as seen in an article entitled "How I Became a Writer," published in the *Manitoba Free Press* opposite its review of the novel, reprinted in this volume: "In my latest story, *Rilla of Ingleside*, I have tried, as far as in me lay, to depict the fine and splendid way in which the girls of Canada reacted to the Great War – their bravery, patience and self-sacrifice. The book is theirs in a sense in which none of my other books have been: for my other books were written for anyone who might like to read them: but *Rilla* was written for the girls of the great young land I love, whose destiny it will be their duty and privilege to shape and share." In July 1936, recording in her journal that she had been rereading all her old books, she declared that *Rilla of Ingleside* was "the best book I ever wrote."[49]

Ads for *Rilla of Ingleside* tended to avoid any mention of the war, as if they shared Montgomery's concern that the Great War would hinder rather than help the sales of a novel in 1921. Instead, they emphasized the appeal of the novel for readers of all ages, particularly women aged fifteen to twenty, the same age as the title protagonist. A near-identical ad in *The Bookseller and Stationer* and *The Publishers' Weekly* early in September 1921, just prior to the book's publication, suggested four reasons for its sales success: it is "the one popular Fall novel you can recommend for young girls as well as for grown-ups"; "it is sincere and it is 'nice' without being namby-pamby – no need to skip ahead to see if it's safe to read aloud"; "the lovers of *Anne of Green Gables* will delight in Rilla"; and the "frontispiece, jacket and cover inlay in full color make a splendid display and suggest the book as a gift."[50] An ad appearing the following week in *The Publishers' Weekly* included a direct quote from an unnamed Chicago bookseller: "I am always glad to hear of a new Montgomery novel ... for it fills a want – something clean and wholesome for a young girl." In both the *Boston Herald* and the *New York Times*, the book was referred to as "a wholesome novel of youth and of love which doesn't always run smooth." In an ad appearing in the Toronto *Globe*, a photograph of Montgomery was used to introduce the book: "Canadian readers will recognize in this picture the popular, gifted and widely-read Canadian novelist, L.M. Montgomery, creator of the famous and adorable Anne of Green Gables and other delightful characters in Canadian literature"; it referred to *Rilla* as "a new 'Anne' book – a captivating, sunny story of a very human, impulsive, pretty, warm-hearted young girl, the daughter of Anne Shirley of Green Gables' fame." For its part, the *Dallas Morning News* referred to the title protagonist as "a glowing, impetuous, fun-loving girl, in some ways unlike the young Anne Shirley of Green Gables Days, yet endowed with the same eagerness, the same bubbling enthusiasm, the same warmness of heart."[51]

Published in fall 1921, the book also marked a milestone for Montgomery: the intended end of the Anne books, which she swore in her journals as "a dark and deadly vow." To Ephraim Weber and in near identical form to George Boyd MacMillan, she added that "six books are enough to write about any one girl. I am sick of her and wonder that the public isn't too. Yet it doesn't seem to be." What is perhaps surprising is that she also made this vow publicly: her Scrapbook of Reviews contains an unidentified clipping, entitled "No More of 'Anne' Books, Says Author," in which Montgomery is quoted directly as calling *Rilla* "positively the last of the 'Anne' books."[52] With the Anne books behind her, Montgomery was finally free to work on an entirely new project about an entirely new protagonist: Emily.

## Emily Interrupted, 1923–1927

"I want to create a new heroine now," L.M. Montgomery declared in her journal in August 1920, upon completing the manuscript of *Rilla of Ingleside*. "She is already in embryo in my mind." She began "collect[ing] material" for *Emily of New Moon* by mid-December of that year, and by May of 1921 she had given her American publisher an ultimatum about the protagonist's name, even though she would not begin drafting the manuscript until mid-August: "my heroine *is* Emily, just as Anne was Anne. She has been 'Emily' for the past ten years during which time I have been carrying her in my mind, waiting for the time when I could put her into a book ... And 'Emily' she shall remain." To Weber, she added that the book would be "more autobiographical" than the ones that had come before: "People were never right in saying I was 'Anne' but, *in some respects*, they will be right if they write me down as *Emily*." In a later letter to Weber, she was more tepid in her assessment, calling it "good of its kind" but nevertheless "along the old lines – I cannot yet get the unbroken leisure I want for a more serious attempt."[53]

Ads in North American periodicals went to great lengths to demonstrate the book's quality and "wholesomeness." The *Boston Globe* listed it as among "The Best of the New Fiction," while the Toronto *Globe* promised that "readers will find in Emily a delightful new character who has all the captivating charm, the lovableness and welcome sense of humor that endeared 'Anne of Green Gables' fame to young and old." The *Boston Herald* carried three different ads for the book in the fall of 1923, the first including it in a list of "Novels the Girls or Grandma Can Enjoy without a Blush," and the remaining two making rather bold claims about its appeal: "We've Yet to Find the Girl or Woman Who Doesn't Like *Emily of New Moon*," and "Are You Fed Up with Sex, Mystery and Detective Stories? Read *Emily of New Moon*." According to a short item entitled "Weather Forecast" and published in the *Boston Herald*, "Bright and Clear with no clouds for all who read L.M. Montgomery's new novel, *Emily of New Moon*."[54]

Upon completing the manuscript in mid-February 1922, Montgomery called *Emily of New Moon* "the best book I have ever written ... Of course, I'll have to write several sequels but they will be more or less hackwork I fear. They cannot be to me what this book has been." A year after its publication, she wrote to Ephraim Weber that she was rather dismayed by his suggestion that "'Of course *Emily* is another *Anne*.' Well, she may be but if so I have entirely failed in my attempt to 'get her across' to my readers. In my mental conception of her there was a big difference between reserved *Emily* with her background of family and tradition and the hail-fellow-well-met little orphan from nowhere. I can not see any resemblance between them, save one or two superficial ones in the stage they walk on."[55] Moreover, in June 1924 Montgomery was invited to rework extracts from *Emily of New Moon* and *Emily Climbs* into four stand-alone short stories to be published in *The Delineator*, a major New York periodical to which Montgomery had already contributed two short stories – "The Promise of Lucy Ellen" in 1904 and "Each in His Own Tongue," eventually revised for *Chronicles of Avonlea*, in 1910 – as well as the 1903 poem "In Lovers' Lane." Montgomery was astounded to learn later that one of the stories had been turned down because it featured a Roman Catholic priest, which forced her to write an entirely new story featuring Emily to fill the gap. The four stories appeared in consecutive issues in the first four months of 1925 and were accompanied by an ad that claimed that "girls can not fail to adore Emily. And their mothers will love her, too, for beneath all her laughter and charm there lies a keen study of childhood that no parent can afford to miss."[56]

Fifteen months prior to the publication of *Emily of New Moon* in August 1923, Montgomery reported in her journal that she had already started gathering material for a book to which she had assigned the working title of "*Emily II*. I am sure I won't be able to make it anything as good as *Emily I* but the publishers want a series and it pays and so I'll carry it on." She finished the manuscript early in 1924, explaining in her journal her reasons for concluding that her second volumes about girl characters were "the hardest for me to write – because the public and the publisher won't allow me to write of a young girl as she really is ... you have to depict a sweet, insipid young thing – really a child grown older – to whom the basic realities of life and reactions to them are quite unknown."[57]

Yet the novel that she dismissed to Weber as "hack work" received a highly positive response, not only from reviewers but also close to home: a newspaper from St. Paul, Minnesota, quoted from a letter Montgomery had written to her Canadian publishers about her author's copy of *Emily Climbs*, which "looks quite nice. I haven't had time to 'read' it yet, but my 13-year-old boy, Chester, has and wouldn't stop until he had finished. As he never cared much for any of my other books, I regard this as a good sign – for the book." An ad published in the *Boston Herald* to coincide with its publication in August 1925 declared that Emily's "new story makes even more secure her place beside the well-loved Anne. This tale is of high school days, those delightful years brimful of thrills and joy and work." Montgomery went to work on a third book about Emily almost immediately after completing *Emily Climbs*, referring to it in a November 1924 letter to Ephraim Weber simply as "[Emily's] love story," adding two weeks later, "I really haven't a great deal of interest in it." In a journal entry dated five months earlier, however, she unexpectedly mentioned that she had begun work "on a book I'm trying to write" entitled *The Blue Castle*. It was unusual for Montgomery to work on two novels simultaneously, but after several months of struggling to make headway with her third Emily novel, she put it aside and continued work on a project she would call, upon completing it, "a little comedy for adults."[58] Her only novel set entirely outside Prince Edward Island, *The Blue Castle* takes place in Bala, in the Muskoka region, where she and her family had vacationed in the summer of 1922.

Although Montgomery did not consider her target reading audience as exclusively or even primarily children, that she designated *The Blue Castle* as a book for adults ended up being part of its promotion, particularly in the Australian edition. Perhaps this implied that her earlier fiction was somehow exclusively for children; the *Morning Bulletin* of Rockhampton, Australia, suggested that her preceding novels, "though generally regarded as girls' books, afford enjoyment to all." Another Australian newspaper, the Brisbane *Week*, hastened to add that "though she has not written this time for girls, there is nothing in the book which a girl could not enjoy to the full." *The Blue Castle* also marked another sort of departure: it was her first known serialization of a book-length work since parting company with L.C. Page and Company. *The Canadian Countryman* serialized the novel in twenty-one instalments between August 1927 and January 1928, and the *Plain Dealer*, a Cleveland newspaper, published it with some excisions in a single instalment in April 1927. As well, whereas many of the reviews and ads for *Emily Climbs* claimed that both text and protagonist were "typical" of Montgomery, some of the language used to promote *The Blue Castle* seemed to imply a radically different kind of text than the "little comedy" Montgomery had envisioned. "She Married a Tramp," declared the headline of an ad for the *Plain Dealer* serialization. "The sheltered girl from the town was driven to assert herself, and one of the results of getting away from her oppressing family was that she fell in love with a man who bore the most unsavory reputation. How that came about and what came of it is charmingly told in *The Blue Castle*." Accompanying the serialization itself was this tantalizing subhead: "A girl who was held down by her family finds that after all she has something to her and she demonstrates it."[59]

Ads for the novel itself likewise relied on hyperbole. An ad appearing in the New York *Bookman* (and in slightly different form in the *Boston Herald*) reads as follows: "Told at twenty-nine that she has but a year to live, Valancy Sterling [*sic*] revolts against her dull and proper life and marries a mysterious young tramp from the Canadian woods. What happens is the tantalizing secret of the story." In an ad published closer to the holiday season, the *Boston Herald* recommended *The Blue Castle* "for Big Sister": "A bewitching romance of the cool Canadian woods; a 'mousy' girl whose life had been drab and uneventful, resolves to have one glorious fling!" In spite of this apparent success in targeting an audience specifically of adults, Montgomery cautioned Weber that the book "will be more interesting to a girl than a man but I'll send you a copy."[60] Indeed, she had actually dedicated the book "to Mr. Ephraim Weber, M.A., who understands the architecture of Blue Castles," but the dedication does not appear in any Canadian edition of the novel or in the earliest U.S. editions; in his essay "L.M. Montgomery as a Letter-Writer," reprinted in Volume 1 of *The L.M. Montgomery Review*, Weber mentions that the edition he received from Montgomery was, in fact, the British edition published by Hodder and Stoughton.

In April 1926, five months after completing the manuscript of *The Blue Castle*, Montgomery finally resumed work on her third book about Emily Byrd Starr, to be called *Emily's Quest*. To Weber, she tried to be light-hearted about her difficulties with this project: "just now I am trying to marry *Emily* off and am finding her a bit of a handful. Not because of any special perversity on her part but simply because – alack! – I can't write a young-girl – romantic – love story. My impish sense of humor always spoils everything." In her journal, however, she was far more pessimistic: "The book will be poor stuff I fear. My heart is not in it." Finishing the draft in October 1926, she offered her final verdict once the revisions were completed five weeks later: "It is no good."[61] Montgomery's dedication of the novel to her first cousin "Stella Campbell Keller of the tribe of Joseph" proved so intriguing to Austin Bothwell that he wrote a lengthy article dissecting its possible meaning, an essay reprinted in Volume 1 of *The L.M. Montgomery Reader*.

In September 1925, Montgomery mentioned in her journal that she had just finished four stories about a new protagonist, Marigold, with plans to submit them to *The Delineator*; this was on the heels of its publication of the four "Emily" stories earlier that year. "I think they are very good specimens of their *genre* and 'Marigold' seems very real and enchanting to me." Astounded a month later to discover that she would be paid $1,600 for the stories, which appeared in four consecutive issues between May and August 1926, she was nevertheless miffed when the editor changed all four of her titles. The first, originally called "What's in a Name?" was changed to "Magic for Marigold" and appeared with a note claiming that "Little baby Marigold is destined to grow up to be L.M. Montgomery's most captivating heroine ... 'Better than Anne herself! Better than Emily of New Moon!' you will say." Indeed, an undated clipping evidently from *The Delineator* not only refers to Montgomery as "the mother of Marigold" but "predict[s] that spicy little Marigold will bring L.M. Montgomery even wider fame. Do let us know if you agree with our prophecy!" Moreover, the ad attempted once again to market these stories to as broad an audience as possible: "Fathers, mothers – the entire family, in fact – cannot afford to miss 'em." Evidently, the magazine saw a wider audience for these stories than Montgomery herself did, as she revealed in a letter to MacMillan: "It is about a little girl but some of the chapters may interest an adult."[62]

These stories proved to be quite popular, so, as Montgomery told Weber, she was soon asked to pen an additional four about Marigold. Those, however, were eventually turned down due to a change in editorial direction at the magazine. By the time she began work on a book from these stories, her interest in Marigold had dwindled to indifference: "I don't think I'll love her as well as Anne and Emily – so likely the public won't." By the time she completed the manuscript of the book in October 1928, she was repeating a sentiment she had expressed when finishing *Emily's Quest:* "I have never had such a hard time to get a book finished." Upon receiving a copy of the printed book the following May, she reflected that her lack of interest in the project may have stemmed from the fact that "so much of it" had started off as short stories in *The Delineator*. "It seemed like warming up cold soup."[63]

What Montgomery did not mention in any of these accounts was the extent to which the novel *Magic for Marigold* consisted of "cold soup." In addition to the four stories in *The Delineator*, Montgomery had published not four more Marigold stories but *seven*: "One of Us" in *Canadian Home Journal* in February 1928, "One Clear Call" in *The Household Magazine* in August 1928, "The Punishment of Billy" in *Canadian Home Journal* in February 1929, and "'It'" in *The Chatelaine* in April 1929, as well as three additional entries in Montgomery's ledger of published stories whose sources have not yet been identified: "A Counsel of Perfection," "How It Came to Pass," and "Red Ink or –" (the latter being one of the titles mentioned by Montgomery in her letter to Weber).[64] But the fact that nearly half the book had already appeared in the form of stand-alone short stories did not deter marketing campaigns in the United States and Canada: an ad in the *Boston Herald* referred to the title character as "a new and equally lovable young heroine, … and her adventures will delight readers of any age," whereas the Toronto *Globe* called it "The Choice Gift Book of the Year." Moreover, in a "Books of the Month" listing for mid-September to mid-October 1929, the London edition of *The Bookman* placed *Magic for Marigold* as the top title published by Hodder and Stoughton.[65]

Prior to the release of *Magic for Marigold*, Montgomery reported in her journal an unusual development in her career as a novelist after receiving a semi-annual report from the Stokes Company: "the sales of my *old books* are keeping up *too well* and they cut the market from my new ones to a large extent."[66] Perhaps thinking that she had little to lose financially, she decided to take a bit of a chance with her next project – even though, as it turned out, the timing would not work in her favour.

### Great Depressions, 1929–1935

In February 1929, Montgomery mentioned to MacMillan that she was "gathering together material" for a novel similar to *The Blue Castle*. "It is too chaotic yet to have or give any very clear idea of it but I think I'll make it centre around the adventures of an old heirloom jug in a clan, the members of which all want to fall heir to it." Mentioning in her journals that she had begun work on "an adult story, centering around the old Woolner jug" in May 1929, she added that "my heart isn't in it."[67] She finished writing the manuscript in four months, but the process of assigning a title to the work proved to be arduous. She included four possible titles with the manuscript itself – *The Quest of the Jug*, *Darks and Penhallows*, *The Fun Begins*, and *A Tangled Web*, then suggested *Aunt Becky Began It* and *Crying for the Moon* as alternatives. All of these suggestions were vetoed by both her Canadian and American publishers, whereas she found their suggestions either "ridiculous" or "nice sentimental blue-and-pink sweet-sixteen titles for a humorous novel mainly about middle-aged people, some of whom said *damn*. I got plain mad finally and told them to call it any darned thing they wanted to!!"[68] They eventually settled on *A Tangled Web* after all, but as Montgomery added in her journal, her British publisher, Hodder and Stoughton, had requested a different title because they had just published a book entitled *The Tangled Web*, and so they opted to publish it as *Aunt Becky Began It*.[69] The novel in question was actually entitled *A Tangled Web* and was by Scottish theologian James Moffatt (1870–1944). Another novel entitled *A Tangled Web*, by English novelist Lucy Gertrude Moberly (1861–1931), was first published in 1926 but reprinted in 1931.

Although *A Tangled Web* was warmly received by critics around the world – the *Los Angeles Times* called it "an amusing tale of an eccentric old dame who knew how to treat her greedy relatives," whereas the *Chicago Daily Tribune* recommended it "for Elizabeth Ann, aged 16, who is very romantic" – its sales were a disappointment to both her and her publishers. In part, this reflected that it was published during the depths of the Great Depression.[70] For her next novel, *Pat of Silver Bush*, Montgomery returned to familiar territory, focusing once again on a young girl growing up on a farm in Prince Edward Island. But unlike Emily and Anne, Patricia Gardiner is surrounded by a loving and present nuclear family. Starting the actual writing of the manuscript in April 1932, she commented upon its completion in December that "it has been a desperate struggle to get time to write it," and yet "it has a setting after my own heart." Its production was straightforward and swift: after completing the typescript early in 1933 (this was the first manuscript she had typed since *Anne of Avonlea*), she was already reading proofs by mid-February. "Somehow," she noted upon its publication that August, "I love *Pat* as I have not loved any book since *New Moon*. It seemed to me such an 'escape' while I was writing it." To Weber, she called it "another story of the *Anne and Emily* genre" that, with the possible exception of servant Judy Plum, would appeal only to girls.[71] Also geared specifically to young female readers was a volume of essays, *Courageous Women*, for which Montgomery collaborated with Marian Keith and Mabel Burns McKinley. Montgomery's three chapters on Joan of Arc, Mary Slessor, and Florence Nightingale appear in Volume 1 of *The L.M. Montgomery Reader*.

In July 1933, even before she received her copies of *Pat of Silver Bush*, she told Weber that she had started gathering material for a second volume about those characters, although she referred to it as "a 'sequel' and nothing else." She worked on it for much of 1934, but the writing process was interrupted by a number of complex episodes in her personal life, such as the aftermath of the hasty marriage of her eldest son (including the birth of her first grandchild) and another mental breakdown for her husband, who was eventually hospitalized for several weeks at Homewood Sanatorium in Guelph; as she mentioned in one journal entry, "I compelled myself to write a chapter of *Pat II*."[72] Although Margaret Mackey's review, in *Resource Links*, of Jane Urquhart's biography of Montgomery for the Extraordinary Canadians series refers to *Mistress Pat* as "practically a primer on depression," initial coverage of this novel expressed otherwise: an ad in the *Toronto Daily Star* referred to the book as "A Grown-Up Novel for Grown-Up Readers," adding that "Pat of Silver Bush, now grown to womanhood, has become Mistress Pat of a cheerful farmhouse. A novel filled with unique, charming, unexpected people."[73]

## Return to Anne, 1936–1939

In March 1935, nearly fifteen years after her "dark and deadly vow," made upon the completion of *Rilla of Ingleside*, that she was done with Anne Shirley as a character, she announced in her journal that she had "succumbed at long last to the urgency of publishers and 'fans'" and had started work on a novel set between *Anne of the Island* and *Anne's House of Dreams*. "If it proves possible to 'get back into the past' far enough to do a good book it ought to do well commercially after the film," she added, referring to the RKO "talkie" film that had appeared late in 1934 (her public responses to the film appear in Volume 1 of *The L.M. Montgomery Reader*).[74] She started writing it in mid-August 1935 as *Anne of Windy Willows* and found the writing process easier than she had expected, going so far as to say that writing it "seemed like escaping back into the past." She also admitted, in a speech given to the Canadian Women's Press Club that year, that inserting a new instalment into the overall narrative of Anne's life had proved challenging: as the *Toronto Daily Star* reported her saying, "It was most difficult at first to recapture the atmosphere of the past and to pick up the threads of the story first told many years ago, but now I find myself easily living again all the life-story of my Anne – only I must watch myself carefully lest such modernities as motor cars or radios or even a new-fangled sled creep into the story by mistake." After completing the manuscript that November, she was surprised when her American publisher thought the title too reminiscent of Kenneth Grahame's 1908 book *The Wind in the Willows*. While she thought this "a foolish objection," she readily suggested *Anne of Windy Poplars* instead. As she added to MacMillan, however, her British publisher decided to publish it as *Anne of Windy Willows* and created its own plates from its copy of Montgomery's typescript, so extracts that had been deleted from the North American version of the novel at Stokes's request appeared in the British edition.[75] Prior to the publication of the novel, Montgomery published eight extracts from the book as stand-alone stories in the Montreal paper *The Family Herald and Weekly Star*, beginning with "The Man Who Wouldn't Talk" in its 6 May 1936 issue.

By the time *Anne of Windy Poplars* was published in fall 1936, Montgomery's husband had retired from the ministry and they had moved into an attractive Toronto home near the Humber River. Not surprisingly, her next book, *Jane of Lantern Hill*, would draw on this environment for part of its setting. For this late novel, about a young Toronto girl determined to reunite her estranged parents, Montgomery started collecting material sometime in the spring of 1936, but it was only in August of that year that she began what she called "the real writing of it." That same day, she noted in her journal that she had reread her old book *Chronicles of Avonlea* and admitted something revealing about her view of her later work: "I don't think I could write like that now – I have lost something." She finished writing the novel early in February 1937. In a letter to Weber shortly before its publication, she stated that "*Jane* is a quite different type from any of my other heroines. She is a practical, business-like little body, concerned with domesticity."[76]

And finally, in what was to be her last book published in her lifetime, Montgomery repeated the strategy she had adopted with *Anne of Windy Poplars* by creating a new story to be inserted between *Anne's House of Dreams* and *Rainbow Valley*, depicting Anne as a thirty-something mother of young children. As she confessed to Weber in a letter dated June 1938 about her publisher's suggestion that she undertake the project, "I may do so as a commercial proposition but my heart will not be in it." What she neglected to mention was that, according to her journal, she had begun the spade work for *Anne of Ingleside* two months earlier, even before receiving the proofs for *Jane of Lantern Hill*. Part of her hesitation likely stemmed from her apprehension about actually writing the book. "I *dread* trying to begin it," she admitted in her journal in September 1938. "What if I find I *cannot* write?" When she finally succeeded in starting it a week later, her relief was palpable: "A burden rolled from my spirit. And I was suddenly *back in my own world* with all my dear Avonlea and Glen folks again. It was like going home."[77] In this way, at least, she was in fact very emotionally attached to the project.

In spite of its inauspicious beginning, she managed to complete the draft within three months and had it revised and typed by the end of January 1939. While she recorded her anxieties about her writing ability in her journal, to her correspondents she was much more business-like: "I don't think it is 'up to' the other books in the series," she told MacMillan, whereas to Weber she dismissed it as "just what I have called it – a pot-boiler," adding in a later letter that she disliked the cover art but had chosen it as being the "least worst" among those that had been sent for her consideration.[78] Although the book was published in the summer of 1939, a serialization of sorts appeared in the form of eight stand-alone stories under the title "Chronicles of Ingleside," published in September and October of that year in *Onward: A Paper for Young Canadians*, a Toronto paper published by the United Church of Canada, without any mention of its recent appearance in book form.[79]

Recording in a journal entry dated December 1938 the completion of her twenty-first book (evidently excluding *The Watchman and Other Poems*, *Further Chronicles of Avonlea*, and *Courageous Women* from her mental list), she added, "I always wonder now if I will ever write another one. There are lots I want to write – but I *am* getting a little tired. I love to write still – I will always love it. But –" By November 1939, she had started work on a sequel to *Jane of Lantern Hill* entitled *Jane and Jody*, which she dismissed to Weber as "frankly a pot-boiler, so you need expect nothing else from it."[80] No further records of this late project survive. At some point in the two years that followed she completed a final manuscript, a sequel of sorts to both *Chronicles of Avonlea* and *The Watchman and Other Poems*: rather than create a "pot boiler" interquel as she had done with *Anne of Windy Poplars* and *Anne of Ingleside*, she revised fifteen short stories – many of which had been published in their original form in periodicals throughout the 1930s – to include mentions and appearances of Anne, Gilbert, their children, and their housekeeper. Between these stories she added vignettes comprised of forty-one of her own poems, most of them published in magazines from 1919 onwards, that she attributed to Anne and to her son Walter; these are accompanied by dialogue and private reflections of the Blythe family members. Entitled *The Blythes Are Quoted*, it was apparently submitted to her publisher the day of her death, although the fact that this is noted solely in one of her obituaries makes this detail impossible to verify.[81] From this final manuscript she submitted one poem and its accompanying commentary to *Saturday Night* a mere fortnight before her death, a capstone to her career that is included in Volume 1 of *The L.M. Montgomery Reader*.

Today, more than seventy years after her death, Montgomery's work continues to fascinate and enchant readers all over the world, to whom this reception history and these marketing practices across a thirty-year period have been largely unknown. And yet, at the close of her 1930 journal entry in which she painstakingly transcribed pages and pages of extracts from these reviews, she concluded that, after all, none of these external factors had ever had a real bearing on her career as an author. "All this has never meant very much of pleasure or pain, except superficially. I have written to please myself. It has not mattered much what anyone else thought. I have always tried to catch and express a little of the immortal beauty and enchantment of the world into which I have sometimes been privileged to see for a moment – the moment of 'Emily's' 'flash.' Those who never have that glimpse cannot believe there is such a world. I can but pity them."[82]

NOTES

1 Rubio, *Lucy Maud Montgomery*, 397; Montgomery, 1 March 1930, in *SJLMM*, 4: 38, 36.
2 Montgomery, 1 October 1928, in *SJLMM*, 3: 378–79; Montgomery to Weber, 5 April 1908, in *GGL*, 66; Montgomery to Weber, 10 September 1908, in *GGL*, 71.
3 Montgomery to Weber, 8 May 1939, in *AfGG*, 247.
4 "Saved from the Waste-Basket," unidentified and undated clipping (ca. 1923), in SR, 206; Gene Stratton-Porter (1863–1924), American author and photographer best known for *A Girl of the Limberlost* (1909); Harold Bell Wright (1872–1944), best-selling American author of fiction, non-fiction, and drama; Ethel M. Dell (1881–1939), English author of popular romance novels.
5 Ad for *Emily of New Moon*, unidentified and undated clipping (ca. 1923), in SR, 210; *The New York Tribune* (New York, NY), untitled clipping, 19 November 1929, in SR, 333.
6 Untitled, unidentified, and undated clipping (ca. 1914), in SR, 67.
7 *The New York Observer*, "Best Books for Boys and Girls," 740.
8 *Whit Weekly* (Kingston, ON), review of *Anne of the Island*, undated clipping, in SR, 74; *Philadelphia Record* (Philadelphia, PA), "'Anne' in New Story," review of *Anne's House of Dreams*, 27 October 1917, in SR, 106; "What Do 'Flappers' Read?" unidentified and undated clipping (ca. 1921), in SR, 185. See also F.W.T., review of *Rilla of Ingleside*, 4.
9 *Greensboro Daily News*, "The Montgomery Books," 4.
10 *Journal* (John O'Groats, UK), review of *Rainbow Valley*, date illegible, in SR, 154.
11 Montgomery, 16 August 1907, in *SJLMM*, 1: 331; Montgomery to Weber, 10 September 1908, in *GGL*, 73.
12 *The Publishers' Weekly*, "Notes on Travellers and Their Lines," 953; *The Publishers' Weekly*, "Notes in Season" (14 March 1908), 1113; *The Publishers' Weekly*, "Nineteen Hundred and Eight," 1157; *The Publishers' Weekly*, "Notes in Season" (13 June 1908), 1913; *The Publishers' Weekly*, "Published To-day," front cover. See also *The Publishers' Weekly*, "New Fiction," 1705; *The Publishers' Weekly*, "Ready at Once," 1479.
13 "Agreement between L.M. Montgomery and Her Publisher"; Browne, "Ingenious Novel by Paul Bourget," BR146; *The New York Times*, "Some of L.C. Page & Company's Spring Books," 35; *The Dial*, "Announcements of Spring Books," 188; *The Bookseller, Newsdealer and Stationer*, notice for *Anne of Green Gables*, 226; *The Bookseller, Newsdealer and Stationer*,

"Items of Interest" (15 June 1908), 401; *The New York Times*, "Boston Gossip of Latest Books" (20 June 1908), 358; *The Boston Herald*, "Week-End Book Notes," 7; *The Bookman* (New York), ad for *Anne of Green Gables*, 757; *The Globe*, "The Brightest Book of the Year," 2.

14 *The Boston Herald*, "Three Notable Books," 7; *The Bookman* (New York), "Chronicle and Comment," 348.

15 *The Bookman* (New York), "The Book Mart" (August 1909), 671–72, 674–78. In the July 1908 list, *Anne of Green Gables* appeared first in Cincinnati and Providence, fifth in Norfolk (Virginia), and sixth in Rochester (New York). In August, it appeared second in Norfolk, third in Providence and Rochester, fourth in Cincinnati and Indianapolis, and fifth in Worcester (Massachusetts). In September, it appeared third in Cincinnati and Norfolk, fifth in Baltimore, and sixth in Indianapolis and Portland (Maine). In October, it appeared second in Cleveland. In November, it appeared second in Cincinnati and third in Detroit. In December, it appeared third in Cincinnati, fourth in Indianapolis, and fifth in Denver. In January 1909, it appeared first in Pittsburgh, third in Boston, fifth in Cincinnati, and sixth in Atlanta. In February, on the fiction list, it appeared third in Worcester, fourth in Boston, fifth in Buffalo, and sixth in Cincinnati, and on the juvenile list it appeared second in Indianapolis and Philadelphia and third in Kansas City (Missouri). In March, on the fiction list, it appeared first in Boston, second in Worcester, and fourth in St. Louis (Missouri), and on the juvenile list, it appeared first in Kansas City, New Haven, Philadelphia, and St. Paul, second in Dallas and Seattle, and third in Indianapolis. In April, on the juvenile list, it appeared first in Indianapolis, Kansas City, Philadelphia, Portland, and St. Paul and second in Baltimore. In May, on the fiction list, it appeared fifth in Detroit, and on the juvenile list, it appeared first in Baltimore, Indianapolis, Kansas City, New Orleans, Philadelphia, Toronto, and Worcester and third in Albany and Dallas. See *The Bookman* (New York), "The Book Mart" (September 1908), 92, 94–95; ibid. (October 1908), 189–92; ibid. (November 1908), 293–95; ibid. (December 1908), 405; ibid. (January 1909), 517–18; ibid. (February 1909), 630; ibid. (March 1909), 109–10; ibid. (April 1909), 216–18, 220, 222; ibid. (May 1909), 327–31, 333–34; ibid. (June 1909), 447, 449–53; ibid. (July 1909), 565–68, 570–71, 574.

16 *The New York Times*, "Boston Gossip of Latest Books" (8 May 1909), BR297; *The Los Angeles Times*, "Departmentalized Index of Desirable Holiday Books," 1; *The Los Angeles Times*, "Books for Christmas," 6.

17 *The Bookman* (London), "The Booksellers' Diary," 166; Browne, "Boston Gossip of Latest Books," BR105; *The Boston Herald*, "Mid-Week Book

Notes," 6; *The Athenaeum*, ad for *Anne of Green Gables*, 187; *The Athenaeum*, "Literary Gossip," 76; *The Athenaeum*, notice for *Anne of Green Gables*, 104; *The Bookman* (London), "A Selection of Newly Published Books," 21; second and third ellipses in original.

18  See Lefebvre, "What's in a Name?"

19  Devereux, "'See My Journal for the Full Story,'" 250; Montgomery to Weber, 2 May 1907, in *GGL*, 51. In her entry dated 1907, she stated that she had begun the actual writing of the novel in May 1905, finishing it in January 1906 – "I think." But in a journal entry dated 1914, she wrote that she had written the opening paragraph one "evening in June ten years ago." Montgomery, 16 August 1907, in *SJLMM*, 1: 331; Montgomery, 18 April 1914, in *SJLMM*, 2: 147.

20  Montgomery, 16 August 1907, in *SJLMM*, 1: 331. For more on the professional relationship between Montgomery and the L.C. Page Company in the context of early-twentieth-century publishing, see Gerson, "'Dragged at Anne's Chariot Wheels.'"

21  Montgomery, 3 August 1908, in *SJLMM*, 1: 338; Montgomery to Weber, 10 September 1908, in *GGL*, 74; Montgomery, 28 March 1909, in *GGL*, 85; *The Globe*, "Under the Lamp," 4; Montgomery to MacMillan, 21 May 1909, in *MDMM*, 43. See also Montgomery, 9 October 1907, in *SJLMM*, 1: 332; Montgomery, 30 June 1908, in *SJLMM*, 1: 335–36.

22  *The Christian Advocate*, "Have You Met Her Yet?" 1952; *The Boston Herald*, "Have You Met Her Yet?" 8; *The Boston Globe*, ad for *Anne of Avonlea*, 7; *The Bookman* (New York), "'Leaders' from L.C. Page & Company's Fall List," 933; *The Bookman* (New York), "From Page's List" (August 1910), 687.

23  Montgomery to MacMillan, 21 February 1910, in *MDMM*, 48–49; Montgomery, 23 December 1909, in *SJLMM*, 1: 362; Montgomery, 27 January 1911, in *SJLMM*, 2: 45. See also Montgomery, 4 May 1910, in *SJLMM*, 2: 8.

24  *The Boston Globe*, "Bits from Bookland," 7.

25  *The Bookman* (New York), "From Page's List" (October 1910), 217; *The Boston Globe*, "Ready This Day," 4; *The Toronto Daily Star*, ad for the Robert Simpson Company Limited, 9; *Charlotte Daily Observer*, ad for *Kilmeny of the Orchard*, 6; *The Boston Herald*, "The Big New Novel," 7; *The Bookman* (New York), "From Page's List" (February 1911), 695.

26  Montgomery, 6 January 1910, in *SJLMM*, 1: 368; Montgomery, 29 November 1910, in *SJLMM*, 2: 20. See also Montgomery to MacMillan, 1 September 1910, in *MDMM*, 51.

27 "From L.C. Page & Company's Announcement List," n.pag. Much of this copy was also worked into the reviews for the novel in two newspapers: see *The Boston Globe*, "Very Engaging Novel," 11; *The New York Observer*, review of *The Story Girl*, 373.

28 *The Canadian Courier*, "Literary Notes," 31; *The Boston Herald*, "Indian Wars of New England," 8; *The New York Observer*, "Successful New Books," 635; *The Boston Globe*, ad for *The Story Girl*, 11; *The Boston Herald*, ad for *The Story Girl*, 8; *The Sun*, ad for *The Story Girl*, 8; *The Times–Dispatch*, ad for *The Story Girl*, 2; *The Boston Herald*, "Among Books and Authors" (3 May 1911), 7.

29 See Montgomery, 28 January 1912, in *SJLMM*, 2: 67.

30 Montgomery, 28 January 1912, in *SJLMM*, 2: 94.

31 *The Publishers' Weekly*, "Spring Lines of the Publishers" (24 February 1912), 634; *The Boston Herald*, "Among Books and Authors" (6 May 1912), 7; *The New York Times*, "Literary Boston," BR307; *The Boston Herald*, "The Best Fall Fiction," 8; *The Publishers' Weekly*, "The Best Sellers of 1912," 281; MacMurchy, "Retrospect of a Year's Books," 7; Montgomery to MacMillan, 20 January 1912, in *MDMM*, 66.

32 *The Publishers' Weekly*, "Literary and Trade Notes" (21 June 1913), 2157; *The Publishers' Weekly*, "Spring Lines of the Publishers" (22 February 1913), 666; *The Dial*, "Notes," 28.

33 Montgomery to MacMillan, 13 September 1913, in *MDMM*, 67. See also Montgomery, 21 May 1913, in *SJLMM*, 2: 119; Montgomery, 30 April 1912, in *SJLMM*, 2: 96.

34 *The Publishers' Weekly*, "From Page's List"; *The Publishers' Weekly*, "Educational Books in Demand," 312; *The Publishers' Weekly*, "Two of a Kind," 706; *The Publishers' Weekly*, ad for *The Golden Road*, 74; *The Bookman* (New York), "From Page's List" (September 1913), inside front cover; *The Bookman* (New York), "New Books of Importance," 94; *The Athenaeum*, "Ready Next Week," 285.

35 Montgomery to MacMillan, 20 February 1910, in *MDMM*, 50; Montgomery, 27 September 1913, in *SJLMM*, 2: 133; Montgomery, 11 April 1915, in *SJLMM*, 2: 163. See also Montgomery, 18 April 1914, in *SJLMM*, 2: 147; Montgomery, 20 November 1914, in *SJLMM*, 2: 156; Montgomery, 5 August 1914, in *SJLMM*, 2: 150–51; Montgomery, 30 August 1914, in *SJLMM*, 2: 151–52.

36 Butcher, "Tabloid Book Review," 3; *The Kansas City Star*, "Published Today," 12; *The Dallas Morning News*, "Published Today," 4; *The Bookman* (New York), "Worth While Vacation Reading," 67.

37 *The Publishers' Weekly*, "Literary and Trade Notes" (3 July 1915), 92; Young, "Trials of a Publisher," 27; *The Sun*, "Published Today," 10.

38 *The Independent*, "Folk Who Write," 123; *The Publishers' Weekly*, notice for *Anne of the Island*, 349; *Saint John Globe* (Saint John, NB), notice for *Anne of the Island*, 15 May 1915, in SR, 72; *The Publishers' Weekly*, "Canadian Notes," 2003.

39 Montgomery, 16 August 1907, in *SJLMM*, 1: 331; Gerson, "'Dragged at Anne's Chariot Wheels,'" 57. See also Montgomery, 29 November 1910, in *SJLMM*, 2: 25; Montgomery, 26 July 1915, in *SJLMM*, 2: 171; Montgomery, 25 May 1916, in *SJLMM*, 2: 185; Montgomery, 30 July 1916, in *SJLMM*, 187–88.

40 Montgomery, 16 December 1916, in *SJLMM*, 2: 198; Montgomery, 21 March 1916, in *SJLMM*, 2: 180–81; Benjamin Lefebvre, "L.M. Montgomery and Her Publishers," Historical Perspectives on Canadian Publishing, http://hpcanpub.mcmaster.ca/case-study/lm-montgomery-and-her-publishers. See also Montgomery, 12 April 1916, in *SJLMM*, 2: 182.

41 Montgomery, 11 November 1916, in *SJLMM*, 2: 194; *The Globe*, ad for *The Watchman and Other Poems*, 2; *The Bookseller, Newsdealer and Stationer*, notice for *The Watchman and Other Poems*, 379.

42 Montgomery, 21 July 1917, in *SJLMM*, 2: 222; Montgomery, 20 April 1916, in *SJLMM*, 2: 182; Montgomery to Weber, 25 November 1917, in *AfGG*, 67.

43 *The Publishers' Weekly*, "Literary and Trade Notes" (11 August 1917), 491; *The Publishers' Weekly*, ad for *Anne's House of Dreams*, 476; *The Bookseller, Newsdealer and Stationer*, ad for *Anne's House of Dreams*, 184; *The Publishers' Weekly*, notice for *Anne's House of Dreams*, 608; *The New York Tribune*, ad for *Anne's House of Dreams*, 5; *The New York Times*, ad for *Anne's House of Dreams*, 64; *The Athenaeum*, "Autumn Announcements," 544; *The Bookman* (London), ad for Constable & Co., ii.

44 Montgomery, 26 December 1918, in *SJLMM*, 2: 278.

45 *The Publishers' Weekly*, ad for *Rainbow Valley*, 462; *The Bookseller, Newsdealer and Stationer*, "Stokes Novels Ready August 25th," 118; *The New York Times*, ad for *Rainbow Valley*, 14; *The New York Times*, ad for Frederick A. Stokes Company, 98; *The Globe*, "Canadian Books for Christmas," 16; *Manitoba Free Press*, "Christmas Gifts for Particular People," Book Section, 2; ad for *Rainbow Valley*, unidentified and un-dated clipping, in SR, 151. See also *The Evening World*, "The Pleasant Land of Story Books," 15; *The Globe*, review of *Rainbow Valley*, 17; *The*

*New York Times*, "Christmas Books for Children," 5; *The New Orleans Item*, "Holmes Store News," 4; *The Publishers' Weekly*, "Stokes' Autumn Fiction," 1005.

46  See Montgomery, 14 January 1919, in *SJLMM*, 2: 285; Montgomery, 16 January 1919, in *SJLMM*, 2: 286; Montgomery, 18 December 1919, in *SJLMM*, 2: 358; Montgomery, 10 April 1920, in *SJLMM*, 2: 376; Montgomery to MacMillan, 10 February 1929, in *MDMM*, 140–47.

47  *The Bookseller, Newsdealer and Stationer*, "From Page's List" (15 January 1920), front cover; ibid., "Items of Interest" (15 January 1920), 66; ibid., "From Page's List" (1 February 1920), back cover; ibid., "From Page's List" (15 February 1920), front cover; ibid., "From Page's List" (1 April 1920), back cover; ibid., "From Page's List" (1 May 1920), back cover; *The Syracuse Herald*, "New Books for Girls," 9.

48  Montgomery, 24 August 1920, in *SJLMM*, 2: 390; Montgomery, 3 September 1921, in *SJLMM*, 3: 17.

49  Montgomery, "How I Became a Writer," Christmas Book Section, 3; Montgomery, 13 July 1936, in *SJLMM*, 5: 80.

50  *The Bookseller and Stationer*, ad for *Rilla of Ingleside*, inside front cover. See also *The Publishers' Weekly*, ad for *Rilla of Ingleside*, 620.

51  *The Publishers' Weekly*, "New Stokes Books," 658; *The Boston Herald*, "New Novel," 5; *The New York Times*, ad for *Rilla of Ingleside*, 52; *The Globe* (Toronto), ad for *Rilla of Ingleside*, 20. See also *The Bookseller and Stationer*, notice for *Rilla of Ingleside*, 24; *The Dallas Morning News*, "Books Make the Best Presents," 6; *The Publishers' Weekly*, "The Season's Outstanding Work," 1144; *The Bookseller and Stationer*, "New Stokes Books," 3.

52  Montgomery, 24 August 1920, in *SJLMM*, 2: 390; Montgomery to Weber, 29 September 1920, in *AfGG*, 84; Montgomery to MacMillan, 23 August 1920, in *MDMM*, 103; "No More of 'Anne' Books, Says Author," unidentified and undated clipping, in SR, 181–82.

53  Montgomery, 24 August 1920, in *SJLMM*, 2: 390; Montgomery, 13 December 1920, in *SJLMM*, 2: 391; Montgomery, 11 May 1921, in *SJLMM*, 3: 6. See also Montgomery, 20 August 1921, in *SJLMM*, 3: 16; Montgomery to Weber, 19 October 1921, in *AfGG*, 88; Montgomery to Weber, 25 September 1922, in *AfGG*, 104.

54  *The Boston Globe*, "The Reputation of the Author," 9; *The Globe*, review of *Emily of New Moon*, 22; Minot, "The Herald's Mid-Week Book Page," 21; *The Boston Herald*, ad for *Emily of New Moon* (15 December 1923), 7; ibid. (8 December 1923), 8; *The Boston Herald*, "Weather Forecast," 5.

55 Montgomery, 15 February 1922, in *SJLMM*, 3: 39; Montgomery to Weber, 1 November 1924, in *SJLMM*, 3: 114–15.

56 Montgomery, 23 June 1924, in *SJLMM*, 3: 191; Montgomery, 10 July 1924, in *SJLMM*, 3: 193; ad for Emily stories, *The Delineator*, undated clipping, in SR, 222. "Enter, Emily" condensed chapters 1–4 of *Emily of New Moon*; "Too Few Cooks" borrowed elements from chapters 6–8 of *New Moon* and was later reworked for chapter 17 of *Magic for Marigold*; "Night Watch" and "Her Dog Day" adapted chapters 3 and 22–24 of *Emily Climbs*.

57 Montgomery, 22 May 1922, in *SJLMM*, 3: 56; Montgomery, 20 January 1924, in *SJLMM*, 157. Montgomery felt so strongly about her views about the idealized realism in *Emily Climbs* that she repeated this response in near-identical form in letters to both MacMillan and Weber: see Montgomery to MacMillan, 3 September 1924, in *MDMM*, 118–19; Montgomery to Weber, 1 November 1924, in *AfGG*, 117–18.

58 Untitled and unidentified clipping, newspaper from St. Paul, Minnesota, 6 September 1925, in SR, 245; *The Boston Herald*, ad for *Emily Climbs*, 11. Montgomery to Weber, 1 November 1924, in *AfGG*, 115, 117; Montgomery, 10 April 1924, in *SJLMM*, 3: 180; Montgomery, 8 February 1925, in *SJLMM*, 3: 218. Mary Rubio suggests that Montgomery was so blocked creatively by the inevitability of having to push Emily toward a romantic resolution that she needed a different project to unblock her first. See her essay "Subverting the Trite: L.M. Montgomery's 'Room of Her Own'" in Volume 2 of *The L.M. Montgomery Reader*.

59 *The Morning Bulletin*, review of *The Blue Castle*, 12; *The Week* (Brisbane, Australia), "A Girl's Day Dreams," review of *The Blue Castle*, 20 August 1926, in SR, 264; *The Plain Dealer*, "She Married a Tramp," 7; Montgomery, "The Blue Castle" (*The Plain Dealer*), 2.

60 *The Boston Herald*, ad for *The Blue Castle*, 6; *The Bookman* (New York), "New Stokes Books," inside front cover; *The Boston Herald*, "Stokes Books for Christmas Giving," 21; Montgomery to Weber, 18 July 1926, in *AfGG*, 135.

61 Montgomery to Weber, 18 July 1926, in *AfGG*, 134; Montgomery, 2 April 1926, in *SJLMM*, 3: 292; Montgomery, 20 November 1926, in *SJLMM*, 3: 313. See also Montgomery, 30 June 1926, in *SJLMM*, 3: 298; Montgomery, 13 October 1926, in *SJLMM*, 3: 310.

62 Montgomery, 24 September 1925, in *SJLMM*, 3: 251; Montgomery, 30 October 1925, in *SJLMM*, 3: 259; Montgomery to Weber, 18 July 1926, in *AfGG*, 135; Montgomery, "Magic for Marigold," 85; "L.M. Montgomery:

A Maker of Magic Who Sends Her Best to *The Delineator*," unidentified
and undated clipping, in SR, 237; Montgomery to MacMillan, 10 February
1929, in *MDMM*, 140.

63 Montgomery to Weber, 16 November 1927, in *AfGG*, 154; Montgomery, 1
June 1927, in *SJLMM*, 3: 335; Montgomery, 17 October 1928, in *SJLMM*,
3: 379; Montgomery, 3 May 1929, in *SJLMM*, 3: 396.

64 See Russell, Russell, and Wilmshurst, *Lucy Maud Montgomery*, 92–94.

65 *The Boston Herald*, ad for Frederick A. Stokes Company, 19; *The Globe*,
ad for *Magic for Marigold*, 22; *The Bookman* (London), "Books of the
Month," 155.

66 Montgomery, 1 October 1928, in *SJLMM*, 3: 379.

67 Montgomery to MacMillan, 10 February 1929, in *MDMM*, 138;
Montgomery, 3 May 1929, in *SJLMM*, 3: 396.

68 Montgomery to Weber, 27 December 1931, in *AfGG*, 193–94. See
also Montgomery, 1 June 1931, in *SJLMM*, 4: 121.

69 Montgomery, 11 July 1931, in *SJLMM*, 4: 139, 142.

70 *The Los Angeles Times*, "Romance Opens Door to Joy," 14; *The Chicago
Daily Tribune*, "Here Are Christmas Books," 21. See also Lefebvre,
"Pigsties and Sunsets," 130n9, 142.

71 Montgomery, 3 December 1932, in *SJLMM*, 4: 211; Montgomery, 1 August
1933, in *SJLMM*, 4: 227; Montgomery to Weber, 16 July 1933, in *AfGG*,
209. See also Montgomery, 2 April 1932, in *SJLMM*, 4: 178; Montgomery,
6 January 1933, in *SJLMM*, 4: 213; Montgomery, 17 February 1933, in
*SJLMM*, 4: 217.

72 Montgomery to Weber, 16 July 1933, in *AfGG*, 211; Montgomery, 15
June 1934, in *SJLMM*, 4: 270. See also Montgomery, 15 January 1934, in
*SJLMM*, 4: 252; Montgomery, 31 March 1934, in *SJLMM*, 4: 257.

73 Mackey, review of *L.M. Montgomery*, 62; *The Toronto Daily Star*, ad for
*Mistress Pat*, 28.

74 Montgomery, 9 March 1935, in *SJLMM*, 4: 356–57. See also Montgomery
to Weber, 22 June 1936, in *AfGG*, 227–28; Montgomery to MacMillan, 1
March 1936, in *MDMM*, 177; Montgomery, 6 May 1935, in *SJLMM*, 5:
10.

75 Montgomery, 8 November 1935, in *SJLMM*, 5: 45; *The Toronto Daily
Star*, "Creator of 'Anne' Addresses Women," 25; Montgomery, 11 January
1936, in *SJLMM*, 5: 54; Montgomery to MacMillan, 27 December 1936,
in *MDMM*, 180–81. See also Montgomery, 12 August 1935, in *SJLMM*,
5: 31; Montgomery, 23 August 1935, in *SJLMM*, 5: 32; Montgomery, 25
November 1935, in *SJLMM*, 5: 47.

76  Montgomery, 21 August 1936, in *SJLMM*, 5: 85; Montgomery to Weber, 18 June 1937, in *AfGG*, 236. See also Montgomery, 11 May 1936, in *SJLMM*, 5: 67.

77  Montgomery to Weber, 18 June 1937, in *AfGG*, 236; Montgomery, 26 April 1937, in *SJLMM*, 5: 161; Montgomery, 7 September 1938, in *SJLMM*, 5: 277; Montgomery, 12 September 1938, in *SJLMM*, 5: 278.

78  Montgomery to MacMillan, 7 March 1939, in *MDMM*, 195; Montgomery to Weber, 8 May 1939, in *AfGG*, 248; Montgomery to Weber, 13 February 1940, in *AfGG*, 255.

79  The eight instalments were adapted from the following chapters of *Anne of Ingleside*: 4–6; 7–10; 18–20; 28–29; 25–26; 23–24; 34; 35–36. See also Montgomery, 6 March 1939, in *SJLMM*, 5: 310.

80  Montgomery, 8 December 1938, in *SJLMM*, 5: 295; Rubio, *Lucy Maud Montgomery*, 562; Montgomery to Weber, 13 February 1940, in *AfGG*, 256.

81  For more on *The Blythes Are Quoted* and Montgomery's death, see Lefebvre, Afterword; Rubio, "Uncertainties Surrounding the Death of L.M. Montgomery."

82  Montgomery, 1 March 1930, in *SJLMM*, 4: 43.

# A Note on the Text

This volume consists of 370 reviews published in newspapers, magazines, and journals in Canada, the United States, the United Kingdom, Cuba, India, South Africa, Australia, and New Zealand – an indication of the impressive reach of L.M. Montgomery's books throughout the English-speaking world. Beginning in 1912, after her move to Leaskdale, Ontario, Montgomery began pasting clippings of reviews and notices into a six-hundred-page scrapbook that is now housed at the University of Guelph archives and known as "Scrapbook of Reviews from Around the World Which Her Clipping Service Sent to Her, 1910–1935." The earliest reviews are of her third book, *Kilmeny of the Orchard*, published in 1910, and although there are mentions in her journals of scrapbooks containing reviews of *Anne of Green Gables* and *Anne of Avonlea*, those clippings appear to have gone astray. In most cases, Montgomery also included a tag from various clipping services that identified the periodical and the date (although not the page number), but in other cases Montgomery provided any bibliographical information she had or included clippings with no identifying information at all. Also included in this scrapbook are clippings of her essays, interviews, and published letters, many of which are reprinted in Volume 1 of *The L.M. Montgomery Reader,* as well as extensive reports on the 1919 and 1934 screen adaptations of *Anne of Green Gables,* even though she had no creative involvement with either project and did not benefit financially from their success.

# A Note on the Text

In my role as hunter and gatherer, I have attempted to supplement the reviews in Montgomery's scrapbook, first by locating as many of these clippings as possible in their original sources (thus confirming or correcting the publication date and adding pagination as well), and second by adding to them a significant amount of reviews that are not found in Montgomery's scrapbook and that I have located after numerous searches of online repositories and print collections in university libraries. The 370 reviews included in their entirety are a representative sample of a much wider range of reviews, many of which are summarized in the headnotes that open each chapter.

As with the preceding two volumes of *The L.M. Montgomery Reader*, I have refrained from making excessive editorial interventions. Although I have silently corrected obvious errors in spelling and punctuation and standardized the capitalization of titles and subheads, I have retained the inconsistent use of American and British spellings and styles, given that Canadian newspapers, in particular, seemed to draw on both conventions equally. I have italicized the titles of books and films as well as words and phrases that are bolded, underlined, or capitalized for emphasis in the copy texts. I have also corrected misspellings of names (including "Annie Shirley," "Beverly King," "Cicely King," "Davey Keith," "L.H. Montgomery," "L.W. Montgomery," "Ludivic Speed," "Ludovick Speed," "Miss Lavender," "Mrs. Evan MacDonald," "Mrs. Ewan McDonald") and places ("Alvonlea, "Prince Edward's Island," "Prince Edward's Isle"), but I comment on these corrections and other substantive corrections in the notes. I have refrained from correcting factual errors (including misconceptions about the setting of these books) and the occasional misgendering of L.M. Montgomery. I have almost always retained the title of a review, but if a review was untitled, as was most often the case, I have provided a descriptive title within square brackets. All reviews are presented in full, except in a few cases in which excessive quotations from the book in question are deleted and noted with [* * *].

It is also worth noting that many of these reviews give away crucial plot details (what we now call "spoilers") from the books in question, including the way they end.

For an exhaustive list of reviews and other resources pertaining to L.M. Montgomery's work, see the website for L.M. Montgomery Online at http://lmmonline.org.

# 1

## *Anne of Green Gables*

—— 1908 ——

When Montgomery provided Ephraim Weber with an account of the sixty reviews of *Anne of Green Gables* that she had received by early September 1908, she noted that "two were harsh, one contemptuous, two mixed praise and blame and the remaining fifty-five were kind and flattering beyond my highest expectations."[1] The twenty-two reviews from Canada, the United States, and the United Kingdom included in their entirety below reflect this range in terms of reviewers' overall high praise for the novel; while the first known review, in the *New York Times Saturday Review*, is rather negative, it certainly did not set the tone for those that followed. And as with all chapters in this volume, the ones included in full are a small fraction of the vast amount of reviews that appeared in newspapers and magazines. Anne Henszey Bradford, for instance, opined in the *Boston Budget and Beacon* that "of course Anne is altogether too precocious a youngster to find in real life, but she is a most diverting book heroine," whereas George Murray was highly enthusiastic in his review, published in the *Montreal Daily Star* the same day:

> We have much pleasure in drawing attention to this novel, not only
> because it is, in our opinion, the most fascinating book of the season,
> but because its author, Miss Montgomery, is a resident of Prince Edward
> Island, where the scene of the story is laid, and is evidently a keen student
> of both nature and human nature. The fact that the volume was published
> quite recently, and is now in its second large edition, is a sufficient guar-
> antee of its unusual merit; but it is almost impossible for readers to guess
> even vaguely the treat that awaits them in its perusal.[2]

Later reviews were equally full of praise: "It could have been written only by a woman of deep and wide sympathy with child nature, one able to look beyond the trammels of conventionality and discover the hidden jewel uncut and unpolished," declared the *Boston Herald*. The *Springfield Republican* of Massachusetts added that "the author has written a book that should prove one of the most popular of the holiday stories; it certainly deserves to be." While most of the reviews treated *Anne of Green Gables* as a novel for adults, a good number wrote about it as a wholesome book for young girls: "The teaching of the novel is wholesome, and the book is a suitable present for a young girl at school," *The Oregonian* declared, adding that "there ought to be more sensible books like *Anne of Green Gables*." The *Grand Rapids Press* made a similar pronouncement, calling it "a girl story with the real flavor." And in a review published in 1925, at which point the novel was reissued with new illustrations, the *Wilmington Every Evening* of Delaware called the novel "clean and wholesome, full of lively humor, and most interesting to all readers, most appropriately to young girls. It is well to have such books, especially in these days of erratic literature."[3]

## A Heroine from an Asylum
### *The New York Times Saturday Review* (New York, NY)

A farmer in Prince Edward Island[4] ordered a boy from a Nova Scotia asylum, but the order got twisted and the result was that a girl was sent the farmer instead of a boy. That girl is the heroine of L.M. Montgomery's story, *Anne of Green Gables*, and it is no exaggeration to say that she is one of the most extraordinary girls that ever came out of an ink pot.[5]

The author undoubtedly meant her to be queer, but she is altogether too queer. She was only 11 years old when she reached the house in Prince Edward Island that was to be her home, but, in spite of her tender years, and in spite of the fact that, excepting for four months spent in the asylum, she had passed all her life with illiterate folks, and had had almost no schooling, she talked to the farmer and his sister as though she had borrowed Bernard Shaw's vocabulary, Alfred Austin's sentimentality, and the reasoning powers of a Justice of the Supreme Court.[6] She knew so much that she spoiled the author's plan at the very outset and greatly marred a story that had in it quaint and charming possibilities.

The author's probable intention was to exhibit a unique development in this little asylum waif, but there is no real difference between the girl at the end of the story and the one at the beginning of it. All the other characters in the book are human enough.

## [Will Appeal to Every Reader]
### *The Montreal Daily Herald* (Montreal, QC)

Whether Miss L.M. Montgomery is a Canadian or not, we know not, but if she isn't she has taken a Canadian countryside, and peopled it, in a manner marvellously natural, and if she is a Canadian she has succeeded in writing one of the few Canadian stories that can appeal to the whole English-speaking world. *Anne of Green Gables* is a charmingly-told story of life on the north shore of Prince Edward Island, but the local coloring is most delicately placed on the canvas and in no respect weakens the impression created by the central figure, Anne. This waif from an orphan asylum in Nova Scotia, adopted by an old farmer and his maiden sister, is covered with a sensitive and imaginative mind and the story of her hopes, struggles and ambitions, will appeal to every reader, old and young. She is certainly one of the most attractive figures Canadian fiction has yet produced, while the characters of the farmer and his sister are drawn with a delicacy of touch that is most refreshing and charming. The book is an ideal volume for growing girls, being as pure and sweet as the wild flowers of the Island which Miss Montgomery describes so lovingly. In fact, one of the great attractions of the story is the author's love of nature which finds expression everywhere, without once appearing exaggerated or forced. The story is one which will give profit and pleasure to all its readers.

## [An Imaginative, Eager Child]
### *The Sun* (New York, NY)

A pretty story in which the opportunities the author allows to go by are as marked as those she puts to good use is *Anne of Green Gables*, by L.M. Montgomery. The author understands thoroughly the rural surroundings and makes the reader understand them too. The old farmer, his sister, who to some will seem the real heroine, and two or three other women are drawn with vigor and truth. The blunder by which the eleven-year-old young person is introduced into the story is ingenious and natural and the episode is handled very delicately. She is a nice little girl and in her the author has shown as we have never seen before the inner workings of the mind of an imaginative, eager child. The volubility with which she is endowed is probably true to nature too, but there are too many specimens of it, and the vocabulary with which she expresses her feelings is that of a grown up person and not that of a child. That seems to be one opportunity missed. Another is in the setting: this is in Prince Edward Island, which is virgin ground for the story teller, yet there is little to mark the place in the story. It might be at any country village near the seashore. Again, as the heroine grows up she drops into pretty conventional lines. It is a good story in its way and it is no discredit to the author if she makes us see that there were greater possibilities in it.

## [A Pathetic Little Tale]
### *Saint John Globe* (Saint John, NB)

Anne is a truly delightful little girl who goes from an orphan asylum in Nova Scotia to a home on Prince Edward Island. The people to whom she was to go had written for a boy, and when Anne, with her undeniable freckles, her tawny head and lively little tongue, appeared, she was so far from the original idea of some one to "save steps now and lean upon later," that was in the good people's mind when they had decided upon the adoption of a child, that it was felt wiser to return her to the asylum. However, Anne's ready acceptance of her fate, her willingness to make the best of whatever came to her, and the pathetic revelations she unconsciously made of the bareness of her life win over the friends and she finds with them a home, "a really truly home,"[7] where she is wanted, and where later she makes herself a necessity. Her career in the village among her friends, and with her school mates, the development under kindly influences of a generous impulsive nature, form the background of a pretty story that by its naturalness will charm its readers. "Green Gables" is the name of the home to which Anne comes and where she finds a happiness that even in her wildest flight of imagination she had never compassed. She is not by any means an unusual girl, but falls into all sorts of mischief, her impulsiveness carrying her far into the world of mistakes, but having had to depend upon her own resources through eleven dreary years of "living out," she has a well developed mind and on more than one occasion comes to a timely rescue. She is lovable, naughty, bright and stubborn, but under kindly influences develops into a fine young woman, and one leaves her reluctantly on the threshold of a romance, feeling that he would like to hear more of her. Like Miss Alcott's girls,[8] she has become in this story of her life at Green Gables a friend.

## [Picture of Prince Edward Island Life and Character]
### *The Gazette* (Montreal, QC)

This picture of Prince Edward Island life and character by a Prince Edward Islander of genius, Miss L.M. Montgomery, cannot fail to delight every Canadian who reads it. It is only necessary to read a few pages of the book to be assured that *Anne of Green Gables* is in conception and style, the fruit (the first fruit, we believe) of a richly endowed mind of rare imaginative capacity. Her scenes and the personages with which she peoples them become real as one reads. It is our privilege to know Avonlea and Lynde's Hollow and Bright River and The Avenue. It is our greater privilege to know Anne herself. As she says in her happy confidences to the kind old Matthew, Is it not delightful when your imaginations come true? Anne of Green Gables, when we meet her first at the Bright River station, seems in truth to be of imagination all compact. To Matthew her presence is at first a hard, negative and puzzling fact, Anne being anything but the boy that he expected to find, he had to give an account of himself to Marilla. Anne's poetic raptures soon held him captive. But he knew that Marilla would not be easily won by flights of fancy, and he dreaded the substitution of the boy, lately so much desired. But Anne was born to conquer spinsters and matrons as well as men and ultimately even boys. Droll, pathetic, sometimes all but tragic, is the story of her sayings and doings, but the apprenticeship, which ends at Marilla's gate and another ripens Anne of Green Gables into a very charming woman, while it makes us acquainted with some Prince Edward Islanders that are well worth knowing. The book is handsomely bound and illustrated.

## [A Pleasant Book of the Hour]
### *The Boston Journal* (Boston, MA)

A most charming personality is the heroine of this bright tale, and the author has drawn her vividly and sympathetically, but with discretion. Her parents by adoption – the gruff old farmer and his spinster sister – are also pictured with an unusual fidelity to nature. With these central personages the story moves along briskly, making entertainment to the reader by the development of the characters and by the interest in the plot. It is a pleasant book of the hour.

## [A Story So Pure and Sweet]
### *The Globe* (Toronto, ON)

The craze for problem novels has at present seized a large section of the reading public, and it must be confessed that several recent stories have not been healthy reading, and can serve no useful purpose that we can see. In these days of unhealthy literature it is, however, a real pleasure to come across a story so pure and sweet as *Anne of Green Gables*, by L.M. Montgomery, from the press of Messrs. L.C. Page & Co., of Boston, Mass. There are no pretensions to a great plot in the story, but from the first line to the last the reader is fascinated by the sayings and doings of the girl child taken from a Nova Scotia home, adopted by the old Scotch maid and bachelor, brother and sister, who owned Green Gables, a Prince Edward Island farm, situated in one of the garden spots of the beautiful Island Province in the St. Lawrence Gulf.

The quaintness of the child, the funny scene when the old bachelor brother finds a girl waiting at the station for him, and not a boy, as ordered from the home, are pictured in irresistible drollery. Then the reader's interest is evoked as the author pictures how the poorly-trained and often harshly-treated little maiden develops into womanhood, under the strict yet kindly training of the strange couple who loved her so dearly, and who, Scotch like, could not find words to give utterance to that love. Every Canadian boy and girl who has had the happy chance of going to a rural school, and who has had ambitions to be something different to the ordinary individual, will take "Anne of Green Gables" to heart, and will laugh and cry with her in her school and home troubles, and many will easily call to mind people who are the very doubles of the tart, the gossipy yet always lovable characters sketched so faithfully by Miss Montgomery in her story; and those who have had the privilege to visit the Island Province will revel in the simple, yet splendid descriptions of the people and scenery of the Island which are to be found on almost every page of this excellent story. *Anne of Green Gables* is worth a thousand of the problem stories with which the bookshelves are crowded to-day, and we venture the opinion that this simple story of rural life in Canada will be read and reread when many of the more pretentious stories are all forgotten. There is not a dull page in the whole volume, and the comedy and tragedy are so deftly woven together that it is at times difficult to divide them. The story is told by an author who knows the Island of Prince Edward thoroughly, and who has carefully observed the human tide which flows through that Island, as it does over all places where human beings live. With the pen of an artiste she has painted that tide so that its deep tragedies are just lightly revealed, for she evidently prefers to show us the placid flow, with its steadiness, its sweetness, and witchery, until the reader stands still to watch the play of sunshine and shadow as it is deftly pictured by the hand of the author of *Anne of Green Gables*.

## [A Girl to Remember]
### *The Living Age* (New York, NY)

Let it be said at the beginning that *Anne of Green Gables*, by L.M. Montgomery, is not a second Rebecca, for, as there are already some twenty-five "second Rebeccas," without counting the apparently intentional Rebecca Mary,[9] such an introduction might not be a recommendation. Anne Shirley, Anne with an "e," comes from a Nova Scotia orphan asylum to Prince Edward Island to be informally adopted by an elderly brother and sister to whom she discourses endlessly.[10] "Ten minutes by the clock" is one listener's measure of her eloquence.[11] More than two pages by the eye is the reader's observation, but it is amusing talk, and so entirely American that one fully expects that the inevitable sequel will reveal her American birth. This book leaves her crowned with the highest honors of Queen's College, and showing herself worthy of them by unselfish devotion to the good woman who has sheltered her for five years. She is but sixteen years of age and many things may yet happen. Meantime, no one who has made her acquaintance is likely to forget her or to neglect the sequel when it arrives. Anne of Green Gables is a girl to remember.

## [An "Ugly Duckling" Story, After All]
### *The Plain Dealer* (Cleveland, OH)

*Anne of Green Gables*, by L.M. Montgomery, is one of those books for girls that will be found as worth reading by grown ups as by little readers. Anne is a "skinny," plain featured, brick haired orphan, with an ugly temper and a superabundance of self-consciousness. She gets herself and her friends into all kinds of trouble. But it turns out to be an "ugly duckling" story, after all, for Anne develops into a handsome and lovable young lady. The book is exceptionally well written and stands quite above the average of its kind, a composite of Kate Douglas Wiggin and Louisa Alcott.

## *Anne of Green Gables* Is a Story for Girls
### *The Evening News* (San Jose, CA)

*Anne of Green Gables* is a story for girls by L.M. Montgomery. The book is very attractively bound and illustrated, and the plot centers on an orphan girl who is adopted by a crabbed maiden lady and her brother. Anne is an interesting character and her queer doings and sayings quite make up for the absence of an interesting plot. She is a personality who proves fascinating not only to girls, but to people of all ages.

## [An Engaging Bit of Juvenilia]
### *The New York Tribune* (New York, NY)

An engaging bit of juvenilia is Miss L.M. Montgomery's *Anne of Green Gables*, the story of a little orphan whose tongue is hung in the middle. Never was there so prodigious a talker as Miss Anne Shirley. When old Matthew Cuthbert and his sister Marilla decide to adopt a boy out of an asylum it is bad enough for them to have a girl unexpectedly placed upon their hands instead of the desired urchin. The situation promises to become quite impossible when Anne turns out to be possessed of a burning imagination and an inexhaustible power of speech. There is something innocent as well as amusing about her, however, and she very soon makes herself indispensable to the lonely pair. Her sallies are cleverly hit off and the author shrewdly develops her difficult little heroine's character. The story closes only after Anne has been exhibited as emerging into admirable womanliness from her too talkative and self-assertive girlhood.

## [Lively Story of an Orphan Girl]
### *ALA Booklist* (Chicago, IL)

Lively story of an orphan girl, sent from an asylum by mistake to an elderly brother and sister, who wanted a boy to assist on the farm. Anne is a lovable, impulsive, imaginative but obedient child who gets all there is out of her narrow life, receives a good education and becomes a great source of pride and comfort in the Green Gables home. A story that all girls from 12 to 15, and many grown-ups, will enjoy.

## [A Winner of Hearts]
### *The Book News Monthly* (Philadelphia, PA)

Anne is a creation – a quaint, talkative little being with a big imagination and the gift of a facile expression. They had wanted a boy, but the "boy" proved to be a girl, and she was taken from an orphan asylum to be adopted into the household of a hard-hearted spinster who lives with a bachelor brother. Naturally Anne is a winner of hearts, with her old-young wisdom and her droll, queer little ways.

The story of Anne is being compared to that of *Rebecca*, the winning child of Sunnybrook Farm, and the comparison brings no discredit upon Anne. Mrs. Wiggin has accomplished no more charming little tale and no more engaging small character than Miss Montgomery has achieved in *Anne of Green Gables*. Says the maiden lady: "No house will ever be dull that [Anne's] in,"[12] and that is the plain truth. Young and old will find in this book an enjoyment as whole-souled as it will be wholesome, and a refreshment that certainly will not come amiss.

## [A Charming Character Study]
### *The Canadian Magazine* (Toronto, ON)

In the whole range of Canadian fiction one might search a long time for a character study of equal charm with *Anne of Green Gables*, a novel that easily places the author, Miss L.M. Montgomery, in the first rank of our native writers. The story of Anne, of her "ups and downs" in life is excellent in technique, development and consistency. It contains much genuine, quaint and wholesome humour, and it also appeals in a very intense way to the best human sympathies. Anne is indeed a most interesting and entertaining person, and she might well be placed with the best character creations in recent fiction. Her environment, a picturesque section of Prince Edward Island, is thoroughly Canadian, and Miss Montgomery presents it in a piquant literary style, full of grace and whole-heartedness.

Anne is an orphan who, owing to an error, is sent instead of a boy from an orphanage to live at "Green Gables" with Marilla Cuthbert, a spinster, and her brother, Matthew, a bachelor, both persons of rather set and precise notions of propriety. Anne is an extremely impetuous girl, and early in life she is bowed down in sorrow with red hair and freckles and an angular form, almost as angular as Marilla's. But she has a very accommodating imagination, a faculty that relieves her of many a heartache. She is continuously seeking "scope for imagination." On her first morning at "Green Gables" she looked out from her bedroom window and saw an apple tree in full bloom. Her delight was unbounded, and she expressed it generously to Marilla, whose appreciation of picturesqueness and romance is not very keen. [* * *]13

The author is a resident of Cavendish, P.E.I., and is a young woman of unusual ability as a writer.


## [Fresh Tale of Country Life]
### *Colorado Springs Gazette* (Colorado Springs, CO)

One looking for a bright, fresh tale of country life need search no further. Mr. Montgomery has drawn an attractive picture of life on Victoria island near Nova Scotia. So far away one may doubt the actual existence of Victoria island, but we have the testimony of geographies as to the actuality of Nova Scotia. The interest of the story does not depend upon whether there is such a place surrounded by water; the author has surrounded it by a deep interest that is better. A little girl, Anne, capable of more blunders and accidents than any other girl of her age, has fallen into kindly hands, those of folks who will make light of them, even to the point of causing the reader to think more of Anne because of them.

Anne, when she is presented, is red-headed, freckled, dressed in poor clothes, with an imagination that colors everything the brightest. She is presented in a home where she is not wanted, the old bachelor and his sister having sent to the asylum for a boy, but she comes in such a way that they decide to keep her. As told by Mr. Montgomery, it is the luckiest disappointment of their lives, for they learn to take an interest in the affairs of people not living at Green Gables, and there is a zest put into human affairs which did not exist for them before.

## [Arcadian Purity and Simplicity]
### *The National Magazine* (Boston, MA)

It came about in this way: The book came to my desk after going the round of the family circle. It had been read aloud, read in silence, read in bed, read on street cars, in fact, it had been read everywhere in every way. Somehow, I felt slightly acquainted with Anne of Green Gables even before I had opened the book. Far into the morning I sat beneath the rooflight of a speeding night train, until I had finished reading this delightful story, leaving Anne walking in the lane with her lover.

The book is redolent with the charm of Prince Edward Island; the characters are delicately drawn, and every page has its own interest as the author tells how the orphan child wins all hearts, beginning with the elderly bachelor and old maid, Matthew and Marilla. The former is touched by little Anne's fancies and childish imaginings as he drives her from the station to Green Gables. She looks with wide-eyed delight at the scenery, and promptly proceeds to christen the beauty spots with more suitable names than those they bear. Hereafter to her they are "The White Way of Delight," the "Lake of Shining Waters," and the plants and trees become "Bonny" and "Snow Queen." When Anne has been at Green Gables a few hours, Marilla is obliged to admit to herself that "there's nothing rude or slangy in what she does say," though she "talk[s] entirely too much for a little girl."[14]

At about the thirty-seventh page the story begins to "draw blood" – I mean tears. At supper, Anne cannot eat because of the lump in her throat, brought there by the knowledge that a boy was wanted, and not a girl; that she is unwelcome at Green Gables and may be obliged to return to the orphan asylum. She has already made a conquest of Matthew, who confides later to his sister that "she's a real interesting little thing,"[15] and is evidently willing, much to Marilla's disgust, that the child should remain at Green Gables. Anne's own story, – Anne spelled with an "e" – told in her own romantic way, and a sight of the woman to whom she will be consigned if Marilla refuses to keep her, soften the heart of the woman, and the announcement that she may remain at Green Gables and have the "real home" for which she has always longed is received with such delight that Marilla again remonstrates.

Charming pictures of rural life follow, interspersed with the story of Anne's struggles with her temper and the difficulties into which her vivid imagination leads her. The people really move and talk, diffusing an atmosphere of Arcadian purity and simplicity that is refreshing.

Marilla discovers that Anne needs instructions in other matters than housekeeping, when the child announces, "I never say any prayers."

She explains her reason for this omission: "People who haven't red hair don't know what trouble is. Mrs. Thomas told me that God made my hair red *on purpose*, and I've never cared about Him since."

Marilla insists that Anne shall pray, and the child cheerfully assents: "I'd do anything to oblige you," though she regrets she has not time to make her utterances as flowery as she would wish.[16]

The red hair continues to be a source of grief, reaching the climax when, on being left alone in the house, her fertile imagination suggests a remedy on the appearance of a peddler in whom she "believes *implicitly*." Later her faith in human veracity is somewhat shaken when the dye, warranted to turn her hair "a beautiful raven black" and never wash out, fulfills only the latter part of the promise, and the green hair absolutely refuses to turn red again, despite a week of washing, and the despised locks have to be cut close to Anne's head, while she laments:

"Such an unromantic affliction – there is no comfort in having your hair cut off because you've dyed it a dreadful color – it seems such a tragic thing."[17]

Occasionally her romance and love for the beautiful get her into difficulties, but even a tough old editor can feel for the child when she yearns unavailingly for "puffed sleeves," an indulgence which finally comes to her through the kindness of her fast friend, Matthew, who never fails to be delighted with her outspoken comments on life and character. Her "utterances" and "expert opinions" are often more profound than those authoritative minds consider. Her naive simplicity and affection are invincible, and for her obstacles arise only to be surmounted, even to the extent of inventing a falsehood in order to please Marilla. If for this once she must depart from the straight path of truth, she does it artistically, and makes the fabrication "as interesting as possible."[18] At times she is a trial to her guardian's sense of propriety, as when she goes to Sunday school with real flowers in her hat, because her beauty-loving soul detests the Spartan severity of the raiment provided for her. Despite it all, Marilla grows to love the child, and it is not long until her heart is wrapped around the little waif whom she and Matthew have rescued from slavish drudgery or the orphan asylum, where "there is never enough to go around."[19]

The annals of the country school are very real, and one feels personally acquainted with teachers and scholars and sympathizes with Anne in the indignity of a "take notice" and the rasping influence of the Pye family, whose mission in life, Mrs. Lynde opines, is "to keep schoolteachers reminded that earth isn't their home."[20]

The one thing that Anne cannot endure is an allusion to her red hair, and when Gilbert Blythe calls her "carrots,"[21] she arises and smashes her slate over his head; for years she refuses his efforts at reconciliation, and they become rivals in scholarship. At last the seeds of a tender romance begin to grow and blossom, and Anne has dreams of "the turn in the road."[22]

Anne's errors are many and remarkable. She puts liniment in the cake instead of flavoring, just when she wants it especially good for her new friends, the minister and his wife. Yet she is always optimistic, and assures Marilla that she must come to an end of her mistakes after a time, because she never makes the same one twice. Even the "unfortunate Lily Maid" episode does not permanently damp her spirits. After a good cry in the solitude of her little room, she tells Marilla:

"I think my prospects of becoming sensible are brighter now than ever ... each mistake has helped to cure me of some great shortcoming." Her final conclusion that "it is no use trying to be romantic in Avonlea ... romance is not appreciated now," meets with dissent from Matthew, who comes and lays a kindly hand on her shoulder and says:

"Don't give up all your romance, Anne ... keep a little of it, Anne, keep a little of it."[23]

The reader is disposed to agree with Mrs. Lynde – who has forgotten her first stormy meeting with Anne and grown to love her – that there is no danger of her ever becoming "too sensible."

Yes, I was looking for trouble with her "bosom friend" all through, but reached the last page and failed to find even a single "fuss" with Diana or a gloomy thought, as the "chatterbox child" grew to womanhood and developed a sweet reticence as attractive as her former freedom of speech. When the last page is read and the book is laid down, one feels that it really is possible to find something lovable in every human being – could more be said of any book?

## [A Delightful Book]
*The New York Observer* (New York, NY)

One of the most delightful books of the year is *Anne of Green Gables*, the Christian name spelled with an "e" as she herself insisted because that means a great deal more. L.C. Page & Company are the fortunate publishers and L.M. Montgomery,[24] whose portrait is here presented, is the author. The story is cleverly written and Anne's words and ways hold the interest of the reader from the beginning to the end of the book. Her imagination is most wonderfully developed, clothing ordinary every day affairs with a garment of bright colors. Often as the pages are turned, the reader is made to laugh at the quaint sayings and queer doings of Anne and often too some sweet and tender touch brings a lump to the throat and a dimness to the eyes. Little by little as Anne's life unfolds from the time when she is taken from the orphanage into the home of Marilla and Matthew Cuthbert there to win her way into both their hearts until her devotion to her benefactors and her appreciation of their goodness is proved beyond question, the reader becomes more and more in love with the dear mistake-making girl who in the end develops into a sweet young woman capable of supreme self sacrifice. The public need only to realize how enjoyable a book *Anne of Green Gables* is to insure its being a deserved success.

## [A Canadian Tale of Domestic Sentiment]
*The Times Literary Supplement* (London, UK)

A Canadian tale of domestic sentiment which seems to have attained popularity across the Atlantic – Anne being a little orphan girl adopted by farming folk on the Gulf of St. Lawrence.

## [An Irrepressible Idealist and Optimist]
*Vogue* (New York, NY)

*Anne of Green Gables*, by L.M. Montgomery, is a story for girls of almost any age between eleven and eighteen, and one that should bring something of value to almost any young reader. The central character is an irrepressible idealist and optimist, one whom ill fortune cannot really touch, because she herself, as Whitman says, is good fortune.[25] The little orphan child from the asylum brings sunshine wherever she comes, and that without being figured to us as a prig or a prodigy. She sees whatever is beautiful in the aspects of men, in the character of those about her, enjoys all good things, and turns toward the world a face of unsuspicious and untroubled good-will. This book has in it great possibilities of character-building.

## [An Alternative Entertainment]
### *The Spectator* (London, UK)

We can pay the author of *Anne of Green Gables* no higher compliment than to say that she has given us a perfect Canadian companion picture to *Rebecca of Sunnybrook Farm*. There is no question of imitation or borrowing: it is merely that the scheme is similar and the spirit akin. To all novel-readers weary of problems, the duel of sex, broken Commandments, and gratuitous suicides, Miss Montgomery provides an alternative entertainment, all the more welcome because what we get in place of those hackneyed features is at once wholesome and attractive. As for Prince Edward Island, in which the scene is laid, no better advertisement of the charm of its landscape could be devised than the admirable descriptions of its sylvan glories which lend decorative relief to the narrative. Miss Montgomery has not merely succeeded in winning our sympathies for her *dramatis personae*; she makes us fall in love with their surroundings, and long to visit the Lake of Shining Waters, the White Way of Delight, Idlewild, and other favourite resorts of "the Anne-girl."

The mechanism of the plot is simple enough. An elderly farmer and his unmarried sister decide to adopt an orphan boy and bring him up to assist them on the farm; but owing to a blunder on the part of an intermediary, a girl, and not a boy, is sent from the asylum in Nova Scotia. Anne Shirley, an "outspoken morsel of neglected humanity,"[26] with a riotous imagination, a genius for "pretending," a passionate love of beauty, and a boundless flow of words, bursts like a bombshell on the inarticulate farmer and his dour, honest, undemonstrative sister. But the law of extremes prevails. Matthew succumbs on the spot, and after a short space Anne casts her spell over Marilla as well, for in three weeks that excellent dragon admitted to her brother that it seemed as if Anne had been always with them: – "I can't imagine the place without her. Now, don't be looking I-told-you-so, Matthew. That's bad enough in a woman, but it isn't to be endured in a man. I'm perfectly willing to own up that I'm glad I consented to keep the child and that I'm getting fond of her, but don't you rub it in, Matthew Cuthbert."[27] The process of Anne's education both at home and at school is chequered and dramatic, and the way in which this little lump of human quicksilver and her grim but just mistress act and react on each other is brought out by scores of happy touches and diverting incidents. Anne is a creature of irresistible loquacity when we first meet her, and meeting with kindness and consideration for the first time after years of poverty and neglect, she expands in a way that is at once ludicrous and touching. Perhaps her literary instinct is a little overdone, but otherwise Miss Montgomery shows no disposition to idealise her child heroine, and one can readily forgive exaggeration when it leads to such pleasing conceits as the child's suggestion that amethysts were the souls of good violets, or her precocious appreciation of the "tragical" sound of the lines: –

> *"Quick as the slaughtered squadrons fell*
> *In Midian's evil day."*[28]

The book lends itself to quotation at every turn, but we must content ourselves with the passage describing Marilla's effort to teach Anne to say her prayers, after her *protégée* had confessed that she never said any at all: – [* * *][29]

Miss Montgomery has given us a most enjoyable and delightful book, which, when allowance is made for altered conditions, is in direct lineal descent from the works of Miss Alcott. It needed considerable restraint on her part to leave off where she did without developing the romantic interest hinted at in the last chapter, but the result is so excellent that we trust she will refrain from running the greater risk of writing a sequel. Having sown her wild oats, "the Anne-girl" could never be so attractive as the little witch, half imp, half angel, whose mental and spiritual growth is vividly set forth in these genial pages.

## [Straight to the Heart]
### *Home Needlework Magazine* (Florence, MA)

One of the most delightful books we have read in many a day, and of a most unusual sort. It finds its way straight to the heart, and one reads it with mingled smiles and tears. It is a book to own for a companion, one to be picked up and read again and again. A chapter of it now and then will do one a world of good, but one will hardly be content with a chapter. It is the story of a little orphan girl adopted by an elderly spinster and her bachelor brother, her mistakes, quaint and humorous, her love of romance, and her sweet, generous, open spirit, and is one of the rare books to be read aloud. Old and young alike will fall beneath its charm, and it will mellow even the most cynical.

## [Lifelike – Never]
### *The Bookman* (London, UK)

It requires a genius (so it seems) to evolve a satisfactory child's character in a book for grown-ups. At least three-quarters of the children of whom we have read are either so priggish as entirely to alienate our sympathies or so precocious that we cannot believe they ever could have lived. To her credit be it said that Miss Montgomery has avoided the first of these pitfalls, but there can be no doubt she falls into the second. We cannot believe that such a child as Anne is possible; amusing she is, humorous, attractive, but lifelike – never. The book is a study of the growth of her character – from the age of eleven to thirteen at considerable length, from thirteen to seventeen with much less detail. The plot is simple. Anne is adopted by Matthew and Marilla Cuthbert – two delightful people – a brother and sister living on a farm in Prince Edward Island. She is educated by them, makes numerous friends among the neighbours' children, and at the end of the book is a school-teacher and the supporter of the lonely Marilla. By that time she is a fairly normal girl. We cannot help liking Anne; her story is full of entertainment – a story of the light, healthy, and amusing kind that deserves success and is pretty sure to win it.

### NOTES

1 Montgomery to Weber, 10 September 1908, in *GGL*, 71.
2 Bradford, review of *Anne of Green Gables*, 4; G. Murray, review of *Anne of Green Gables*, 2.
3 *The Boston Herald*, review of *Anne of Green Gables*, 8; *The Springfield Republican*, "Books for Young People," 23; *The Oregonian*, review of *Anne of Green Gables*, 11; *Grand Rapids Press*, review of *Anne of Green*

*Gables*, 10; *Wilmington Every Evening* (Wilmington, DE), review of *Anne of Green Gables*, 6 June 1925, in SR, 242.

4  Here and in the next paragraph, I have corrected the original, which reads "Prince Edward's Island."

5  I have corrected the original, which reads "'Anne of the Green Gables.'"

6  George Bernard Shaw (1856–1950), Irish playwright; Alfred Austin (1835–1913), English poet who became Poet Laureate after the death of Alfred, Lord Tennyson (1809–1892).

7  *AGG*, 19.

8  Louisa May Alcott (1832–1888), American author best known today for *Little Women* (1868–69) and numerous sequels.

9  Title protagonist of *Rebecca Mary* (1905), a novel by Annie Hamilton Donnell (1862–?), American author.

10  I have corrected the original, which reads "Prince Edward's Island."

11  *AGG*, 93.

12  *AGG*, 104.

13  An exceedingly long quotation from the novel, appearing in the original review, has been omitted here.

14  *AGG*, 41, 33.

15  *AGG*, 29.

16  *AGG*, 49, 50.

17  See *AGG*, 216, 218.

18  See *AGG*, 103.

19  *AGG*, 27.

20  *AGG*, 109, 305.

21  I have corrected the original, which reads "Gilbert Blythe calls 'carrots.'"

22  Properly, "The Bend in the Road," the name of the final chapter in the novel.

23  *AGG*, 227–28.

24  I have corrected the original, which reads "L.H. Montgomery."

25  Properly, "I myself am good fortune." From "Song of the Open Road," from *Leaves of Grass* (1856), by Walt Whitman (1819–1892), American poet.

26  *AGG*, 83.

27  *AGG*, 89.

28  *AGG*, 82.

29  An exceedingly long quotation from the novel, appearing in the original review, has been omitted here.

# 2

## *Anne of Avonlea*

—— 1909 ——

Although the London *Spectator*, in its review of *Anne of Green Gables*, had expressed its hope that Montgomery would refrain from writing a sequel, the consensus among reviewers was that this second novel was successful overall even though it did not quite live up to the standard of its predecessor. "This is a story of real life, of rather primitive types, and yet the emotions and purposes are set forth so well that we feel as if we knew the people," declared the *Philadelphia Inquirer*. *The Christian Advocate* of New York took a somewhat different tack, noting that "the characters and incidents are much like those of the New England before 'the foreign invasion,'" adding that "even the ripples of true love do not became dangerous rapids." Questions of target audience persisted, with the *ALA Booklist* of Chicago decreeing that "while it will be enjoyed by older girls, it is scarcely suitable for a juvenile collection," whereas the *Seattle Sunday Times* declared that "it is a young folks' book but every one likes it." An ad in the *Boston Herald* quoted a review by Edwin Markham that had appeared in the *New York American*: "Welcome back, Anne. You're a bit more grown up to be sure, but you're still our old, earnest, impulsive, imaginative Anne." Across the ocean, the *Times Literary Supplement* summarized the plot as "a pretty tale about a young American 'school-marm' – her school, her village life, and her foreshadowed love affair," and in Australia, the *Register* summed up what are some of Montgomery's greatest strengths as an author: "The story has no sensational plot, and there is no chronicling of violent emotion. There are, however, quaint fancies and word pictures of country scenes and life; there are humour and dry philosophy, and an abundance of really human interest." The *New York Tribune* went so far as to complement the interior art: "Mr. Gibbs's frontispiece looks as if he really had read the book before attempting to draw Anne's imaginary portrait, and, what is more, as if he, too, had come under her spell in the reading."[1]

And in a later review in the *Des Moines News*, Robert A. Turner zeroed in on what is perhaps the enduring appeal of Montgomery's work: "Such delightful stories are much to be desired, both for their clean, wholesome influence and the fact that they are in utter contrast to the many silly, sentimental love stories of the day and the tiresome mystery and problem stories of exceedingly doubtful literary value. The reading public is surfeited with such stories. Let us hope to hear more of Anne in the not too far distant future – to say nothing of Gilbert."[2]

## [The Next Few Years of Anne's Life]
### *The Nation* (New York, NY)

Readers of *Anne of Green Gables* do not need to be told that the story of the next few years of Anne's life is a story of crystal clearness, of tenderness, humor, and fancy. If the fancy is sometimes exaggerated, it is not in the least morbid, but walks always in lock-step between fun and common sense. To an Anne who has reached the age of discretion and become a teacher in her old school at Avonlea, it is naturally not permitted to be so consistently impossible and so hilariously freakish as in her tender years; nor may she dream quite so recklessly. Accordingly the author, with happy respect to her own forte, provides an orphan boy who is all pranks and a half-orphan boy who is all aerial dreams, and the two supply what was earlier found in Anne.

Anne herself, meanwhile, has by no means wholly graduated from either her imaginings or her talent for predicament. When she is found telling the irrepressible Davy that it is "wrong for little boys to use slang,"[3] it seems that Anne must have been changed at rebirth. But again, there are reassuring scenes of catastrophe in respect to mistaken potions which link her joyously with the past. Interest in sentimental adventure naturally waxes, but it does not even yet carry the drama beyond the bounds of youth. As before, the atmosphere of Prince Edward Island prettily surrounds the story.

## [A Pretty Story Prettily Told]
### *The Boston Globe* (Boston, MA)

### This Book Will Be Welcomed by Those Who Loved
### *Anne of Green Gables*

Those who learned to love *Anne of Green Gables* will be glad to know the *Anne of Avonlea*, whom the sequel to the earlier book makes them acquainted with. It is a pretty story prettily told of a young school teacher's experiences, not only with her pupils, but with the neighbors, who make up the little community on Prince Edward Island.

For Anne and her friends do not limit their activity to training the infant mind, but resolve to make Avonlea a better place to live in, both mentally and physically, and the efforts of the enthusiastic members of the village improvement society to better the looks of the town form some of the most interesting chapters of the book. Folks are pretty much the same, no matter where you find them, and Avonlea is as typical as Cranford.[4]

The characters, many of them children, are painted in bright colors, and the queer men and women have their oddities shown up as seen through not unfriendly eyes. Two interrupted romances are brought to happy endings; and as the reader closes the book it is with a promise that romance will follow Anne throughout life, and that when her four years of college are ended Anne herself will enter upon that happiness which seems to be her reward for the kindness she has shown to others.

## [Anne of the Bronze Tresses]
### *The Evening Star* (Washington, DC)

Following *Anne of Green Gables*, this book is for girls alone. It is very simple in construction, without much of a plot. It is as light as the proverbial feather and the reader has much difficulty in getting his mind on Anne of the bronze tresses. Anne is no heroine, but far from this, though her exploits are of such a mild character as to satisfy the censors of a boarding school volume. The scene at a country homestead, where cows break through the fence and partake of the neighbor's corn, is probably the most complex situation in the story. *Anne of Avonlea* can be labeled "light fiction," for it is indeed of the "lighter-than-air" variety.[5]

# [A Prose Lyric of Rural Life]
## *The Globe* (Toronto, ON)

That delightfully fresh idyll of Prince Edward Island life, *Anne of Green Gables*, has now a sequel in *Anne of Avonlea*, which Miss L.M. Montgomery has just given to the public. It is the same Anne, only a lady who has made much headway mentally and in maturity of viewpoint. Anne has advanced from a frisky child to the dignity and social position of a country schoolma'am. The roof of Green Gables no longer limits her activity and influence; she is the property of Avonlea, the poetical name of the nearest post office,[6] and consequently of the whole countryside.

It should be said at once that the sequel is no disappointment. Miss Montgomery's success in *Green Gables* has but deepened her sense of responsibility as a writer. *Anne of Avonlea* is, if the expression may be permitted, a prose lyric of rural life in many parts of Canada. It is the uneventful life of an Ontario countryside all over again. Lacking excitement and incident, the most insignificant happenings are food for conversation for days. Contact with the outside world being infrequent, each individual develops in more or less his own fashion, and there ripens material for an extensive portrait gallery for the novelist. Miss Montgomery is doing for Canadian village and country life what Mary E. Wilkins has done for the types of New England.[7]

True, the reader who thirsts for excitement will find little to please him in this book. The collapse of a kitchen roof, suspending a curious girl seeking a willowware platter from an absent neighbor until she was chopped out by the house-owner, is not very thrilling. Neither is the panic which faced a girl cleaning feather beds when stormed by three stylish visitors from the city an hour before dinner-time, with only a ham-bone in the house. Nor is a meeting of the Improvement Society when the news was spread that Farmer Parker out of necessity and cussedness had decided to rent his road fence for patent medicine advertisements. Yet these are the things of which country life is made, and they are faithfully pictured by Miss Montgomery.

The author is quite successful in a number of her character studies. Old Mrs. Lynde, the neighborhood busybody, reappears, but in a somewhat more favorable light. The character of Miss Lavendar Lewis is an especially happy etching. She was "an old maid," who, disappointed in love 25 years before, lived on in dreams, did as she pleased, and indulged her fancy by such caprices as preparing her table for an imaginary tea party. Her wistful romance with its happy culmination is really the climax of the story. When Anne was entrusted by the returned "prince" to ask if Miss Lavendar would see him, she mused: "Would she not? Oh, indeed she would! Yes, this was romance, the very, the real thing, with all the charm of rhyme and story and dream. It was a little belated, perhaps, like a rose blooming in October which should have bloomed in June; but none the less a rose, all sweetness and fragrance, with the gleam of gold in its heart."[8] The author's child characters are happily interpreted, though their conversation is sometimes "stagey." Davy, one of the twins adopted in the Green Gables household, is an untamed sprite, withal of good intentions and wisdom beyond his years. When urged one night to say his prayers he answered that "he didn't see the good of praying until he got big enough to be of some importance to God."[9] Paul Irving, a boy of eleven, was of a dreamy, poetical disposition that promises wonders if Miss Montgomery continues her neighborhood chronicles. Priscilla is another imaginative person, one of whose expressions is, "If a kiss could be seen I think it would look like a violet." Anne herself when the story opens is "a tall, slim girl, 'half-past sixteen,' with serious gray eyes and hair which her friends called auburn."[10] Throughout, the pages are illuminated by flashes of her fecund fancies, and as the story closes she leaves Avonlea for a term at college to be succeeded by – but that is another story.

## [Quiet Days in a Country Village]
### *Los Angeles Sunday Herald* (Los Angeles, CA)
FLORENCE BOSARD LAWRENCE

A delightful story of quiet days in a country village is found in *Anne of Avonlea*. This is by L.M. Montgomery, whose *Anne of Green Gables* introduced many of the same folk and enough of the same atmosphere of romantic rural beauty to make one eager to read this book quite through.

Anne is now become a sweet, high-minded girl, with all the beautiful ideals of her girlhood still undisturbed by any serious disappointments or by the jar which more intimate association with the world will give. Her newly assumed womanly dignity, put on in recognition of the fact that she is to teach the village school, is frequently interrupted by sudden dashes into her old-time reckless extravagance, and these little incursions from the prosaic existence only serve to endear her more to the reader.

Anne teaches school for two years to earn money so that she may go away to college, and the book deals only with those two years of her life, although it closes with a promise of many interesting chapters yet to be told, and it is probable that the author will write still more of this interesting young woman. The heroine has so many charmingly feminine characteristics that the reader will be anxious to know just how these traits work out when submitted to the cold, stern realities of everyday college life.

## [Radiating Sunshine]
### *The Lethbridge Daily Herald* (Lethbridge, AB)

If you enjoyed *Anne of Green Gables* you will be glad to see *Anne of Avonlea* which is now out. The heroine has grown to be a "tall, slim girl, 'half-past sixteen,' with serious gray eyes and hair which her friends called auburn,"[11] and is engaged in teaching the village school at Avonlea. The vivid imagination is still there, and the unfortunate propensity for getting into scrapes. Anne would not be Anne shorn of these attributes. She has grown in knowledge, however, as well as in years, and if not quite so amusing, is even more charming – you must read for yourself the story of the Avonlea Village Improvement Society adoption of the twins, the sad tale of the selling in haste of the wrong cow and the romance of Miss Lavendar. It is all delightful and Anne is the presiding genius, radiating sunshine. Davy, who is the better half of the twins, so far as interest goes, and Paul Irving, a kindred spirit of Anne's, a child with an imagination, share the honors, but neither one wins us as did the childish dreamer in the old days at Green Gables.

It is often lamented that Louise Alcott has no modern prototype, and that the youth of this age are so much the poorer. Miss Montgomery has given us a wholesome, delightful company that cannot fail to attract both young and old readers. Many a young person, we predict, will go to sleep with Anne under her pillow.

We leave our heroine with her Prince charming under the silver poplar, not quite the same Anne of impetuous emotions. "Perhaps, after all, romance did not come into one's life with pomp and blare, like a gay knight riding down; perhaps it crept to one's side like an old friend through quiet ways; perhaps it revealed itself in seeming prose, until some sudden shaft of illumination flung athwart its pages betrayed the rhythm and the music; perhaps ... perhaps ... love unfolded naturally out of a beautiful friendship, as a golden-hearted rose slipping from its green sheath."[12]

And so we say good-bye to the young girl who has crept into our affections, and hope that her fairy godmother may have good things in store during the coming years at college, – and afterwards.

## ["Let Well Enough Alone"]
### *The San Francisco Call* (San Francisco, CA)

*Anne of Green Gables* was a deservedly popular book and the reading public will not quarrel with the author when they hear that *Anne of Avonlea* is a continuation of adventures for that charming young person. One thing only is feared, that we may get another book yet, for the author, L.M. Montgomery, leaves the characters so at the end that they could easily be started off again on another series of adventures. There are several new characters in this book, one of which, in particular, Paul Irving, will be a joy to the young people. The book is interesting, but not quite up to the mark of the first, and one hopes the author will "let well enough alone."

## [Not Quite as Bewitching]
### *The Bookman* (New York, NY)
#### MARGARET MERWIN

To do a thing twice and to be as successful with the latter as with the former effort is apparently almost impossible to humanity. Either the second attempt is really not so good as the first, or else the rest of the world, mixing up its memories with subsequent fancies and glamours, is disappointed, however unjustly, with number two. Especially in books and their sequels does this statement hold. The sequel to a successful book is no other than a poor stepchild, labouring under invidious comparisons, sure only of being found fault with, damned before it is convicted.

*Anne of Avonlea* contains much the same gentle charm that made *Anne of Green Gables* so delectable a book. Anne is now past sixteen, which is evidently maturity in Prince Edward Island, and begins to teach school in the place where she herself was taught. Her old chums are similarly occupied in nearby villages; and she and they, with several of the old characters and some new ones, continue their hushed, secluded, leisurely lives in a way calculated to yield the reader weary of the steam riveter and the automobile, the career and the fad, a refreshing sense of peace. None of the problems of modern life enter the quiet pages. But there is plenty of sunshine and green shadow, of the timid and yet serene faith of untried youth, and not a little blue and silver love making. Childhood still pervades the pages, for Anne has her schoolful of youngsters, and Marilla adopts twins – twins as opposed as the poles and filling every waking hour with mischief perpetrated or endured.

There is a Miss Lavendar, sweet as her name, pretty, faded, full of quaint fancies, pretending people out of fairyland to fill her lonely life, and ending in a bloom of romance. And that is all. The book is as simple as a daisy, and if not quite as bewitching as the first we were given, the fault is doubtless with ourselves rather than the little flower.

## [A Little More Sentimental]
### *The Outlook* (New York, NY)

An unknown Canadian writer published a girls' story a year ago or so which had that peculiar quality which makes the person who reads it tell some one else to do the same; and just this thing probably has more to do with the success of play or story than any amount of booming. *Anne of Green Gables* was funny without being silly, quite naïve, but honest as it was simple. Naturally Miss Montgomery has written a sequel, and evidently meditates another. *Anne of Avonlea* is a little more sentimental than the earlier Anne, but it is jolly and friendly, and a "rambunctious" boy-child supplies the irrepressible fun formerly due to the now young-ladyish Anne. The story will surely be read.

## The Reappearance of Anne
### *The Boston Herald* (Boston, MA)

Miss L.M. Montgomery's *Anne of Green Gables* reappears in all the charming seriousness and simplicity that she wore in *Anne of Avonlea*. Anne is "half-past sixteen" now and has been appointed the Avonlea school teacher. After some trouble she quite wins the hearts of her young charges, as she had formerly won the hearts of the grown-ups in Avonlea. Her girlish blunders relieve her efforts to reform the town and placate her neighbors. At the end of the book she is starting off for college with Gilbert Blythe, her old-time schoolmate. Her friendship with Gilbert bids fair to ripen into an intimacy which Miss Montgomery may tell us more about in another book.

The story has a good deal of quiet charm. It does not try to go very deep. It has all the faults of the work of Elizabeth Gaskell and Jane Austen,[13] with few of their redeeming virtues of genuineness of character drawing and sustained interest in narrative. But, like *Anne of Green Gables*, it is sure to command a large sale, perhaps because so many people prefer not to think seriously when reading novels. Anne is never mischievous. Her conception of life is narrow, sober and uninteresting. Her chief fault is her overzeal for doing good. An occasional flash of infectious humor is all that saves the book from dulness.

## [Studies in Canadian Village Life]
### *The Scotsman* (Edinburgh, UK)

Sequels are often disappointing, but not this one. It continues the story of *Anne of the Green Gables* with conspicuous success. Now "half-past sixteen" and a teacher in Prince Edward Island, the book tells of her experiences in this out-of-the-way corner of the globe. It is a charming series of studies in Canadian village life and the ways of children rather than a novel in the ordinary sense of the term. Anne herself simply brims over with graceful fancies and noble enthusiasms, and altogether is a wonderfully dainty creation. Some of her charges are as good fun as Helen's Babies; others are as full of quaint imaginings as Alice in Wonderland; and one small chap is just another Little Lord Fauntleroy.[14] The adult characters are every bit as delightful as the juveniles. In its old-world flavour and pure sentiment the book breathes a spirit as different from many modern novels as sunlight is from ditchwater.

## [An Ideal Heroine]
### *The Bookman* (London, UK)

This is one of the most delightful and refreshing of books – a book that stands quite apart from the ordinary run of "novels." It is a successor to *Anne of Green Gables*; the author continues in it the story of the quaintly imaginative and lovable Anne (now grown to "half-past" sixteen), in a decidedly clever and sympathetic manner. There is a great charm about the book; it possesses a fund of irresistible, quiet humour, and is written simply and naturally. Anne – with the hair "which her friends called auburn," and the seven freckles on her nose, with the vivid imagination and broad-minded views, good intentions, and unlucky blunders – is an ideal heroine. She becomes school teacher to the children of Avonlea village, and sets out valiantly to win the love and respect of her pupils by kindness and firmness (she does not believe in caning); and how she succeeds with all but one small boy, and how she eventually wins him over by a totally unexpected act, rival in interest the episodes of the Improvement Society; Anne's admiration for Mrs. Charlotte E. Morgan (a well-known authoress) and the visit Mrs. Morgan pays her; Uncle Abe's weather prophesies, and how he was once (accidentally) right in his prophesies; Miss Lavendar's romance; troublesome Davy and prim Dora; Mr. Harrison's Jersey cow – and numerous others, are all equally entertaining. We hope sincerely to meet Anne again, and trust that the author will give us the pleasure of renewing her acquaintance by writing a successor to *Anne of Avonlea*. There is an excellent frontispiece and coloured cover by George Gibbs.

## [Sympathetic Prose Epic]
### *Vogue* (New York, NY)

We retain a fragrant memory of a certain wholesome, cheery story of a year or two ago that had as heroine a very charming little girl named Anne Shirley. The book entitled *Anne of Green Gables* was indeed such a remarkable artistic success in its unpretentious way that it was a risky experiment perhaps to write a sequel to that engaging first fruits of the author's pen. While the present novel may lack in a measure the spontaneity and simplicity of the earlier work, it should, none the less, prove refreshing reading for most of us, young or old. As before, the scene is laid in picturesque Prince Edward Island. Anne has become a tall, slim girl of "half-past sixteen" and is a teacher in the same school where she herself imbibed knowledge but a few years back. As a schoolma'am Anne was so progressive and clever in her methods that the tale of her experience might well be helpful to rural educators everywhere. At the same time *Anne of Avonlea* is not so much the story of a school teacher as it is the sympathetic prose epic of the healthy, bithesome *jeunesse* in a small community. There are interesting older people, too, some of whom, like most of Anne's chums, we have met before. Quaint, kindly Miss Lavendar, a lovable spinster soul addicted to harmless "pretendings," who is yet not too old to achieve the consummation of a beautiful, long-cherished romance of her own, must surely be related, we think, to one Dr. Lavendar of old Chester.[15]

Mr. Gibbs's frontispiece in color of the heroine fairly realizes our private conception of the winsome Anne of Avonlea.

## [A Pleasing Chapter in Canadian Fiction]
### *The Canadian Courier* (Toronto, ON)
#### JEAN GRAHAM

Miss Lucy Montgomery of Cavendish, Prince Edward Island, gave us a delightful chronicle of a schoolgirl's fancies and aspirations in *Anne of Green Gables*, in 1908, and this year has contributed *Anne of Avonlea* for our edification. We are pleased to greet a more mature Anne, who is teaching school this time and is as "aspiring" as ever. The fresh naturalness of her enthusiasm and beliefs infects the reader, who finds Anne a comrade to be desired who improves on a sequel acquaintance. However, one may venture the hope that *Anne of Avonlea* is not to be followed by Anne as a Fiancee, and so on, for eighteen volumes – after the fashion of the immortal and unbearable "Elsie" books.[16] One of the most charming features in the story is the picturesque island setting, with gardens – always gardens – old-fashioned, demure and fragrant. These books are a pleasing chapter in Canadian fiction and should bring the author much kudos and Prince Edward Island many tourists, all intent upon discovering the real and original Green Gables.

## [A Separate Entity]
### *The Canadian Magazine* (Toronto, ON)

It would be almost too much to expect as abundant enjoyment from *Anne of Avonlea* as from *Anne of Green Gables*. A sequel to a novel is usually unsatisfactory, particularly to the person who has not read its antecedent, but the first reading in this instance is not necessary, because *Anne of Avonlea* is sufficiently removed from the original *Anne* to be regarded as a separate entity. Like the first, the second is in all important respects a character study, but it is doubtful if the author, Miss L.M. Montgomery, realised how completely she was creating for us a new *Anne*. Nevertheless the metamorphosis is natural, but instead of the child we have a young girl in the first impulses of womanhood; instead of the homely, self-conscious, physically unattractive, ultra-impulsive and highly imaginative sprite, we have the nervous yet confident, elusively beautiful, subtle, womanly maiden – a true development, but a decided one. In these two books there is a good example of miscalculated objective. No doubt the author wrote the first to attract juvenile readers, but it went beyond that modest mark and was an unqualified success among adults. With equal confidence it might be said that the sequel was written with the intention of continuing that mature interest, but in this instance the attraction will be mostly for the young. In *Anne of Avonlea* the adult reader fails to encounter any dramatic or tense moments, and the characters, although excellently depicted, fail to do anything extraordinary. The charm of everyday incident in a quaint rural community must be admitted, but back of that there is demanded a strong coherent play on at least one outstanding human passion. Coherence is wanting in *Anne of Avonlea*, and the reader is not enthralled even by love as a passion. Love scenes there are, but they do not absorb the sympathies. Well would they play their part if *Anne* herself were concerned in a more engaging, more indefinite encounter. We find *Anne* about to begin the career of schoolma'am, and we leave her on the eve of a college career. There is promise of a stirring of emotions later on, and we are therefore free to hope that Miss Montgomery has a trilogy in mind, and, if so, the third of the series will undoubtedly prove to be the best.

## [An Exceedingly Pretty Story of Young Girlhood]
*The Living Age* (New York, NY)

It is seldom that a story and its sequel are so nearly similar in literary quality as *Anne of Green Gables* and *Anne of Avonlea*, published this autumn; evidently Miss L.M. Montgomery is to be congratulated on having preserved her original conception unaltered during the two years which have elapsed since the publication of the first volume. In the present book Anne's mind is occupied not only with her pupils, whose compositions are magnificently original, but with a Village Improvement Society, which after the manner of a half organized organization makes quite as much trouble as it mends. Also, one of a pair of twins of whom she and her aunt assume charge misbehaves in a score of embarrassing ways and excuses himself with immense ingenuity, but Anne is almost invariably admirable, although occasionally her celebrated red-headed temper betrays her. *Anne of Avonlea* is an exceedingly pretty story of young girlhood, and as it leaves the heroine four years before her marriage, Miss Montgomery has no excuse for not writing four more, and making a pretty "set." Therefore the small girls must not neglect *Anne of Avonlea* lest they should not quite understand those four. The grown-ups need no admonition.

## Anne Grows Up
### *The Salt Lake Tribune* (Salt Lake City, UT)

The public has had from this author a former book of which the present one is a sequel, *Anne of Green Gables*; and Anne Shirley, the heroine of this book, as of the former one, moves along in fine girlhood fashion, making friends everywhere and deserving them by her graceful, warm-hearted and pleasant ways. She is hearty and helpful, a firm friend, a fine neighbor, deeply interested in the welfare of all her associates. She gradually reaches the stage of young ladyhood, however, and she finds that the young man of her heart has also reached the proper maturity, and the two find themselves in sentiment and regard in the most lover-like fashion. The author has made a fine story of this, a fit sequel to the very entertaining story which first introduced Anne to the reading public.

## [A Somewhat Commonplace Story]
### *The Independent* (New York, NY)

In *Anne of Avonlea* we have a contribution to the holiday fiction. It is by no means a great work but is rather a somewhat commonplace story of a school teacher of some imagination, a type of thousands of other teachers all over the land who are doing conscientious work in and out of school and who draw old and young to them by means of pleasing personality. The character drawing is sketchy and in no instance does it rise into the realm of a masterpiece. Anne of Avonlea is the same as *Anne of Green Gables*. "She's not like other girls," as the author says, and those who found her popular in the earlier book will be glad to hear more of her in the present story into which the author has introduced several new characters. *Anne of Avonlea* has the remarkable distinction of figuring among the best selling books of both the adult and juvenile class at the same time. The cover decoration by George Gibbs appears in this issue in color.

# [Commonplace, If Pretty]
## *Saturday Night* (Toronto, ON)

There are some literary critics whose reviews are more entertaining than informing, and I regard Mr. Kerfoot, of *Life*, as one of these. But what he says of this book strikes me as being a judgment so exact, so excellent that I make no apology – except to Mr. Kerfoot – in reproducing it as being my own opinion expressed with most admirable deftness:

"Any one who has to do with dogs knows that between their irresistible puppyhood, when humans of all ages love them, and their comradely maturity, when human grown-ups chum with them, there is an interval during which children avoid them, grown-ups lose patience with them and they would be quite neglected, did not idealistic youth lead them about with a string around their necks. So, at times, with books. Last year, we met 'Anne of Green Gables,' an irresistible child-woman, and loved her. Some day – who knows? – we may meet her full grown and chum with her. But *Anne of Avonlea*, by L.M. Montgomery, is Anne betwixt and between – a book for girls."[17]

Miss Montgomery is one of the most promising of younger Canadian writers, but *Anne of Avonlea*, to tell the truth, is commonplace, if pretty. This bright Prince Edward Island girl has done much better work, and will do more. It may be added that *Life*'s judgment of her latest work is here reproduced not only for the reason that it is a fair one smartly worded, but because it is unprejudiced – for Canadian reviewers are often accused of being prejudiced – sometimes for, sometimes against – Canadian books.


## NOTES

1 *The Philadelphia Inquirer*, "A Sequel to *Anne of Green Gables*," 5; *The Christian Advocate*, review of *Anne of Avonlea*, 2034; *ALA Booklist*, review of *Anne of Avonlea*, 134; *The Seattle Sunday Times*, review of *Anne of Avonlea*, 8; *The Boston Herald*, "'A Girl in a Class,'" 2; *The Times Literary Supplement*, review of *Anne of Avonlea*, 379; *The Register*, "Peaceful, Helpful Lives," 4; *The New York Tribune*, review of *Anne of Avonlea*, 8.

2 Turner, review of *Anne of Avonlea*, 5.

3 *AA*, 79.

4  *Cranford*, by Elizabeth Gaskell (1810–1865), English author, published serially in 1851 and in book form in 1853.

5  I have corrected the original, which reads "'Annie of Avonlea.'"

6  I have corrected the original, which reads "postoffice."

7  Mary Eleanor Wilkins Freeman (1852–1930), American author of three dozen novels and collections of short stories published between 1883 to 1918, including *A New England Nun and Other Stories* (1891).

8  *AA*, 256.

9  *AA*, 82.

10  *AA*, 103, 1.

11  *AA*, 1.

12  *AA*, 276; ellipses in original.

13  Jane Austen (1775–1817), English author of many books, including *Sense and Sensibility* (1811). I have corrected the original, which reads "Gaskill."

14  *Helen's Babies* (1876), by John Habberton (1842–1921), American author; *Alice's Adventures in Wonderland* (1865), by Lewis Carroll (1832–1898), British author; *Little Lord Fauntleroy* (1886), by Frances Hodgson Burnett (1849–1924), British author.

15  Dr. Lavendar, a character appearing in several books by Margaret Deland (1857–1945), American novelist, including *Old Chester Tales* (1898).

16  *Elsie Dinsmore* (1867), a novel by Martha Finley (1828–1909), American author, was followed by twenty-seven sequels, the last published in 1905.

17  See Kerfoot, review of *Anne of Avonlea*, 746.

# 3

## Kilmeny of the Orchard

—— 1910 ——

Although Montgomery had reservations about her third novel, reviews were enthusiastic about this unusual romance, which the *Boston Globe* proclaimed "a fascinating novel and love story." According to the *Idaho Daily Statesman*, Montgomery "has sympathetic knowledge of human nature, joined to high ideals, a reasonably romantic view point and a distinct gift of description." The *San Francisco Call* cautioned that "the two earlier 'Anne' stories are better from a literary view point, but this story is sure to win all that class of readers who think a book is fine if it makes them weep," particularly "girls from 14 to 16." And yet, in the Cleveland *Plain Dealer*, Carl T. Robertson argued that whereas the two Annes were primarily for girls, *Kilmeny* "will be enjoyed by young and old," arguing that Montgomery "has made a somewhat radical departure in her latest volume," including "much romance, considerable dramatic material and a sustained plot with a slightly melodramatic climax." These departures did not detract from the quality of the novel, however: according to the *Hennebec Journal* of Maine, "The book leaves a good taste in one's mouth – a tribute, by the way, that cannot be honestly paid to all novels." An unidentified clipping published in an Australian newspaper added, "The story of Kilmeny reads like a poem, and undoubtedly ought to have been told in verse. It is one of the most charming love idyls written for many years." The Toronto *Globe* picked up on this thread, noting that "some writers would have made more of the emotional struggles which mark the plot, but Miss Montgomery has chosen to leave in the mouth the taste of a poem, as it were, and from her standpoint and regarding the manner of her writing, which is now pretty well defined, we feel that her course was the wise one."[1]

An article in the December 1910 issue of *The Atlantic Monthly*, a magazine published in Boston and New York, offered one of the earliest sustained responses to Montgomery's work. In "Lying Like Truth," Margaret Sherwood attributed the phrase to a statement made about Daniel Defoe to refer to "the art of making the unreal, perhaps even the impossible, more evident than that which happens before your very eyes, because amazing improbabilities are told with such close attention to immediate detail that you can but believe; and, by the side of his fictitious tales, newspaper accounts of actual happenings seem, in their sketchy presentation, unreal and improbable." Claiming that she had been "searching, among the novels of the last six months, for the truth that comes from close observation," she offered the following analysis of *Kilmeny of the Orchard* as a successor to *Anne of Green Gables*:

> It is partly a lessening of this quality of close study which makes Miss Montgomery's *Kilmeny* less appealing than *Anne of Green Gables*. There was a distinctness about the former, an artistic truth in the portrait of the quaint child with individual fancies. This story is pretty and fanciful, in the green and gray setting of a Prince Edward Island orchard, but vagueness replaces the close rendering of real things, and, in spite of the poetic touch, the tale does not hold the reader. Only the genuine poet, one to whom the invisible is more real than the visible, dare write the story "all made up of the poet's brain."[2]

## [Perpetual Fitness for Romance]
### *The Nation* (New York, NY)

The author omits Anne of Green Gables from this her third venture into fiction, although we have the familiar setting of Anne's Prince Edward Island. Its salt shore and spring blossoming have their wonted charm, and one reflects that an island is a portion of land bounded by perpetual fitness for romance. Never, surely, did romance glide onward so gently, so balmily, so florally as this. Never did the roughnesses inherent in the course of true love disappear so gracefully. Hard-hearted guardians are melted by a kind word. Prohibiting parents yield at a touch. Critical friendship melts under beauty's first glance. How mildly the eerie mystery of Kilmeny's dumbness unfolds and later clears itself! How amiably the lions in the path of young affection take themselves off! How lightly falls the foot of crime that only treads on flowers! But "the pleasure that's almost a pain" stirs at the self-taught violinist girl who plays "an airy delicate little melody that sounded like the laughter of daisies"; who lures from her violin divine music – music that revealed "the whole soul and nature of the girl … the beauty and purity of her thoughts, her childhood dreams and her maiden reveries."[3]

## [A Vision of Springtime]
### *The Times–Dispatch* (Richmond, VA)

The author of *Anne of Green Gables* and *Anne of Avonlea* has written her latest book from a romantic, not to say a melodramatic, standpoint.

Its Canadian setting is beautifully drawn in, with the firm yet delicate and assured touch that characterizes everything the author of the "Anne" books writes. *Kilmeny of the Orchard* is a vision of springtime and apple blossoms, and the vision is dainty in the extreme. But in the describing of a heroine that, having been dumb all her life, is enabled at once to break out into speech, there is an incongruity that taxes the mind of the reader and deprives "Kilmeny," attractive and gentle as she is, from possessing the spontaneous and irresistible charm exhaled by Anne in every word.

The book is pure and sweet, and the characterization in the main is admirable, so that while it has undoubted faults, it yet has much that can be commended and thoroughly enjoyed.

## [An Idyll of Prince Edward Island]
### *Saturday Night* (Toronto, ON)

There is one thing at least that Miss Montgomery may be depended on to do for her stories, and that is to select a pretty name for them. It may seem, of course, that there is considerable similarity between the titles, but they are none the less pretty for that. Her process seems to be to take a girl's name – a charming name like Anne or Kilmeny – and tack onto it some equally delightful name of a place. What could be better than "Green Gables," for instance, or "Avonlea"? And certainly it would be difficult to find a name with more charming associations than "The Orchard." And so Miss Montgomery has taken two very pretty names and combined them to produce *Kilmeny of the Orchard*.

As for the story itself, it is all that might be expected from the title – simple and sweet and wholesome, an idyll of Prince Edward Island, with something at times of the delicate tints and fragrance of apple-blossoms.

There is nothing particularly original about the plot, nothing particularly clever or vigorous about the characters. But it is a pretty story, that of Kilmeny, the beautiful dumb girl, who lived secluded in the old orchard on account of the unfortunate circumstances of her birth. But, of course, Prince Charming found her out, and came along to woo her in the guise of a young college graduate teaching the village school. But she would not marry him because of her dumbness. Then came the crisis when she saw him in mortal danger from a jealous rival, and her emotion caused her to break the barriers that with-held her speech, and she found her voice to warn him. So it all ended happily as pretty stories should.

Like all Miss Montgomery's work, this novel is very nicely written, and has many passages of descriptive beauty. The dialogue, however, is often conventional and even somewhat mawkish at times. But these defects do not prevent the book from being a very enjoyable piece of work in the sentimental vein. Miss Montgomery has the art of telling a pretty story very prettily, but it might be well if she kept her work by her a little longer, and did a little more filing and polishing. Of course, the temptations are many to induce a young and successful author to force the output somewhat. But it is a mistake which always affects the quality of the work done, and which is apt to prove even poor business in the end.

## [Some Delightful People]
### *The Washington Herald* (Washington, DC)

In *Anne of Green Gables* and *Anne of Avonlea*, Miss L.M. Montgomery gave us two tales of Prince Edward Island that were delightful, and in her latest book, *Kilmeny of the Orchard*, she has returned to that locality. Of this work it may be said, as it once was of Hall Caine, "that the author succeeds because of the intimate knowledge he has of his people."[4] In Hall Caine's case it was of the inhabitants of the Isle of Wight; in Miss Montgomery's of those of Prince Edward Island.

This detached portion of land near Newfoundland has been sadly neglected by fiction writers looking for out-of-the-way places to lay their plots; but as pictured by this authoress, it must be an exquisite bit of scenery, peopled with lovable, enjoyable folks. All three of her books show an intimate knowledge of the habits and the life of the Prince Edward Islanders, and her descriptions of the landscapes and effect of the hills and orchards of the islands are wholly delightful.

In the present story Eric Marshall, a young man with a fortune in his own name, goes to the island to teach school for a friend of his for a time. While roaming around the surrounding country he strays into an orchard, where he hears the sound of a violin. On surprising the player he discovers a beautiful girl, who runs away from him in apparent terror, and he loses her in the woods.

On making inquiry, he hears that she has been dumb from her birth, but that the doctors say that a great shock may restore her powers of speech, as they have not been impaired, but have simply become somewhat atrophied through disuse. This shock is administered through the discovery by the girl that one of her rejected lovers is about to kill Eric. Being too far off to interfere, she realizes that, to save his life, she must make some outcry. The effort is successful, the blow is averted, and the girl recovers her speech.

As will be seen, the plot is not particularly novel, but the charm and beauty of the story rest in its descriptive passages and in the manner in which it is told. It is one of those tales of the outdoors that are especially pleasing in summer – and, as all summer reading should be, it is not too long – merely a well-told, simple narrative of a little known part of the world and some delightful people.

## [Happy in Setting and Plot]
### *The Times Literary Supplement* (London, UK)

A shortish Canadian story, happy in its setting (Prince Edward Island) and in its plot. It tells of the wooing of a beautiful young girl who is dumb, with a touch of dramatic originality both in the origin and the cure of her affliction.

## [Romantic as It Should Be]
### *The Living Age* (New York, NY)

The title chosen by L.M. Montgomery for her third novel, *Kilmeny of the Orchard*, would make friends for it wheresoever Scottish verse is loved, but it will win favor for itself wheresoever it is read. Kilmeny is a dumb girl, beautiful exceedingly but growing up in the belief inculcated by her mother that she is very ugly. She is a self-taught violinist of rare genius, and the young school-master who hears and sees her as she is playing in the orchard loses his heart at once. He happens to be not only a school-master, but a modern version of the fairy prince, being the clever son of a rich man, upright, well-bred and handsome, and his love story moves swiftly and smoothly to its end. The minor personages, the quaint dwellers on the adjacent farms, all represent well-defined but not overdrawn rustic types with a background of Scottish virtue for their inheritance. The scene is Prince Edward Island of which the inhabitants are said to speak as "the Island," asking "What other island is there?" when requested to be more definite.5 As Miss Montgomery describes it, it is lovely enough, on Wordsworthian theory, to account for Kilmeny's beauty and for her music. The tale is an idyll with all its unhappiness, "an auld sang"6 and its actual events forming a pleasant succession with a glimpse at the end of the happiest of coming lives for Kilmeny and the master. How can the husband of a dumb wife expect happiness? There be those who could see something reasonable in the prospect, but Miss Montgomery's solution of the question is not cynical, but as romantic as it should be to harmonize with Kilmeny's lovely face and nature.

## [Not So Good, but Good Enough]
### *The Bookman* (London, UK)

This is a pretty idyll of Prince Edward Island, in which a dumb beauty suddenly recovers her voice in a shock of fear for her lover. Many readers of *Anne of Green Gables* and *Anne of Avonlea* will turn eagerly to another novel from the same pen. They will not get so good a story; still, it is good enough to read and enjoy. The charm of it is twofold: partly the atmosphere and partly the dramatic interest of Kilmeny's fate. The girl appears in the last scene, dressed in blue; "her glossy black hair was wound about her head in a braided coronet, against which a spray of wild asters shone like pale purple stars. Her face was flushed delicately with excitement. She looked like a young princess, crowned with a ruddy splash of sunlight that fell through the old trees."7 This is the heroine, and the story of her awakening to love is as pretty and unsophisticated as herself.

## [The Charm of Naive Innocence]
### *Vogue* (New York, NY)

L.M. Montgomery, whose *Anne of Green Gables* is likely to be for many years a favorite with young people, and even with many of mature age, has written *Kilmeny of the Orchard*, a love story of Prince Edward Island.[8] The sole touch of originality in this story lies in the invention of a heroine who can hear perfectly, but is unable to speak. As the inhibition upon her speech lies in causes psychological and not organic, the cure is not a thing for surgeons or physicians, but for the person who can make the proper appeal to the mind and heart of the subject. The interest of the tale lies in the solution of the problem presented by the girl's defect, but there is charm in the naive innocence of this long sequestered and beautiful young woman. *Anne of Green Gables*, however, is worth a great many such books as this new story.

## [Wholesome as Bread and Milk]
### *The Independent* (New York, NY)

*Kilmeny of the Orchard* [* * *] is a title connoting a blossom romance – a romance as wholesome as the bread and milk that the hero eats at dusk. This hero is a young school teacher; his Kilmeny a gentle figure out of that sentimental fiction we seem about to lose. To the young man who discovers her, and loves her in the fragrant coolness of the orchard, she is a lady in distress – not any problematic distress of morals or mind, such as civilization imposes, but that kinder distress imposed by Nature. She is dumb. The lover, who is too modern to agree with her relatives in their acceptance of what seems to them an inexorable visitation of the sins of the fathers, calls science to the rescue, and Kilmeny gains her speech. This story is as refreshing – and perhaps rather more stimulating – as a drink from a cool spring set back from the novel reader's dusty road.

The story of Kilmeny, however, in spite of its rural garb, could be set in the sophisticated garden of some fashionable country house and lose none of its atmosphere thereby.

## [More for Sentimentalists Than Realists]
### *The English Review* (London, UK)

"Kilmeny's mouth is like a love-song made incarnate in sweet flesh," says Eric Marshall to his father in the excitement of an approved engagement.[9] Now young men do not say things like that to their fathers about young women, even in Canada. Consequently, no realistically inclined person, after catching sight of this sentence, is likely to attempt to read

Miss Montgomery's book. The sentimentalists are a wider audience than the realists, however, and thousands will read with eagerness this pleasant, somewhat high-flown tale of the college-bred young townsman who goes off to Prince Edward Island to teach a school in place of an invalid friend, and who there meets Kilmeny of the mouth. Kilmeny, unhappily, is dumb, but, when she sees Eric about to be murdered with an axe, she suddenly recovers her speech and shouts aloud. As the curtain falls, we see on Eric's face "a light as of one who sees a great glory widening and deepening down the vista of his future."[10]

## NOTES

1  *The Boston Globe*, "Shock Gave Her Speech," 11; *The Idaho Daily Statesman*, review of *Kilmeny of the Orchard*, 4; *The San Francisco Call*, review of *Kilmeny of the Orchard*, 15; Roberston, "On the Book Shop Shelves," 6; *Hennebec Journal* (Augusta, ME), review of *Kilmeny of the Orchard*, undated clipping (September 1911), in SR, 1; unidentified and undated clipping (Australian newspaper), review of *Kilmeny of the Orchard*, in SR, 1; *The Globe*, review of *Kilmeny of the Orchard*, 18. See also *The Boston Herald*, review of *Kilmeny of the Orchard*, 8.
2  Sherwood, "Lying Like Truth," 806, 807, 808.
3  *KO*, 55, 57.
4  Sir Thomas Henry Hall Caine (1853–1931), British-born novelist and playwright.
5  I have corrected the original, which reads "Prince Edward's Island."
6  The phrase "There's the end of an auld sang" was spoken by the Earl of Seafield upon the signing of the Act of Union in 1707, at which point Scotland lost its independence and was united with England. The phrase "an auld sang" is also in *Waverley* (1814), a historical novel by Sir Walter Scott (1771–1832), Scottish author.
7  *KO*, 134.
8  I have corrected the original, which reads "Prince Edward's Island."
9  *KO*, 133.
10  *KO*, 134.

# 4

## *The Story Girl*

—— 1911 ——

As these reviews demonstrate, Montgomery's prediction about *The Story Girl* – that it was superior to *Anne of Green Gables* in terms of literary quality but would not prove as appealing to the public – was entirely correct. Although some reviewers already insisted that no book could live up to the high standard of her first, *The Christian Science Monitor* opined that "there is a skill in the construction and a finish of style about the book which marks it as the most artistic production of Miss Montgomery's pen." A review in the *Alloa Journal* of Scotland agreed, stating that the novel "embodies all the freshness and charm which characterised the famous 'Anne' stories, and a dash of that subtle suggestion of the mysterious which made *Kilmeny of the Orchard* outstanding; and in addition there is a marked advance in the purely literary aspect of the author's style of writing." The *New York Herald* added that "the book is not only out of the ordinary, both in conception and development, but it is always delightfully enthralling." According to the *Pittsburgh Post*, "Miss Montgomery possesses the enviable faculty of writing with simplicity and at the same time weaving into her stories an imaginative quality that lifts them somewhat above the plane of everyday life, even while they deal with that life"; this review added that "the book, while dealing with the lives of children, is for adult readers ... And to all who read it will come the remembrance of the days of early youth." Indeed, an unidentified clipping in Montgomery's scrapbook made what is perhaps the highest compliment: "It is even better than the author's former works, and that is saying a great deal."[1]

The book's depiction of children was also highly praised, particularly in a review in the *Montrose Standard* of Scotland, parts of which Montgomery underlined in ink; this review called the book "one of the best interpretations of child-life we have seen for a long time, natural, wholesome, attractive, charming ... From cover to cover it is full of freshness, and we sincerely hope Miss Montgomery will soon give us a sequel." *The Book News Monthly* of Philadelphia, in contrast, cautioned that the child characters of the novel "are more or less repetitions of her children in the earlier books," adding that "if *Anne of Green Gables* had never been written *The Story Girl* would have a better chance." Still, *The National Magazine* of Boston argued that "child life is mirrored in such a charming manner that the reader is unconsciously carried back to the happy, carefree days of his own childhood."[2]

## [Attractive Children]
### *The Sun* (New York, NY)

Prince Edward Island,[3] which Miss L.M. Montgomery has made her own domain in fiction, is again her scene in *The Story Girl*. It is a story of children, who are natural and attractive, and it gives the author better opportunity to display her gifts than her more ambitious tales. She can describe quiet country scenes delightfully, she appreciates the simple islanders and the children, and in the mouth of the little girl who tells them, the legends and stories have a peculiar charm. It is a pity that ideas of future lovemaking should be made to trouble these healthy youngsters, but there is not much of that.

## [An Intuitive Knowledge of Child Nature]
### *The Bookseller, Newsdealer and Stationer* (New York, NY)

*The Story Girl*, by L.M. Montgomery, is an exquisitely written narrative of the doings of eight children during a summer spent on an old farm near Charlottetown, Prince Edward Island.[4] Chief among them is the Story Girl – a child of fourteen, with a wonderfully vivid and original imagination and exceptional histrionic powers, whose fanciful tales are interspersed through the record of the joys and petty sorrows which are the lot of healthy, happy children. The author has an intuitive knowledge of child nature and the characters are all real flesh and blood children. Few and far between are books like this, and hence they give a greater pleasure to the reader who is carried back to his or her own childhood to live again those joyous carefree days.

## [Romance, Vitality, and Barbarian Instinct]
### *The Boston Herald* (Boston, MA)

It was Robert Louis Stevenson who wrote:

> "I have just to shut my eyes
> To go sailing through the skies –
> To go sailing far away
> To the pleasant Land of Play."[5]

It is something of this sort which happens to the reader of Miss Montgomery's latest book. It is a veritable land of play into which we find ourselves transported, and not so far away, for the author's foot is still upon her native heath. And what a group of playmates we are introduced to – eight children, whose ages run from 11 to 14 years, with all the romance, vitality and barbarian instinct which real children everywhere possess.

Unlike her other books – *Anne of Avonlea*, *Kilmeny of the Orchard*, etc., Miss Montgomery has written this story in the first person, and has eliminated from it both plot and love element – unless the growing sense of affinity which Felicity stirs in the heart of Peter Craig may suggest the latter. The absence of these, however, in no way intercepts the interest of the reader. On the contrary, it is a relief from the stereotyped novel with its more or less intricate plot, thrilling episodes and illicit loves. Assuredly the person who finds in childlife a never ending charm, who delights in rural simplicity, "musky winds," "sweet-scented" grass,[6] orchards aglow with apple blossoms, and an open sky whose cloud effects stir all sorts of poetic fancy, to say nothing of dark spruce woods with their uncanny noises, will welcome this unassuming, finely written, idyllic story.

Its scene is laid on a hill farm of Prince Edward Island, and it narrates the events and experiences which come to those children during "a delectable summer."[7] With the exception of Peter Craig, Uncle Roger's handy boy, and Sara Ray, a neighbor's child, they are related to each other, and Uncle Alec and Aunt Janet, to whom the farm and three of the children belong, are lovable "grown-ups." Differing greatly in temperament, as well as in physical features and accomplishments, these boys and girls seldom allow the reader's interest to flag. The environment in which they have grown up makes itself evident in their thought and action, but they have much in common with all children. Sara Stanley, the "Story Girl" and the principal character of the book, is a fine creation.

As a character study she will compare favorably with any which Miss Montgomery has produced. She has the dream temperament, and has inherited from her father an artistic quality. She is fascinating in her personality, and her talent for telling a story rises to genius. Indeed, her repertoire of stories, for a country lassie, is surprisingly large – ranging from the classic myths of the ancients and the folklore of the northland to the lore of her own kith and kin. Peter Craig is also strongly drawn, and the narrow-grooved but practical Felicity stands out, too, as a real character. There is ample character material here for another volume on a somewhat different plan, which we hope to see in the near future. Meanwhile we heartily commend this story for its intrinsic worth and pleasure giving quality.

## [A Remarkably Vivid Little Personality]
### *The Scotsman* (Edinburgh, UK)

A winter spent in an old farm in Prince Edward Island by a set of young people, their ages ranging from eleven to fourteen, supplies the simple materials of a story whose charm depends mainly on the atmosphere of country life in a part of the Empire which is still unhackneyed in the eyes of the readers of fiction, in its knowledge of child nature, ways, and ideas, and in its delicate power of character-drawing. The "Story Girl," especially, is a remarkably vivid little personality, and her sayings and doings will be followed by the grown-ups and by the young people who make her acquaintance in the book with an interest resembling the fascination she exercises over her male cousins and others that come under her spell. The story is illustrated by a frontispiece and cover, in colour, by George Gibbs.

## [The Far, Fair Land of Youth]
### *Chicago Record–Herald* (Chicago, IL)

Once upon a time – to be a little personal! – a rainy night came to Chicago. Pouring torrents overhead, muddy streets beneath, about and around an inclement wind that rendered the carrying of an umbrella a gymnastic feat of difficulty and distinction. A certain reviewer, buffeting her wet and weary way across town, felt the book she carried, L.M. Montgomery's new study of *The Story Girl*, to be the last straw of hampering provocation. But, once safely ensconced in the train, she "took it all back" because of that very volume. For *The Story Girl* is a dear, delightful whiff of fragrance from the far, fair land of youth.

There's not a deal of plot to the simple narrative. Those who are happy enough to remember this author's earlier tales, *Anne of Green Gables*, *Anne of Avonlea* and *Kilmeny of the Orchard*, will recall that her strength lies less in plot than in spirit, atmosphere, sympathetic and telling characterization of childhood. So it is in regard to the "story girl," Sara Stanley of Carlisle, Canada, with whom and her likable, natural companions, Felicity, Cecily, Sara Ray, Dan, Beverley, Felix and Peter, the reader longs to play and revel. And this, indeed, is precisely what happens. The children – the reader and all! – join hands merrily and frolic about in the fields, the orchards, the lanes of a rural locality as real as the one in which you spent your last vacation, while the no less natural "grown folks," whom it sometimes is so hard for childish natures to comprehend, look on and encourage and scold and tease and reprove just as they did when – well, when we were just such joyous, unthinking little grigs and shavers. And the childish plays and tragedies depicted are so fascinating and lifelike that – well, again, it must indeed be a cold-hearted "grown up" who wouldn't grow young again in their vicarious sharing. It was still pouring when the train stopped at the reviewer's station, the wind was blowing strong, the street still muddy, but – *The Story Girl* was no longer a burden. It was a cherished treasure that had endowed the dripping, gray-tinted world with a colorful, sunshiny smile.

## [A Magnetic Personality]
### *Pittsburgh Chronicle Telegraph* (Pittsburgh, PA)

Not since *Anne of Green Gables* has Miss Montgomery written anything so charming as this new story. Indeed, it is likely that many of her admirers will declare that *The Story Girl* is superior to even the first great success scored by the author. Prince Edward Island is again made the scene of a story by this gifted writer, and although the principal characters are children the novel will be read with deep interest by adults, for the delightful heroine charms old and young alike with her magnetic personality and her wonderful stories. There is a rich vein of humor running through the book, but more noteworthy is the evidence that Miss Montgomery has made a thorough study of human nature and has put her knowledge to good use in the development of her new romance.

# [The Tender Sweetness of Childhood]
## *The Globe* (Toronto, ON)

Surely there is not in all Canada one human heart which cannot be soft-
ened by a baby's touch and which does not feel when mixing freely with
healthy, happy boys and girls that a corner of Eden is yet left for hu-
mankind. We would also ask if there is to be found anyone who rejoices
to see happy childhood and happy youth blooming into manhood and
womanhood who does not in his heart of hearts love a good story about
young folks. "If you do not care for the baby's touch, if you cannot
be young again, God's pity on you," said the Gypsy mother, and it is useless to invite such a one to read Miss L.M. Montgomery's latest work,
*The Story Girl*. This latest volume has all the charm of *Anne of Green
Gables*. The author always invests the heroine of her stories with a charm
which is delightful because it is natural. The story girl of this new volume
is a fascinating creature. In voice and manner she captivates her listeners as she tells of the "Mystery of the Golden Milestone," "How Kissing
Was Discovered," "How the Milky Way Was Placed in the Heavens,"
of ghosts and other weird instances, until there come back to the oldest
reader the memories of his own "childish terrors of the night" or of his
boyhood's pranks. Plot, in the accepted sense of the word in its relation
to a book, there is none, but in the sequel which all will hope to hear of
by-and-bye there will doubtless be a plot and the worries of happy, innocent love for Sara Stanley. In *The Story Girl*, as in *Anne of Green Gables*,
*Anne of Avonlea*, or *Kilmeny of the Orchard*, one tastes afresh the tender
sweetness of childhood and youth; one loves to wander among greening
fields, to enjoy the glamor of moonlight nights, to live in summer time
out in the open of the beautiful Prince Edward Island climate, and then,
as the evenings lengthen, to come in to enjoy books and music and
"hearthstone stories." The reader of *The Story Girl* may, like the critic,
be unable to say just wherein lies the charm of the book, but every line of
it will be read and, we venture to predict, re-read many times, for there
is a freshness and a sweetness about it which will help to lift the load of
care, to cheer the weary and to make brighter still the life of the carefree
and the happy.

## [A Far-Off Golden Age]
### *The Christian Advocate* (New York, NY)

The popularity of L.M. Montgomery's stories of the simple life of Prince Edward Island is readily accounted for by the fact that to the average American city dweller the peace and happiness of that isle seems like that of some far-off golden age. The audience that *Anne of Green Gables*, *Anne of Avonlea* and *Kilmeny of the Orchard* have won will listen eagerly as *The Story Girl* exercises her gift in the little cousinly circle in that orchard that seems so far away. The freshness is not crudity, and the cleverness and grace are literary art of a fine sort. The humor is so natural and spontaneous that it brings many a smile, but never a guffaw. Read it, young folk and old, and let it sweeten the taste that the problem-novel has corrupted. Mark Twain's estimate of Miss Montgomery's art may be seen from his letter to Francis Wilson: "In Anne you will find the dearest and most moving and delightful child since the immortal Alice."

## Charming Children
### *The Register* (Adelaide, Australia)

Those who have enjoyed the "Anne" books will be prepared to love the "Story Girl" and her friends for Anne's sake, before making their acquaintance, and for their own afterwards. Miss Montgomery is an artist at drawing children, but not even she could create a second character so altogether delightful as the vivacious "Anne of Green Gables." Still, if the subject of this book suffers by comparison, it is not on account of her own lack of charm, but because of the brilliancy of her rival. When an author can compel "grown-ups" hardened to all sorts and conditions of books to enter deeply into the joys and sorrows of imaginary children, he or she has achieved something to be proud of. And that is what Miss Montgomery can do and does. "The Story Girl" and her companions are not the angelic darlings to be found in some books; they deserve chastisement just as often as the children of everyday life. Quarrelsome often, selfish sometimes, but lovable always, their innocent escapades are unfolded with a rare skill and sympathy. [* * *]8 Miss Montgomery has a keen insight into the child-mind. She never overdraws or makes one of her characters say or do anything unnatural. She can take those who have "put away childish things"9 back to the days when their outlook upon life was not dimmed by troubles which cramp and kill – the days that come only once and stay such a little while. Her book is for the young children, or for the old children who never grow old.

## Arcadia
### *The Young Woman* (London, UK)

In her new book, *The Story Girl*, the author of *Anne of Green Gables*, Miss L.M. Montgomery, has, I am glad to say, not given us another novel, as her last book led one to fear. She has returned to her earlier manner, that of *Anne of Green Gables*, and has given us a delightful history of a summer spent by a group of children in the enchanting surroundings of an American "Arcadia."

The standard to which one refers books of this kind is, of course, the work of Louisa Alcott. Louisa Alcott's mantle seems to have been divided in two parts, one fallen upon Ethel Turner, the Australian writer, and the other upon Miss Montgomery.[10]

Miss Montgomery in this book also shows a certain kinship with Kenneth Grahame, whose *Dream Days* and *The Golden Age* have charmed thousands of readers.[11] There is one thing, however, that mars the work of all the well-known writers for children of the present day, and which is present in Kenneth Grahame's work, and also in that of another charming writer, E. Nesbit.[12]

Their children are all too conscious of the inferiority of the "grown-up," and this consciousness makes them too sophisticated for perfect naturalness. It seems as if the "child-study," that is so marked and so welcome a feature of modern psychology, has so permeated the minds of these writers that they cannot refrain from pointing the moral to the "grown-up" even when writing books ostensibly for young people. This may be very salutary for the "grown-up," but it is very bad for the children.

Miss Montgomery shows signs of being infected with this sophistication; but in justice it must be noticed that she errs less in this way than any of the other writers mentioned. Yet such touches as "Never you mind him, Felicity. He's only a grown-up." And again, "It's no wonder we can't understand the grown-ups, ... because we've never been grown-up ourselves. But *they* have been children, and I don't see why they can't understand us" are not to be found in any of Louisa Alcott's books, and I think they gain by their absence.[13]

Miss Montgomery's book, too, would have been better if she had not insisted quite so much upon the "Story Girl's" genius. The author does "protest too much"[14] about the magic of her voice, so that she fails to convince us, and an element of artificiality is introduced.

Some of her stories, too, we have heard before. "The Story of the Poet Who Was Kissed" must be an American version surely of the kiss bestowed by Margaret upon Alain Chartier, and one prefers it in its native garb.[15]

However, having cavilled at these slight flaws, one has nothing left but praise. Miss Montgomery has the power of suggesting atmosphere, and we really see and feel the environment in which she places her young people. The old homestead where the children's father had been "raised," the orchard, with its well and the cup of cloudy blue, and the spruce wood are all vividly real.

The orchard, which in the opinion of "sensible" people should have been a money-bringing cornfield, was the realisation of one of grandfather King's delightful ideas. "A vision of the years to be, and in that vision he saw, not rippling acres of harvest gold, but great, leafy avenues of wide-spreading trees laden with fruit to gladden the eyes of children and grandchildren yet unborn." So on his home-coming with his bride, they planted their bridal trees, and for every child that was born a tree was planted, and for every grandchild. "Every family festival was commemorated in like fashion, and every beloved visitor who spent a night under their roof was expected to plant a tree in the orchard. So it came to pass that every tree in it was a fair green monument to some love or delight of the vanished years."[16] Also when Miss Montgomery describes the other perfectly natural and normal children, she is quite equal to Miss Alcott.

She has advanced both in her method of telling a story and in powers of characterisation. Peter, the hired-boy, is a masterpiece, and one would like to hear of his subsequent career: it is certain to be a successful one. It is Peter who wins in the "sermon contest," in spite of Beverley's[17] painstaking efforts and his "thumps," written in red ink, at exciting passages. Peter, too, wins in the "Ordeal of Bitter Apples," a truly appalling competition.

The Story Girl succeeds in getting him to church; but, alas, the paper prophesies the end of the world for a certain Sunday, and the children live in deadly terror until it is over.

Peter is distressed because he has not made up his mind before whether to be a Presbyterian or a Methodist.

"Oh, that doesn't matter," said Cecily earnestly. "If – if you're a Christian, Peter, that is all that's necessary."

"But it's too late for that," said Peter miserably. "I can't turn into a Christian between this and two o'clock to-morrow. I'll just have to be satisfied with making up my mind to be a Presbyterian or a – Methodist."[18]

Among the children's many amusements is that of keeping "dream-books," in which they write down their dreams to be read to the others, until, discovering the efficacy of heavy suppers, Cecily nearly kills herself with cucumber and milk.

The scene where the children try to propitiate the local "witch" is perfectly done, but once begin quoting and one would never stop.

Miss Montgomery is to be congratulated on having written a wholesome, refreshing, and altogether delightful story.

## [A Group of Merry Children]
### *The Nation* (New York, NY)

The many admirers of this author will welcome her new book. And those who, in the cases of the later Anne and of "Kilmeny," found cause to temper praise with comparison will give double welcome to a story which returns to the plane of the author's best work. The scene is still in Prince Edward Island, the actors are a group of merry children spending their lives or their vacations on ancestral acres. The acres bloom in the old picturesque and fragrant way. The children are of all sorts, except very bad. Inevitably one of them must be dowered with a fantastic soul, and this one is the Story Girl who has the gift of remembering, inventing, and, above all, of telling. Fairy tales, Norse legends, the family ghost stories, the domestic ancestral joke are alike fuel for her fire. She becomes, in a way, the mouthpiece for much anecdotage, but through it all preserves a marked personality, compounded, in the author's agreeable manner, of fancy, fun, loftiness, and perversity. She is the leading spirit, but there is no lack of individuality among the boys and girls with whom we spend the summer, and pass long hours in the old grand-paternal orchard, where every member of the clan is represented by a tree. We go to school, do chores, gather apples, burn potato stalks, and after the manner of youth attack the problems of the universe. To sit in the grassy aisles of the orchard with the cousins and listen to the Story Girl's witching voice, to assist at counsels of mischief, at the drolleries, scrapes, and inter-squabbles of the young folk, and to have clear if brief glimpses of the elders is to be left with a lively sense of lively and actual acquaintance.

## Childhood Days
### *The Springfield Union* (Springfield, MA)

Miss L.M. Montgomery, whose *Anne of Avonlea* still stands at the top notch of modern stories of childhood, in *The Story Girl*, her latest book, has excelled herself. It is one of the most natural and wholesome stories of childhood ever written and we have in mind Louisa Alcott and the host of other women writers who have told stories of childhood experiences. Although there is no intimation that the story is other than fiction, yet one is impressed with the belief that Miss Montgomery has woven into the story incidents of her own childhood and that many of the happenings of the story are chronicles of actual events, though perhaps the author has exercised the privilege of her art as a story-teller in embellishing the incidents. However, the essential thing is not whether or no it is a "true story" but whether it is true to life. There can be no question on that point. Many of us have lived similar experiences and all of us can hark back to the days when we played and scrapped with a group of children much the same as the group of which Miss Montgomery writes so lovingly.

The story purports to be the reminiscences of one of the boys of a group of eight children who played together one summer in one of those small towns on Prince Edward Island with which Miss Montgomery is so familiar. "The Story Girl," who was known to her elders as Sara Stanley, had a remarkable gift for telling stories. She would read some old myth, or learn of some old legend, and then she would retell these stories in her own words to the group of children. She held them spellbound and fascinated. They saw the incidents pictured to them through the vivid realism of the little story-teller. When she told a ghost story, even the grown-up reader of the book experiences a furtive shiver. "The Story Girl" dramatized even the most commonplace of incidents. It was a most remarkable gift and the "Story Girl" seems to have preserved the gift, even when she grew up to be a real author.

But the "Story Girl" is not the only interesting one in the group of children. There is the delicate and lovable Cecily; the vain, but housewifely

Felicity; the lachrymose Sara Ray; Peter, the hired boy who was not above his place, but won friends through his sturdiness and honesty. The other boys are equally of interest, as they are real boys. In fact you have some of them as your neighbors. What scrapes these children got into and though they were solemn affairs to the children they are laughable in the reading. Then again there are incidents of genuine pathos. Peter's illness brings a sob to the throat of the most blase reader. Peter's realistic sermon is ludicrous, despite its somewhat tragic conclusion. But one could go on citing incidents from the book. The real pleasure is to be found not in the telling but in the reading. The author is remarkably gifted in child psychology, the best exemplification of which is in the compound letter to Peter.

The story is graceful in style, rich in imagination, poetic in description, gay with humorous haps and mishaps and grown-ups will obtain from it an equal amount of pleasure with that of younger readers. It reveals Miss Montgomery as a writer of ripened art.

### *The Story Girl*, by the Creator of Kilmeny
*The Feilding Star* (Feilding, New Zealand)

After reading *Anne of Green Gables*,[19] Mark Twain, who had grown very critical in his latter days, wrote that Anne "is beyond question the most popular girl heroine in recent years." In America this was as great a tribute of praise as was a postcard from Gladstone in England. Of *Kilmeny of the Orchard* praise was again showered upon Miss L.M. Montgomery, who had by this time "arrived," her books being amongst the best sellers. Now comes her very latest, *The Story Girl*, published by Messrs L.C. Page and Co., of Boston, with a beautiful coloured frontispiece by George Gibbs. Critics who were charmed by Anne and Kilmeny will rave over Sara Stanley, the Story-teller, who is a most fascinating creation; and we can imagine no present more suitable for a birthday or any other day sort of present than a copy of *The Story Girl*, which might have been written especially for the delectation of young people, but will delight even an octogenarian who has a young heart. Sara is a modernised Scheherazade, with tales for daytime as well as for nights.[20] And the voice of her! After beguiling a crusty old bachelor with the story of "How Betty Sherman Won a Husband," the old man startled Sara and her company by requesting her to recite "the multiplication table." After the Story Girl had done, the bachelor, when he had cheerfully handed out the fee for the story, exclaimed: "I thought you could do it … The other day I found this statement in a book. 'Her voice would have made the multiplication table charming!' I thought of it when I heard yours. I didn't believe it before, but I do now."[21] And that is exactly how the reading of *The Story Girl* will impress everyone – old or young or not so old or so young – who has the privilege of buying, begging, or borrowing it.

## [Capital Reading]
### *The Outlook* (New York, NY)

It is a genuine pleasure to be able to say of a new story that it is equal to the very best thing the author has previously done. *The Outlook* was one of the first journals to point out the charm and genuineness and fun in Miss L.M. Montgomery's *Anne of Green Gables*. Her other stories have also been liked, but none, we suppose, has pleased readers quite as much as the first "Anne" book. Now Miss Montgomery's *The Story Girl* is being read everywhere, and everywhere it is liked and praised. Again the scene is in Nova Scotia, and again the subject is child life; but instead of one interesting child, as in *Anne of Green Gables*, we have a group of several girls and boys, quite unlike one another, each with characteristics which are strongly marked. Their play and adventures, and, above all, the stories told them by the girl who has gained the name of *The Story Girl*, make capital reading. Like its predecessors, this story is clean, wholesome, and unsensational, but alive with character and rich in amusement.

## [A Far More Finished and Subtle Art]
### *The Montreal Daily Star* (Montreal, QC)

There are great children's books and there are great books about children; and there are a very few which are both. To write a great book about children one must have retained in full power the inspired vision to behold those "clouds of glory"[22] and of wonder and mystery which enwrap even the common phenomena in our infant days – and of whose existence and glory the child himself is so blissfully unconscious until he wakes up one mature morning to find it gone. America has produced no writer who can clothe a picture in those strange, misty, elusive and fairy-like colors of childish imagination with such perfect art as the Prince Edward Island girl, who a few years ago made all us Canadians so proud of her *Anne of Green Gables*. Miss L.M. Montgomery's new volume, *The Story Girl*, narrates a series of incidents in the budding days of a group of children in "The Island." Less ambitious in its effort than some of her previous works, it shows a far more finished and subtle art. The comparison that leaps to mind at once – a comparison most honorable to Miss Montgomery, and in some respects to her considerable advantage – is that of Kenneth Grahame's *The Golden Age*, but Miss Montgomery is more effective than the English writer at making the reader feel himself an actual part of the group of youngsters; Grahame seldom gets away from the impression of a grown-up outsider looking on – and how unutterably outside is a grown-up in all the affairs of youth! When you get to the end of Miss Montgomery's story you feel just as certain as you would if you were a real boy or girl that you are going back next summer and will meet Sara Stanley, the girl with the voice that "made words live,"[23] and pretty and self-conscious Felicity, and Peter who couldn't make up his mind whether to be a Methodist or a Presbyterian, and all the rest of the fascinating crew who worked out the puzzles of the world for themselves that summer in the old island orchards. There will have to be a sequel. After three hundred and sixty-five pages one's prevailing feeling is that it is a shame to cut the whole visit short just as one was getting really to know the girls and boys; and besides, Sara obviously has a destiny before her. There may be something of autobiography in her; if there is not, then Miss Montgomery's fertility in providing her with an incessant supply of weird and characteristic ideas and remarks and actions is nothing short of marvellous. When the Story Girl and her companions were waiting for the end of the world in full belief that it was due at 2 p.m., that Sunday, one of them asked her to tell a story to alleviate the horrors of suspense. "No, it would be no use to try," she answered. "But if this isn't the Judgment Day I'll have a great one to tell of us being so scared."[24] You can't stop a story-teller like that in one volume. Especially when it is such a delightful volume.

## [The Essence of Girlhood and Boyhood]
### *Westminster Gazette* (London, UK)

The "Story Girl's" personality made every story she had to tell alive and vivid; her voice made even the multiplication table charming. But these are just the qualities which the novelist finds it hard to convey. The personality of the "Story Girl" herself is admirably suggested, but it does not make her stories glow; they remain a series of little episodes very varied, told cleverly enough but lacking the electricity which we are so frequently told made them vibrate with intense drama to the listeners of the individual little raconteuse. Miss L.M. Montgomery paints a pleasant picture of the children's life in the old homestead in Prince Edward Island.[25] She has made her way into the intimacies of child life and has looked through their eyes at the things that matter. Her book will recall "old days, old dreams, and old laughter,"[26] to many of us, for it has caught the essence of girlhood and boyhood. But to speak truth, the tales told by the "Story Girl" are of far less interest than many of the smaller daily happenings that befell Felix or Beverley, Felicity or Cecily, Peter or Dan, or the "Story Girl" herself.[27] Miss Montgomery gives us clever sketches of character half developed and countless little incidents which appeal by reason of their familiarity.

## [A Story of Children for Grown-Ups]
### *The Catholic World* (New York, NY)

Among the popular new books is *The Story Girl*, by L.M. Montgomery. Like the author's first success, *Anne of Green Gables*, it is a story of children for grown-ups. It makes pleasant reading.

## [Simple Realism]
### *Vogue* (New York, NY)

This new book of Miss Montgomery's is by far her best since *Anne of Green Gables*. She has abandoned the rather cheap and weak romanticism of *Kilmeny of the Orchard*, but has not gone back to the juvenility of her earlier books. *The Story Girl* is a book for adults, but one that wholesomely mature girls and boys will enjoy. It is not, properly speaking, a single story, but many, though there is a slender thread of unification running through the volume. The scene is laid in Cape Breton Island, and the characters are the natives of all ranks whom the author knows so well. There is a deal of excellent and piquant characterization throughout the book, whether in the group of persons clustered about her of the title rôle or in the stories she tells. One feels the charm of that far northern climate, and the sturdy and picturesque character of the people. As to the stories thrown in episodically, they are of great variety, of invariable interest, often of delightful humor, as occasionally touched with a genuine passion, and almost always strongly human. The author will make a grievous mistake if she attempts again the purely romantic, and there seems no reason why one who writes so effectively for adults should narrow her audience by confining herself to "juveniles." She has demonstrated that she can do extremely well the sort of thing that appears in this book and in the charming and wholesome *Anne of Green Gables*. Perhaps in time she can widen her sphere. Meanwhile the world is by no means tired of her Cape Breton folk in their simple realism.

## [An Entertainment for the Young]
### *The Canadian Magazine* (Toronto, ON)

The average girl of from twelve to twenty years would read *The Story Girl*, Miss L.M. Montgomery's latest story, with juvenile delight. Therefore to that extent at least the book is a noteworthy achievement. And if it has the magic that charms, even though the charmed be of tender years, it should be heralded as such and treated as an entertainment for the young. Miss Montgomery possesses rare gifts of phantasy, and there is in all her novels a wholesome yet piquant humour, a humour that is not too elusive for the teens. Her humour and phantasy appear at best in *Anne of Green Gables*, a book which, according to the author herself, was written for juveniles but which appealed more to adults. Her exquisite aptness of expression and fine sense of the picturesque appear again in *Anne of Avonlea*, and although *Kilmeny of the Orchard* appealed less to the common emotions, even to the vulgar emotions, it equalled the others in imagery and excelled them in genuine artistry. Now we have in *The Story Girl*, a piece of fiction that is not easily estimated. It is not a novel, as we use the term. It has no plot. It has no apparent design. It is merely the sketch of a summer passed by two Ontario boys with relatives in Prince Edward Island. In reality these boys do not exist, and if the author had not in one or two instances used their Christian names we should suppose that they were girls. One of them tells the story in the first person, or, rather, gives an account of their experiences during the summer. The experiences consist of the little, everyday affairs common to children of prosperous farmers in Ontario or, we presume, in Prince Edward Island, with this exception, that these everyday affairs are garnished by the fairy tales of the *Story Girl*. Although we feel that there is a plethora of garniture, the girl of sixteen would not likely think so, and while we might find tedium in the successive tales related by this almost phenomenal girl we should not forget to hand the book to someone more attuned to their spirit and more in sympathy with the sentiment of the book apart from the *Story Girl*. The whole structure is redolent of the orchard, the wooded lane, the spacious welkin, the farmhouse kitchen, the pleasant countryside. There are hints of romance, but no consummation, and one sets the book down with a natural curiosity as to whether *Felicity* has yet become reconciled to the fact that *Peter* was only a hired boy. *Peter* is perhaps the best character in the book. He is a quaint urchin, blunt to the point of being comical, particularly when in a preaching contest in the orchard he announces that he is going to talk about the future abode of the damned, in short, about Hell.

## [Simple Life in a Fascinating Land]
### *The Christian Work and the Evangelist* (New York, NY)

We have learned to look forward with much eagerness to any story from the pen of L.M. Montgomery. *Kilmeny of the Orchard* is already known to most of our readers, and those who have read that book will immediately order *The Story Girl*, by Miss Montgomery. The story is again laid in the author's beloved Prince Edward Island, and takes one back to all the freshness and vigor of the simple life in that fascinating land. There is art in every page of this new book, and her insight into the hearts of girls and young men is hardly surpassed by any of the authors who are devoting themselves to stories for the young. The story girl herself is a fascinating creature, and will delight and thrill our readers with her weird tales of ghosts and things. In spite of *Kilmeny of the Orchard*, *The Story Girl* is perhaps the most original creation that has yet come from Miss Montgomery's mind. It has a beautiful style, and we heartily recommend it.

## [The Gift of Telling a Story]
### *The Dallas Morning News* (Dallas, TX)

The special gift of the young girl who gives this book its name is one that young people ought to cultivate – the gift of telling a story in such a way that it not only does not lose interest in the telling, but gains in piquancy and dramatic force through the narrator's personal magnetism. Perhaps one of the "story girl's" sayings, "I do like a road, because you can be always wondering what is at the end of it,"[28] may explain a little of the charm of the book, for the road to Prince Edward Island, via Toronto, is long and unknown enough to kindle the imagination into "wondering what is at the end of it." On the far-away island of the Dominion the young folks, who had made the long journey to spend a season in their father's old homestead, find a warm welcome and likeable friends among the neighbors' girls and boys. The story girl's stories and all the gay young life on the island are as bubbling with interest and fun as a picnic or a camping party. The stories are so simply told as to be within the mental grasp of quite young readers, while their undeniable literary quality will appeal to grown-ups who are wise enough to remember their own youthful fancies and pleasures. The author's vocabulary is so extensive and varied as to be educative in the way of fertility and facility of expression.

## [Vivid and Real Children]
### *The Lexington Herald* (Lexington, KY)

A story by the author of *Anne of Green Gables* is sure to be sought without other recommendation. But it is only an introduction that the Story Girl needs; she will make her way afterward without other assistance than her beautiful gift of story telling and her wonderful voice. Of all natural attractions a lovely speaking voice is the greatest and the only one that can be shown at all times, for the most perfect beauty can have things happen to her looks. Besides, nobody is beautiful to all eyes, and everybody is charmed by a beautiful voice.

There is, perhaps, a little too much story-telling for a grown-up, but that is one thing children do not tire of, and the little party of gay friends who gathered at the King Orchard gate were extremely vivid and real children.

The hired boy is a New England type that appeals some way to a southern heart. His position seems so pathetic. One hates to believe that snobs are born – we had believed them made by the devil – but Felicity certainly was a full-fledged snob. If any young people have been overlooked in the Christmas giving of gifts, *The Herald* cordially advises a hasty search of book stores for *The Story Girl*.

## [A Dangerous Rival for Anne]
*The Republic* (Boston, MA)

Those who read the first of the "Anne" books three years ago, had much to justify them in the thought that here was a juvenile which for originality in conception and setting, for magnetism and wholesome sweetness could hardly be surpassed. But the surprising thing has happened. In her *Story Girl*, Miss Montgomery has created a dangerous rival for "Anne." Sara Stanley, to give the heroine of the new book her real name, is not in the least like her famous predecessor, but to many readers she will be even more attractive. Again the scene of the story is a country town in Prince Edward Island. The story of that memorable summer in their child-life is told by Beverley King,[29] who with his brother Felix, has been sent from Toronto to remain at the old King homestead in the Island during the prolonged absence of the widower father on business for his firm in Rio de Janeiro. Uncle Alec and Aunt Janet, with their children, Felicity, Cecily and Dan, inhabit the homestead. Another cousin, "the Story Girl," lives with her unmarried aunt and uncle on a farm adjoining the homestead aforementioned. Two other characters are part of the story, Peter Craig, Uncle Alec's hired boy, and Sara Ray, the only child of a widowed neighbor. Beverley and Felix come back to live again in the home of their ancestors, with whose customs and traditions their father has made them familiar. In the long vacation they all do children's tasks about the farms; in schooltime they attend the Carlisle school. It is a place where "nothing happens but days," to quote from the Story Girl;[30] and no one but a genius could have made anything out of material at first sight so meagre. But Miss Montgomery is a genius in her capacity for understanding the child-heart, and making the most of the possibilities of the simplest of lives; and here we have a story for which children will have boundless enthusiasm, and which will hardly less delight the most sophisticated of novel readers among their elders. The wonder of the book is the way in which its author has contrived to make the individuality of every one of these children – whose ages range between eleven and fifteen – appear clear-cut, and to make the little incidents of their innocent days stand out with as much importance in the reader's mind as in the children's. "The Story Girl," who alone of all the little group is destined to a career, is certainly a remarkable creation. Yet, she has had no advantages beyond those of her mates, unless the possession of a rather Bohemian father, much given to travel, may be so accounted by us. It gave no pride to her relations. She is not pretty, but she is fascinating, by reason of her wonderful eyes and voice, and a memory which has retained all the histories of her own and other families in the section; all her father has written her from foreign parts; all she has read, even in Aunt Olivia's "Early Victorian" scrap-book, with the power to tell old tales and traditions, to recount classic legends and sentimental stories in a fashion which holds every hearer. She can make herself look like the characters of whom she speaks, and her magic is as potent with the grown-ups as with her child-companions. To her in largest measure it is due that the summer had been so beautiful, and that there was no weariness in "the sweetness of common joys, the delight of dawns, the dream and glamour of noontides, the long, purple peace of carefree nights."[31] She thought of all the new games, and Romance blossomed wherever her footsteps fell. As usual, Miss Montgomery gives us lovely pictures of her Island home. We wonder if she realizes what she is doing for it. We fully expect to see Prince Edward Island a favorite summer resort for American travelers, just because of her presence and her stories.

## [An Irresistible Appeal]
### *Southport Guardian* (Southport, UK)

The author of *Anne of Avonlea* and *Kilmeny* has proved herself a mistress of sentimental romance and a trained observer of life, especially young life. In *The Story Girl* she again treats of young life, not in a keen analytical introspective way, but with rare instinct and intuition. She possesses the real faculty of endowing her characters with sentimental fascination; she quickly creates an atmosphere in which her characters may move not as skeletons but as living persons; and though her books have only the slenderest of plots their wholesomeness, their humour, their humanity make an irresistible appeal. So it is here. The children of Prince Edward Island, whose minor excitements, and romances, and ambitions, and desires, and collections for school libraries and the like are here related for us, may be the veriest of lay figures, but at Miss Montgomery's touch they become the heroes and the heroines of romance, with the Story Girl as the particular Queen. She has a wonderful personality and her influence extends over the whole book; the other children, even Peter and Felicity, and the fat Felix, who inhabit the old world home on Prince Edward Island, only deriving their power and attractiveness from being associated with her. The whole book is instinct with youth, and though the sentimental strain may sometimes get a little tiresome it is the natural note for a character so alluring as "the story girl," who, though in real life she might prove rather tiring, in fiction is peculiarly charming.

## [A Story of Simple Sweetness]
### *Simmons Magazine* (New York, NY)

Miss L.M. Montgomery's novels have been read world-widely. *Anne of Green Gables* outsold all of the other novels of its season and is still selling rapidly, several thousand copies a week being demanded of the publishers to keep up with the demand. When a book takes so strong a hold on the reading public, it may safely be wagered that it is the *true worth* of the story and not the extravagant ravings of a press agent that makes it go. A story spiced with salaciousness may sell extraordinarily well for a few weeks (and it speaks volumes for the moral purity of the American mind at large that it is only for a few weeks), while a story of simple sweetness sells just as well, and continues selling as well, for as many years. The reading public will undoubtedly receive with avid joy the new story by this author, *The Story Girl*, a companion to *Anne of Green Gables*.

Sara Stanley, the Story Girl, is one of a group of young girls and children of the neighborhood who gather round her to listen to her marvelous tales. Sara is spending a year with her uncle in an old family mansion cosily situated on the border of a lovely wood of spicy balsam and fir trees, and with a grand, leafy old orchard in front. In this ideal environment the Story Girl romps and plays with her friends and entertains them with marvelous stories, quaint and imaginative. Edwin Markham was charmed with the book, and says, "The children touch on big problems of religion and morality, and, like grown folk, answer in the dry, hard terms of the creed that has formed their opinions. They reach out into the mysterious unknown through the dreams that visit their pillows, each vieing with the other for a vision of splendor or terror. They have their secret dread in believing some prophetic announcement reported in the 'reliable family paper' that the world is coming to an end on a given date. How they prepare for and spend that fateful day is pleasant reading; but so are all the chapters in this clean, high-minded book."[32]

Miss Montgomery finds her scenes once more in Prince Edward Island.[33] Two brothers from Toronto spend a summer there, and have joyful adventures with the Story Girl and other young companions. The book is full of the sprightly humor, the quaint conceits and the genuine understanding of youth which mark so excellently the various chronicles of Anne.[34]

### NOTES

1 *The Christian Science Monitor*, review of *The Story Girl*, 5; *The Alloa Journal* (Alloa, UK), "An Ideal Christmas Gift-Book," review of *The Story Girl*, undated clipping (1911), in SR, 24; *The New York Herald* (New York, NY), review of *The Story Girl*, undated clipping, in SR, 15; *Pittsburgh Post* (Pittsburgh, PA), review of *The Story Girl*, undated clipping (1912), in SR, 36; review of *The Story Girl*, unidentified and undated clipping, in SR, 18.

2 *Montrose Standard* (Montrose, UK), review of *The Story Girl*, undated clipping (July 1911), in SR, 29; *The Book News Monthly* (Philadelphia, PA), review of *The Story Girl*, undated clipping, in SR, 15; *The National Magazine*, review of *The Story Girl*, 711.

3 I have corrected the original, which reads "Prince Edward's Island."

4 I have corrected the original, which reads "Prince Edward's Isle."

5 From "The Little Land," part of *A Child's Garden of Verses* (1885), by Robert Louis Stevenson (1850–1894), Scottish writer.

6 SG, 165.

7 SG, 218.

8 A long description of the chapters "A Dread Prophecy" and "The Judgment Sunday," appearing in the original review, has been omitted here.

9 1 Corinthians 13:11 (KJV).

10 Ethel Turner (1872–1958), Australian author whose books include *Seven Little Australians* (1894).

11 Kenneth Grahame (1859–1921), Scottish author best known for *The Wind in the Willows* (1908). For a discussion of Montgomery's *The Story Girl* and *The Golden Road* in relation to Grahame's *Dream Days* (1898) and *The Golden Age* (1895), see Jennifer H. Litster's "'The Golden Road of Youth': L.M. Montgomery and British Children's Books" in Volume 2 of *The L.M. Montgomery Reader*.

12 E. Nesbit (1858–1924), English author of forty books, including *The Wouldbegoods* (1901).

13 SG, 117, 206.

14 An allusion to *Hamlet* (1603), a play by William Shakespeare (ca. 1564–1616), British playwright and poet.

15  The mythical story of the kiss bestowed on Alain Chartier (ca. 1385–1430), French poet and political writer, by Margaret of Scotland (1424–1445), Dauphine of France and eldest daughter of James I of Scotland, has been depicted several times in poetry and painting.

16  *SG*, 8.

17  I have corrected the original, which reads "Beverly's."

18  *SG*, 145. Here and below, I have corrected the original, which reads "Cicely."

19  I have corrected the original, which reads "'Anne of the Green Gables.'"

20  A storytelling character in *One Thousand and One Nights*, a Persian text that was first translated into English in 1706 and is also known as *Arabian Nights*.

21  *SG*, 56.

22  From "Ode: Intimations of Immortality from Recollections of Early Childhood," a poem by William Wordsworth (1770–1850), British poet.

23  See *SG*, 9.

24  *SG*, 156.

25  I have corrected the original, which reads "Prince Edward's Island."

26  From the dedication to "Frederica E. Campbell in remembrance of old days, old dreams, and old laughter."

27  I have corrected the original, which reads "Beverly" and "Cecil."

28  *SG*, 1.

29  Here and throughout, I have corrected the original, which reads "Beverly."

30  Properly, "Nothing ever happens here, except days" (*SG*, 11).

31  *SG*, 258.

32  Edwin Markham (1852–1940), American poet best known for *The Man with the Hoe and Other Poems* (1899).

33  I have corrected the original, which reads "Prince Edward's Island."

34  The last paragraph appears in identical form in the *New York World* (New York, NY), "Sara, a Teller of Tales," review of *The Story Girl*, undated clipping (June 1911), in SR, 6.

# 5

## Chronicles of Avonlea

—— 1912 ——

Although this book was put together as an imperfect substitute for a new full-length Anne novel, and although some reviewers lamented the fact that Anne does not appear as frequently as the cover copy implied, ultimately this volume received high praise because, as the *Oakland Tribune* of California put it, "In this volume the author establishes her right to be considered one of the best short story writers in our country." *The Christian Science Monitor* echoed this view, arguing that "all the insight and charm of the Anne books, with the added grace of a more finished craftsmanship, render this an exceptional collection; and a few of the chapters will take very high rank in the short-story domain." In Toronto, the *Mail and Empire* noted that "to say that one sketch was better than another would be to insinuate that the latter was not just as good as it possibly could be. Which would be insinuating something utterly untrue." Moreover, the depiction of rural community was seen not only as appealing but as universal: as Mary Alden Hopkins stated in *The Publishers' Weekly*, "Avonlea might be any one of those home towns to which wandering sons and daughters hurry back for their summer holiday; a village where every little white house has its grass plot, flower beds and vegetable garden; where the air is sweet with rose odors in June and apples in September; an out-of-the-way spot where quaint characters develop idiosyncrasies." Indeed, the *National Magazine* of Boston declared that *Chronicles* was "just the book for a college girl."[1]

Once again, too, this book was praised not only for what it contained but also for what it lacked: the *Pittsburgh Post* declared that "Miss Montgomery is both artistic and human in her work, a combination all too seldom met with nowadays," whereas the *San Francisco Evening Post* noted that "there is a charming old-fashioned sentimentality about all the Chronicles of Avonlea that is not unpleasant in the present-day mass of realism, red blood and abysmal brutes." A review in the *Boston Times* declared, "The charm of the author's style was never more in evidence. The stories 'tell themselves' with a readiness and naturalness which is the perfection of literary skill … These 'Chronicles of Avonlea' demonstrate anew the truth that simple, quiet lives may be full of romance and of tragedy, even if the latter be bloodless." To this an unidentified clipping added, "What the stories lack in action is more than made up in the drawing of the unusual characters which the author delights in portraying." And finally, several more newspapers chimed in with their praise, including the *Nashville Banner* ("Miss Montgomery has a very refined art and deserves more than ordinary praise for her clean simple style, and her power to convey the sweetness and charm of such a heroine"), the *San Francisco Argonaut* ("Avonlea is evidently full of interesting people, or perhaps it is Miss Montgomery's romantic clairvoyance that is able to see the interest in characters usually supposed to be past the age of ordinary sentiment"), and the *Buffalo Commercial* ("As one reads of her sayings and doings one is reminded of some sweet girl known away back in the halcyon days of youth, and one finds oneself wondering whether this is a creation of fancy or a real living, moving, loving personality of flesh and blood").[2]

Finally, two more reviewers saw the change in format as an organic expression of her strengths as a writer, rather than as a disappointment. As the *Philadelphia Press* noted, "Contrary to her usual custom, Mrs. Montgomery has produced a volume of short stories rather than a connected narrative; but, after all, the total effect of the book is not different, for example, from that of *The Story Girl*, which consisted of a series of episodes centering round a single character." The *Morning Post* of London admitted that "perhaps Miss Montgomery is right in not giving us too much of Anne. She is a clever enough writer to be able to picture many other personages equally as vivid and alluring."[3]

## Book of Smiles and Tears
### *The Boston Globe* (Boston, MA)

*Chronicles of Avonlea*, by L.M. Montgomery, Bears
Eloquent Testimony to the Skill of the Author

Exquisite in color and perfect in drawing are the many short stories found in the volume entitled *Chronicles of Avonlea*, by L.M. Montgomery, the author of *Anne of Green Gables, Anne of Avonlea* and *The Story Girl*, etc.

It is rare that such a wide scope is found in the grouping of a number of short stories as is the case in this new publication. Any one story in the volume is eloquent testimony to the skill and literary ability of the author.

The stories possess real, alluring charm, they are filled with whimsical, searching humor and quaint, delightful characters, whose doings are bound to cause both smiles and tears to almost any reader.

The author shows a wonderful knowledge of humanity, great insight and warm heartedness in the manner in which some of the scenes are treated, and the sympathetic way the gentle peculiarities of the characters are brought out.

There certainly is nothing gentle in the character of one woman she writes of, a martinette who has dominated the life of her gentle and timid sister for so long that the other is in terror of her.

The strong-minded and strong-willed sister undertakes to hinder her timid relative becoming engaged, and the story is one bubbling over with rich humor and ridiculous situations.

A story which causes smiles and tears to lie close is that of an old maid who announces she is about to marry. Then when her lover appears her habits of years assert themselves and she cannot submit to his manly ways and disregard for tidiness.

She drives him forth and later almost founders a horse striving to reach the railroad station in time to call him back. Every story is different, but all are unusually clever and good.


## Down East Idyls
### *The Boston Herald* (Boston, MA)


The readers of L.M. Montgomery – now Mrs. Ewen Macdonald – will welcome this new book saturated with the life and environment of Avonlea. One hardly opens its pages ere one breathes the ozone of the sea and becomes sensible of the odors of orchards and firs and spruces and pines and Mayflowers and the blooms of old-fashioned gardens. Then, too, we plunge at once into the romance of the region, the common drab of its everyday activities and its tragedies. What James M. Barrie has done for Kirriemuir (Thrums), with its Auld Licht weavers, and John Watson for Logiealmond (Drumtochty) in the Perthshire glen, Miss Montgomery has done for Prince Edward Island.[4] And there is something suggestive of both of those men in her work. Anne Shirley, the Story Girl, Kilmeny, to mention no others, have a Barriesque flavor about them, and the pen pictures of those down East farmers and their wives are not unworthy of being placed alongside the characters that figure in *The Bonnie Brier Bush*.

These chronicles are practically 12 short stories, which are woven around local interests, and in which Anne Shirley once more appears among the actors. It would be difficult to select any one of them as of especial merit. There is a remarkable evenness of treatment and interest. "Old Lady Lloyd," "Little Joscelyn," "The Winning of Lucinda," "Old Man Shaw's Girl" and "Aunt Olivia's Beau," are all charming, but hardly better than some others which are mentioned. There are enough humorous situations, and they usually centre about the courtships of old maids. What a paradise for the left-overs is Avonlea! And how coy, and discerning, and resourceful, and loveable and sensible they really are! Fifteen-year courtships, too! Think of that. Put this book in your satchel or trunk by all means. It will fit in well with the hammock on the mountainside or the piazza on the seashore, and, best of all, it will give you a pleasant relief from the society novel and the modern thriller.

## [An Intrinsic Worth of Their Own]
### *Saint John Globe* (Saint John, NB)

Friends of Anne Shirley will be glad to read these chronicles of the many interesting and lovable persons among whom the heroine of Green Gables spent her childhood and her girlhood days. The "chronicles" is not a continued story, it is twelve complete stories in which Anne with her brilliant hair and no less brilliant personality sometimes appears, oftener she does not. The stories are held together by the fact that they pertain to Avonlea and Carmody folks, and by the interest that attaches and will continue to attach itself to those places and persons that are connected ever so slightly with Anne. These stories have, however, an intrinsic worth of their own, and are each in its own way complete and finished examples of the art to which short story writing may attain. Miss Montgomery writes with a simplicity and a naturalness that is convincing. Instinctively one feels that the men and women, the boys and girls, the very cats and dogs of her stories are human and real; and they remain not creatures of the imagination but actual friends whose pleasures we have shared, whose griefs we have borne, and whose good fortunes we rejoice over. The authoress, too, is not without a saving sense of humor that lends the quaint charm to her stories that mark their individuality. *The Chronicles of Avonlea*, bound in cloth with a colored inset and a colored frontispiece of Anne by George Gibbs, is published at one dollar and a quarter.

## [Gently Sentimental and Enjoyably Humorous]
### *The Outlook* (New York, NY)

This is, we believe, the fourth or fifth of the Anne books. It is less distinctively an Anne book than its predecessors, as that charming and energetic girl appears only incidentally in one or two of the stories. The several tales which make up this volume are in turn gently sentimental and enjoyably humorous. Miss Montgomery seems to have great store of excellent material for this kind of writing.

## [Chronicles of Perfect Characters]
### *The Lexington Herald* (Lexington, KY)

One of the most beautiful stories in the world is in this volume, "Each in His Own Tongue." Its tender beauty is so great it almost seems inspiration. The other tales are far above the average; each one has a distinct and vivid color of its own.

The author of *Anne of Green Gables* is one from whom we might expect no disappointment, and surely in this volume of stories there is fulfillment of all promise. It is the tender, loving, simple side of life that the author of these and many other lovable volumes appeals to and writes about. There are not breathless climaxes, no vehement avowals, only sweet reasonableness throughout, and the tone is always sincere and satisfying. But "Each in His Own Tongue" is a really wonderful story, with insight, understanding and sympathy for a strangely assorted group of people. If only true goodness were not so often made hideous by mistaking Ego for Deo![5] Avonlea is a much newer, more concentrated Cranford,[6] and the characters in these Chronicles are perfect.

## Re-enter Anne of Avonlea
### *The San Francisco Call* (San Francisco, CA)

The friends of Anne Shirley of Green Gables and Avonlea (and their name is legion) will welcome another book from the hand of L.M. Montgomery, in which Anne, more mature, but no less sprightly, no less fascinating, again appears. The title of the book is *Chronicles of Avonlea*, and it introduces a number of new persons and personalities of the community in and about Avonlea. This distinction between persons and personalities is made advisedly, for out of Miss Montgomery's little group of characters there emerges now and then one of those images of life that appear occasionally in fiction and make one feel their essential humanness. They are salient without being detached; they are part of the picture and yet the atmosphere and light seem to flow around them – to envelop them completely.

Such a one, of course, is Anne herself, and such a one, most distinctly, is Old Lady Lloyd. Her story is a pathetic one, but it is told with such consistent sweetness and delicacy that it stands out not only as the most charming tale in the volume, but one of the most charming that has appeared for many a day.

The story of the impoverished old lady's secret beneficence to Sylvia, the orphan of the man she had once loved, is told with an exquisite fineness; the mere narrative is admirably conducted; the touch and the effect are sure and subtle and unspoiled by sentimentality.

The substance and the style of Miss Montgomery's work may be likened to a miniature painting. She depicts her Avonlea folk in the colors of fancy, but colors that are transparent and through which, here and there, the high light of reality may be seen like the ivory through the artist's pigment.

Anne Shirley appears as a participant only in the first story, "The Hurrying of Ludovic," through which she dances mischievously. She seems, however, to be hovering near in some of the other stories, even though the allusions to her are casual. Undoubtedly Avonlea and its environs can not even be mentioned without conjuring thoughts of Anne of Green Gables. In these "Chronicles" the author's purpose is, in the main, to amuse as most of the tales are humorous, and as such they make most excellent reading. Yet, tempering the tone of the book, are such stories as "Old Lady Lloyd" and "Little Joscelyn," wherein her purpose may have been to tempt tears. There will be few to say that she has failed, although the moving quality of these tales is not due to any feelings of sadness that they arouse, but rather to that form of pathos which has for its foundation the nobler aspects of human relations.

## [Middle-Aged Love Stories of Unusual Type]
### *Boston Evening Transcript* (Boston, MA)

In spite of the colored frontispiece portrait of the charming Anne Shirley of Green Gables and Avonlea, that popular and delightful young woman appears in only one of these stories, and then only casually. Clearly this is not another Anne book. But many other people of Avonlea and nearby towns in Prince Edward Island, most of them older than Anne, appear in well-written and entertaining little tales, which are middle-aged love stories of unusual type. They improve as we near the end; indeed the last story, "The End of a Quarrel," which relates the sad result of a young woman's insistence upon "kerrect" language from her husband, is quite the best of the collection. Prince Edward Island women evidently are good housekeepers, for several broken romances are mended with a broom and a dishpan. There is quaint humor as well as subtle romance in the story of "The Quarantine," and "Each in His Own Tongue" is a pathetic little tale.

It is to be hoped, however, that there will be another "Anne" story. There are other interesting people in Avonlea, but there is only one Anne.

## [Each Tale a Gem]
### *The Brooklyn Daily Eagle* (Brooklyn, NY)

Avonlea is a charming place and a number of charming and interesting people live there. The author of *Chronicles of Avonlea*, L.M. Montgomery, tells us all about it in a series of delightful tales. The publishers of the book are L.C. Page & Co. It is true that you can only visit the place through the medium of her writings, for it exists only in her imagination. But it is all very real and the persons to whom she introduces her readers are fast friends before the last page is turned down, for they are a lovable lot. Simplicity marks the telling about these people and humanity the people themselves. In the telling of these tales the author plays on all the chords of human emotion. If you laugh at the way that lovable but dilatory lover with the incongruous name, Ludovic Speed,[7] was brought to book after a deliberate courtship of fifteen years and forced in a hurry to marry, you will have difficulty in suppressing the tears over "Each in His Own Tongue," in which a very much loved clergyman was taught that there were more ways of serving his Master than he had chosen, and that the Almighty had many ways of expressing His will and desire.

The author has won a fine reputation as a depictor of child life, but it is a mistake to consider that she is limited to that life. Indeed her finest work is to be found wherein she gives us the relation of the child and the adult. Mark Twain was responsible, in a degree, in fixing the idea that the author was a depictor of child life only, when he said, "In *Anne of Green Gables* you will find the dearest and most moving and delightful child since the immortal Alice." All that he said was true but without saying so he conveyed the idea that there were limitations. Miss Montgomery has an intuitive insight into human nature and with her delightful style has ease in expressing what she sees and she finds it in all "sorts and conditions of men" at every age.[8] The book under consideration is a series of tales, each one of which is a gem.

## [Romances of Middle Age]
### *The Nation* (New York, NY)

Miss Montgomery continues to follow up the vein she opened in *Anne of Green Gables*. These stories are all of Spencervale or Avonlea. Anne herself – or what we hope to be a caricature of her – appears on the cover, and is mentioned now and again within. But she is not the leading figure in any of the tales, which might have been called "Romances of Middle Age," so strongly does a single motive dominate them. Ten out of the dozen stories deal with belated love-affairs, or with the pathetic devotion of age for youth. Perhaps this is why the group as a whole reminds one of Mrs. Deland's *Old Chester Tales*[9] – this and certain resemblances of style which are probably not due altogether to accident. The resemblance does not go very deep. The essential difference between the two chroniclers is the difference between sentiment and sentimentality, restraint and exuberance. Mrs. Deland looks upon her Old Chester scene with an eye both keen and affectionate; it lies peopled in her imagination, a thing real and complete. She is incapable of inventing pretty stories about these people. Miss Montgomery's Avonlea, on the other hand, is a place which furnishes types about which pretty stories may be invented. This writer has that fatal gift of neatness which is ready to sacrifice everything else to finish of plot. So she does not balk at the absurdity of a twelve-year-old boy who has never been taught to fiddle improvising masterpieces on the slightest provocation. This is a pity, because Miss Montgomery has certainly the story-teller's instinct, genuine humor, and a sentiment altogether clear of sentimentality – when she chooses to keep it so.

## [Happy Sentiment]
### *Newport Daily News* (Newport, RI)

A new book by L.M. Montgomery will be eagerly welcomed by the admirers of *Anne of Green Gables*, *Anne of Avonlea*, *The Story Girl* and *Kilmeny of the Orchard*. Anne Shirley plays some part in *Chronicles of Avonlea*, but there are many events in which she has no share. Anne's absence, however, does not detract from the interest of the stories, for they are full of humor, a gay sprightliness and happy sentiment.

The author's love of nature and of all growing things is evidenced by her word pictures of woods and sea. In the tale "Old Man Shaw's Girl," in which father and daughter meet after an absence of three years, there is this exquisite pen sketch: "at sunset they came back and sat down on the old garden bench. Before them a sea of splendour, burning like a great jewel, stretched to the gateways of the west. The long headlands on either side were darkly purple, and the sun left behind him a vast, cloudless arc of fiery daffodil and elusive rose. Back over the orchard in a cool, green sky glimmered a crystal planet, and the night poured over them a clear wine of dew from her airy chalice. The spruces were rejoicing in the wind, and even the battered firs were singing of the sea. Old memories trooped into their hearts like shining spirits."[10]

The "chronicles" describe some ridiculous happenings and ludicrous situations. "The Winning of Lucinda" will evoke a hearty laugh even from the gravest and most serious of men, while "The Courting of Prissy Strong" will quickly chase away the blues. In "Aunt Olivia's Beau" humor and sentiment both abound. The transformation of a prim little old maid who gave up her lover because he tracked mud into her house is worth reading about. "The Quarantine at Alexander Abraham's," in which a woman-hater and a man-hater are compelled to live together in the same house for a few weeks, is perhaps the most amusing of all the stories. The woman has always hated men and dogs. As she says:

"The more I saw of men, the more I liked cats."[11] The man in question had threatened that if any woman came into his yard he would chase her out with a pitchfork.

"Old Lady Lloyd," the longest of the dozen stories, is an appealing tale, showing the wonders that love can work. "Each in His Own Tongue" teaches a lesson which all strict moralists may well heed. Other stories are "The Hurrying of Ludovic," who had courted for 15 years; "Little Joscelyn," telling of a famous singer and a dear old lady; "Pa Sloane's Purchase," which was a baby boy; "The Miracle at Carmody" and "The End of a Quarrel."

## [Miss Montgomery's Best Work]
### *The Canadian Magazine* (Toronto, ON)

The wholesome and naïve qualities that distinguish all of Miss L.M. Montgomery's essays in fiction are present to a marked degree in her volume of short stories entitled *Chronicles of Avonlea*. The word "Avonlea" will resound in many responsive ears, because it is a word which, with Anne Shirley, has achieved international fame. These chronicles are of the best work that Miss Montgomery has done. The characters are real, living people, full of human weaknesses and homely virtues. Perhaps it is fortunate for Miss Montgomery that she has not found it necessary to go farther afield for her material, because by this time there has been established in Carmody and its people a bond of sympathy that will endure. Besides that, Miss Montgomery writes of these people with a sure pen, and one feels that she is drawing from life. *Old Lady Lloyd, Ludovic Speed, the Reverend Mr. Leonard, Naomi Clark, Prissy Strong* and most of the others are so much of the flesh that one hesitates before writing their names in italics.[12] Anne Shirley herself has got beyond that stage, and so we must respect her now as something more than a mere creation of imagination. She reappears in these pages, and indeed the first two words of the first story in the book compose her name. The sentence containing them is a good example of what one might expect to find in the book: "Anne Shirley was curled up on the window seat of Theodora Dix's sitting-room one Saturday evening, looking dreamily afar at some fair starland beyond the hills of sunset." Then after a few other sentences, the story continues: "She leaned her shapely head, with its braided coronet of dark red hair, against the window-casing, and her gray eyes were like the moonlight gleam of shadowy pools."[13]

This first story, which is called "The Hurrying of Ludovic," has to do with the courtship of *Theodora Dix* and *Ludovic Speed*. These two have been sweethearts of a kind for fifteen years but Ludovic, who has belied his name in showing less speed than inclination, has failed lamentably to see that he and *Theodora* are away past the grown-up stages; in short that *Theodora* is almost passé. Anne soon discovers that *Ludovic* needs a little baiting and she openly charges *Theodora* with failure to arouse the lover to a sense of his responsibility. *Theodora* admits that she "*did* try once," and she recounts that: "When I realized that I was getting sere and mellow, and all the girls of my generation were going off on either hand, I tried to give Ludovic a hint. But it stuck in my throat. And now I don't mind. If I don't change Dix to Speed until I take the initiative, it will be Dix to the end of life."[14] With that Anne determines to take the initiative. She induces a city-bred cousin of her own to make pretence at courting *Theodora*, with the result that *Ludovic*, spurred by jealousy, proposes before he knows it, and the thing is settled. But the subtlest passage is the suggestion that the cousin in the end was not very sure that his own courtship of *Theodora* was only a sham. There is about the others of the set a wholesomeness and charm that attracts attention and merits admiration.

## [Thoroughly Delightful Sketches]
### *The Globe* (Toronto, ON)

A new and altogether charming department of letters is entered by L.M. Montgomery, author of *Anne of Green Gables*, in her new book, *Chronicles of Avonlea*. Forsaking the long novel, Miss Montgomery gives in short story form a series of thoroughly delightful sketches of Prince Edward Island life. For sustained literary finish this book contains the author's best work to date. It reminds one of the early stories of Mary E. Wilkins,[15] describing New England life, and that is paying Miss Montgomery a high compliment. The author has chosen types and incidents from commonplace village and rural life, and invested them with a sympathetic realism that makes almost every story live in one's memory.

Over the realism of the characters there is the unmistakable atmosphere of the author's Island home, the sweep of the sea, the long, shady lanes, the quiet countryside, the glamor of the setting sun, the mystery and romance of moonlit nights. Into these pages are placed characters that would attract little attention from the world at large except perhaps from their eccentricities.

True, there are records of persons of genius, but they only make the home folks the more real by contrast. [* * *]16

Now that Miss Montgomery – or Mrs. Ewen Macdonald, as she has become – has settled in an Ontario village, it is interesting to speculate if she will transfer her literary affections. Or will the memories of childhood, of the Island garden and its wholesome, quiet life by the sea be her abiding inspiration?

## Charming Stories
### *The Register* (Adelaide, Australia)

Miss Montgomery's books are as fresh flowers floating on the flood of drab fiction poured forth by the printing presses to-day. Their influence is wholesome and sweetening, and refreshing to the mind jaded with "problem" novels. They make no claim to greatness, but merely depict everyday men and women and children with everyday failings and virtues; and the fact that they have sold by the hundred-thousand is an indication of the healthy condition of the reading public. The present volume of short stories is a fitting succession to the "Anne" books, although it rather lacks the piquant flavour of the narratives in which that young lady figures. The title was evidently chosen for advertisement purposes, as in reality Avonlea, made famous by Anne Shirley, is hardly mentioned in the book; and Anne herself is dragged in here and there – quite without justification – solely because of the interest which her name is sure to excite among readers of Miss Montgomery's previous volumes. Still, the stories are well able to stand on their own merits. They are uniformly delightful – never melodramatic or farcical, but gently humorous, with touches of true human pathos. There is one sad blot on the otherwise pure pages – a swear word! One would as soon have expected to find a pig in a parlour as a strong adjective in a Montgomery book. But there it is – in italics, too. It came about in this way:– Romney Penhallow was engaged to his cousin Lucinda, but they had quarrelled, and for 15 long years the Penhallow pride would not let either of them break the silence. Then one night they found themselves walking home together after a dance. Came a brook, with no bridge; and Romney in grim silence picked Lucinda up and proceeded to carry her across. Halfway over he slipped – and they both sat down in the middle of the stream. "Lucinda was the first to regain her feet. About her clung, in heart-breaking limpness, the ruined voile. The remembrance of all her wrongs that night rushed over her soul, and her eyes blazed in the moonlight. Lucinda Penhallow had never been so angry in her life. 'You d – d idiot!' she said, in a voice that literally shook with rage." Thus was the silence rudely broken, and the twain made friends again. Afterwards the family discussed the affair. "'Lucinda has spoken to Romney *at last,*' [said Mrs. Nathaniel Penhallow.] 'Oh, *what* do you suppose she said to him?' cried Mrs. George. 'My dear Cecilia,' said Mrs. Frederick, 'we shall never know.' They never did know."[17] And perhaps it was just as well.

## [Clean, Sparkling Humor]
### *The Catholic World* (New York, NY)

Miss Montgomery has written a series of short stories full of pathos and humor. *Old Lady Lloyd* and *Old Man Shaw's Girl* are quaint and original stories of foolish pride and perfect human love. We can see before us *Old Man Shaw* sitting on the old bench in the garden, wondering whether the little girl he sent away to be educated will return to him spoiled, as Mrs. Blewett informed him, "after three years of fashionable life among rich, stylish folks, and at a swell school"; but we are glad when *Baby Blossom* returns "a little taller, a little more womanly, but his own dear Blossom, and no stranger." "'The world out there is a good place,' she said thoughtfully. 'There are wonderful things out there to see and learn, fine, noble people to meet, beautiful deeds to admire; but,' she wound her arms about his neck and laid her cheek against his – 'there was no daddy!'"[18]

For quaint, clean sparkling humor, *The Winning of Lucinda, Aunt Olivia's Beau, The Courting of Prissy Strong*, and *The Quarantine* are remarkable. The author is very fond of one particular theme, namely, the marrying of old spinsters to their lovers of twenty or thirty years ago. She succeeds in disposing of at least five such hopeless cases.

Frequently in these stories we are reminded of J.M. Barrie; the author has not his finished style, but she does share his sympathetic and kindly understanding of human nature.

## [Leisurely Love-Making]
### *The Scotsman* (Edinburgh, UK)

An obscure nook in an unconsidered province of Maritime Canada – Prince Edward Island[19] – has been rendered familiar and beloved to many readers on both sides of the Atlantic by the penetrating and sympathetic study which Miss L.M. Montgomery (now Mrs. Ewan Macdonald[20]) has lavished on the humorous and pathetic sides of the local characters and history. A further instalment of *The Chronicles of Avonlea* will be hailed with pleasant expectations by the widening circle who have made acquaintance with "Anne of Green Gables" and her friends and neighbours. Anne Shirley makes intermittent, but characteristic reappearance in these stories. She "speeds up" the lagging love affairs of Ludovic Speed,[21] who for fifteen years has been seeing home from meeting house the lady on whom he has fixed his tranquil affections without attempting to bring the affair to a crisis, and she accomplishes the wedding of Prissy Strong, in spite of the precautions of Prissy's dragon of a sister, although the bride has to hold out her arm from an upper window which the bridegroom reaches by means of a ladder, while the minister reads the service from the ground below. But in Avonlea love-making, like everything else, is usually done in a leisurely fashion, varied by sudden spurts, the result, as we may understand, of a mixture of blood of Celtic impulse breaking through Lowland Scottish caution.

## [Engaging "Heart-Interest Stories"]
### *The Times Literary Supplement* (London, UK)

Miss Montgomery, a Canadian authoress (of Prince Edward Island) made a success with her *Anne of Green Gables* and *Anne of Avonlea* – tales of the engaging type known to the trade as "heart-interest stories"; and the episodes she here puts together in which Anne again plays her part will no doubt be warmly welcomed.

## [A Little Disappointed]
### *The Bookman* (London, UK)

Those of us who have enjoyed the stories of Anne of Green Gables and Avonlea, will take up Miss Montgomery's new Avonlea book *Chronicles of Avonlea* with eagerness and high expectations. And I fear we shall find ourselves a little disappointed. For, entertaining as the stories undoubtedly are, yet they do not all reach the level of their author's previous work. One or two are a trifle unconvincing, and at times the pathos is overdrawn, notably in "Old Lady Lloyd" and "Little Joscelyn." Also there is not quite enough variety in the plots – too much tendency to elderly lovers' quarrels and reconciliations. Still, these remarks apply to only a few of the tales. "Each in His Own Tongue" is a powerful piece of work, and there are several other fine little stories. Anne Shirley flits through the book like a ghost, appearing for a few seconds from time to time but taking little or no definite action in any of the plots. Yet these brief glimpses of her make us long for another book all about Anne, and hope that Miss Montgomery will give us one in the near future. There is a beautiful frontispiece to the book, a picture in colour of Anne, by Mr. George Gibbs.

## [Delightful Summer Reading]
### *The Boston Watchman* (Boston, MA)

The charming little stories in this volume all have the home town of the famous "Anne of Green Gables" for their setting. Although Anne herself never holds the center of the stage in any of the scenes, there are many glimpses of her which show various attitudes towards her among her townspeople. Whimsicalities and idiosyncrasies among these island people have made these stories sometimes amusing, but more often sad. They all, however, breathe a peaceful, quiet, rural charm which makes them delightful summer reading. So greatly has the author endeared herself to her readers, that the popularity of one of her new books is a foregone conclusion.

## [Chronicles of Autumn Flowers]
### *The Republic* (Boston, MA)

Since the appearance of this author's first delightful and most deservedly fortunate book, the public has looked with interest for everything which she has been pleased to give them. *Anne of Green Gables*, however, remains on a height of beauty and freshness unreached of any of its successors. We must admit, however, the near approach of its excellence of *The Story Girl*. Nevertheless, we love "Avonlea" for Anne's sake; and we gladly enter its intimate life, as set forth in Miss Montgomery's latest, in the hope of meeting Anne herself once more; or, of at least getting close to the characters with whom her childhood was associated. We find Anne in the first of "The Chronicles" – "The Hurrying of Ludovic," in the unexpected guise of a match-maker. She actually precipitates the mis-named Ludovic Speed, who for fifteen years has been courting Theodora Dix, into his long delayed proposal of marriage by the simple expedient of getting Arnold Sherman to pay some small attentions to Theodora. Fortunately, Ludovic for once in his life acts promptly; for, although Anne doesn't realize it, the grown-up reader sees that a little more delay, and there would have been a tragedy instead of a gentle comedy, as Arnold Sherman began to take his part too seriously. Four more of the stories turn on belated marriages. They are autumn flowers, sweet and daintily colored, but with a faint chill from the uncharted regions of the other world blowing over them. There is one exception: "The Quarantine at Alexander Abraham's," where the "old maid" is a decidedly jolly and amusing person; the more so, as she takes herself so dreadfully in earnest. There's a snap in it which might suit Anne herself, if she ever attained to mature single blessedness, but that, of course, is out of the question. Let Angelina MacPherson talk a little, and see if she is not a kinswoman of Anne:

"Mrs. Allan is famous for her tact. Tact is a faculty for meandering around to a given point instead of making a bee-line. I have no tact. I am noted for that." Angelina, to her intimates Peter, is accounted a man-hater; but when it comes to taking a Sunday School class, her philanthropy gets the best of her aversion. "'Then I shall take the boys,' I said decidedly. I am noted for my decision '… Nuisances they are bound to become under any circumstances; but if they are taken in hand young enough, they may not grow up to be such nuisances as they otherwise would and that will be some unfortunate woman's gain."[22]

Strangely enough, Miss MacPherson became intensely interested in Jimmy Spencer, a peculiarly aggravating type of the genus Boy, even to the extent of bearding Alexander Abraham Bennett, an inveterate woman-hater, in his den, otherwise his neglected farmhouse, in her quest of the truant.

"As usual, I took William Adolphus with me for company. William Adolphus is my favourite among my six cats … He sat up on the seat beside me and looked far more like a gentleman than many a man I've seen in a similar position."[23]

The reader must find out what befell Miss Angelina when she made her unconventional entrance into the Bennett homestead, and found herself in a house that had just been quarantined in a small-pox scare. The story is funny enough to have carried the book before us to success, of itself. But there are other good, if pathetic stories, as "Old Man Shaw's Girl," "Each in His Own Tongue," and "Pa Sloane's Purchase." The development of marked individualities in a small town, as contrasted with the sameness of the residents in a section of a great city is brought out well. It is safe to predict for *Chronicles of Avonlea* a wide popularity.

## [Stories of Real People]
### *The Rochester Herald* (Rochester, NY)

To say that the *Chronicles of Avonlea* is a better book than Miss Montgomery's other books is in the nature of trying to gild refined gold. But as impossible as the feat may seem, this delightful Canadian woman is improving as her pen becomes more practiced. In the new volume we have some of the old people – notably her famous Anne of Green Gables – and some that are new to us. However, they are all real people, without a suggestion of artificiality about them. There is one thing about Miss Montgomery's work that we like, and in these times it is worth a good deal to booklovers. We can place one of her books in the hands of a person whom we respect without fear of its containing something which one would rather have had omitted. And Miss Montgomery's books do not come in the "goody goody" class either. They are just wholesome, healthy and enjoyable.

## [Full of a True Human Nature]
### *The Toronto News* (Toronto, ON)

Anne of Green Gables flits through a page or two of these *Chronicles of Avonlea*, by L.M. Montgomery, now Mrs. Ewan Macdonald.[24] But Anne's winsome personality is not needed to make this book a success on its own account. The volume contains what seems to be Miss Montgomery's best work so far. What made Anne so delightful a little friend was her happy spirit and abundant life. No one could read about Anne without feeling more hopeful and more confident that good would come true. This same spirit has been set free in all the stories which make up *The Chronicles of Avonlea*, and, besides this, all the stories are full of a true human nature as it is to be found in a country a little shut off from the rest of the world.

There are oddities and frankness and queer tales and the coming back of those who have gone away into the world outside and the warping of one soul and the setting free of another. Miss Montgomery's Prince Edward Island people in this book remind the reader a little of Miss Jewett's New Englanders.[25] To say so is to give high praise. Perhaps the finest quality in the book is its happy humor. Miss Montgomery shows in these chronicles that she has a sure hold on character. The touch of unreality which belongs to her other work is not present here. The men and women in "The End of a Quarrel" and in "The Quarantine" are masterly delineations in miniature of just such people as belong to everyday life in Canada. The style of writing is easy and pleasant. When Miss Montgomery writes a longer story about grown-up people in the same mood as that in which she has written *Chronicles of Avonlea* the story cannot help being again a marked success.

## [The Concealment of Art]
### *The Toronto World* (Toronto, ON)

Art is greatest when it conceals itself. It does not often do so in the sentimental novel. The aim of the author to probe the tear-ducts of the reader is often too painfully apparent. From flowing wells of pathos we turn to be surfeited with lovey-dovey gush. In our fight from these we are arrested by the strident voice of the preacher in the "problem" or "purpose" novel. Do we regard any of these as types of the real art of fiction, or do we derive real and lasting pleasure from the reading of them? Not unless our taste has been sadly warped and vitiated.

It is of a book which does not belong to any of these types that I desire to speak to you. In *Chronicles of Avonlea*, by L.M. Montgomery, what impresses one most is the concealment of art, the power to make our inner chords of sympathy thrill without any obvious attempt at doing so, but merely by a simple and straight-forward recital of the facts of the story. An excellent example of this is the short story "Each in His Own Tongue" – a story which deserves to rank as a classic of its kind. This story shows how the message of salvation is revealed to a dying soul thru the medium of music – the music of the violin, which the minister had hitherto regarded as something profane. The pathos and beauty of the simple description of the young boy's violin playing at the bedside of the dying woman will strike a responsive chord in the heart of every reader capable of real and adequate emotion.

A strong vein of humor is a marked characteristic of much of the work of this writer, but this is quiet and persuasive rather than any way obtrusive – a sort of domesticated humor of everyday life as it were. We might perhaps call L.M. Montgomery the Jane Austen of Canadian literature. Those who object to classification and comparison on the ground of the misquoted quotation "comparisons are odious"[26] must remember that without comparison we would have no criticism, no standard of values or tastes in anything. Without comparison, or the presence of things or qualities admitting of comparison, the world would be one vast monotone. Let us then not be afraid to accord our author some distinctive place in our, perhaps narrow, national field of letters. There are others, as Sir Walter Scott said of himself, who "can do the big bow-wow strain,"[27] but we have ample room in Canadian literature for a writer who can depict faithfully and with real art the simple happenings of our quiet rural communities.

Again, the optimism of the creator of "the adorable Anne" is a characteristic quality. Here, too, the real artist is apparent. No other Canadian author (no, not even our clergymen-novelists[28]) preaches so effectively the gospel of love and hope, faith and kindness. And why? Simply because she does not preach at all. The stories are told with the art of naturalness; they do their own preaching. It is idle to discuss such topics as "Shall the novel teach something?" The novel or story cannot help itself. If the reader has an intellect to understand and a soul to be affected, the story will teach him something, good or ill. If you change your brief to "Shall the novelist preach?" then you have a question which at least admits of a difference of opinion.

Going back to the characterization of the author as the Jane Austen of Canadian literature, let it not be understood that we are regardless of the difference in the scope of the work of the two writers. Jane Austen's canvas is immensely broader, yet, let me note, that L.M. Montgomery's portrayal of her fellowmen and fellowwomen shows a much keener personal sympathy; her work has more heart to it.

We hope that the urgent and unreasoning demand of the reader and the publisher will not compel this continuous output of a book or more each year from this author's pen. The work she has to do, if she is to fill the place which there is for her in Canadian literature, requires time for a broader and deeper treatment of her future themes.

## [Aroma of New England]
### *Trenton Times–Advertiser* (Trenton, NJ)

The author of *Anne of Green Gables* here offers a collection of short stories with all the aroma of choice New England about them, much true characterization of folk of those parts, and a great deal of fine-spun, wholesome, and inviting sentiment. She writes with much of the charm of Alice Brown and not a little of Mrs. Wilkins' insight.[29] There is a great place for stories of this sort. In this day of the drab and the outre, the straining for cleverness, the remote, and the suggestive, those writers who keep before the public the high ideals of rural simplicity and abiding traits should be given first place. "Old Lady Lloyd," "Little Joscelyn," "Prissy Strong," and Nancy and Peter in "The End of a Quarrel" are real people, with vital affairs and worthy missions.

## [The Simple Life of Homely People]
### *Eastern Western Review* (Boston, MA)

A dozen short stories make up this book of "chronicles." Separate in theme, they are closely related by the nature of the material. It is New England life which the author describes – life in which she is at home and in which she must have grown up. Her imagination compasses a variety of situations; she shows considerable insight into character. The literary touch is graceful rather than pretentious. None of the stories carry us off our feet; all give a quiet kind of pleasure which is restful amid the noise and din of the "best-sellers." In some of them the incident is of the slightest, as where a daughter comes home to her "old daddy," or an old woman dies peacefully after hearing the songs that delighted her in earlier years. But the simple life of homely people is always with us in these pages, and the author's natural way of presenting it convinces us that "it really happened."

Among Miss Montgomery's favorite situations is a long period of courtship with only a remote prospect of marriage in sight. Two of the stories are thus founded, and 15 years is the period of exasperating delay in each. In one the procrastinating lover is brought to the proposal stage by the expedient of arousing his jealousy; in the other, the lady – such is the mystery of woman – is melted to tenderness by being compelled to call her worshipper a "damned idiot."[30] In "Each in His Own Tongue," the author uses the violin, as a variant from her resort to the voice, for an effective illustration of the power of music. "Aunt Olivia's Beau" is the amusing story of a lady who is obdurate as long as her lover leaves mud on her doorstep, but undertakes the capture of him when she learns that he is at the railway station on his way west. And of such are the other narratives in Miss Montgomery's book.

## [Whether or Not an Anne Book]
### *The Independent* (New York, NY)

We are not quite certain whether or not the *Chronicles of Avonlea* is an "Anne" book, but it is by L.M. Montgomery and is in the same class as those well-known tales, and is about an Anne – Anne Shirley of Green Gables. 'Tis a book with which one may pleasantly pass an hour now and then, until it is ended. It has been likened to *David Harum*,[31] in its human charm; tho we would not have thought of that simile.

## [Plain Everyday Folk]
### *Kansas City Post* (Kansas City, KS)

The *Chronicles of Avonlea*, by L.M. Montgomery, is a really charming new book. There are twelve chronicles, each a story complete in itself, since they are connected by locality, rather than plot. They are narratives of the tragedies and comedies everywhere about us and ring true to life. They are told so simply and unaffectedly that we almost lose sight of the art back of the telling.

There are no melancholy, black browed heroes, and no romantic, melo-dramatic heroines, just plain everyday folk, the stories of whose lives are exalted, and made appealing by the comprehending heart of the author.

There are exquisite bits of description, but they are not studied efforts at word painting. They serve only as a setting for the story, or spring naturally from the story itself.

There are passages of real pathos, but they grow out of incidents really pathetic, not strained sentimentality.

There are paragraphs and pages of real humor, but they are the result of a sympathetic comprehension of ludicrous situations, not of an effort to make some one ridiculous. In a word, the pathos and humor are spontaneous.

Barring an absence of dialect they bring to mind Ian Maclaren's stories of "Drumtotchy." There is a similar mingling of the pathetic, the humorous and the reverential.

As we read them, "Each in His Own Tongue" is the best example of the serious themes, and "The Quarantine at Alexander Abraham's" the best of the stories in lighter vein.[32]

The whole book is so human, the character delineations so deftly drawn, the moral tone so pure and sweet, that we believe a warm welcome awaits it.

## [Harmless and Easy Reading]
### *The Louisville Post* (Louisville, KY)

From the standpoint of the unexacting, these are quite pretty stories, with enough and not too much of humor and of pathos. For the other sort – the fastidious, the exacting, the folk who know – there is very little here. A touch of lavender and old lace, a hint of Mary Wilkins, a reminder here and there of the older New England novelists – these are the best and most important qualities. As for the matter of variety, one tale is much like another – or, rather, there are but two or three orders and all of the stories are included in this small number. "The Hurrying of Ludovic," for instance, is much like "The Courting of Prissy Strong" and "Old Lady Lloyd" like "Little Joscelyn."[33] Of their order, however, they will do very well. There are many readers in the world, and this is but harmless and easy reading.

### NOTES

1  *The Oakland Tribune*, review of *Chronicles of Avonlea*, 10; *The Christian Science Monitor*, review of *Chronicles of Avonlea*, 2; *The Mail and Empire* (Toronto, ON), review of *Chronicles of Avonlea*, undated clipping, in SR, 46; Hopkins, review of *Chronicles of Avonlea*, 814; *The National Magazine*, "The Vacation Girl Reads," 680.
2  *Pittsburgh Post* (Pittsburgh, PA), review of *Chronicles of Avonlea*, undated clipping (1912), in SR, 37; *San Francisco Evening Post* (San Francisco, CA), review of *Chronicles of Avonlea*, undated clipping (1912), in SR, 34; *Boston Times* (Boston, MA), review of *Chronicles of Avonlea*, signed D.S.K., undated clipping (1912), in SR, 37; "Anne of Avonlea Reappears in New Volume of Stories," review of *Chronicles of Avonlea*, unidentified

and undated clipping, in SR, 38; *The Nashville Banner* (Nashville, TN), review of *Chronicles of Avonlea*, undated clipping, in SR, 37; *San Francisco Argonaut* (San Francisco, CA), review of *Chronicles of Avonlea*, undated clipping (1912), in SR, 39; *Buffalo Commercial* (Buffalo, NY), review of *Chronicles of Avonlea*, undated clipping (1912), in SR, 39.

3 *Philadelphia Press* (Philadelphia, PA), review of *Chronicles of Avonlea*, undated clipping (1912), in SR, 34; *Morning Post* (London, UK), review of *Chronicles of Avonlea*, undated clipping, in SR, 47.

4 J.M. Barrie (1860–1937), Scottish novelist and playwright best known for *Peter Pan,* who wrote about Thrums (based on the village of Kirriemuir) in his earliest work, including *A Window in Thrums*. John Watson (1850–1907), Scottish author and theologian who wrote many books about Drumtochty under the pseudonym Ian Maclaren, including *Beside the Bonnie Brier Bush* (1894).

5 In other words, mistaking the self for the divine.

6 See "*Anne of Avonlea*," note 4, above.

7 I have corrected the original, which reads "Ludivic Speed."

8 *All Sorts and Conditions of Men* (1882), a novel by Walter Besant (1836–1901), English author.

9. See "*Anne of Avonlea*," note 15, above.

10 *CA*, 105–6.

11 *CA*, 122.

12 I have corrected the original, which reads "Ludoric Speed."

13 *CA*, 1.

14 *CA*, 5.

15 See "*Anne of Avonlea*," note 7, above.

16 Several paragraphs of detailed plot summaries of three stories – "Little Joscelyn," "Each in His Own Tongue," and "The Winning of Lucinda" – have been omitted.

17 *CA*, 92, 94.

18 *CA*, 100, 104, 106.

19 I have corrected the original, which reads "Prince Edward's Island."

20 I have corrected the original, which reads "Mrs. Evan Macdonald."

21 I have corrected the original, which reads "Ludovick Speed."

22 *CA*, 122, 123.

23 *CA*, 124–25.

24 I have corrected the original, which reads "McDonald."

25 Sarah Orne Jewett (1849–1909), American author of several "local color" novels set along the seacoast of Maine.

26 The phrase "comparisons are odious" can be traced back to the long

poem "Horse, Goose and Sheep" (ca. 1440), by John Lydgate (ca. 1370–ca. 1451), English monk and poet. In Shakespeare's play *Much Ado about Nothing*, a character transforms this phrase into "comparisons are odorous."

27 The phrase "The big bow-wow strain I can do myself" appears in Scott's journal entry dated March 1826, upon reading Jane Austen's *Pride and Prejudice*.

28 Among the Canadian novelists who were also Presbyterian ministers during this period are Charles W. Gordon (1860–1937), a best-selling author better known as Ralph Connor, and R.E. Knowles (1868–1946), whose first novel, *St. Cuthbert's*, was published in 1905.

29 Alice Brown (1857–1948), American author of "local color" fiction.

30 The actual quotation, in the story "The Winning of Lucinda," is "*You d – d idiot!*" (*CA*, 92).

31 *David Harum: A Story of American Life* (1899), a novel by Edward Noyes Westcott (1846–98), American author and banker.

32 I have corrected the original, which reads "The Quarantine of Alexander Abraham."

33 I have corrected the original, which reads "Jocelyn."

# 6

## *The Golden Road*

—— 1913 ——

"The spirit of youth pulsates throughout the volume," declared *The Canadian Magazine* in its review of this sequel to *The Story Girl*, a statement that was echoed in many other reviews of this book. As the *Evening Star* of Washington, DC, observed in its review of the novel, "The young people who skip and dance and sometimes stumble along the especially golden way that stretches from cover to cover of this refreshing book are merry pilgrims with just enough faults to make them lovably human, and who are good without being prigs." According to a review in the *Springfield Union* of Massachusetts, moreover, the book's "delightful romp through Boy and Girl Land" is "full of the flowers and joys of the spring of life's year, with just a raindrop or two to keep the flowers fresh and the road from getting dusty." To this the *Boston Times* added, "We make a note of many of the witty sayings in the book for future reference, then resolve to copy them, and then, despairing of culling them all, we decide that some evening, when the storm keeps us indoors and we are threatened with the blues, we will read the whole story again. It will prove a sure cure." Whereas the *Winnipeg Telegram* opined that "like all of Miss Montgomery's stories this one is so charmingly told that it will interest the entire household from the oldest to the youngest member," Marjory MacMurchy in the *Toronto News* insisted that "Miss Montgomery has kept a very complete sympathy with what girls care for most and with what they think, believe and worship." For MacMurchy, this limited readership was not a detraction but a strength:

> There is no strain or effort from the beginning to the end of *The Golden Road*. The narrative flows on as simply and naturally as a brook through

a meadow. It is scarcely possible that girls have a better friend to-day than Miss Montgomery. Without seeming to do so, she teaches them how lovely and delightful are simple, natural and wholesome ways. Wealth and luxury are wholly absent from her stories. The natural daily life of girlhood is made the most attractive thing in the world for a girl. There is nothing sentimental or exaggerated in these stories. Here are no false standards, but gayety and good times and an intellectual and moral sturdiness that will act like a touchstone by which a girl may judge the false and the true. *The Golden Road* may justly be called an ideal book for girls.

Nevertheless, the *Utica Press* of New York stated that the book would appeal to a wider range of readers: "Many who have walked the golden road and perhaps left it behind will in reading this story look backward to their youth."[1]

A review in the *Lexington Herald* in Kentucky was also full of praise, but it, too, saw Montgomery's world view and messages as important for a broader audience: "These delightful books of L.M. Montgomery's teach the religion of pleasantness and good cheer in every line – just simple, uncomplicated, pleasant little things. It is so easy to make little things seem all drudgery and ill-humored duty. Until we can arrive at the perfect poise which makes our duty our pleasure and pleasantness our duty, it is well to try and look on life just a little less soddenly than many of us do. But all this dear little story does is to make simple pleasure seem delight just by letting the sunshine flood the pages of the story." A review in an Australian magazine pondered the same notion: "What is Miss Montgomery's charm? It is difficult to say, but she undoubtedly has it. It doesn't matter what she writes about, she has the knack of being readable. We can imagine that, if she were shipwrecked on a desert island with a pencil and a few quires of paper, she would at once sit down under a tree and commence writing a most enchanting story."[2]

Not all reviews were full of praise for Montgomery's sixth novel, however. *The Ladies Field* of London called it "an unequal book, sometimes crisp, sometimes dragging, never exciting, but occasionally amusing ... There are occasional happy turns of phrase and bits of unexpected humour wrapped round in a blanket of dulness; but we are disappointed with Miss Montgomery's new work, it does not come up to the standard we were led to expect, basing our expectations, of course, on *Anne of Green Gables*." The *Indianapolis News* was equally tepid in its reaction: "The book, like so many sequels, lacks the spontaneous, vivid charm of its predecessor; it is colorless. However, like all that Miss Montgomery has written, it is clean, simple, well written and, in places, mildly humorous." In contrast to this perceived decline in literary quality, *The Bookseller, Newsdealer and Stationer* declared that "like all her other books this one will be greatly liked, for the spirit of her stories is fine and her humor free from malice."[3]

These detractions aside, some reviewers even expressed their hope for a third volume about the Story Girl and her friends. As the *Daily Picayune* of New Orleans stated, "We hope Miss Montgomery will follow their fortunes in some future book, for she has interested too many persons in these young people to let them be lost entirely to their loyal readers." And the *Chicago Inter Ocean* noted that the novel "ends with Sara Stanley's departure for Paris, under the protection of her artist-father, and it seems probable that her experiences abroad may form the nucleus of a volume to come."[4]

## [The Power to Charm]
### *The Bookseller, Newsdealer and Stationer* (New York, NY)

The popular author further emphasizes her power to charm by this story which again acquaints the reader with life of the simple folk of Prince Edward Island, where old acquaintances are renewed and where new life and incident is introduced and romance walks side by side with the sunny humor and philosophy that are marked characteristics of this dispeller of gloom. The book like others by this author will have a big sale for it reaches so many different types of readers.

## [Merry, Bright Young People]
### *Boston Evening Transcript* (Boston, MA)

The story girl, who a few years ago told us pleasant little stories of adventures in Prince Edward Island, which the author has made the field for several entertaining books, comes again to tell us more in *The Golden Road*. Her efforts are aided by several boys and girls in the King family and many of the pages of the book are filled with conversation relating to the everyday life of the happy family. By way of giving all the family a chance to become a story girl or story boy they publish a magazine, and all contribute to the several departments of the paper, which is reproduced in full in the course of the book.

The story girl tells an occasional romance which she does even better than her colleagues; and they are all merry, bright young people who enjoy life and evidently are trying to show others how to be cheerful. As the narrative ends, the story girl's father, an artist, arrives and takes her to Paris, where she may be expected to find material for many more pleasant tales.

## [An Arcadian Byway]
### *The Globe* (Toronto, ON)

There must be more than a coincidence between the antagonism to automobiles in Prince Edward Island and the pictures of country life on the Island in the stories of L.M. Montgomery. In actual life we witness a determined resistance by the farmers to this modern instrument for "getting there"; in Miss Montgomery's pages the Islanders lead an isolated, dream-like existence, apparently untouched by the hurry of the western Provinces. In fact, she has painted the Island as an Arcadian byway, away from the currents of travel, where men live long, and where people of imagination may indulge their fancies and look upon Toronto or Paris as beyond hope of visitation.

Such at least is the feeling after reading Miss Montgomery's latest book, *The Golden Road*. Its very title suggests the poetic fancy with which the author clothes her stories. It is the road of youth, and along it fare once more Sara Stanley and the other principal characters in *The Story Girl*. They are a little older now, and they are carried along in this Arcadian atmosphere until returning fathers and enlarged duties sweep them off, and the charming circle is broken. One almost drops a tear at the conclusion of such a happy existence. There are radical differences of temper and temperament, there are various degrees of brain-power, and dissimilarity of tastes, but under the genius of leadership of "The Story Girl" herself the double household of "small fry" leads an idyllic existence. Peg Bowen, the old witch, lends contrast, and yet how fitting is her action when she goes to church, blurts out her opinion of the various members as they enter, to the great scandal of everyone, and when she is reproached she says:

"Bless you, boy, ... the only difference between me and other folks is that I say these things out loud and they just think them."[5]

The beautiful romance of The Awkward Man and Alice Reade, the music teacher, is perhaps the choicest part of this story. Jasper Dale is a creation to place alongside Blair Stanley and even Anne herself, though The Awkward Man is only etched in with few lines. A victim to shyness and aloofness, he possessed a "nature full of delicate romance and poesy, which, denied expression in the common ways of life, bloomed out in the realm of fancy and imagination."[6] His fancy created a woman, which creation developed until he set aside a room for her, which he furnished suitably, even to buying a dress and slippers. The sequel came through the advent of Alice Reade. Alice had her dreams of a possible Prince Charming; she soon heard of the recluse of Golden Milestone, who was different from everyone else, and it is not difficult to found on these conditions a romantic relationship, ending in an idyllic love match.

Amid the clamor of strenuous novels dealing with sex problems, social ambitions, the suffrage cause, and a hundred other struggles, it is a treat to turn to *The Golden Road*. Its pages teem with references to elfs and pixies, dryads and sprites, but there is a wholesomeness, a simplicity, and a poetic touch that are refreshing, and like the cool breezes on the hilltop after the nauseous fumes of the valley.

## [A Wholesome, Out-of-Door Atmosphere]
### *The Publishers' Weekly* (New York, NY)
#### DORIS WEBB

Nothing really thrilling ever happened to the "Story Girl" and her group – in Prince Edward Island as of old – yet Cecily declared she hated to go to sleep for fear she might miss something. And the moral of that is – how full the world is of a number of things! For instance, what a drama was that when Cyrus Brisk stole a piece of Cecily's hair (the chapter is called "The Rape of the Lock") and further transgressed by writing her notes in school time, one of which travelled across the room by inter-desk carriage and fell under the eye of Mr. Perkins! Mr. Perkins did not read the note, but he ordered Cecily to write its contents on the blackboard or else sit for three days beside – a casual choice – Cyrus Brisk! And Cecily copied the note.

"Our Magazine," issued monthly by these young people travelling the "golden road," is an original sheet with plenty of personals. It fills up the time when nothing else is doing.

Aunt Olivia's romance is headlined in this racy paper, whose editors have the journalistic knack of giving the public just those interesting details that the public wants. Even the etiquette department has its personal touch, with its gentle and quite unsolicited advice to an eager youth who pursues too ardently the lady of his choice.

*The Golden Road* has the wholesome, out-of-door atmosphere of *Kilmeny* and plenty of *The Story Girl*'s humor. Like the egg that fell to the lot of the curate when he breakfasted with the Bishop, "parts of it are excellent."

## [Entertaining Family Chronicles]
### *The Boston Herald* (Boston, MA)

Doubtless there are certain readers to whom Miss Montgomery's delightful *Golden Road* will make but slight appeal, but we hope they are few, since we have found it capital reading. The story is concerned with the entertaining family chronicles of some seven or eight engaging young folk of varying ages whose home is Prince Edward Island, which to them is the centre of the universe. As in previous tales by Miss Montgomery in which several of the young dramatis personae figure, the atmosphere is entirely natural; there is no exaggeration and no gush apparent in the conduct of the story, which is intended for adult readers, though the principal personages are just in and out of their teens. Touches of pathos appear now and then, and the dialogue and descriptions are full of wit and humor. Prince Edward Island may well be proud of its distinguished novelist.

## [More or Less Delightful]
### *The Book News Monthly* (Philadelphia, PA)

Miss Montgomery must do better than this if she is to hold the audience she won with *Anne of Green Gables*. No author can go on indefinitely selling on the strength of her first books. *The Golden Road* is more "Story Girl" stories, as usual done in a more or less delightful way, but certainly the only reader to whom this book can be really recommended is the young reader of sixteen or eighteen, who will find interesting matter in the paper the King children ran; and in the pleasant times they and the "story girl" had. For such readers the book is appropriate and wholesome.

## [Excessively Commonplace Young People]
### *The Mail and Empire* (Toronto, ON)

The occurrence of such expressions as "sorter," "ain't," and "real cute," with many more of a like nature, and the general conversation of a group of excessively provincial and commonplace young people does not produce a particularly favorable impression in the reader of *The Golden Road*, another of the "Story Girl" semi-juvenile books by L.M. Montgomery (Mrs. Lucy Maud Macdonald[7]).

The present volume is a collection of short stories held together in much the same manner as the various "turns" in a modern revue by an underlying thread which is not a plot, and the stories are worked in whenever an opportunity occurs. The scene is a farmhouse in the author's native Prince Edward Island, and one is introduced to a family group sitting in front of the wide open fire place in "Uncle Alec's kitchen." As a method of whiling away the long Winter evenings the beforementioned young people decide to issue a monthly magazine for circulation among themselves, and this magazine is made the excuse for introducing a lot of rubbish into the book, which is neither interesting nor amusing, and which one strongly suspects of being actual material gathered in the form of essays in a district school on some part of the island.

There is a suggestion of Louisa M. Alcott's works in the present volume, though it by no means deserves to be classed with the work of the justly popular American writer. The unnecessarily poor English which the writer puts into the mouths of her characters does not make the book particularly good for young people.

### [Intelligent and Resourceful Children]
*Philadelphia Press* (Philadelphia, PA)

More of Miss Montgomery's brightly engaging and wholesomely vivacious chronicles of life on Prince Edward Island are presented in this story, which introduces her "Story Girl" of established popularity and all the intelligent and resourceful King children. Very entertaining is the account of their activities as presented through the medium of their newspaper, "Our Magazine," which is conducted in the most approved manner. The comments on topics of general interest are interesting on their own merits; the outlook on life that is held by the young people is healthy and wide awake, and the narrative is easy and natural in style throughout.

The spirit of the book is symbolized in the title, for, in the author's conception, "the golden road" is the road of joyous, zestful youth, the road of those who are keenly appreciative of the beauties of life, and instinct with an inarticulate poetry.

## [A Genius for Understanding Youth]
### *The Canadian Courier* (Toronto, ON)
MARJORY MacMURCHY

Such a book as *The Golden Road*, by L.M. Montgomery, seems easy enough to explain. It is a pretty book for girls, the continuation of another work of fiction, *The Story Girl*. The author is a lover of her native province, Prince Edward Island. She is a lover, too, of girlhood, and she is a story writer. These facts are simple and sufficient, or they seem sufficient at first sight. But there is a point when the love of one's native country becomes a passion which shuts out other things. There is an absorption in young life which becomes a genius for understanding youth. There is a quality in such a book as *The Golden Road* which is not just exactly defined as the common light of day. Girls and women care too much about it somehow; they are too much moved. It is not just story telling; there is some magic in it. Only genius of a certain variety can make an old woman feel like a young girl.

## [Chronicles of a Group]
### *Grand Rapids Press* (Grand Rapids, MI)

Prince Edward Island[8] seldom is the scene of the story writer's labors but it is the background for *The Golden Road*, a story of child life at that interesting period where some of the youngsters are nearing their majority. The story is filled with amusing incidents and it has a very wholesome character. It is more the chronicles of a group than a tale with a plot but it is certain to interest the young.

## Childhood Days
### *The Los Angeles Times* (Los Angeles, CA)

To have a new book by the author of *Anne of Green Gables* usually means an easy chair by the grate fire and a sigh first of contentment and then a bit of sadness because the end comes all too soon.

It matters not how long ago since last we walked on the golden road – we will live again in its memories as we read this book. Every character in it is alive, from sweet Cecily, who resolves on New Year's eve to believe only one-half of what she hears, the best half, to little Sara Ray, who resolves not to be jealous of other girls who have been sick, because it makes them important. Then there's the story girl's resolution not to be vexed when people interrupt her story telling, and Felix resolves to taboo apples for fear of becoming fat.

In "Our Magazine," which this fun-loving group edit each month, the happenings of the King family are set forth, and such delightful nonsense as it is.

While the book treats of young people barely 15 years old, yet the love story of the Awkward Man and Alice, as told by the story girl, will linger in the memory of young and old.

Miss Montgomery has the gift of description, and in none of her books is it more evident than in this one, where

"Life was a rose-lipped comrade
With purple flowers dripping from her fingers."[9]

## Youthful Memories
### *The Register* (Adelaide, Australia)

This writer won her public with *Anne of Green Gables*,[10] and those who fell in love with that original orphan will welcome a new volume from the same pen. Miss Montgomery, however, is perhaps not wise in dealing so freely in sequels. The first of the three "Anne" books was the best, and this second volume about "The Story Girl" lacks something in freshness. Possibly the memories of childhood in Canada may be real, and the narratives gathered from the memories of actual people; but the execution is not quite finished enough for the material. There are less description and less reflection – some critic may have suggested to the author in American phraseology to "keep on sawing wood." But the charm of her stories is in the telling, and this example seems rather hasty – only a sketch for a charming study of child life.

## [Bog of Shoddy Sentiment]
### *Saturday Night* (Toronto, ON)

Miss Montgomery once wrote a really delightful book about a little girl, *Anne of Green Gables*. That book instantly established for itself an international popularity. Since then she has produced a book every year. These books, we presume, have found numerous readers – possibly even admirers. But their literary merit has steadily diminished, until now the clear rippling stream of the first charming book is lost in a bog of shoddy sentiment.

*The Golden Road* is in the nature of a sequel to *The Story Girl*. In this volume, as in the other, that extremely tiresome young female, who is called throughout the Story Girl till one hates the sight of the words, officiates as the weaver of silly stories and the leader in silly adventures by an extremely silly lot of people. Of course, we realize that this book will perhaps be popular with young girls. But then we are not a young girl – except possibly in figurative allusion to our sweet innocence of heart – and we got so tired in the middle of *The Golden Road* that we lay right down in the gold dust and went to sleep.

## [A Merry Party of Young Folks]
### *The Scotsman* (Edinburgh, UK)

*The Golden Road*, by L.M. Montgomery, is a story of a merry party of young folks who entertained themselves and one another in their leisure time by running a magazine and listening to the recital of stories by one of their number so skilled in the art that she had earned an appropriate soubriquet. And the reader is enabled to participate in their amusement by perusing their journalistic achievements and their essays into the realm of fiction. The American origin of the book is unmistakable, but young people of school age in Charlottetown or Carlisle are pretty much the same in temperament, disposition, inclination, and desire as the young people of Birmingham or Edinburgh, and their revels by the great wood fire in the cosy kitchen or in the old orchard where so often they kept tryst, will be read with a sense of genuine refreshment by boys and girls, young and old, everywhere. The humours and the sentiment are skilfully handled by the author, but some readers will probably find most to pleasure them in the delightful descriptions of Nature's moods as the seasons pass in these young folks' lives.

## [Transatlantic Young People]
### *The Times Literary Supplement* (London, UK)

A company of Transatlantic young people, the magazine they produced, the stories the "Story Girl" told them, and other matters which may please equally cheery and simple young folk over here.

## [The Simple Life of American Country Children]
### *The Glasgow Herald* (Glasgow, UK)

*The Golden Road* is that of childhood and youth, and the book deals with some American country children. They are not demons or angels, but are interesting in no unnatural or out of the way fashion. One has a touch of gentle goodness about her, another has a spark of poetry and histrionicism while a third is an amusing mixture of complacent vanity and clever housewifery. The life too of these children is simple. There are no cinemas, but walks on starlit nights; there are no grand children's parties, but school concerts. The writer too has the art of rendering vivid these healthy simplicities, and a quiet gift of humour which can draw fun from the little incidents of ordinary existence. She can make us see the children dressed up in their best for the school entertainment, she forces us to realise the poor schoolmaster's pride and concern, she can rouse our interest in the performance of the artistic pupil, and she can bring before us the mingled comedy and tragedy when the stupid pupil spoils the great climax of the clever girl. Along with this picture of old social country life the authoress gives us descriptions of nature which convey the delicate impalpability of her beauty in a magical way.

## [A Certain Homely Appeal]
### *The Bookman* (London, UK)

On "The Golden Road of Youth," which is the road of which Miss Montgomery writes, we meet the little group of boys and girls who have already seen light in a former volume, we understand. They live on Prince Edward Island, in Canada, and have a happy, unconventional life together. This narrative begins with plans for the starting of a monthly magazine among themselves; and the magazine appears at intervals in the pages of the book, and chronicles the children's doings. They have their adventures and their pleasures and squabbles; and the style of life has freshness and interest to an English public of young people. We get an outline of a grown-up romance now and again. There is nothing markedly impressive about the volume, which is a chronicle rather than a story, but it has a certain homely appeal, and is successful in its characterisation. We are sorry that we could not rid ourselves of the impression that it is all told by a girl, instead of by a boy.

## [Apt to Wear Thin]
### *London Post* (London, UK)

The diversions and daily occupations of a band of young people in a rural district of Prince Edward Island loosely strung together without any real continuous plot are here related by the author of that over-praised book, *Anne of Green Gables*. It is the sort of thing which, if one is actually a participant and not more than fifteen years of age and an inhabitant of a place where pleasure and excitement do not run beyond the limits of the farm and the school, is quite good fun; but as set forth chapter after chapter throughout a fairly long book, the fun which no doubt was very real is apt to wear rather thin in the colder medium of print. We can say, however, that it was a buoyant troupe, pressing a very wholesome wine from the joys and even the minor sorrows of life, and if the vintage seems a little thin on our palate that is, perhaps, entirely our own fault.

## [Transatlantic Farm Life]
### *The Globe* (London, UK)

A story of some Canadian children, mostly cousins, and so extremely grown up in their amativeness, and so babyish in their diversions that it is quite a time before we are able to realise that they are children, in years, at any rate. The tale improves as it goes on, there being much genuine feeling mixed up with false sentimentality. The quotations from the family Magazine frequently prove diverting, and it is with some regret that we read the last of these, and part from the young hopefuls of Prince Edward Island.[11] On the whole, perhaps our English girls will be more interested in the story than their elders can be, in spite of the entirely different point of view of the home-bred and the colonial. The writer spares us much of the usual Transatlantic jargon, leaving us the better able to enjoy the freshness and romance of simple farm life as realised by an author of taste and sympathy.

## [At Times Wearisome]
### *The Montreal Daily Star* (Montreal, QC)

*The Golden Road*, by Miss L.M. Montgomery, will be welcomed by those who delighted in *The Story Girl*, to which it forms a sequel. It contains a good deal of the charm of Miss Montgomery's earlier writings, quite enough to indicate the delightful books that gifted delineator of children's drollness and sweetness may have to give up when she strikes a new vein of characters and incidents. To tell the truth the flavor which distinguished *Anne of Green Gables* and following works rather palls upon the appetite when served up too frequently. It is hard to believe that Miss Montgomery is to be incapable of a further inspiration. We meet the sweet little Story Girl, the gentle Cecily, the judicious Beverley, the corpulent Peter, the Awkward One, the witch "Paddy" and all the rest of them again teasing, rejoicing, sorrowing along The Golden Road of youth.[12] There are a few good yarns told, and some that are indifferent, the wit and innocence of childhood is at times wearisome, though generally true enough. It is possible to have too much of the youngsters however, especially when incidents are not frequent, nor very exciting. The idea of a family newspaper written by the children has been worked so often in juvenile stories, one cannot but be sorry to find it employed by the very original creator of the glorious "Anne." Still, all Miss Montgomery's friends will want her latest book to complete their sets, and, as has been said already, it is exceedingly likely that we shall yet enjoy some new creations from the hand to which the story-loving public is already greatly indebted.

## [More of a "Juvenile"]
### *The Toronto World* (Toronto, ON)

In her writings it seems to me that L.M. Montgomery is accomplishing two very important results; she is keeping before her readers the ideals, the hopes and the fancies of youth; and she is picturing, as no other Canadian writer is doing, the quiet romance of the rural Canadian community. It takes a finer skill in literary composition to handle effectively such themes as are dealt with in *Anne of Green Gables*, *Anne of Avonlea*, *The Chronicles of Avonlea* and *The Golden Road*, than it does to write a thrilling adventure tale of fur-trade days, or to elaborate some melodramatic plot. In *The Golden Road*, we meet again Sara Stanley, the Story Girl and her circle of young friends. As an explanation of the title and a suggestion of the tone and general atmosphere of the book, we may quote from the author's foreword: –[13]

Perhaps the most noticeable thing about the book, comparing it with the other productions of the author, is that it is more of a "juvenile" than its predecessors. I note that the book monthlies have usually classed *Anne of Green Gables* and the other books by this writer as "juvenile." They had, however, the broad appeal that made them equally acceptable to readers of all ages. *The Golden Road* has much of the same quality, but there are portions of it – the "extracts from our magazine" – which scarcely rise beyond the purely juvenile attitude.[14] This is not mentioned by the way of disparagement of the book, but simply as a statement arising out of a critical analysis. In the first place, Miss Montgomery (Mrs. Ewan Macdonald[15]) began writing with only a juvenile audience in mind. It was a happy quality of her literary powers that enabled her to captivate also the older readers, so that now, if she may seem to give the really juveniles a little more attention, we may notice it, but we have no ground for complaint.

We are asked to imagine a "day of wild November wind, closing down into a wet, eerie twilight."[16] It was the beginning of winter, a time when the domestic circle was drawn together closer than usual; when the time, unless the persons of that circle were resourceful, began to hang heavily in the long evenings. The Story Girl's inventiveness was likely to be severely taxed during the coming months, so as a possible relief or "shift" she had set things going for the introduction of a little scheme of entertainment which would involve the assistance of nearly everybody in the circle.

From this suggestion developed "Our Magazine," to be issued once a month – circulation, one copy, carefully handwritten. Its limited circulation and primitive mechanical department was not allowed to detract from the scope of its editorial aims, so there were many departments – etiquette, household, beauty hints – besides fiction, poetry and everything to make up an all-round magazine. Of course, the "Story Girl" contributes her share and her tales vary from pure fairy stories to the recounting of neighborhood romances. Of these stories within a story, perhaps the tenderest is the love story of the "awkward man." This is an idyllic prose gem. Intertwined with the magazine numbers and the various sketches and stories are the no less interesting adventures of the circle itself. Our former friends, Peter and Dan, Cecily and Felicity, are all there, tho a little "older grown"; and they are all just as much filled with youthful superstition, youthful cantankerousness, and youthful lovableness as ever.

Thruout the story runs that vein of wholesome but mischievous humor which this author so skilfully employs in most of her stories. At the same time there is a fine, sympathetic understanding of human troubles and an appreciation of hidden human longings. That the writer's love of nature and nature's moods expresses itself occasionally in verse and in nature sketches, we can readily understand from the highly poetic language and atmosphere of the descriptive passages that make the appropriate scenic background of this story. In conclusion let me quote one of these passages, which is doubly appropriate because of its further explanation of the story's title:

"June was crowded full of interest that year. We gathered in with its sheaf of fragrant days the choicest harvest of childhood ... There were so many dear delights along the golden road to give us pleasure – the earth dappled with new blossom, the dance of shadows in the fields, the rustling, rain-wet ways of the woods, the faint fragrance in meadow lanes, liltings of birds and croon of bees in the old orchard, windy pipings on the hills, sunset behind the pines, limpid dews filling primrose cups, crescent moons through darkling boughs, soft nights alight with blinking stars. We enjoyed all these boons, unthinkingly and light-heartedly, as children do."[17]

Can you recall these joys of the golden road? Ten thousand pities, it is, if you can't! Can you enjoy these dear delights of the "golden road" now? – still more pitiful your case, if you have lost so much of the spirit of youth! Nothing else can take its place.

## NOTES

1 *The Canadian Magazine*, review of *The Golden Road*, 106; *The Evening Star*, review of *The Golden Road*, 9; *The Springfield Union*, "Another 'Story Girl' Book," 3; *Boston Times* (Boston, MA), review of *The Golden*

*Road*, signed D.S.K., 2 September 1913, in SR, 53; *Winnipeg Telegram* (Winnipeg, MB), review of *The Golden Road*, undated clipping, in SR, 54; Marjory MacMurchy, review of *The Golden Road*, *The Toronto News* (Toronto, ON), undated clipping, in SR, 53–54; *The Utica Press* (Utica, NY), review of *The Golden Road*, undated clipping, in SR, 58.

2  *The Lexington Herald*, review of *The Golden Road*, 4; review of *The Golden Road*, undated clipping (identified simply as "Australian"), in SR, 62.

3  *The Ladies Field* (London, UK), review of *The Golden Road*, 14 May 1914, in SR, 64; *Indianapolis News* (Indianapolis, IN), "A Sequel to 'The Story Girl,'" review of *The Golden Road*, 6 December 1913, in SR, 65; *The Bookseller, Newsdealer and Stationer*, review of *The Golden Road*, 320.

4  *The Daily Picayune*, review of *The Golden Road*, 5; *Chicago Inter Ocean* (Chicago, IL), review of *The Golden Road*, undated clipping, in SR, 48.

5  GR, 143.

6  GR, 165.

7  I have corrected the original, which reads "McDonald."

8  I have corrected the original, which reads "Prince Edward's Island."

9  The epigraph in the original edition of *The Golden Road*, signed "The Author," is excerpted from Montgomery's foreword to the novel.

10  Here and throughout, I have corrected the original, which reads "'Ann.'"

11  I have corrected the original, which reads "Prince Edward's Island."

12  I have corrected the original, which reads "Cicely." In *The Golden Road*, the "corpulent" character is actually Felix, not Peter; Jasper Dale's derogatory nickname is the Awkward Man, not the Awkward One; and "Paddy" is a cat, whereas Peg Bowen is presumed to be a witch.

13  The original review proceeds to quote all three paragraphs from the foreword, omitted here; see GR, vii.

14  Chapter 20 of *The Golden Road* is entitled "Extracts from *Our Magazine*."

15  I have corrected the original, which reads "Mrs. Evan MacDonald."

16  GR, 1.

17  GR, 104.

# 7

## *Anne of the Island*

—— 1915 ——

As I mentioned in the introduction to this volume, Montgomery had some reservations about this highly anticipated second sequel to *Anne of Green Gables*, and oddly enough, some of the reviewers of *Anne of the Island* seemed to have read Montgomery's mind about the limits of its appeal in terms of both genre and form. According to the *Rochester Post*, "Anne's romance has in it nothing very exciting. All along the perspicacious reader knows that Gilbert is to be the favored lover." As another unidentified clipping pointed out, "it would have been a pity if Anne Shirley had dropped out of sight just when she was grown up and ready for the greatest adventure of all." At the same time, the *Chicago Record–Herald* called it "as sweet, as sane, as sunny and as sensible – not to say sentimental – as its predecessors," and according to the *Atlanta Christian Index* of Georgia, "This is an example of the kind of fiction which ought to be more generally read." The *Lexington Herald* of Kentucky noted that "this is a pleasant and graceful story, with much good sense and cleverly concealed moralizing, a cheering gift to help many homesick schoolgirls through the first hard days away from home."[1]

## A Trilogy Completed
### *The Montreal Daily Herald* (Montreal, QC)

It seems as though we had always known Anne Shirley. In our minds she is associated with such life long friends as Maggie Tulliver, who was created by George Eliot as long ago as 1860.[2] It is with surprise, then, that we find, on looking the matter up, that nobody heard of Anne until 1908, when *Anne of Green Gables* was published. It was not long, however, before we began to realize, to paraphrase a trade mark, that she "was the girl who made Prince Edward Island famous," for now *Anne of Green Gables* is in her 310th thousand. Still the reading public wanted more Anne and *Anne of Avonlea* was the response, in 1909. She, the publishers tell us, is now in her 109th thousand and "going strong," as the horsemen say. Now there issues from the press a more mature Anne, an almost grown up Anne, and she has broadened her horizon so that she becomes "Anne of the Island."

"L.M. Montgomery" is now the wife of a Presbyterian minister, the Rev. Ewen Macdonald,[3] of Leaskdale, Ontario. We do not know whether he is a Prince Edward Islander but we fancy he must be in order to have carried off, as a bride four years ago, so thorough and so loyal a lover of her native province, as Miss Montgomery. Be that as it may, her own marriage induced Miss Montgomery to which the new book deals; she experiences the delightful days of courtship – we were going to say of romance, but Anne's days were all days of romance.

Even if we had never known the Anne of Green Gables or the Anne of Avonlea we should have been hugely pleased with the Anne of Prince Edward Island, so sweet and captivating has she been drawn for us. No great tragedy marked her college days with which the new book deals; she experienced none of the great sorrows that deepen and widen natures such as hers but she proceeded calmly and serenely through the college halls until she reached the threshold of matrimony and there we take leave of her – leave that is evidently final – for Miss Montgomery's publishers announce this book as completing the trilogy. As Canadians we are proud of Anne; she is a girl of whom any of our provinces would be proud; we are proud, too, of Miss Montgomery, whose brain evolved her described by Mark Twain as "the dearest and most moving and delightful child since the immortal Alice."

Though the Island Anne is more mature than the Green Gables Anne she does not lose that peculiar combination of youth's fresh outlook upon life with the quaint wisdom, that, while occasionally inbred, is usually the product of experience. Pure and sweet, interesting and elevating, humorous and philosophical, *Anne of the Island* is a cure for the blues, an antidote to the coarser literature of the day, and absolutely certain of a circulation as large as either of the chronicles of the earlier life of one who will always occupy a foremost place among the heroines of Canadian fiction.

## [Busy with Affairs of the Heart]
### *The Sun* (New York, NY)

Those who have met in previous books the heroine of L.M. Montgomery's *Anne of the Island* will be glad to hear more about her, which may not be the case with those who make her acquaintance first in this story. As too often happens in "series" tales, the author takes her heroine for granted and puts more life into the new people she brings in. Here Anne is put through college in a rather perfunctory way and is busied with affairs of the heart. Little sympathy will be felt with the blunder she comes near making because the author hints pretty strongly throughout that she will not let the girl make a fool of herself. The book is redeemed by a bright and amusing girl with a real love story, by some delightful old ladies and by several vigorously drawn country people, whose stories have little to do with the heroine.

## The New Page Book
### *The Waterbury American* (Waterbury, CT)

"Anne" of Green Gables and of Avonlea, is one of the girls of fiction destined to be as immortal as Miss Alcott's famous quartet or "Pollyanna."[4] L.M. Montgomery now tells another delightful story of her Prince Edward Island heroine under the title of *Anne of the Island*. This tells the story of her life at Redmond, a co-educational college, and is just as full of humor, pathos and all the elements of real girl life as were its predecessors which is saying a good deal in its praise. "Davy," the irrepressible twin, is a never-ceasing source of amusement, the things he "wants to know" being as highly original and unexpected as can be imagined, yet thoroughly in keeping with the character of the bright, inquisitive youngster in real life. Philippa or Phil Gordon, one of the college girls, is another refreshingly original character, and the girls who chum together at "Patty's Place," under the chaperonage of Aunt Jamesina and in company with the trio of felines, the Sarah-Cat, Joseph and Rusty, are real girls, not stilted imaginary creations. *Anne of the Island* is one of the best and most amusing books of this season, and is sure to be thoroughly enjoyed by all readers, whether or not they are familiar with the previous books.

## [Ever Charming, Ever Heartsome]
### *Pittsburgh Leader* (Pittsburgh, PA)

From *Anne of Green Gables* to *Anne of the Island*, the new Anne book is a short step in bookmaking, but a long journey in life. The Anne of the first book we all remember as a delightful child. The "Anne of Avonlea" was growing up, but still delightful. In *Anne of the Island* the child becomes a young woman, but ever charming, ever heartsome. This new Anne story tells of Anne's college life, her new friends and, finally, of her romance. That Anne should have a lover is natural, for the reading world has loved her since, as a child, she smiled from the pages of a book. It is sincerely hoped that Anne's arrival at woman's stature will not end her history. There cannot be too many Annes in books and in the world.

## [The Same Old Anne]
### *Boston Evening Transcript* (Boston, MA)

After wandering around among chronicles, story girls and indulging in other more or less entertaining adventures, Anne Shirley comes back, the same old Anne, beautiful, brilliant, charming, the good angel of Prince Edward Island. Now she oscillates between Avonlea, where so many have met her, and Redmond, where she acquires a B.A., and few stories of a girl's college life have been better told than this. College life and romance are carried along in attractive proportions, and there is an occasional holiday at Green Gables where we hear more stories by the garrulous natives which are told in the quaint manner that has been a striking feature of the several Anne books.

Aunt Atossa, a new character in Avonlea, figures in several of these. One relates her adventures at a prayer meeting. After the customary remarks by the preacher, who was very deaf, and various members of the congregation, Aunt Atossa "bounced up. She didn't either pray or preach. Instead, she lit into everybody else in the church and gave them a fearful raking down, calling them right out by name and telling them how they had all behaved, and casting up all the quarrels and scandals of the past ten years. Finally she wound up by saying that she was disgusted with [the] church and she never meant to darken its door again, and she hoped a fearful judgment would come upon it." Then she sat down. The minister, who had not heard a word, fervently prayed in a strong, devout voice: "Amen! The Lord grant our dear sister's prayer!"[5]

Anne's career at college where she and Philippa, Stella and Priscilla "keep house" in a quaint little edifice known as "Patty's Place" is an attractive bit of college life, and even such minor details as Gog and Magog, the china dogs and Sarah-Cat and Rusty are made necessary parts of the happy family.

Friends of Anne will remember the twins and be glad to meet them again. "Are you clean?" asks Mrs. Lynde of Davy, as he reports ready for Sunday school. "Yes – all of me that shows," replies Davy, which indicates that the author has met some real boys. Davy expects to live to be a hundred years old, like Thomas Blewett, who says, "he's lived so long 'cause he always smoked tobacco and it killed all the germs," and Davy suggests that he, at eight years of age, start the slaughter of the germs.[6]

In many ways this new story is the author's best. Anne has not the humorous proclivities that she had as Anne of Green Gables, nor is she so mischievous; natural changes with the accumulation of years; but she is the same sweet-tempered, cheerful girl that has made Prince Edward Island famous. The story as a whole is better finished and the plot has more definite strength than that of any of the Anne books. There are numerous little love stories, some serious, some humorous, some frivolous, all capital little diversions, and, of course, best of all is the roaming romance of Anne herself, which takes an unexpected devious course, but ends in the expected happy way.

## [Possibly the Last, Possibly the Best]
### *Wilmington Every Evening* (Wilmington, DE)

Possibly the last, as it carries Anne Shirley through college and to the close of a somewhat troubled but happily ending romance, *Anne of the Island* may be set down as the best of those very popular stories the author has written about this most charming personage and the other interesting folk of Prince Edward Island. It should be as much a favorite as *Anne of Green Gables*, which has reached an edition of enormous size.

More pleasing than ever is Anne Shirley as a young woman facing the graver problems of life. Her course in college is detailed with much attraction, as her hard and conscientious work is mingled with a moderate extent of enjoyment and congenial intercourse with friends and acquaintances. Her school friends are charming, and they have a delightful home in an old house in the aristocratic part of Kingsport, the seat of Redmond College, where Anne was graduated. Here she passed through the most troublesome part of her romance, temporarily setting aside real love in a belief that she loved another, but fortunately, in the end, making the right choice and opening the way to true happiness.

While Anne is a delightful personality, there is nothing abnormal about her. She is human to the core, natural and vivacious, and not in any sense a prig. Her story is told with such appreciation of a really lovable person, one with human faults and failings as well as many virtues, that she seems real all the time. Seldom is such skill displayed in portrayal as in this presentation of the daily life and doings of Anne. No wonder all the stories about her and about the quaint and original Avonlea folk, have been exceedingly popular.

## [A Fluctuating Participant in Romance]
### *The Springfield Republican* (Springfield, MA)

With *Anne of the Island*, L.M. Montgomery completes a trilogy in which Anne Shirley is the center of interest. Like most "series" stories, Anne's activities have become a bit forced, and the author must needs resort to new characters and matters connected with these in order to put sufficient "body" in this volume to hold the interest. In the two preceding books Anne passed through childhood and young girlhood, and, with the advent of the third, she is ready for a wider sphere. Its opening coincides with her determination to enter college, and the story's scope covers the four years passed within "the studious (?) cloister's pale."[7] Her college career is rather perfunctory, aside from the romance in which she is a hesitating and fluctuating participant. The reader feels a livelier interest in her chum "Phil," who, in spite of an apparently light and frivolous character, is caught up in a love affair – after a series of like experiences – that has a surprising outcome. The author further digresses from Anne's affairs to introduce several well-drawn people of different ages and pursuits. This phase is perhaps the most engaging of the entire story. The action of the trilogy is in Prince Edward Island and neighboring portions of Nova Scotia, and attractive descriptions of scenery are included in the book.

## The Third Book of Anne
### *The New York World* (New York, NY)

Miss Montgomery's Charming Heroine
Out of College and in Love

The trilogy of "Anne" is complete. She of Green Gables and of Avonlea comes to us now as *Anne of the Island*, and Miss L.M. Montgomery leaves her at the end of forty-one chapters happy in the possession of a college education and an accepted lover [8]

She is the same Anne we have known through her earlier years – a maiden bright, fair and frank, yet elusive, full of clever thoughts and with her own alluring oddities of expression. Along with her in the last book of the trilogy appear Diana Barry, Gilbert Blythe, Charlie Sloane, Ruby Gillis and other old friends, of course including Marilla. Philippa Gordon is a new girl, met at Redmond College, fitting admirably into a place in our group of familiars.

It has been well worth while to watch the growing up of Anne, and the privilege of being on intimate terms with her throughout that process has been properly valued. The once little girl of Green Gables should have a permanent fictional place of high yet tender esteem.

## [A Perfunctory Fumbling with Obstacles]
### *The Nation* (New York, NY)

If it is painful to reflect that the better order of American fiction has become almost hopelessly feminized, it is still more ominous that the same thing should be happening to popular fiction. Melodrama has its faults, but it is not all slush and mush; at its best there is a kind of male strength about it. Perhaps it is better that the national type of auditor should be even the tired business man, rather than the silly high school girl – the flapper, as Britain hath it.

We have here the latest goods of two successful dealers in flapper literature. They have established their "line," and have only to keep up the output. [* * *][9]

Miss Montgomery's Anne of the Island is of course none other than the Anne of Green Gables and of Avonlea, who has hitherto found a market (say her publishers) to the tune of some half a million copies, and who threatens to become another Elsie for sequels.[10] She is here brought to the verge of matrimony; so the worst may be over, since this is the kind of fiction which naturally ends with wedding bells. It is an altogether foolish and adequate account of Anne as a "co-ed." An adoring Gilbert appears on page three, who is clearly Anne's chosen, but, of course, the author puts him off by a series of transparent expedients till it is convenient for him to do the trick. It all "comes out right" in the end, which is the main thing. All that is desirable in this kind of fable is a perfunctory fumbling with obstacles in the interest of sentimental contrast.

## More about Anne
### *The Mail and Empire* (Toronto, ON)

Nobody can accuse the lady novelists of being unfaithful to the characters who serve them well. If they create a girl to whom the public takes a fancy, that girl is fairly sure to have a long life. Of course people will immediately think that this is a reference to Elsie, that Methuselah of American fiction, but while Elsie established a record in the number of books through which she traveled, a record that will probably never be approached, many others have imitated her performance in a small way. There were Mildred and Bessie, one remembers, some time ago. In recent years we have had Miss Billy and Pollyanna.[11] And right here in Canada, is there not Anne? *Anne of the Island* is, of course, "Anne of Green Gables" and "Anne of Avonlea," and one must remark in passing that Miss L.M. Montgomery selects better titles for exploiting her heroine than any of the other possessors of serial female characters. Would it be flippant to suggest that the series might some day come to an end with a novel entitled *How Old Is Anne*? In the new novel, Anne has become a co-ed, and her adventures carry her to the steps of the altar, where they cease. Of course matrimony is in sight all through the book. One scents it when Gilbert Blythe is introduced on the fourth page, but things are not finally settled until the final chapter is reached. The authoress has arranged misunderstandings and other expedients, which keep Anne and Gilbert apart until both of them are almost in despair, but finally on the last page we find him saying, "Oh, Anne, this makes up for everything, doesn't it?" While she chirrups blithely, "We'll just be happy, waiting and working for each other – and dreaming. Oh, dreams will be very sweet now."[12]

To those who know the novels of Miss L.M. Montgomery it is only necessary to say that *Anne of the Island* is a characteristic little story. The reason it was written is probably indicated in the dedication to "all the girls all over the world who have 'wanted more' about Anne." By the girls who have "wanted more" about Anne the new book will be welcomed.

## [Presumably the Last]
### *The Duluth News Tribune* (Duluth, MN)

When *Anne of Green Gables* was introduced to the reading public she became a popular heroine at once. *Anne of Avonlea* was a second volume showing the development of this fascinating little girl and now comes the third and last *Anne of the Island*. At least the reader will presume it is the last, as it takes Anne through college and leaves her "crowned ... queen in the bridal realm of love."[13] It is a clever, wholesome story for girls of high school age, but if they have been feeding surreptitiously on an overspiced diet of Chambers novels,[14] a nice, every day girl like Anne may seem a little tame and old fashioned.

## [Good Times at College]
### *The Bookseller, Newsdealer and Stationer* (New York, NY)

Another "Anne" book which will delight the hearts of those who have read *Anne of Green Gables* and *Anne of Avonlea*. In this new story Anne goes to college and makes many new friends, and they have such good times that, as one of the girls said, "the time just whizzed away."[15] The vacations spent with many of the same characters in the other books and the romances of the different girls and the final wedding of Anne make this book even more interesting than the previous volumes.

## [A Story of Young Life]
### *The Publishers' Weekly* (New York, NY)
#### REBECCA D. MOORE

Anne is back, not the little prankish Anne, Canadian cousin of Rebecca of Sunnybrook Farm yet with an individuality and charm quite her own, but a grown up Anne ready for college and the more serious things of life. As one says of the delectable bit of fur and mischief, the romping kitten, one is tempted to say of Anne, – Why does she have to grow up?

But it had to be. Anne-lovers, testified to by forty printings of *Anne of Green Gables*, twenty-two of *Anne of Avonlea* not to mention statistics of others of the author's in which Anne figured to a greater or less degree, demanded it. And so Miss Montgomery, or rather Mrs. Macdonald,[16] attempted the difficult and thankless task of trying to suit everybody in the delicate matter of settling Anne in life and love.

*Anne of the Island* is the chronicle of the doings of Anne and her friends during four years spent at Redmond, pleasant adventures of the sort which might happen to any likable young people in a small co-educational college. Anne herself, now a beautiful, clever, and charming young woman, has many admirers. Among them is the faithful Gilbert Blythe, her childhood friend who is also a student at Redmond, and eventually Anne discovers that her heart has always been his.

In the intervening vacations, the scene shifts from Kingsport, Nova Scotia, the seat of Redmond, back to the Island, Prince Edward Island where the author's pen and heart are so much at home. Here are the old school friends of former books, the gossipy but usually warmhearted old ladies, and a pair of twins whose liveliness suggests early Green Gable days.

One wonders why an unmistakable Halifax has been veiled behind the name Kingsport, but to Anne-lovers, it will not be of serious moment whether she is educated at Halifax or Honolulu, so long as Anne occupies the centre of the screen. And they as well as others will find in *Anne of the Island* a wholesome and pleasant story of young life in the Maritime Provinces.

## [A Sunny Young Woman]
### *ALA Booklist* (Chicago, IL)

This completes the trilogy of which *Anne of Green Gables* and *Anne of Avonlea* were the first two stories. Anne grows up and proves the promise of her youth by being a lovable, sunny young woman with an infinite capacity for enjoying "Patty's Place" at college and life in general, especially when it brings her own love story.

## [Anne Goes to College]
### *Wisconsin Library Bulletin* (Madison, WI)

"Anne of Green Gables" goes to a coeducational college on Prince Edward Island, and combines good times with work in a manner highly satisfactory to herself and her many friends. A happy future is assured at the book's close. Girls will like it, but adults will find it cloying.

## "Anne of Green Gables" in a New Role
### *Boston Advertiser* (Boston, MA)

*Anne of the Island*, by L.M. Montgomery, brings an old favorite to us once more. In this Anne leaves Avonlea for college and the story tells of school and home life for four years and introduces a few new characters. The book may not hold and charm us as the first one did – few serials do live up to the promise of their initial numbers – but the college girl, Anne Shirley, is little Anne of Green Gables grown-up, and is bright and refreshing. She still finds "scope for the imagination," and while her fancy does not indulge in the wild flights that it did in her little girlhood, it still gives much pleasure to her and to those around her. The accounts of her many conquests and her attempts at authorship furnish some very enjoyable chapters. We wonder if we can expect more "Anne" stories; so charming a character we are loathe to lose.

## [Plenty to Entertain]
### *The New York Herald* (New York, NY)

In *Anne of the Island* Miss L.M. Montgomery takes that delightful person to college, brings her through one or two mild romances and leaves her with her feet set on the path of future happiness. When an author describes as charming a child as Anne of Green Gables she may make up her mind that no peace will be given her until she has carried that child through to her wedding day. But these second volumes are seldom equal to the first, and expectation is not often fulfilled.

This being granted, we find much that is entertaining in this third volume of Miss Montgomery's trilogy. We follow Anne through her college career at Redmond and her vacations at Avonlea with pleasure. While at Redmond she and three other girls, with an old lady to look after them, take a little cottage and keep house. Redmond is "co-ed," and besides Anne there is Philippa Gordon, one of those born fascinators whose trail is strewn with masculine hearts, so between the two there are enough boys on hand to keep things going.

The author is good at character drawing, and among the old friends and the new are some delightful people. Davy and Dora, the twins, are admirable, especially Davy, and the story of his Sunday escapade and consequent remorse is quite harrowing. "Phil" Gordon is also a delight, with her many suitors and her final surrender to the ugly but earnest young clergyman. Aunt Jamesina, who keeps house for the girls at Kingsport, is full of humor and wisdom, and the three cats, Joseph, Rusty and the Sarah cat, are evidently drawn from life.[17]

One of the most amusing episodes in the book describes the writing of Anne's first story, "Averil's Atonement," and the remorseless criticism pronounced on it by Mr. Harrison. There is plenty to entertain in *Anne of the Island*.

## [Sentiment and Fun]
### *The Living Age* (New York, NY)

The new "Anne" book, *Anne of the Island*, by L.M. Montgomery, completes the trilogy, according to the statement on its cover, but this by no means indicates who leads Anne to the altar, or who is left lamenting on the shore of P.E. Island, and these secrets are revealed in a very pretty story, a wholesome blending of sentiment and fun. It is difficult to analyze the charm of the "Anne" books, but it seems to be that they are the coinage of a mind which refuses to admit evil thoughts, and hospitably welcomes beauty and mirth and goodness, and most certainly Anne herself is a creature of delight. In this book, Davy, the youngster who "wants to know," and inquires concerning every topic on land or sea, or under the whole Heaven, makes himself manifest. The severe lady who decides doubtful matters with a sharp "That's what" is also in a state of constant activity. As for Anne, she is mistress of herself even when a guest sits down upon a cushion concealing a chocolate cake, to the utter ruin of both cake and cushion. Could more be said for a girl? The sale of *Anne of Green Gables* already exceeds 310,000, *Anne of Avonlea* has passed the 100,000 limit and the Christmas holidays may be expected to send both still further aloft among the best sellers. It speaks well for American morality that this can be said of such books as Mrs. Montgomery's, and they have enough literary merit to maintain their present vogue for many a year.

## [The Simple but Sentimental Chronicle Continued]
### *The Times Literary Supplement* (London, UK)

Continues the simple but sentimental chronicle of Anne Shirley,[18] as already told by Miss Montgomery in *Anne of Green Gables* and *Anne of Avonlea*, and conducts her safely, though with one dreadful episode, to matrimony through a Nova Scotian college.

## [Slips between the Cup and the Lip]
### *The Scotsman* (Edinburgh, UK)

Another instalment of the story of Anne Shirley, and of the Chronicles of Avonlea, in New England, is provided by Miss L.M. Montgomery under the title of *Anne of the Island*, for the delectation of "the girls all over the world who have asked for more." Here the career of Anne is carried forward from her eighteenth year until she completes her college course by taking her B.A. degree and becomes engaged to an old fellow-student and friend of her childhood. As Anne's own history illustrates, there are many slips between the cup and the lip in the affairs of love as well as of school. But this time she seems to be finally booked for matrimony; and if there are further demands for more of her they will have to be satisfied from her experiences of wedlock.

## Irresistible Heroine of Green Gables and Avonlea
### *North American* (Philadelphia, PA)

There have been editions without end of Miss Montgomery's fascinating "Anne Shirley" series – *Anne of Green Gables, Anne of Avonlea* – and now the final volume of a notable trilogy of girlhood, *Anne of the Island*. The island is Prince Edwards, and the scenes are laid at Avonlea, in the old Green Gables house, and around Redmond College, on the mainland, where Anne finally takes her B.A. degree and later cries hail and farewell to simple girlish ideals.

Anne, grown to womanhood, is quite as sprightly and quick witted as was the midget girl who came to Green Gables years ago. If she is a shade more precise, and readier to fall into an ingenue pose, that is the novelist's lookout. Her simple story of love and loyalty and sturdy endeavor is none the less attractive because it deals with things of everyday life as every one would have them, and portrays an ideal society in which all share each other's burdens and laugh in turn at grim fate.

Many of the people whom the reader encountered in the author's earlier chronicles of Avonlea are here introduced again, making the book seem like some reunion of old and loved friends.

But, after all, it is the love affair – or affairs – of Anne herself, now grown to womanhood, with stately carriage, glorious Titian hair, and large powers of expression, that are chief matters of importance.

Before many months at Redmond the heroine is off with her old love of childhood days, and on with another. They are unselfish people, these islanders and bluenoses of Miss Montgomery's creation, and nothing happens dramatically to intervene.

Anne must go over the predestined course of every fair heroine who is constrained by a downcast destiny. This means intrusion of unwelcome suitors, dismissal of the prince charming, and later reversion to the one true love.

These heart adventures really happen where Anne is concerned – nor does the fictionist permit her love shallop to rest in still waters. She must still wait three years for her lover – opportunity, it would seem, for still another chronicle of one of the most charming girlish careers that has been recorded in present-day fiction.

Few romancers in this genre have succeeded in presenting the simple life in its up-to-date, sophisticated aspect, without running afoul of breakers of irreverence or stranding on shoals of affectation. Miss Montgomery's trilogy is free from these drawbacks. Its moral soundness is untinged by vapidity, its common sense is as salient as its humor is natural and unforced.

The books are wholesome, natural and sympathetic from cover to cover. But – the trilogy ought to be a tetralogy.

## Anne Engaged
### *The Daily Graphic* (London, UK)

#### More about the Heroine of the Green Gables

Anne Shirley as the child of the "Green Gables," and then Anne Shirley of "Avonlea" as a grown-up girl, have given infinite pleasure to thousands of readers. They have discovered in that native of Prince Edward Island a lineal descendant of the inimitable children created by Miss Alcott. To all such the mere announcement that Miss L.M. Montgomery has completed her Anne trilogy with *Anne of the Island* will be sufficient to suggest several hours' delightful reading in store.

Nor will they be disappointed. If Miss Montgomery lost a little of her hold on Anne the girl, she has regained it on Anne the young woman of eighteen. Perhaps that is partly due to the fact that she has now dealt with a period of a maiden's career which is fresh in her own experience. In the new story, then, we have Anne Shirley as what the Americans call a "freshette," in other words, an undergraduate at a girls' college. She is, in brief, seen in these chapters undergoing training for a schoolmarm's vocation. She imagines she is quite grown up at eighteen. "When I was ten I thought twenty was a green old age." Diana chides her friend that she will "marry somebody splendid and handsome and rich."[19]

At least a part of that programme is on the way to fulfilment when the book ends. Anne has a faithful lover in the person of a medical student, Gilbert Blythe, whom she does not know she loves in return until she is within an ace of losing him through a dangerous illness. It is all capitally suspended by Miss Montgomery, with pretty scenes and episodes to retain her reader's interest. But on the last page Gilbert draws Anne to his side and kisses her. Then they walked home together "crowned king and queen in the bridal realm of love."[20]

## [Anne's College Life and Engagement]
### *The Spectator* (London, UK)

Lovers of Anne will be delighted at her reappearance; this book tells of her college life, and of her engagement to Gilbert Blythe.

## [Completed Trilogy]
### *The Bookman* (London, UK)

Miss Montgomery completes the trilogy of her "Anne" books with the story of Anne's college career and matrimonial settlement. Honesty compels us to admit that this is our first introduction to Anne, although her praises have often sounded in our ears. We have the feeling that Anne must have been more arresting as a child than she is as a young woman. When she essayed to write stories, a candid critic to whom she submitted the manuscript, advised her to "cut out all those flowery passages." We share the critic's feelings when we find Anne, a girl of eighteen, in the woods with her lover with "her face upturned to the sky" rhapsodising in this strain: "The silence here is like a prayer, isn't it? ... How I love the pines! They seem to strike their roots deep into the romance of all the ages ... I think, if ever any great sorrow came to me, I would come to the pines for comfort."[21] The picture of college life which Miss Montgomery draws is strangely unfamiliar to an English reader acquainted, say, with Girton.[22] Anne, we are told, partly owed her rapid social success to her friendship with a girl who was the daughter of a rich and well-known man who belonged to an old and exclusive "blue-nose family." Such odious snobbery is happily not one of the vices of our colleges. Miss Montgomery obviously writes chiefly for her many American readers, but there are myriads of English readers who will no doubt be as delighted with this latest "Anne" book as they were with the earlier ones.

### NOTES

1  *Rochester Post* (Rochester, NY), review of *Anne of the Island*, 4 August 1915, in SR, 73; review of *Anne of the Island*, unidentified and undated clipping, in SR, 83; *Chicago Record–Herald* (Chicago, IL), review of *Anne of the Island*, 31 July 1915, in SR, 72; *Atlanta Christian Index* (Atlanta, GA), review of *Anne of the Island*, 20 January 1916, in SR, 88; *The Lexington Herald*, review of *Anne of the Island*, 3.
2  Maggie Tulliver, protagonist in *The Mill on the Floss* (1860), a novel by George Eliot, pseudonym of Mary Anne Evans (1819–1880), English novelist.
3  I have corrected the original, which reads "McDonald," but have retained the original spelling of "Ewen."

4 Title character of the best-selling novel *Pollyanna* (1913), by Eleanor H. Porter (1868–1920), American novelist, and published by L.C. Page and Company. It was followed by a number of sequels, only one of which was written by Porter.

5 *AIs*, 83.

6 *AIs*, 93–94, 110.

7 The quotation "the studious cloister's pale," from "Poems on Several Occasions," by John Milton (1608–1674), English poet best known for the epic poem *Paradise Lost*. The editorial interjection "(?)" appears in the original review.

8 I have corrected the original, which reads "M.L. Montgomery."

9 Omitted here are portions of the review pertaining to Gene Stratton-Porter's novel *Michael O'Halloran*, also published in 1915.

10 See "*Anne of Avonlea*," note 16, above.

11 *Mildred Keith* (1876), by Martha Finley, the author of *Elsie Dinsmore* and its twenty-seven sequels, was followed by five sequels, the last published in 1894. *Bessie at the Sea-Side* (1867), by Joanna Mathews (1849–1901), American author, was followed by five sequels, the last published in 1870. *Miss Billy* (1911), by Eleanor H. Porter, author of *Pollyanna* and one of its sequels, was followed by two sequels of its own. I have corrected the original, which reads "Miss Billie" and "Pollyanny."

12 *AIs*, 243.

13 *AIs*, 243.

14 Robert W. Chambers (1865–1933), American author best known for the collection of weird short stories *The King in Yellow* (1895).

15 Properly, "The second term at Redmond sped as quickly as had the first – 'actually whizzed away,' Philippa said" (*AIs*, 62).

16 I have corrected the original, which reads "MacDonald."

17 I have corrected the original, which reads "Jamieson."

18 I have corrected the original, which reads "Annie Shirley."

19 *AIs*, 4.

20 *AIs*, 243.

21 *AIs*, 89, 45, 46.

22 Girton College, a constituent college of the University of Cambridge in England.

# 8

## *The Watchman and Other Poems*

### — 1916 —

Given that Montgomery's poetry has been largely overlooked in the last several decades, it may surprise today's readers that her book of poems, released in November 1916, received high praise from reviewers in Canada, the United States, and the United Kingdom. The *Montreal Witness* referred to Montgomery as "a poetess of rather notable calibre" and celebrated the volume for the "naturalness of picture, depth of feeling and delicacy of touch which has characterized her earlier writings." According to an unidentified clipping in Montgomery's scrapbook, "The entire volume breathes of the sea, the shore, country meadows and hills, morning and evening, storm and calm, laughter, tears and sentiment, and through all is the spirit of reverence and the lilt of music." Another unidentified clipping added that the book "contains many exquisite lines and bears the unmistakable mark of the nature-loving Canadian poet. There are here and there verses that contain more than a haunting reminiscence of places and times in the well-known 'Anne' books. While none of the poems are outstanding, they maintain a high level of beauty and will continue to charm a host of friends and make many new ones for the sweet singer of Prince Edward Island." Noting that the title poem, in free verse, is "ambitious" in its subject, a review in the Toronto *Mail and Empire* added that it "hardly shows Miss Montgomery's gifts to the best advantage. We prefer the little lyrics, often delightfully delicate and full of music. They are fragrant and one feels that they are written by a woman who loves the good and the beautiful in the world. *The Watchman* will be read by those persons who like gentle poetry."[1]

A review in the *Montreal News* also went into detail as to Montgomery's strengths as a poet: "Miss Montgomery has an extraordinary gift of imagery.

Like so many of the big people of her craft she has a sensuous instinct for color, and she displays her skill in this direction in almost every line. The piece which gives the title to the volume is a powerful account of the Resurrection, told in verse that swings along like music; with a wealth of description that makes it like a poem painted in rich colors; and with a dignity and a restrained tenderness that scarcely fail in a single line." To this the *Chicago Evening Post* added that "in her love of nature she is, of course, following the true Canadian tradition, for somehow all Canadian poets since the very first of them have found their chief inspiration in their beautiful countryside. And still following the Canadian tradition, Miss Montgomery writes singingly, fluently, uncritically, letting imagery come and go as it will." Commenting on the book's dedication to the memory of fallen Canadian soldiers in the Great War, an unidentified clipping adds that "it is not a book of war poems; it is a 'book of life,' wherein the author sings of those familiar things of every day," whereas a second unidentified clipping calls it "the outpouring, surely, of a beautiful soul." And in a joint review in the *Springfield Union* of both *The Watchman* and John W. Garvin's anthology *Canadian Poets and Poetry*, in which some of Montgomery's poems also appear, Montgomery, referred to as "a writer of technique and inspiration," receives the following evaluation: "Her poetry does not compare with the best poetry being written today, but it is full of a wholesome beauty and sincere love of nature in all its phases that make it of value. A kinship with the sea is strongly apparent throughout the book. This trait, one that is apparently common to the majority of Canadian poets, finds expression in a number of excellent sea-pieces. Delicate lyrics and a number of suggestively presented outlooks on the deeper moods of life may be found in the volume."[2]

## [A Volume Full of Charming Things]
### *The Globe* (Toronto, ON)

Those familiar with the work of Miss L.M. Montgomery as novelist will not be surprised to learn that she has also written a volume of poetry. One with her joyous outlook on life, vivid imagination, instinct for words, and facility in expression could not help being a poet. More than that, she has lived nearly all her life in Prince Edward Island, where the fairies are said to live. In truth, Miss Montgomery was a poet long before she began to write prose; indeed, it is doubtful if she has ever been anything else, for Anne Shirley – the Anne of Green Gables in that brood of wonderfully successful books that have proved conspicuous features of the Christmas book trade during the past half dozen years – is essentially a creature of sentiment, of imagination, and of those qualities of heart and brain which are the products of the poetic mind.[3]

This year, instead of a new "Anne" book, we have a volume of poetry, *The Watchman, and Other Poems* – a book quite in keeping with her reputation as novelist, and one that will add materially to her standing as a foremost Canadian writer.

## Full of Music

Her verse is quite as perfect as her prose, though without its human touch, and her lyrics, especially those dealing with the smiling aspects of her native Province, its fragrant fields of red earth, and the "blue sea coming up on every side," are of rare quality, delicate, lilting and full of music.[4]

The title poem, and the most ambitious, is an excellent and dignified poem in blank verse concerning the keepers who watched over the grave of Christ, and who, "for fear of Him ... did shake and become as dead men."[5] But the bulk of the volume, and that upon which her reputation as artist and poet is to be based, are her songs of the sea and songs of the hills and woods.

## A Writer of the Sea

Curiously enough, in spite of Canada's splendid length of sea coast and her great wealth in shipping and in fisheries, Miss Montgomery is almost the first Canadian poet to write of the sea, of the sailors and of the fisher folk. Miss Montgomery was born by the sea, and from infancy she has lived on the north shore of the Island. Here she has absorbed the glories of landscape and sea, and developed that wonderful appreciation of nature and sympathy with all those who go down to the sea in ships.

This verse from "Off to the Fishing Ground" is but one of a score of exquisite touches:

> Oh, 'tis a glad and heartsome thing
>   To wake ere the night be done
> And steer the course that our fathers steered
>   In the path of the rising sun.
> The wind and welkin and wave are ours
>   Wherever our bourne is found,

And we envy no landsman his dream and sleep
When we're off to the fishing ground.[6]

## "The Old Man's Grave"

There is something very kindly and tender in her touch, a gentle sympathy with the varying moods of nature, and a singular charm and nimbleness of expression. "The Old Man's Grave" is a good example: [* * *][7]

## A Dainty Conceit

The little poem, "Fancies," however, is one of the daintiest conceits in a volume full of charming things: [* * *][8]

## Made in Canada

As readers of Miss Montgomery's novels will remember, her books have always been beautiful specimens of book-making, and quite in keeping with their character. This present volume is the first to be made throughout in Canada, and is a dainty piece of work, and in every way quite up to the standard of the others in paper, printing and binding.

## [The Fancies of a Young Heart]
### *The Toronto World* (Toronto, ON)

This book of verse which tells about the sea, a loved country and the fancies of a young heart, is a companion book to *Anne of Green Gables* and the other stories of Anne. It reflects faithfully the joys, dreams and imaginings of poetical fancy. There are three poems which merit special praise as being of a higher order: "At Nightfall" for its mystery and "If Mary Had Known" and "The Mother" for their deep poetical interpretation of motherhood.

## Canadian Verse
### *The Christian Guardian* (Toronto, ON)

There are no doubt some who have been charmed with Miss Montgomery's stories who have never yet learned to think of her as a poet at all. And yet it is a question if she will not be remembered in the future more by her verse than by her prose. She has delicate sentiment and a deft gift of versification that make her work very charming.

## [This Gifted Canadian Writer]
### *The Canadian Magazine* (Toronto, ON)

Although the author of *Anne of Green Gables* and *Anne of Avonlea* has been known for years to all readers of *The Canadian Magazine* as a poet of fine sense and fancy, this is the first volume of her poems that has appeared. That fact is perhaps not so noteworthy as the gratifying circumstance that this time this gifted Canadian writer's work is offered to the public by Canadian publishers. Heretofore her books have been published by a Boston firm. The change, of course, does not mean that Mrs. Macdonald (L.M. Montgomery is in private life the mistress of the manse in an Ontario town) is neglecting her large American audience. Her novels have made her sure of that, so that if the copyright laws permit it, she might well publish her next novels first in Canada. Her verse is marked by gentle rhythm, exquisite conceits, and actually breathes out the fragrance and beauty of field and wood and murmuring brook. She is above all else a nature poet. [* * *]9

## Poems by Author of *Anne of Green Gables*
### *The Family Herald and Weekly Star* (Montreal, QC)

Nothing written by "L.M. Montgomery," author of some of the most popular serials published in *The Family Herald and Weekly Star*, can be neglected by the reviewer who wants to deal with the best of the output of publishers. On their own merits the verses contained in *The Watchman and Other Poems*, by L.M. Montgomery, author of *Anne of Green Gables*, etc., must be judged worthy of attention even just now when a great deal of good poetry is being produced under the stress of feeling occasioned by the war.

"The Watchman" is a fantasy in blank verse, depicting the thoughts of the centurion who watched the tomb in Joseph's garden on the first Easter Eve. The dramatic instinct is there but not the dramatic force required to carry home the great picture, though the story is of course well told by the deft-handed novelist.

Perhaps as distinctive as anything in the book is the following somewhat quaint conception.

### To My Enemy

Let those who will of friendship sing,
    And to its guerdon grateful be,
But I a lyric garland bring
    To crown thee, O, mine enemy!

Thanks, endless thanks, to thee I owe
    For that my lifelong journey through
Thine honest hate has done for me
    What love perchance had failed to do.

I had not scaled such weary heights
    But that I held thy scorn in fear,
And never keenest lure might match
    The subtle goading of thy sneer.

Thine anger struck from me a fire
    That purged all dull content away,
Our mortal strife to me has been
    Unflagging spur from day to day.

And thus, while all the world may laud
    The gifts of love and loyalty,
I lay my meed of gratitude
    Before thy feet, mine enemy![10]

There has gone a deal of thought into some of these apparently simple verses, as witness some lines from the little poem on "Genius":

Their victory and their laughter for this have strong men given,
    For this have sweet, dead women paid in patience which survives –
That a great soul might bring the world, as from the gate of heaven,
    All that was rich and beautiful in those forgotten lives.[11]

Or take the second part of the prettily conceived ode entitled "Forever," which runs as follows:

O, my friend, nothing shall ever part
My soul from yours, yours from my heart!
I am yours and you mine, in silence and in speech,
Death will only seal us each to each.
Through the darkness we shall fare with fearless jest,
Starward we shall go on a joyous new quest;
There be many worlds, as we shall prove,
Many suns and systems, but only one love![12]

There is reminiscence here of the actor manager Frohman's last words, on the sinking *Lusitania*,[13] about the Great Adventure on which his and so many souls were then about to embark. Some of these last lines have already crept into popular use, and if there is no great poetic value in them, they contain that which appeals to the minds and affections of men and which may confer a measure of immortality upon them.

## [Breezy and Inspiriting Book of Poems]
### *The Scotsman* (Edinburgh, UK)

That it comes from Canada must commend this breezy and inspiriting book of poems to many readers on this side of the water, though its sturdy and sweetly moving outpourings about the sea and the storm, the beauty of the hills and woods, and the healthy fascination of the open air, are not marked by noticeably distinctive local touches. The piece mentioned in the title is an exception to the general expansiveness of the poems, which as a rule sing heartily in the face of Nature. In "The Watchman" the singer goes to church, and sets out an effective dramatic monologue supposed to be spoken by a Roman-born sentinel, who was on duty under Pontius Pilate when the stone was rolled back from the gate of the tomb.

### NOTES

1  *Montreal Witness* (Montreal, QC), review of *The Watchman and Other Poems*, 9 January 1917, in SR, 90; "The Watchman and Other Poems," unidentified and undated clipping, in SR, 91; "If Mary Had Known," unidentified and undated clipping, in SR, 92; *The Mail and Empire* (Toronto,

ON), "Three Little Volumes by Our Minor Poets," 9 December 1916, in SR, 93.

2 *Montreal News* (Montreal, QC), review of *The Watchman and Other Poems*, 27 November 1916, in SR, 92; S.W., review of *The Road to Castaly and Later Poems*, 8; "Miss Montgomery's Poetry," unidentified and undated clipping, in SR, 209; review of *The Watchman and Other Poems*, unidentified and undated clipping, in SR, 119; *The Springfield Union* (Springfield, MA), "Canadian Poetry Presented in Excellent Anthology," review of *Canadian Poets and Poetry*, chosen and edited by John W. Garvin, and *The Watchman and Other Poems*, 13 May 1917, in SR, 123.

3 With the exception of the phrase surrounded by dashes, this paragraph appears in nearly identical form in E.J. Hathaway's headnote on Montgomery in John W. Garvin's collection *Canadian Poets*, also published by McClelland, Goodchild and Stewart in 1916. The anthology includes five poems by Montgomery, including "Off to the Fishing Ground" and "The Old Man's Grave," discussed here. This volume appeared as *Canadian Poets and Poetry* in the U.S.

4 This paragraph also appears in near identical form in Hathaway's headnote. The quotation "blue sea coming up from every side" is from Marjory MacMurchy's profile "L.M. Montgomery: Story Writer," which appears in Volume 1 of *The L.M. Montgomery Reader*.

5 From Matthew 23:4, used as an epigraph for the poem "The Watchman" (*WOP*, 3).

6 *WOP*, 26.

7 The full text of Montgomery's poem "The Old Man's Grave," cited in the original review, is omitted here. See *WOP*, 156.

8 The full text of Montgomery's poem "Fancies," cited in the original review, is omitted here. See *WOP*, 109.

9 The original review also quotes all nine stanzas from "Fancies" as "an example of her work." See *WOP*, 109.

10 *WOP*, 93.

11 *WOP*, 132.

12 *WOP*, 157.

13 Charles Frohman (1856–1915), American theatre producer, whose reported last words were a paraphrase from J.M. Barrie's *Peter Pan*: "Why fear death? It is the most beautiful adventure that life gives us." For Montgomery's response to the sinking of the ocean liner the *Lusitania* in May 1915, see Montgomery to MacMillan, 2 August 1915, in *MDMM*, 76.

# 9

## Anne's House of Dreams

—— 1917 ——

Montgomery's fourth novel about Anne received fairly positive reviews, yet
the fact that it appeared with new publishers in Canada and the United States
appears to have been largely unnoticed. But its publication in the midst of the
Great War was commented on by several reviewers. As the *Boston Post* noted,
"For relief from all the horrors of these days no recent novel is better than
*Anne's House of Dreams* ... It is an attractive romance without great excitement, but wholesome and refreshing." The *San Jose Mercury Herald* called it
"a bright little volume but one that few people have time for in these busy, busy
war times. However, we need such tales occasionally to keep the mind from
dwelling altogether on the tragedies and sadness of war." To this the *Liverpool
Courier* added, "In these dark days of war such a book has a mission, and
it fulfils it precisely as one can imagine the idyll of Ruth doing in the days of
the Judges." While the *Chicago Daily Tribune* commented favourably on the
"generous share of agreeable humor, gently satirical at times," the *New York
World* added that "like each Anne book before it, *Anne's House of Dreams* is
a composite. It holds stories within a story ... Certainly all this is matter for
sentimentalists, but we confess to being just a little sorry for fiction readers
who truly do not care for it."[1]

Moreover, although the novel depicts a woman trapped in a nightmarish
marriage and mentions numerous violent deaths, *The Bookseller, Newsdealer
and Stationer* called it "a simple and kindly tale, permeated with the spirit of
common sense and the essence of happiness." And according to the *American
Jewish Chronicle*, which called the novel "a clean, sweet, wholesome book for
girls in their 'teens," "It is a compound of sweet romance, very mild humor, salt

tears, and just enough mystery to add the necessary spice. Not that the book could really be called spicy by the wildest stretch of the imagination; but it is sufficiently interesting for all practical purposes throughout ... and, presumably, they all live happily ever after." Additional reviews expressed some ambivalence with the characters and the plot: according to a review in the Toronto *Mail and Empire*, "sometimes a reviewer has to forget his own personal preferences and say, 'This is just the very book that the persons who read this sort of book will like,'" adding that "Miss Montgomery's views of life and people are very conventional but she gives us a pleasant picture of married bliss. She is a Canadian novelist who does not attempt to do things that are beyond her. She seems quite satisfied to do a modest thing fairly well." In a retrospective of work by Canadian writers published in 1917, this same newspaper added that Montgomery's "gentle and wholesome little stories are much beloved by a great number of women who like pretty fiction, and this authoress maintains her standard." This time, the question of target audience led to a rather contradictory explanation: a review in the *Brooklyn Daily Eagle* suggested that "this is not a little girl's story, as in it the heroine, Anne Shirley, becomes engaged and is married," then added that, "though technically a story for grownups, girls will enjoy it."[2]

Although the *Pittsburgh Chronicle Telegraph* referred to the book as "a pleasant surprise for those who had believed the preceding story of the beloved heroine was the last," to which an unidentified clipping from a Michigan newspaper added that "the reader need fear no let-down when he approaches this book, as is too often the case where one or more characters are made to live again and again in the customary 'series,'" several more reviews had reservations about the changes to Anne's character after her marriage. As the *Cincinnati Enquirer* noted, "The new neighbors include some original and lovable New England characters ... though Anne has lost much of the sparkle that gave zest and charm to the first volume of the series." Meanwhile, Baird Leonard of the New York *Morning Telegraph* revealed that "the adventures of Anne, Miss Montgomery's charming serial heroine, have always interested me, although it is too bad that the demands of an avid public have forced the author to drag her past the period where brook and river meet." An unidentified clipping from the United Kingdom argued that "the author must really relinquish Anne (though she is obviously loath to do so) if she would not lose her gift of story-telling. Miss Montgomery loves Anne so dearly that she allows her no difficulties or problems in her married life, which runs along so smoothly as to seem to the reader almost tame and monotonous." And yet, another unidentified clipping went to the opposite extreme: "Let us have a few more of the Anne books."[3]

## [Charm and Action]
### *Saint John Globe* (Saint John, NB)

These Anne books are in the hardy perennial class, and may be likened to such old time favorites as the bright and fragrant Sweet William, and the spicy Southernwood. "No one makes a mistake in investing in this new one," to quote a seed catalogue, which lies on the desk, and is as neat a garden as we may get. Anne, whom we last left teaching school, is now the wife of Gilbert. They make their home in the country, and have many quaint friends whose sayings and doings add greatly to the charm of the story. There is much more action than in the preceding books, and Miss Montgomery's work is showing more than ever the touch of the true artist.

## [A Love-Nook in the Hearts of Innumerable Readers]
### *The Globe* (Toronto, ON)
#### JOHN W. GARVIN

It is nine years this fall since Lucy Maud Montgomery of Prince Edward Island published her first and most popular novel, *Anne of Green Gables*;[4] and since then the immortal Anne, declared by Mark Twain to be "the sweetest creation of child life yet written," has journeyed far afield and won the enduring friendship of hundreds of thousands of readers.

It seems to me that *Anne's House of Dreams* must also find a love-nook in the hearts of innumerable readers. Old friends reappear and are welcomed, but there are three new and original characters introduced who leave a vivid and lasting impression: Captain Jim, Miss Cornelia and Leslie Moore.[5] Captain Jim is an old sea captain and lighthouse keeper, honest and wise and delightfully loquacious; Miss Cornelia is a middle-aged spinster, who is never so happy as when engaged in man-baiting; and Leslie Moore is a young woman with an embittered soul (in a surpassingly beautiful body), due to an early and tragic marriage.

But the chief interest continues to centre in the lovable Anne, whose engagement to Dr. Gilbert Blythe is announced as the story opens, and who shortly marries him and accompanies her husband to the "House of Dreams" at the Four Winds Harbor. But I must not disclose the joys and the sorrows of this sweet home-nest and of the dear new friendships, or the reader would have a grievance. Suffice it to say that the story is fresh and wholesome, the characters original with vivid portraiture, and the dialogue throughout spontaneous and natural. In this record of interesting experiences of real people there is much humor and some pathos, and the eternal wisdom of the pure in heart.

The publishers must also share in the acceptability of this book. Their part is admirably done. The Frontispiece in colors, by M.L. Kirk, is a work of art, and its beauty on the cover is enhanced by a border of roses.

Some who read this review may not know that this popular author was married in 1911 to the Rev. Ewan Macdonald, Presbyterian minister at Leaskdale, Ontario county, Ontario.

## [Happenings and Vistas]
### *The New York Times Book Review* (New York, NY)

Continuing the characters that have appeared in several previous stories Miss Montgomery carries on into wifehood and motherhood the same Anne Shirley of the red locks and the gay, sweet spirit who was the young heroine of *Anne of Green Gables* and *Anne of Avonlea*. The scene is still Prince Edward Island, with the wide blue waters of St. Lawrence Gulf hemming in the lives of all the people of the tale. Readers of the former stories will find many of their old friends in the early chapters, but when Anne marries Dr. Gilbert Blythe in the fourth chapter and goes to live at Four Winds Harbor in another part of the island a new set of characters comes on the stage and not much is seen or heard of the old ones after that. The home to which the young husband takes his bride is her "house of dreams," so charming is it in its simple hominess, with its garden and Lombardy poplars and circling ring of white birches, and its windows looking out on a great blue harbor and a lighthouse.

New friends, of the kind Anne calls "kindred spirits," soon come into her life and make her "house of dreams" very much alive with new interests, new hopes, new plans. Among these friends one of the most important is the lighthouse keeper, an old man with a history and a kindly, philosophic tongue, who tells Anne and her husband many a tale that is linked with the romantic history of their home. Another is a beautiful girl with something of a mystery about her at first, until it is resolved into a near-tragedy that threatens to be with her all her life. This is finally brushed away and leaves the possibility of happiness. So the story of the two or three years that Anne spends in her "house of dreams" is full of happenings for herself and others, and unfolds many vistas of mingled gladness and sorrow.

## Anne Shirley
### *The Oakland Tribune* (Oakland, CA)

*Anne's House of Dreams* Is Another Book Concerning
L.M. Montgomery's Lovable Heroine and Friends

L.M. Montgomery has found in Anne Shirley a heroine of undying popularity. Her *Anne's House of Dreams* is of the same charm as *Anne of Green Gables*,[6] and it may be that there are more planned.

In this latest volume Miss Montgomery marries Anne to Gilbert and they go to live in the house of dreams. Their married life is marked by happiness, friendship of interesting neighbors, and some exciting and deeply moving events. The neighbors furnish the material for the best of what is in the book. Miss Cornelia, whose tongue is never so sharp as when talking of men and who talks of but little else, is caught at last. The beautiful Leslie Moore, Captain Jim the old lighthouse keeper, and the aristocratic, long-haired Marshall Elliott, all come under Anne's spell.

The romance of Anne and Gilbert is not the only one in the book. She and Miss Cornelia help toward the happy outcome of another that brightens the story. There is much in the book to bring laughter and much to call for deserved praise. The sharp sayings of Miss Cornelia are tinged with real humor and the pictures of the neighborly folk about the house of dreams are those of likable, gossipy, big-hearted, everyday country people.[7] And so Anne's house of dreams is built in an atmosphere of simplicity and the wholesome. Gaiety, common sense and happiness pervade her story. Miss Montgomery has written her book with joy for the task and her enthusiasm is evidenced in the result.

## [All the Elements of "Sixteen-ness"]
### *The Times–Picayune* (New Orleans, LA)
#### CARMELITE JANVIER

We have all been sixteen, that is, all women have, some men may have slipped by but only a few! Therefore we know that it is not so much an age as a state of mind and can be brought back for a fleeting moment at least by a sound or a scent or a book – most easily, perhaps, by a book.

*Anne's House of Dreams* has all the elements of "sixteen-ness," if we might invent the word. It is the sort of book which we used to spend the whole day reading, only stopping now and then to think those "long, long thoughts" which were our heritage of Youth.[8] It is the sort of book that girls even today will be interested in in spite of the moving pictures, because it talks about the things they think about and it is sweet and wholesome. Of course, nothing over the age of ten will swallow the bare hook of "lived happily ever after," but that is the essence of what we all secretly want in our books. In *Anne's House of Dreams* we find it skillfully concealed but present nevertheless for all of the characters! Indeed, it is a book which we are glad to read and enjoy ourselves and more than glad to see our little sisters reading. It is as good food for the girls of today as Louisa M. Alcott and Charlotte Yonge were for those of another age.[9]

## Anne the Matron
### *The New York Tribune* (New York, NY)

Anne Shirley, whom we knew as a sweet girl at Avonlea and at Green Gables, is now a matron and a mother, Mrs. Gilbert Blythe; and the blitheness and beauty of her girlhood prevail also in her womanhood, particularly since the house which Dr. Blythe prepared for her at Four Winds Harbor proves a waking realization of her "little house of dreams," as all that her home should be. There she dwells in peace and happiness, surrounded by interesting neighbors, and playing the good goddess toward other romances which follow on as happily as her own has led.

It is sometimes a perilous thing to continue the same leading character on through a second and a third story, but in this series of Prince Edward Island tales about Anne Shirley Miss Montgomery has triumphed over the peril and attained a most delightful and gratifying success.

## [The Puzzling Business of Being Married]
### *The Evening Star* (Washington, DC)

Anne is an old friend to readers who have followed her through more than one story by this author. These will be glad to go with her on this marriage adventure, for already she has proved the good sense that is bound to stand her in hand upon this new and most perilous voyage. And so it does. Good sense and enough humor to carry one through the day's work help out amazingly in the puzzling business of being married.

So, possessed of these, Anne gives an uncommonly good account of herself, making friends with certain very much alive and interesting people around her, as she does with the reader himself. This is one of the stories that comes under the term "wholesome." There are no problems arising from the apparently endless mis-matings of the world and none of the modern to-do that ties up so many of the current novels in the inextricably hard knots of domestic infelicity. An open and engaging story for some easy half hour.

## A Scotch-Canadian Village
### *The Evening Post* (New York, NY)

One of a series of novels dealing with a heroine of southeastern Canada, Miss Montgomery's book will be enjoyed by those who value descriptions of nature and character above dramatic quality or structure. The story is practically the setting forth of a situation, illumined by episode. Anne Shirley marries Gilbert Blythe and goes to live in a picturesque cottage in Four Winds Harbor, Prince Edward Island.[10] Here she comes to know the characters of her Scotch-Canadian neighborhood – Captain Jim, Miss Cornelia, Marshall Elliot,[11] Leslie Moore. Their lives and emotions are revealed and blend with hers in a leisurely and interesting manner. Anne does no more than absorb these outside elements, watch sunsets, bear her two children, and part at the end with the House of Dreams which has been the centre of her married life and the point of outlook upon these new acquaintances. Captain Jim's gentle nature finds expression in his "Life-Book," a diary that Owen Ford, the pleasant visiting author, dresses for a successful publication. Miss Cornelia, for all her railing at men, marries the curious Marshall Elliot when the Liberals return to power and permit the enthusiastic politician to cut the beard and hair that by a vow had been left to grow for twenty years. Leslie Moore furnishes such genuine plot interest as is offered. The story of her unfortunate marriage to a husband at first incompatible, later an imbecile, and of the operation that brought back his memory and gave her release indicates that the book, had the author desired, might have been a compact novel instead of a leisurely tale. As it stands, it gives a picture of happy young married life and its environment in which suggested tragedy and comedy are alike subdued to a somewhat conventional view of life.

## A New Anne Book
### *The Montreal Daily Herald* (Montreal, QC)

When one sees a particularly sweet and winsome child, one is sometimes tempted to wish it need not grow up. One is sure it will never be as charming again, in any future phase or state of its being. If this is the case in real life it is still more so in story-book land. Most readers, we are of the opinion, are sorry that Anne Shirley, the Anne whom we first knew and loved at Green Gables, has grown up. Anne seems to have grown up rapidly. It seems but a short time since she was making things lively at the old Green Gables home. Then we shared with her the experiences and new friendships and triumphs of her ambitious quest for higher education. Now Anne is married and settled in a home of her own.

One is glad to meet Anne again under any circumstances. Since she had to marry somebody sometime, one is satisfied that her choice fell upon Gilbert Blythe, her old school-fellow, whom, indeed, it needed no prophet to foresee was destined to become the husband of Anne, from the day she broke her slate over his head when he called her "Carrots." It was still more evident when we saw Anne as the charmingly eager maiden of Avonlea, just home from school, and full of plans for the future.

When we again see Anne, she is back at Green Gables, talking with Diana Wright, erstwhile Diana Barry, over the plans for her wedding. "It was a happy and beautiful bride who came down the old, homespun-carpeted stairs that September noon – the first bride of Green Gables, slender and shining-eyed, in the mist of her maiden veil, with her arms full of roses. Gilbert, waiting for her in the hall below, looked up at her with adoring eyes."[12]

Gilbert is now a full-fledged doctor, with a practice at Four Winds Harbor, so Anne's house of dreams is on her beloved Prince Edward Island. It is a little house, and an old house, hallowed by a past that commends it to its new mistress, who is the third bride it has welcomed. To the little house come friendly neighbors – Miss Cornelia Bryant, whose tongue is sharp, especially when some erring man body is in question; Captain Jim, the high-minded old keeper of the lighthouse; Susan, the spinster help; Marshall Elliott, rabid party politician; Leslie Moore, whose life story furnishes a touch of drama, unexpected in the quiet surroundings of Four Winds Harbor. There are birth and death, joy and sorrow in the house of dreams, which grows too small a dwelling before the story ends.

Miss Montgomery has given her readers many glimpses of the beauties of Prince Edward Island in the Avonlea books, and in this one she takes us to a point where she can show us the changing lights and moods of the harbor, the sand dunes, and the sea-ward glens. She has a good descriptive pen. Miss Montgomery's character drawing is most convincing when her people are what in their own neighborhood would be called "characters." Miss Cornelia is more living than the beautiful Leslie Moore.

As for Anne, – well, there isn't enough of Anne in "The House of Dreams." And it has to be admitted that she is a more subdued Anne. Perhaps her three years of teaching had something to do with it. Anyhow, one misses the old spirit and spontaneity from Anne's speech and action. Except for occasional flashes of her old self, she might be almost any nice, lovable young matron. Or perhaps it is that we do not like to realize that she is quite grown up. Still, as said before, we are always glad to meet and greet Anne.

The book has a very pretty colored frontispiece.

## [More or Less Exciting Events]
### *The Hartford Courant* (Hartford, CT)

*Anne's House of Dreams* is a novel whose scene is laid in a sea-coast community. There, in their "house of dreams," Anne and her husband live their happy life with interesting neighbors whose lives are interwoven with theirs by more or less exciting events. It is a story of simple and wholesome life, in which pathos and humor are mingled, such as might be expected from the author of *Anne of Green Gables* and *Avonlea*.

## [Hard on the Shut-Outs]
### *Life* (New York, NY)

Books on etiquette are agreed that it is bad manners to make conversational references (such as "What do you hear from Jim?" and "I understand that Nora is divorcing her fourth husband") that are meaningless to a portion of the company present. They're all right for those in the know, but hard on the shut-outs who must somehow contrive to look both incurious and intelligent at the same time. L.M. Montgomery's *Anne's House of Dreams*, which deals with the early married life of the heroine of *Anne of Green Gables* and *Anne of Avonlea* in an out-of-the-world village on Prince Edward Island,[13] is a thoroughly twinkly and likable story, except for the fact that (like many sequels) it is badly brought up in this one regard. It is constantly dragging in irrelevant references to people and events that its readers may or may not be familiar with.

## [A Gem of a Love Story]
### *Portland Express–Advertiser* (Portland, ME)

Miss L.M. Montgomery has varied her story but not her methods in *Anne's House of Dreams* and the result is a novel characterized by delightful plot and the unique exchange of repartee which made *Anne of Green Gables* and its successors so tantalizingly fascinating to a host of readers. Anne now undertakes the perilous journey of matrimony and the story concerns itself with a variety of characters, some of them old and some of them new. Throughout there is an underlying spirit of tolerance, broad sympathy and an appreciation of difficulties which make each episode delightful and all-convincing. The reader feels that the content with which Anne turns to Gilbert at the end is prophetic of future happiness and true love. Indeed, the author's latest effort is a gem of a love story having a refreshment and daintiness all its own and told in Miss Montgomery's well known, inimitable way.

## [Outside and Inside]
### *Troy Record* (Troy, NY)

How would you like to live in a tiny white cottage surrounded by a lovely garden through which babbled a singing brook? That is the sort of place Anne's House of Dreams was – from the outside. The inside? Well, that would be telling and Miss Montgomery does that far better than anybody else could, for "Anne of Green Gables" is the same enchanting person who inhabits the House of Dreams, only in this new volume the author tells of the joys that come to Anne when she goes as a bride to the little white house on the beach. It is a story brimming over with love and hope and charm and pathos, and it is full of interesting and unusual characters. For instance, consider Miss Cornelia. Have you ever known such an entertaining old maid? And then Cap'n Jim, the lighthouse keeper.

There is a wealth of human interest in the novel, and yet it is so free from any of the sordid things of life that, if you have a young daughter in your house, it is just the kind of a tale you will love to have her read. For it is natural, vivid and fascinating; yet it does not find it necessary to attract the reader's attention by the tiresome reiteration of the problems of the world that arise from the loss of self-control or the presence of unrestrained selfishness. So read the book yourself and then give it to your daughter; only do not blame her if she burns the midnight oil in finishing it.

## An Old Friend Again
### *The Hartford Times* (Hartford, CT)

Many readers who have followed Anne's fortunes thus far will welcome their continuance in this delightful account of her marriage to Dr. Gilbert Blythe, and the setting up of their household gods in a little house by the sea, quite after her own heart.

Miss Montgomery's story is unique and irresistible in its northern flavor; Four Winds Harbor is really located on Prince Edward Island, but it might have been some remote and lovely part of the Maine coast, for its feeling of clean sea-winds and sea-spaces, the tang of its air, and the tang of its people – such as Captain Jim, retired from seafaring to tend the harbor light, a man wise with the wisdom of those who have dared and pondered much; and sharp-tongued Miss Cornelia, with her never-failing mother-wit, her bedrock prejudices against men and Methodists, and her staunchness at the core.

The gay, tender atmosphere of this little seaside house, whose devoted mistress has a fund of humor, true sentiment and interest in her environment, makes the reader as well as the neighbor loath to leave it when the tale is done.

Dull it never becomes; the writer has a feeling for the color and lure of the northern landscape – she makes us realize all autumn in the flapping black crown blown across the sky's deep blueness; nor does she come to the end of good conversation – one never desires Miss Cornelia, or the captain, "to take in the slack of [his] jaw and go home";[14] skill is shown, too, in weaving a mystery to shadow the life of Anne's youngest neighbor and dear friend – an attractive wife near her own age.

All in all, Miss Montgomery is justified of her devoted circle of readers.

## [A Simple and Pleasant Story]
### *Everywoman's World* (Toronto, ON)

All who have followed with interest the career of Miss Montgomery's charming child heroine, "Anne of Green Gables," will be glad to renew their acquaintance with her in the author's latest volume, *Anne's House of Dreams*. This is the chronicle of the first few years of Anne's married life and while in it we renew our friendship with many old friends, we are introduced to several new characters. Of these the most striking are "Miss Cornelia," and "Captain Jim." Miss Cornelia, "who did not hate men, but just naturally despised them,"[15] is a quaint and laughable figure, while "Captain Jim," with his tender heart and keen sense of the ridiculous, his love of cats and dogs and friendly interest in all his neighbors' concerns, will be dear to the heart of all who read. The story is a simple and pleasant little one and will be greatly enjoyed by girls, old and young. There is nothing morbid about Miss Montgomery's writings. They are thoroughly wholesome reading, taking the place, for this generation, of the *Little Women* and *Good Wives*,[16] dear to the hearts of the girls of that which has just passed.

## [A Splendid Sequel]
### *The Canadian Churchman* (Toronto, ON)

Mrs. Macdonald's throng of readers will welcome another volume from her pen. It has lost none of its winsome attractiveness. In this story our friend, Anne, withdraws to the background, and brings into her "House of Dreams" new and strikingly original characters. They develop under the magic of her friendship and home life in a natural but strong manner, and the longings and passions of the human race are as clearly portrayed in the isolated gulf land, as they could be in the busy life of the city. "Captain Jim," "Miss Cornelia" and others form a group which holds one's attention to the end.[17] The tragedy which seems to envelop Leslie Moore lifts in a most ingenious and skilful way, and into her sombre life, sunshine comes with the great glory of love fulfilled. This is a wholesome, refreshing, and strong story, a splendid sequel to *Anne of Green Gables*.

## Anne of Green Gables in Her New House of Dreams
### *North American* (Philadelphia, PA)

A new book by the author of *Anne of Green Gables* and *Anne of Avonlea*, with the title *Anne's House of Dreams*, makes further record in fiction of a bright and charming heroine – so realistic, engaging and surcharged with human nature that to most of Miss Montgomery's clientele of readers Anne Shirley is a veritable living creature, and no creation of imagination. In this later volume the clever, sprightly girl of Green Gables is done with study and teaching – becoming, in fact, the bride of Dr. Gilbert Blythe, and returning shortly from a honeymoon journey, ready to take up her new task of homemaking. They are going to Four Winds Harbor, on the island which Anne has helped to make famous, where she has "a little house o' dreams all furnished in my imagination – a tiny, delightful castle in Spain."[18] It is a fine old house, and Anne is the third bride to enter it since it was first built, half a century ago.

Here begin what might be termed the simple annals of a wholesome, happy life – into which, before long, the romancer introduces new characters and situations, interesting neighbors and moving, exciting events.

There is the same electric atmosphere, created by Anne at Avonlea, to stir natives and visitors into unusual activities – the veteran lighthouse keeper is induced to write the story of his sea adventures; the sharp-tongued old maid of the vicinage is brought under subjection to Anne's persistent and pervasive geniality, and her new neighbors become as devoted to her as were the people of Avonlea.

Later a new romance appears, centering in the personality of beautiful Leslie Moore, yoked, to all appearances, with an imbecile in a sort of living death. This, too, in the novelist's skillful hands, develops into an extended episode of pure, ingratiating romance – introducing, in truth, a new heroine to share the honors and fortunes of Four Winds life.

In the end the house of dreams changes occupants, and a wider sphere of social interest is opened for Anne and her little group of loyal friends. But this, it is to be trusted, will prove matter for another story – the real Anne, in fact, seems to have only begun her joyous and beneficent career.

## [Meeting with Real People]
*The Bookseller, Newsdealer and Stationer* (New York, NY)

*Anne's House of Dreams*, by L.M. Montgomery, renews acquaintance with many of the characters who appeared in the author's earlier novel, solving their difficulties and bringing joy and sorrow into their lives. Almost no other writer has Miss Montgomery's rare sense of humor, her understanding of life and her power to visualize the scenes and characters she describes. She writes of every-day life and every-day people, and yet she puts into her story a quality of interest that is seldom found, an interest that holds the attention of thousands of readers where a story of more pretentious plot would entirely fail. Anne, Captain Jim, Diana Wright, Leslie, Gilbert, even Mrs. Harmon Andrews are people we all know, people whose prototypes are found in the stress of city life as well as in the peaceful seclusion of Prince Edward Island.[19] It is this meeting with real people in Miss Montgomery's story that makes it a pleasure to everyone, old and young. A charming colored frontispiece, reproduced both on cover and jacket, gives the book a holiday appearance that catches the eye of the Christmas shopper who may not already be familiar with the story, while those who have read it will be eager to give the same pleasure to their friends.

## With Many a Sparkle
*Chicago Continent* (Chicago, IL)

The literature of healthy-mindedness has a new addition in this winsome story of a glad girl's married life. Prince Edward Island and its environs afford ample scope for the expression of Miss Montgomery's unfeigned love of nature and her glowing descriptive powers. The mystic appeal of the sea and the charm and witchery of the natural world are interwoven with the loves and dreams, the poetry and pathos of very human characters. Anne Shirley, whose life story began in *Anne of Green Gables*, marries and goes to live in her "house of dreams." The radiant geniality of the bride, the piquant humor of Miss Cornelia, the shrewd sense of Captain Jim and the pathos which envelops the life of Leslie Moore enliven and enrich the story. The style is lucid, pictorial and unlabored. The characters are of the sort that have foibles but no sins. *Anne's House of Dreams* is a wholesome, lovable romance of a wife whose home was a house of dreams.

## [Mr. Montgomery's New Book]
*Minneapolis Bellman* (Minneapolis, MN)

Those who recall the vivacious Anne, heroine of Mr. Montgomery's earlier novel, *Anne of Green Gables*, will welcome her reappearance in the author's new book, *Anne's House of Dreams*.

The House of Dreams is the pleasant cottage on the harbor shore outside the little village Glen St. Mary, Prince Edward Island,[20] where Anne goes to make a new home with her husband, Dr. Gilbert Blythe, who has opened his first office in the village.

The young couple themselves hardly form the chief figures of the story, for they and their pleasant home are rather the attracting force which draws together a group of the village people in whom center the interest of the book. There is Captain Jim, the retired sailor, now keeper of the light at Four Winds Point, a wholesome and philosophical old man, who greets the bridal couple on the night of their arrival and tells them the story of the schoolmaster's bride, the first bride to occupy the house.

Then there is Miss Cornelia Bryant, a vigorous and breezy person who in Captain Jim's words "seems to have been born with a sort of chronic spite agin men and Methodists. She's got the bitterest tongue and the kindest heart in Four Winds."[21] A third of the major characters is the beautiful and baffling Mrs. Leslie Moore, whose tragic story forms a considerable part of the novel.

In spite of the episodical character of the novel and its frank reliance on anecdote and character sketches for much of its interest, its plot is by no means at loose ends. With very considerable skill the author gathers together the rather dispersed material into a consistent and unforced unity. A reality of characterization and a fresh, unpretentious style make the novel pleasant reading.

## Montgomery Book Is Good Reading
*Spokane Chronicle* (Spokane, WA)

Characters in New Novel Are Clearly Drawn by Clever Writer

The sort of people one feels he should like to know are the types that comprise the characters of *Anne's House of Dreams*, a new book by L.M. Montgomery, published by Stokes. They are well and clearly drawn, likewise, so the reader feels he does know them by the time he has completed the book.

The story is one of a seashore settlement on Prince Edward Island, and tells of the early married life of a young doctor and his bride, with their first baby.

It is unfortunate that Mr. Montgomery felt called upon to expend so many of his first pages in reference to events that have supposedly gone before in the life of the heroine, and to characters who have appeared in earlier books dealing with former adventures of Anne.

One might have hoped that when Elsie Dinsmore of hallowed memory expired her last, after having been celebrated in unnumbered volumes, and Little Rollo had globe-trotted his juvenile life away, this sort of thing were to be spared the fiction reader.[22] It makes one feel like he might to be set down in a company of total strangers and be forced to listen to their personal gossip of intimate friends, unknown to him.

After one is permitted to forget these earlier experiences and friends, however, and once is fairly launched into the story, he finds it worth having waited for.

## [Delightful and Womanly Novel]
### *The Scotsman* (Edinburgh, UK)

Those readers who are best qualified to make the most of the charming heroine in Miss L.M. Montgomery's delightful and womanly novel, *Anne's House of Dreams*, probably know her already, for she has appeared in prior novels by the same author. But in this novel she begins where most heroines leave off. She gets married in the opening chapters, and is brought home by her husband to a small house near the sea in Prince Edward Island, to share his fate and fortunes as a busy doctor there. They live in a house which, even realistically regarded, is fascinating, but which takes on a peculiar charm from its mistress's dreams and from the stories, romantic and interesting, that centre in it as the abode from which she exercises a motherly influence, both within and without its walls. The story illustrates also with a rare and tender radiance of spirit some usual and unusual incidents of domesticity.

## [Fresh, Charming, but Sentimental Anne]
### *The Times Literary Supplement* (London, UK)

Readers of *Anne of Green Gables* and *Anne of Avonlea* will here find Miss Anne Shirley happily settled as the wife of Dr. Gilbert Blythe in her new home at Four Winds Harbour, 60 miles away, but still in Prince Edward Island. Though a little inclined to be sentimental, Anne remains a fresh and charming character with a saving grace of humour, and she has the good fortune to be provided by Miss Montgomery with an unusual number of human and interesting neighbours. But while as an ex-school teacher she may be excused for a fondness for making poetical quotations, sometimes with the name of the author solemnly stated, it seems rather incongruous to find an old seaman, whose spelling and grammar were both "sadly askew,"[23] dragging in an allusion to Tennyson.

## An Island Heroine
### *The Globe* (London, UK)

The Prince Edward Island novelist, Miss L.M. Montgomery, instantly created an English circle of admirers by her first story, *Anne of Green Gables*, because of the instinctive sympathy which our island race always feels towards an island people, and because her tender and graceful fancy revealed a branch of her own family which, although the broad Atlantic has long rolled between us, reveal so many quaint and homely likenesses to the Motherland. *Anne's House of Dreams* is not the first sequel with the same heroine, who is now married and having her babes, but she is still as charming and interesting as ever.

## [The Story of Anne's Happy-Ever-After]
### *Punch, or the London Charivari* (London, UK)

*Anne's House of Dreams* strikes me as a good example of what I might call the Economical Sequel. You will take my meaning when I explain that Miss L.M. MONTGOMERY, having safely – and to my recollection very agreeably – got her heroine, *Anne*, engaged in a previous volume, expends no fewer than sixty pages of the present over her marriage and settling-down. Moreover, with a wedding so diffuse it is safe guessing in fiction of this kind that in due course another interesting event may be expected to demand its meed of chapters. As indeed is the case here, and not only once. For the rest, the story of *Anne's* happy-ever-after is a record of no very sensational events in the charming scenery (caught by Miss MONTGOMERY with equal sympathy and skill) of the St. Lawrence Gulf. What drama there is has to be supplied by *Anne's* neighbours, especially beautiful *Mrs. Moore*, whose husband, after making her miserable, ran away to sea, but was unfortunately restored to her some time later, childish from brain injury. More unfortunately still, *Anne's* husband, being a doctor, saw that a simple operation would restore the smiling imbecile to his original capacities – which of course was precisely the last thing that his wife or anybody else in the least wanted. However, he had his way, and behold, when they got (so to speak) to *Mr. Moore's* vital spark, they found – but in spite of almost overwhelming temptation I will not spoil the one situation in the story by telling you what they found. Anyhow, they found a comfortable end to a pretty tale – a tale, however, which neither in style nor scheme can I regard as quite worthy of the quotation from RUPERT BROOKE that forms its text.[24]

## A Canadian Idyll
### *The Saturday Review* (London, UK)

This little romance is played out to the wholesome motto of right is might, in a Canadian fishing village among simple lovable people. The book, we gather, is a sequel to *Anne of Green Gables* and *Anne of Avonlea*, and it tells the story of Anne's early married life at Four Winds Harbour. We are ashamed to confess that this is our first introduction to Anne, and we regret that we missed the opportunity of knowing her earlier. We like her gift of intimacy, and the friends with which she fills her house of dreams. There is about them something of the flavour and the fragrance which we have always thought of as belonging to New England characters. If you were of their circle you would most likely be called Job, or Dave or Eliphalet, or, if you were a woman, Marilla, or Persis, or Cordelia. When you wanted to emphasize a remark, you would ejaculate "believe *me*!" and when you were angry you would say you were "real mad." You would make cherry-pies and frosted cakes and love your neighbour as yourself. And if you were an old maid, you would wear a chocolate print wrapper patterned in pink roses. And you would never be allowed to remain an old maid for long. Miss Montgomery's touch is delicate and sincere. She has a real feeling for the haunting magic of the sea, and a real love for human beings. In her book she makes us realize both.

## NOTES

1 *The Boston Post* (Boston, MA), review of *Anne's House of Dreams*, 1 September 1917, in SR, 116; *San Jose Mercury Herald*, review of *Anne's House of Dreams*, 6; *Liverpool Courier* (Liverpool, UK), review of *Anne's House of Dreams*, 8 May 1918, in SR, 105; *The Chicago Daily Tribune*, review of *Anne's House of Dreams*, 7; *The New York World* (New York, NY), "Her 'House of Dreams,'" review of *Anne's House of Dreams*, 26 August 1917, in SR, 114.

2 *The Bookseller, Newsdealer and Stationer*, review of *Anne's House of Dreams*, 205; *The American Jewish Chronicle*, review of *Anne's House of Dreams*, 141; *The Mail and Empire*, "Pleasant Little Tale though Very Light," 19; *The Mail and Empire*, "Canadian Writers and a Year's Work," 19; *The Brooklyn Daily Eagle* (Brooklyn, NY), review of *Anne's House of Dreams*, 8 September 1917, in SR, 123.

3 *Pittsburgh Chronicle Telegraph* (Pittsburgh, PA), review of *Anne's House of Dreams*, 31 August 1917, in SR, 111; review of *Anne's House of Dreams*, unidentified periodical (Grand Rapids, MI), 27 October 1917, in SR, 98; *Cincinnati Enquirer* (Cincinnati, OH), review of *Anne's House of Dreams*, 3 September 1917, in SR, 116; Baird Leonard, review of *Anne's House of Dreams*, *The Morning Telegraph* (New York, NY), 8 September 1917, in SR, 111; "Another Story Concerning Anne," review of *Anne's House of Dreams*, unidentified clipping, 22 June 1918, in SR, 126; review of *Anne's House of Dreams*, unidentified and undated clipping, in SR, 95. The title of chapter 31 of *Anne of Green Gables*, "Where the Brook and River Meet," alludes to the poem "Maidenhood" by Henry Wadsworth Longfellow (1807–1882), American poet.

4 *Anne of Green Gables* was, in fact, published in June 1908.

5 Here and throughout, I have corrected the original, which reads "Lester Moore."

6 I have corrected the original, which reads "'Anne of the Green Gables.'"

7 I have corrected the original, which reads "sharp saying," "and tinged," "house of dream."

8 Montgomery selected the line "the thoughts of youth are long, long thoughts," from Henry Wadsworth Longfellow's (1807–1882) poem "My Lost Youth," as the epigraph for her later novel *Rainbow Valley*.

9 See "*Anne of Green Gables*," note 7, above. Charlotte Yonge (1823–1901), English editor and author of numerous novels, including *The Heir of Redclyffe* (1853).

10 I have corrected the original, which reads "Prince Edward's Island."

11 Here and below, I have corrected the original, which reads "Marshall Eliot."

12 *AHD*, 20.

13 I have corrected the original, which reads "'Anne of Green-gables'" and "Prince Edward's Island."

14 *AHD*, 39.

15 When Anne asks Miss Cornelia why the latter "hate[s] the men so," Miss Cornelia replies, "Lord, dearie, I don't hate them ... I just sort of despise them" (*AHD*, 48).

16 Alcott's *Little Women* was published in two volumes in 1868 and 1869, the second of which is frequently known as *Good Wives*, particularly in England.

17 I have corrected the original, which reads "'Captain Jo'" and "'Aunt Cordelia.'"

18 *AHD*, 4.

19 I have corrected the original, which reads "Prince Edward's Island."

20 I have corrected the original, which reads "Prince Edward's Island."

21 *AHD*, 30.

22 See "*Anne of Avonlea*," note 16, above. Jacob Abbott (1803–1879), an American children's author, published ten volumes about the character Rollo between 1853 and 1858, beginning with *Rollo on the Atlantic*.

23 *AHD*, 105.

24 The original edition of *Anne's House of Dreams* uses as its epigraph a quotation from "The Song of the Pilgrims," a poem by Rupert Brooke (1887–1915), English poet: "Our kin / Have built them temples, and therein / pray to the gods we know; and dwell in little houses lovable."

# 10

## *Rainbow Valley*

—— 1919 ——

Reviews of this book focusing on Anne's children were largely positive, yet the subtext of the Great War went largely unnoticed. The Philadelphia *Evening Public Ledger* called it "wholesome and entertaining to all who do not want highly spiced fiction and are content with the simple joys and sorrows of everyday folk in the country," whereas the *Boston Herald* noted of the characters that "our author makes amusing play of their impulsive activities and interwoven episodes of neighborhood life." Orphaned Mary Vance received particular mention in the *San Jose Mercury Herald* as "a character to captivate and astonish fiction readers everywhere," whereas the London periodical *The Lady* proclaimed that "this writer strikes a note of sunshine and charm which makes her books a joy to read, and there is no one who can excel her in a sympathetic delineation of the character of the young girl." Perhaps not surprisingly, reviews of *Rainbow Valley* started to express minor fatigue with Anne and what Montgomery referred to as a certain "type" of story: as the London *Observer* noted,

One knows the "Anne of Green Gables" mixture by this time. It is feeblish, but not always entirely feeble; saccharine but with an occasional touch of the salt of humour; sentimental, but not consistently or wearily so. It appeals by its pleasant mediocrity to a large circle of people who like to weep a very little, smile gently often, laugh outright just now and then, and not be roused to face anything perplexing, much less anything grim. Without the grim and the perplexing you cannot get the thing called life; but facts prove that you can get a highly successful work of fiction.

Moreover, as *The Family Herald and Weekly Star* noted, the novel "harps too much on the same old string, the mischievous and useful happenings of little girls, to be altogether pleasing to those who have followed the writings of the clever Prince Edward Island writer." A review in the *Boston Evening Transcript* suggested that Montgomery "has come into her own," but added that "perhaps this is because she has succeeded in keeping the excellent Anne almost entirely out of it, and has dealt with wickeder people."[1]

## The Manse Children
### *The Publishers' Weekly* (New York, NY)
#### CHRISTINE McALLISTER

*Anne of Green Gables* put Prince Edward Island, the smallest of Canada's maritime provinces, on the fiction map and later "Anne" stories have persistently kept it there. Here is another "Anne" story in which Miss Montgomery has succeeded in recapturing some of the elements which made her first book such a popular success. She is at her best in creating without exaggeration delightfully natural children – naughty or rather lively ones, in particular – and in reflecting with an insight not always found in the native writer the rural life of her beloved Island. The present book keeps the adults well in the background and confines itself for scene to a little village near Anne's first Island home.

Anne Shirley, now in village parlance Mrs. Dr. Blythe, has six healthy youngsters who figure in the story and contribute the title, their own name for their favorite playground, but it is the manse family of four which holds the center of the stage. Now minister's children are always entertaining in fiction and the Merediths are no exception, not because they have to scrimp and save to keep up appearances, but because the word "appearances" is not in their vocabulary at all.

Of course the goings on of this motherless neglected brood excite much unfavorable comment both in their father's own Presbyterian flock and among the rival denomination, the Methodist, but even their most serious escapades, such as cleaning the house very conspicuously on Sunday and drowning out the Methodist prayer meeting with a rival concert, including secular songs, are always capable of explanation. But it is "The Good Conduct Club," organized by the children to bring themselves up since there was no one else to do it, as they remarked, that finally roused their affectionate but absent-minded father to providing a proper person, and here enters the romance.

The Meredith children are a jolly engaging set of youngsters who are likely to have a large following among youthful and older readers.

## [A Story of Love and Life]
### *The Philadelphia Inquirer* (Philadelphia, PA)

*Rainbow Valley*, by Mrs. L.M. Montgomery, is a story complete in itself, but it has the advantage of telling something more of the history of Anne of Avonlea, who by this time is a mother. The story is laid in the same old haunts in Prince Edward Island,[2] which is interestedly known to more Americans through her stories than through all the geographies studied and promptly forgotten.

Mrs. Montgomery has a charming outlook on life. She is not hyper-sentimental or gushy, she does not take pictures of things for the things themselves and she knows the true value of the emotions in human life as well as their limitations. This story has clever people, mostly young, but some are old friends now grown older and they give a picture of life which is illuminating and helpful. A story of love and life.

## [Nothing Wild or Thrilling]
### *The Chicago Daily Tribune* (Chicago, IL)

*Rainbow Valley*, L.M. Montgomery's latest novel, continues the Anne of Green Gables tales. Anne's six children and four young neighbors are the characters of the wholesome, romantic little story. There's nothing wild nor thrilling about Miss Montgomery's stories, but neither are they the sort of books which must be locked away when mother comes home from the country.

## Prince Edward Island Tale
### *Trenton Times–Advertiser* (Trenton, NJ)

*Rainbow Valley* is an independent story, able to stand by itself, but for those who have been reading Miss L.M. Montgomery's previous fiction there is the added pleasure of renewing some old acquaintance-ships. Again we have the charming figure of Anne and of other people of Prince Edward Island. Miss Montgomery is devotedly attached to the old home surroundings. Her new tale, *Rainbow Valley*, deals with the adventures of the four children of Anne of Green Gables, married, as everyone knows, to Gilbert Blythe,[3] and with the pranks of the motherless children of the pastor of the Presbyterian Church in the village. Rainbow Valley is a playground for the children and the meeting place for lovers. The children of the minister are natural, prankish youngsters, always getting into mischief. The people in the village think he ought to marry again in order to have someone to bring up the children. What plot the story has revolves around this second marriage.

Of course, it's all a fairy story, but it's a fairy story out of real life. These are real children and real men and women; they do wrong things and they do right things, but one and all they recognize that first principle of happy living, that love will heal and help and strengthen and console, and that without love life is an empty thing at best. It is a cheerful, wholesome book with a delightful outlook upon life.

Miss Montgomery, as she prefers to be known to the outside public, was born in Prince Edward Island. She was educated at the public schools there and at the local college. She taught school for three years, then engaged in newspaper work and wrote short stories and novels and finally married the Rev. Ewan Macdonald,[4] now the pastor of the Presbyterian Churches in Leaskdale and Zephyr, Ontario, two small villages about 15 miles south of Lake Simcoe.

## [Another Story of Prince Edward Island]
### *The Sun* (New York, NY)
CONSTANCE MURRAY GREENE

*Rainbow Valley*, by L.M. Montgomery, the author of *Anne of Green Gables* and several other Anne books, is another story of Prince Edward Island, in which Anne once more takes a wholesome hand, though a light one. She has not been idle during the years, as her six children will prove, but she is as sweet and as understanding – and as insipid, if you will allow the discourtesy – as she ever was. However, she plays a small part here, as do her children. The four young Merediths, motherless and indigenous to the village manse, are more prominently featured, and the book develops into a romance of their absent minded father. There is an orphan also, discovered by the combined youngsters starving in a deserted barn, and a rooster named Adam, pet of Faith Meredith and enemy of the entire parish. He is responsible for a large part of the humor of the book.

"Adam shooed. He was a wise rooster and Mrs. Davis had wrung the necks of so many roosters with her own fair hands in the course of her fifty years that an air of the executioner seemed to hang around her."[5]

The book is easy to read, though not enthralling. We are of the opinion that Anne's day is done and that she is now entitled to rest in peace. She has had a long life and a happy one, as lives are measured in fiction, but now her presence is a hindrance to any story.

## [More Distinctly a Novel]
### *The Outlook* (New York, NY)

The author of *Anne of Green Gables* shows in this book, as in her other popular stories, an unusual knowledge of girls' character, a cheerful spirit, and a sense of humor. This is less distinctly a girls' book and more distinctly a novel, properly speaking, than some of its predecessors.

## [A Homey Charm]
### *The New York Times Book Review* (New York, NY)

It is nearly a dozen years since Miss Montgomery, who is now, in private life, Mrs. Ewen Macdonald, began writing her series of stories about the character and life of Anne Shirley. Through some four or five volumes she has carried the tale, through girlhood, young womanhood and love, marriage and the making of a home on the shores of Four Winds Harbor, Prince Edward Island.[6] In this latest story she has carried the picture of Anne Shirley's developing life forward to the time when half a dozen children, the oldest of whom has arrived at the dignity of thirteen sturdy years, fill their home. The story takes its name from a delectable valley near their house in which these children love to play, especially at eveningtide, when it takes on a fairy-like enchantment. Much of the action of the story takes place in this lovely glen, part of it concerned with the doings of Anne's children and their playmates and part of it with the affairs of their elders, in which also the children are more or less entangled.

It is a pretty story, enlivened with much talk and play, innocent roguery and eager interest in life of a dozen children, part of them Anne's, part of them the new minister's, and one a naughty waif who pops up in the community and develops great ingenuity and energy in the matter of keeping things in general well stirred up. The children are all strongly individualized and each one is portrayed carefully and made to keep his own place in the picture. Miss Montgomery's thousands of admiring readers will welcome many of their old acquaintances whom they have delighted to meet in her previous books. There are also some new people whom the neighborhood takes into its arms and at once begins, after its friendly fashion, to arrange their lives and futures. They are very amusing in their efforts to settle the future of the widowed new minister with his houseful of children. And there is much humor in the conversation and incidents which the author narrates in detail. The reader feels that she loves all these people whom she has created and that she takes keen delight in writing about them. They are racy of their region, each one a sturdy bit of individualism and a true son or daughter of their island soil. The book has a homey charm and its descriptions of the region are likely to make all its readers wish to visit Prince Edward Island.

## [Clean and Healthy Country Life]
*Manitoba Free Press* (Winnipeg, MB)

In *Rainbow Valley*, L.M. Montgomery has given us another comedy of clean and healthy country life in Prince Edward Island. Anne, the erstwhile heroine of Green Gables, is there with all the old charm and winsomeness – but not conspicuously there. Her children and the children of the Manse are the main figures, every one of them lovable children, hearty and happy and original as most children are if not too much pampered. Faith Meredith of the Manse, reminds me of Miss Alcott's immortal Jo, and no more need be said about this most delightful child. Her brother Carl is an embryo naturalist, and typical of the average boy in that. All the children of the two houses take up most of the story, though the church and the community are cleverly inwrought. The Presbyterian pastor is an absent-minded, gentle-souled scholar and widower whose children are left to their own wild, but innocent devices; and there is a love element whose heroine is very attractive in person and in character. Rainbow Valley is a lovely glen where the children play and fish in a well-stocked lake.[7] The hills about look out to the sea.

This is a pleasant, wholesome tale to be recommended to all families where there are children. Miss Montgomery has done for her native island-province precisely what Miss Alcott did for her New England home. There are several very neat psychological touches, and no child is too good, not even Una, for human nature's daily food.

## Some Original Children
*The Post* (New York, NY)

For good measure, Anne of Green Gables appears again in this story amid the pleasant surroundings, the woods, the countryside and the sea of Prince Edward Island,[8] so that the readers of the author's previous tales may feel at home. But as Anne with the years has grown mature and is now the mother of a brood of half a dozen youngsters or so, she is kept in the background with the rest of the grown-ups. It is not even her children who occupy the centre of the stage, though they are the discoverers of a delightful valley which they fill with mystery and adventure. The chief actors are the children of an amazingly absent-minded clergyman, who is a widower and has allowed his offspring to grow up haphazard; chief among them are his two little daughters.

The clergyman, on account of his own absent-mindedness as well as the remarkable performances of his offspring, is regarded with disfavor by a good many of his congregation; in spite of his living in the clouds he manages to fall in love with a desirable spinster, who promises to become the sort of mother the children need. The love story, however, is merely a sop to the tastes of grown-up readers; the real interest lies in the doings of the children. The most striking of these is the older daughter, an independent young person of a dozen years, who is obliged to think things out for herself unduly, owing to her father's peculiarity. She is very amusing, particularly in her startling attempts to set things right, as when she gets up in church at the close of the service and addresses the congregation in explanation of her supposed wrongdoings, or when she sends an extremely frank letter on what is going on among the church people to the local newspaper.

There is a keen-witted and very outspoken little girl from the foundling asylum; there are Anne's poetic boy and the clergyman's little naturalist; there are his smallest girl with her motherly and housewifely instincts and the other bright children, all of whom the reader will like. On all the boys falls a slight shadow of the coming war in which all of Canada's youth is to engage, but that is the author's only allusion to matters beyond her beloved island, and it is in perfectly good taste. Those who have enjoyed the previous "Anne" books will like this one also.

## Sure to Be Liked
### *The New York Herald* (New York, NY)

Miss L.M. Montgomery is sure of her public, although it is a distinctively feminine one, and she who reads *Anne of Green Gables* is pretty certain to let slip no chance of further acquaintance with that delightful young person. In *Rainbow Valley* the scene is shifted from Avonlea to Four Winds Harbor, where Anne, now Mrs. Gilbert Blythe, lives with her husband, the local doctor, and her six children. As is often the case in fiction, though seldom in real life, the interest in a character lessens as time goes on. Anne as a child is delightful; as a woman she is more commonplace and the author, perhaps realizing this, has introduced six Blythe children, four belonging to the Presbyterian minister, and a sharp young waif from the asylum who is the best character in the book. Truth to tell, there is not much that is original in the story. It principally concerns the pranks played by the minister's children, a lively quartette, whose mother is dead and whose father is the learned, absent minded character familiar to all novel readers, so absorbed in his books that his children are left much to their own devices. They are full of life and invention and are continually scandalizing the parish, not only by their goings-on, but still more by their efforts to rehabilitate themselves. One of their performances so horrifies the community that Faith, the eldest little girl, deems it her duty to rise in church while the collection is being taken up and explain matters. On another occasion she comes to church with shoes on but no stockings, this time putting her position before the public in a long letter to the local paper, containing much irrelevant but amusing matter. Of course there is but one way to correct such a state of things and after some difficulties the minister follows it. The descriptions of scenery in the book are really beautiful and it is sure to be read and liked.

## [A Clever Woman Novelist]
### *The Canadian Bookman* (Ste. Anne de Bellevue, QC)

It is perhaps significant of the present state of the Canadian novel that it is much better practiced by women than by men. While the men, following the lead of Ralph Connor, are endeavoring to achieve Canadianism by specialising on the different kinds of fist-fights which occur in different parts of the Dominion, the women are devoting their attention to securing the corresponding national coloring by a depiction of the scenery and the domestic manners of various sections of rural Canada; and of the two subject-matters we are bound to admit that the women's appears to be much the more characteristic of the country. Neither class of novel goes very deep into the essential qualities of Canadian life, but the picture presented by the women is not more sentimental than that of the men and is much truer and more representative.

It may be that the ablest male writers of fiction are lured away from Canada by the superior attractions of the literary field in the United States, while the women, less mobile by nature and circumstance, remain with us, so that the female output in fiction represents the best of which the country is capable while the male output is, with few exceptions, merely the leavings of a process of selection which exports the cream and lets Canada keep the skim milk. Or it may be (but we do not believe it) that life in Canada is less interesting and stimulating to the male mind than to the female, less adapted to male treatment, less productive of the big clashes of character which appeal to the able male novelist. Or it may be that the Canadian public is not yet ready for the stern masculine view of its own life and problems (or that the publishers think it isn't) and that the women writers are cleverer at imparting that roseate tinge which is desired by the unsophisticated reader.

Anyhow, here are four novels, all of them from the autumn list of a single publishing house, all of them about Canadian life and all written by Canadian women; and each one of them in varying degree an honest, presentable piece of workmanship. The best of them, it is true, is the least Canadian. Miss Montgomery, who has long since taken rank as one of the most accomplished of living writers in conveying the elusive charm of healthy family life in which imaginative children and young people are included, has written a tale of the motherless family of a Presbyterian minister, which might doubtless be duplicated in almost any part of this continent – or anywhere else where narrow-minded people exist to take a wrong view of childish purity and ingenuousness. There is less of the characteristic quality of Prince Edward Island in this book than in any of its predecessors, but in other respects it is the equal if not the superior of anything that Miss Montgomery has done, and we know of no writer in the English language who could excel it in delicacy and charm. Beneath the elusiveness and the atmospheric charm of the Montgomery tales there is a wonderful firmness of character-drawing. She never repeats herself; every adult and every youngster whom she introduces is sketched before the reader's mind in a few lines, by little character-revealing actions and utterances, and every one is distinct and separate and consistent. Every

novelist knows how difficult it is to make children stand out as human individuals, but in these three hundred pages or so Miss Montgomery does
this for ten or a dozen of the most lovable and scandalous youngsters
who ever got together in one volume. They elbow into the background a
bunch of adults who would be interesting enough if the youngsters were
not so much more so; and they leave us with a determination to get a
sequel out of their author by hook or by crook, so that we may find out
what becomes of them after they grow up and the Great War has come
to darken their young lives. "Anne" is present in this tale, but only in the
very remote background, and so is Miss Cornelia, with her illuminating
summings-up of every character in the village. And there are a few lovely
bits of description. Is the charming term "cat's light" for twilight a Prince
Edward Islandism or has it wider acceptance?[9]

[* * *][10]

## [Between Sprightly and Pastoral]
### *The Dial* (New York, NY)

*Rainbow Valley*, by L.M. Montgomery, is a story in the gentle jog trot
between sprightly and pastoral; it carries on the tradition of the same
writer's *Anne of Green Gables*.

## [Human and Wholesome, with No Morbidity]
### *The Post Express* (Rochester, NY)

Those who have read Miss Montgomery's idyllic stories *Anne of Green
Gables* and *Anne's House of Dreams* will find in *Rainbow Valley* the
same peculiar charm and the same knowledge of what is best in human
nature which characterized these exquisite tales of Prince Edward Island.
Anne, now married and the mother of several children, figures in this narrative. "Miss Cornelia," as she is persistently called after thirteen years of
wedlock, and Susan Baker, the "gray and grim and faithful handmaiden"
of the Blythe family at Ingleside,[11] supply Anne with enough gossip to
suffice for a year of ordinary life.

But the chief interest in the story centers around the family of the
Rev. Mr. Meredith, the minister of Glen St. Mary, wild boys and girls
who innocently romp among tombstones and a queer little girl named
Mary Vance whom the minister's children find starving in a barn. They

bring the waif into the pantry of the manse, and get her some bread, butter, milk and pie which she greedily devours. Then Mary tells them her history in the graveyard. She had run away from a woman named Mrs. Wiley who had worked her nearly to death and beaten her. Mary is the offspring of unfortunate parents and had been brought up in an orphan asylum. The adoption of the waif by these nice children is one of the finest touches of spontaneous humanity in the story. The minister is too much of a dreamer and an idealist to investigate his children's proceedings. And so it happens that Mary stays at the manse.

Everything that one can think of is discussed in the book by these precocious youngsters, including heaven, hell, Germany and the kaiser. Mr. Meredith is one of those ministers who read even German theology. Faith, his independent little daughter, declares that she will never marry a minister. The reader will find her an interesting personality, and will also want to know what happened to Mary Vance. But this is one of the secrets of Rainbow Valley which are disclosed in Miss Montgomery's beautiful story. The petty squabbles between the Episcopalians, Presbyterians and Methodists of the parish furnish as much fun as George Eliot could have made out of a similar theme. Some rigidly religious persons may object to such matters being dealt with humorously. However, Miss Montgomery is really as reverent as she is natural. In the closing chapter we have the children's version of Browning's "Pied Piper," and we also have that spice of matrimony which somehow all feminine readers love.

*Rainbow Valley* is a human and essentially wholesome tale – one of the few contemporary works of fiction in which there is no morbidity.

## Just Bubbling Over with Whimsical Humor
### *The Boston Globe* (Boston, MA)

*Rainbow Valley*, by L.M. Montgomery, offers the reader 340 pages of pure delight, for the story is as fresh and sparkling as a late October morn, and just bubbling over with the most delicious sort of humor. The scenes are laid in a small community in Prince Edward Island. There is a Presbyterian minister, a widower and his children. It is their long succession of innocent, childish pranks that keeps the reader chuckling, and the Methodist and Presbyterian cohorts of the village in a ferment of laughter or indignation, according to which side is hardest hit. Then there are other well drawn characters, a touch of romance, and just once a touch of sentiment and pathos that is sure to draw tears of sympathy. The author understands human nature and child nature, too, and has written with a keenness of insight and sympathy, embellished with the most wholesome humor. The story is of the kind you wish to tell your friends about.

## [An Infinite Charm All Its Own]
### *The Oregonian* (Portland, OR)

With scenes set in a lovely, quiet, rural district of Prince Edward Island, Canada, and with the principal people the children of a clergyman – this novel has an infinite charm all its own. Rainbow Valley, in the story, must be a charming place in which to live – in the delightful, quiet days, previous to the big war.

## Latest "Anne of Green Gables" Story
### *The Dallas Morning News* (Dallas, TX)

Admirers of *Anne of Green Gables* will gladly learn of another book about their beloved heroine. In this new book Anne is the mother of six interesting children. We find here the same wholesome, happy atmosphere that we find in the earlier stories, and we think that there can be no doubt that the demand for such books springs from some actual need.

## [Back to the Old Ground]
### *The Scotsman* (Edinburgh, UK)

In life and character in the province of Prince Edward Island, and in the gossip, romance, and humour of little coasting places like Four Winds Harbour, the author of *Anne of Green Gables* seems to find an inexhaustible field of material for her pen. We are brought back again in *Rainbow Valley* to the old ground and to the old society, with the elders grown a little more mature, and a young generation cropping up and preparing to make romances of their own. *Rainbow Valley* is a secluded spot, where Anne's children delight to escape to, and where they begin the building of a new set of "houses of dreams," their seniors looking on benignantly or frowningly, according to their nature and their upbringing.

## [Still the Same Person]
### *The Times Literary Supplement* (London, UK)

Anne has survived several volumes. Though many times a parent, she is still the same person; and when in this number the wholesome career of the family is projected one stage further, the old sweetness and simplicity still characterize the narrative. Home life in Prince Edward Island, as indicated by the authoress, is similar to home life elsewhere, only brighter. The pleasure which the "grown-ups" take in discussing one another's pranks by the page shows that they all have good hearts. Anne's will be a slow, happy, and peaceful obsolescence.

## [Might Have Been Worse]
### *The Outlook* (London, UK)

One's general impression on finishing *Rainbow Valley* is that it might have been much worse. When you get a writer of the Kate Douglas Wiggin blend of sentiment let loose on the subject of two families of children, one motherless, you are apt to get something as sticky as treacle. *Rainbow Valley*, of course, has some treacled moments. The valley itself is smeared with it, and the love affair between the preacher Meredith and Rosemary West glistens with it,[12] and most of the self-conscious efforts at self-improvement of the Meredith children. But there is a little maidservant who succeeds in comporting some much-needed salt into the mixture, and some really rather delightful moments, when Walter the poet begins telling ghost stories and fights the village bully. Another is when the children clean house on a Sunday, having mistaken the day of the week, and also when they hold a sacred concert in a jungly, disused churchyard, working themselves so successfully into the shivers that they sing *Polly-wolly-woodle* in order to recover their spirits,[13] to the total destruction of their reputation in the neighbourhood. On the whole, it would appear that Canadian village life is a quintessence of all village life, except that in Canada there appears to be little hope that anyone will take interest in archaeology or botany or something else besides their neighbours' doings. Consequently, thrones are "fine and private places"[14] compared to the homes of doctors and ministers scrutinised by critical eyes made keener by sectarian jealousy. That is obviously not the impression Miss Montgomery intends to leave, but she leaves it nonetheless.[15]

In sum, *Rainbow Valley* might be worse, as has been stated. But when will people learn that childhood, in its charm and pathos, demands above all other subjects restraint in its literary treatment?

## [The Relentless Logic of Childhood]
*The Glasgow Herald* (Glasgow, UK)

*Rainbow Valley* is a book about children written for lovers of children by an authoress who knows how to portray the relentless logic of childhood hidden in apparent inconsequence, and the charm of much that less imaginative people find mere tiresome naughtiness. A slender plot holds together the novel, but the chief interest lies in the doings of the motherless manse children, running wild under the eyes of their absent-minded father and the less astonishing pranks of the Blythe family, in whose mother many readers will greet an old friend, "Anne of Green Gables." Susan, the devoted nurse at Ingleside,[16] is almost too good to be true, even in this idyllic world of Rainbow Valley, and the authoress never succeeds in making her quite convincing.

## A Group of Children
*Glasgow News* (Glasgow, UK)

Miss L.M. Montgomery has added one more to her now lengthy series of stories about a group of children in Prince Edward Island. Her public, which loves her special combination of humour and sentiment, will be delighted with the addition *Rainbow Valley*, and it is really wonderful how she keeps up her brightness and inventiveness without any appearance of forcing. Her children are just as quaintly charming as ever, and she is wise enough to keep the love-story in its proper place, which is strictly subordinate to the demands of these refreshingly original youngsters.

## [A Story of Old World Days]
*The Times of India Illustrated Weekly* (Mumbai, India)

*Rainbow Valley* is the story of a group of Canadian children. It belongs to the old world days when repression not expression was the educational policy adopted towards children. The children of Rainbow Valley were expected to be good, even obedient; a demand which in Montessorian ears sounds almost ghoulish in its invasion of human personality. Needless to say the children were not good, or there would have been no story, but they had all the fun of contravening a moral law, which the modern child with his law-unto-himself upbringing misses. They lived in a constant succession of scrapes, far more awful and exciting than the savourless experiments in self-development of the unrepressed child. They defied the lightning under the impression that Zeus still existed. They watched the on-goings of grown-up people with an idea that grown-ups were of some consequence, and their lives more real than a phantasmagoria of twittering ghosts. The four motherless children of an absent-minded saint have the leading parts in the story. Their father, Mr. Meredith, is a parson, and the cavillings of the rival denominations in a small country-town form a not very humorous setting to the children's escapades.[17] There is a tiresome outspoken old servant who addresses her mistress as "Mrs. Dr. dear" much oftener than is really funny. Most of the humour is on the level of the old servant, but the children are real and charming, especially the sisters Faith and Una, whose endeavours to bring them-selves up (according to the moral code and in the absence of any one else to do so) are both pathetic and amusing. Faith's nonchalant defiance of the Rainbow Valley code and her light-hearted contempt for grown-up propriety lead her into tragedy after tragedy, but fortunately there is a "Dea ex machina" in the shape of the tender-hearted Una who finally, without consulting her father, makes the most delightful spinster in the Parish an offer of marriage on his behalf, so that all is well that ends well.

## [An Absurd Review]
### *The New Age* (London, UK)

We forget what is the chief industry of Prince Edward Island, but Miss Montgomery's manufacture of sentimental fiction is well worth consid-eration in this respect. Imagine a Free Church community all interested in the doings of its minister, imagine that minister a scholar, absent-minded, and a widower with some children, imagine those children to possess the ecstatic qualities (let us say) of the early Christians, add a spinster with maternal feelings and a few cross-currents in them to delay the dénouement, and the story almost writes itself. There is no local, or any other, colour in the story, although "the light that never was on land or sea" except in the best traditions of the Sunday-school movement shines faithfully through Rainbow Valley.[18] Everyone is blue – a most spiritual colour; and "Nokes outdoes Stokes in azure feats: both gorge."[19] Faith has two passages of really delightful humour, her explanation in church of the mistake she and the other children made in doing housework on Sunday, and a letter to the local paper in which she explained why she went to church without wearing stockings; but for the rest, the story touches humanity at the preposterous angle of conventional piety, and has the indefinite universalism of the Mothers' Guild.[20]

## [The Gift of Humour]
### Unidentified clipping
AUSTIN BOTHWELL

L.M. Montgomery ranks, for me, far and away above Sir Gilbert Parker or Ralph Connor or Charles G.D. Roberts as an interpreter of Canadian life, as a realist.[21] I do not say that she tells a better story than these eminent authors, nor that her style is more pleasing (though it is so far as the first two are concerned), but she knows the Canadian people better, gets far closer to their hearts, sees more clearly their faults and their excellencies than they do. But, except for the rather excessive measure of sentiment in her books in *Anne's House of Dreams*, especially where the very title is cloyingly sweet, she presents Canadian life in her stories as it is lived and as we, plain ordinary, everyday Canadians live it and see it lived all about us. Then L.M. Montgomery has a gift strikingly lacking in her more famous fellow craftsmen. It is the gift of humor. This it was which made her first successful book so delightful and won from Mark Twain whole-hearted approval. In a letter to a friend the great humorist wrote, "Anne of Green Gables is the sweetest creation of child life yet written." High praise, indeed! Our author is at her happiest in portraying the humors of child life and *Rainbow Valley* is an especially good example of her power in this line for it has eleven children in it. Six of these are Anne's, a cheerful, well-cared for flock, four are the Presbyterian minister's, just as cheerful but not so well-cared-for as they have lost their mother and the old cousin of their father's mother, who is his housekeeper, is totally incompetent, so that they run wild. The eleventh is Mary Vance, a "Home" girl who has run away from a cruel mistress and is befriended by the manse children, all unknown to their father, who is a book-worm. The manse children get into all sorts of mischief and completely scandalise the little village of Glen St. Mary. Faith Meredith one cannot but like. She is an engaging little miss of eleven, with golden-brown eyes, golden-brown curls and crimson cheeks, who wears her beauty like a rose and laughs too much to please her father's congregation. She is as original as sin, impetuous, spirited, "full of spunk she's bursting with it,"[22] as Norman Douglas, the caretaker, non-church-going widower, declares after she has told him exactly what she thinks of him. While her father is away she and Una, her younger sister, clean house on Sunday by mistake, owing to the Methodist prayer meeting being held on Wednesday instead of Thursday evening. When the enormity of their offense is brought home to them it is Faith who conceives a plan to put things straight and absolve their father from blame. Just after the collection has been taken the next Sunday evening Faith suddenly rises and makes her way to the pulpit platform to explain. Her nerve would have failed her but for Bertie Shakespeare Drew making a face at her. After setting forth how she came to mistake Saturday for Sunday, "It was all Elder Baxter's fault" (sensation in the Baxter pew) she goes on, "and then we thought we'd clean house on Monday and stop old cats from talking about how dirty the manse was ... and we did. I shook rugs in the Methodist graveyard because it was such a convenient place and not because I meant to be disrespectful to the dead. It isn't the dead folks who have made the fuss over this – it's the living folks."[23] It is a case of just one sensation after another for the distracted Presbyterians, much to their chagrin, for there is a standing rivalry between them and the Methodists in the little village, and the pranks of the manse children nullify the advantage which the Presbyterians hold over their rivals in the fact that Mr. Meredith can preach and the Methodist minister can't.

Mr. Meredith has had impressed upon him that it is his duty to marry again for his children's sake, but, though he realises his shortcomings as a father, he is too fine for such a motive to weigh with him. But a romantic encounter with Rosemary West in Rainbow Valley brings developments in its train such as one looks for in a Montgomery story: dawning love, difficulties, the overcoming of the difficulties and a happy ending.

But the salt which is the savor of the book is to be found in the tang and the poignancy of the comments upon the passing show (which the exploits of the children and the minister's romance furnish forth) of the two figures of comedy, Susan Baker and Miss Cornelia, as Mrs. Marshall Elliott continues to be called by her friends. These two good ladies are gifted with tongues as the famous Mrs. Poyser was and it is my considered opinion that as creations of the comic muse they are on an equal plane with George Eliot's masterpiece.[24] Sharp as is their speech, they are amiable withal, "beside them the comic muse," in Meredith's phrase, "is grave and sisterly."[25] When they get together, good night! as Shakespeare was wont to say. When Dr. and Mrs. Blythe return to their home after an absence of three months, it is the duty of the two gossips to put them en rapport (or courant or, even better, in touch) with all that has taken place in their absence. Their manoeuvring for position (i.e. the floor) is pure comedy. A very pleasant time "is had" by Anne and by readers of *Rainbow Valley*.

The scene is frequently repeated; the two ladies are a sort of Greek chorus except on the score of harmony and pulchritude.

It is as plain as a pikestaff that the Blythe boys and the Meredith boys will reach military age in 1914 or thereabouts. I seem to see indications that the part they play in the war and their romances will form the substance of a book to come. Walter Blythe, the dreamer of dreams, poetically inclined, will become an aviator. So long as Mrs. Macdonald[26] (L.M. Montgomery is now a minister's wife and mother of two boys) does not continue the story of Anne until her great grandchildren arrive upon the scene a la Elsie Books, I shall not repine. Anne is a real person, fashioned (it is my surmise) in the image of her creator and her family is a real live bunch of Canadians. And as such quite worth while writing about. O.E.D. in *Rainbow Valley*.

## NOTES

1 *Evening Public Ledger*, "Green Gabling with Anne," 13; Williams, review of *Rainbow Valley*, 4; *San Jose Mercury Herald*, review of *Rainbow Valley*, 6; *The Lady* (London, UK), review of *Rainbow Valley*, 23 September 1920, in SR, 172; *The Observer* (London, UK), review of *Rainbow Valley*, 4 July 1920, in SR, 128; *The Family Herald and Weekly Star* (Montreal, QC), "Another 'Green Gable Anne' Book," undated clipping, in SR, 167; *Boston Evening Transcript* (Boston, MA), "A Clergyman's Family and the Story of Its Upbringing," signed I.W.L., review of *Rainbow Valley*, 29 November 1919, in SR, 150.
2 I have corrected the original, which reads "Prince Edward's Island."
3 I have corrected the original, which reads "Gerald Blythe."
4 I have corrected the original, which reads "Ewan MacDonald."

5   *RV*, 95.

6   Here and below, I have corrected the original, which reads "Prince Edward's Island."

7   I have corrected the original, which reads "Rainbow is a lovely glen."

8   I have corrected the original, which reads "Prince Edward's Island."

9   *RV*, 2.

10  The remainder of this review discusses three additional novels also published by McClelland and Stewart: *Mist of Morning*, by Isabel Ecclestone Mackay (1875–1928), Canadian author; *Janet of Kootenay*, by Evah McKowan (1885–1962), Canadian author; and *Joan at Halfway*, by Grace McLeod Rogers (1865–1928), Canadian author.

11  *RV*, 1.

12  I have corrected the original, which reads "Rosemary Gray."

13  The song sung by the Meredith children is in fact entitled "Polly Wolly Doodle" (*RV*, 186).

14  Properly, "a fine and private place," from "To His Coy Mistress," a poem by Andrew Marvell (1621–1678), English poet.

15  In her "Scrapbook of Reviews," Montgomery adds a handwritten note: "It is exactly what I intended to leave" (SR, 131).

16  I have corrected the original, which reads "Ivyleside."

17  I have corrected the original, which reads "form or not very humorous setting."

18  Properly, "The light that never was on sea or land." From "Nature and the Poet," by William Wordsworth (1770–1850), English poet.

19  Properly, "Nokes outdares Stokes in azure feats, – / Both gorge." From "Popularity," by Robert Browning (1812–1889), English poet.

20  Montgomery's handwritten note appears in her scrapbook: "A very absurd review. There is no 'piety' anywhere in Rainbow Valley."

21  Gilbert Parker (1862–1932), popular author of more than thirty books, including *The Seats of the Mighty* (1896); Charles G.D. Roberts (1860–1943), poet and novelist whose books included *Songs of the Common Day* (1893).

22  *RV*, 182.

23  *RV*, 79, 80.

24  Mrs. Poyser, a character in George Eliot's first novel, *Adam Bede* (1859).

25  From *The Egoist* (1879), a novel by George Meredith (1828–1909), English novelist and poet.

26  I have corrected the original, which reads "Mrs. McDonald."

# 11

## *Further Chronicles of Avonlea*

—— 1920 ——

Although Montgomery was staunchly opposed to the publication of this volume and spent eight years fighting to keep it off the market, she nevertheless added some of the reviews to her scrapbook once the lawsuit had wrapped up in her favour in 1928. In spite of her serious reservations about its contents, reviewers were for the most part quite enthusiastic about this unexpected return to Avonlea. "No other author has done for Prince Edward Island as much as L.M. Montgomery in her 'Avonlea' tales to make it and its people known to outsiders," declared the *Pittsburgh Press*. The *Boston Evening Transcript* opined that "life in Prince Edward Island has always been well portrayed by Miss Montgomery but by no means with consummate artistry; and life in all these tales flows on in the same good way as in her other books." According to the *Wilmington Every Evening* of Delaware, "The 'Avonlea Books' by Miss Montgomery have appealed more potently to readers of fine fiction than any other literary productions of the last decade. They have afforded acquaintance with a people whose homely virtues, whose daily doings, whose romances, loves, purposes and frailties have been presented with such life-like fidelity and such absorbing interest that the reader seemed transported to their little community, to become part and parcel of them." Indeed, most of these reviews expressed no awareness of the existence of two further Anne books that had appeared in recent years with a competing publisher: as one unidentified clipping noted, "The pen of Miss Montgomery has etched on the memory of thousands the beauty and romance of Prince Edward Island, and we will all be glad to remember that the author has not forgotten her many readers and admirers."[1]

And yet, in one unidentified clipping at least, the volume consisted of some of Montgomery's best work: "She sounds a thousand emotional notes with her simple but effective tales, all of them excellent, and all supremely true to the atmosphere of the fertile land of which she writes ... Miss Montgomery is fast becoming one of those writers whose influence will long outlive her. They are not tales of the moment, but stories of the ages. Many years hence those who follow us will select Miss Montgomery's stories naturally as those which faithfully recreate the spirit of their time, and it will be nothing more than they deserve."[2]

## In Avonlea
### *The Boston Herald* (Boston, MA)

### More Chronicles of P.E.I. Life and People

A welcome volume for that vast audience of readers to whom Miss Montgomery has made Avonlea familiar through her earlier books. Avonlea is, of course, on Prince Edward Island,[3] and from Miss Montgomery's first novel, *Anne of Green Gables*, through her later works, *Anne of Avonlea, Anne of the Island, Chronicles of Avonlea*, etc., she has made the scenes and the people of that island increasingly popular with the American fiction reading public.

In *Further Chronicles of Avonlea* she presents 15 short stories that give a series of piquant and fascinating pictures of Prince Edward Island life and characters. Miss Montgomery has the gift of characterizing persons in very few words and of mingling sentiment with a touch of humor that is most delightful. She excels especially in depicting the romantic episodes hidden in the hearts of elderly spinsters and in presenting self-sacrifice as the real basis of happiness.

One story in this collection has an element of the supernatural, and in another a child appears as a solvent of old feuds or domestic quarrels. No reader of the Avonlea stories will ever feel that Prince Edward Island, northern land though it is, is at all cold and barren. The poetic touch that Miss Montgomery gives to her descriptions is sufficient for dispelling any such illusions.[4]

Nathan Haskell Dole of Boston has written an introduction to this volume of charming tales.

## [Further Doings of Widely Popular People]
### *The Bookseller, Newsdealer and Stationer* (New York, NY)

*Further Chronicles of Avonlea*, by L.M. Montgomery, with illustrations by John Goss, will attract many readers for it is devoted to the further doings of the widely popular people who foregathered in and about the home of the heroine of "Green Gables" at Prince Edward Island. Humor and pathos are happily blended in its fifteen tales in which there are pleasant contrasts of character in the engaging personalities who are concerned in the romantic episodes, from the elderly sentimental spinster, who, rather than let her acquaintance believe that she had never had a love affair, invented one. In "Tannis of the Flats" the secret of another woman's spinsterhood is revealed in an incident which illustrates a half-breed Indian Girl's unselfish devotion. Another case of rare unselfishness is disclosed in another story, "Only a Common Fellow," where a young man renounces his fiancée, because his old rival for her affections, supposed to have been killed in France, miraculously returns from the front.

## More about Avonlea
### *Evening Public Ledger* (Philadelphia, PA)

Fifteen short stories about the "Anne of Green Gables" country have been gathered into a volume by L.M. Montgomery and published under the title of *Further Chronicles of Avonlea*. They are written with the simple directness which characterizes this popular author and are as sympathetically human as any of her other stories. This is high praise, for no one now writing has a better understanding of the lives of the plain people. She does not patronize them, but accepts them as her brothers and sisters. Her book will be read by her large following, but there is nothing in it which will gain her new friends.

## [Plain and Simple Lives]
### *The Sunday Sentinel* (Milwaukee, WI)

To the little group of choice storytellers, Miss Brown, Miss Wilkins, Miss Jewett,[5] who have set forth life on the Atlantic seaboard, bleak but bracing and rife with individuality, must be added Miss Montgomery, who has found upon Prince Edward Island further up the coast, material as remunerative as any in New England. Life in its externals is different on Prince Edward Island; its people are of another stamp; yet racially and humanly they are identical with their Puritan neighbors. New England has no monopoly of rugged, cross-grained or wilful natures, of tender hearted spinsters or tart tongued females. Miss Montgomery has sure vision not only for the oddities but for the nobler qualities in humanity, and the poetic touch throws its glamor over her stories and informs their heart. "The Return of Hester" is the kind of ghost story that ought to be true. "The Conscience Case" concerns just such a reticent, sternly upright spirit as was bred by New England Calvinism. "Her Father's Daughter" and "Sara's Way" are Mary E. Wilkins' themes worked out in terms of Avonlea; so is "The Brother Who Failed,"[6] though Miss Wilkins would have allowed no such moment of recompense to the faithful brother, but have left him tragically, with the hurt still in his heart. "The Son of His Mother" is a concept of strong light and deep shadows. Not all reach this high level. But, judged by her best, the author of *Further Chronicles of Avonlea* must be ranked among those given grace to see beauty and meaning in plain and simple lives.

## Chronicles of Avonlea
### *The Evening Missourian* (Columbia, MO)

Miss L.M. Montgomery in *Further Chronicles of Avonlea* brings again her charming humor and pathos into the making of a delightful book. The characters are homely and homelike and yet tinged with beautiful romance. There are fifteen short stories in the new volume, each of which is delightful reading. Only a genius of the first water could conjure up such charming stories as Miss Montgomery has given in her Avonlea incidents.

## [Sentiment a Bit Thick]
### *The Independent* (New York, NY)

Stories of the Avonlea folks first made famous in *Anne of Green Gables*. They are likable, true-to-life people and the stories are good reading, tho the sentiment is sometimes laid on a bit thick.

## Title of Book Warrants Interest
### Unidentified clipping

*Further Chronicles of Avonlea*, by L.M. Montgomery, author of the attractive volumes with unusual covers which seem to be a Page specialty.[7] Beside that, the title of the book warrants much interest among the followers of *Anne of Green Gables*. Anne is in these stories occasionally, but the dominating characters are older maids reviving their lost love affairs. Many of them are fragrant and sweet, but too many of them are stereotyped, along conventional story forms that were outworn years ago. It is Miss Montgomery's manner much more than her matter that a reader commends, for she pictures her Avonlea people in swift, satirical phrases that are photographic in their clearness. All the stories are homely ones, and they are most effective if read at intervals, to avoid a certain incidental monotony which is liable to be troublesome otherwise.

NOTES

1   *The Pittsburgh Press*, "Chronicles of Avonlea," 10; *Boston Evening Transcript* (Boston, MA), "Avonlea Again," review of *Further Chronicles of Avonlea*, 8 April 1920, in SR, 129; *Wilmington Every Evening* (Wilmington, DE), review of *Further Chronicles of Avonlea*, 17 April 1920, in SR, 328; review of *Further Chronicles of Avonlea*, unidentified and undated clipping, in SR, 327.

2   Review of *Further Chronicles of Avonlea*, signed H.L.G., unidentified and undated clipping, in SR, 328.

3   Here and throughout, I have corrected the original, which reads "Prince Edward's Island."

4   I have corrected the original, which reads "her descriptions are sufficient."

5   See "*Chronicles of Avonlea*," note 28; "*Anne of Avonlea*," note 7; and "*Chronicles of Avonlea*," note 24, above.

6   I have corrected the original, which reads "'The Brother Who Tailed.'"

7   In Montgomery's scrapbook, the phrase "unusual covers which seem to be a Page specialty" is underlined in ink (see SR, 330).

# 12

## *Rilla of Ingleside*

—— 1921 ——

While many reviewers of *Rilla of Ingleside* clearly seemed unsure of how to incorporate the Great War in their write-ups about the book, they once again praised the novel for its apparent wholesomeness and simplicity: for the *St. Louis Globe–Democrat* declared it to be "a sweet, simple story of a nice girl and her nice friends, ... the kind of story that nice mothers like their daughters to read." To this the *Brooklyn Daily Eagle* added that "in spite of the flood of war stories, Miss Montgomery will hold many of her 'Anne' admirers with this romance." And in an unidentified and undated clipping, Helen Cody Baker told the story of a young boy whose mother had offered him *Rilla of Ingleside* to read instead of a pulp novel and who consequently loved it. "As long as books like *Rilla of Ingleside* continue to enjoy their present popularity," Baker concluded, "I can't feel too much despair over the coming generation. Children, if given a chance, really like books that tell of courage, self-sacrifice and loyalty when they are as full of fun and as human as this one."[1] Ads for *Rilla of Ingleside* in Toronto newspapers during the Christmas season of 1921 emphasized its optimism and its cross-generational readership: "The Gift Book for Mother, Wife or Daughter ... A Captivating, Sunny Story of Rilla, Daughter of Anne"; "The Most Charming Gift Book for Christmas ... A Gift Which Will Appeal Equally to Mother, Wife or Daughter"; "The Book That Every Woman or Girl Wants to Read ... It is a human story, bright, readable, wholesome and entertaining. Everybody loves Rilla, the impetuous, fun-loving daughter of Anne."[2]

## An Agreeable Romance
### *Trenton Times–Advertiser* (Trenton, NJ)

*Anne of Green Gables* is a gladsome memory for a host of readers, and now we have *Rilla of Ingleside* with the daughter of Anne as the heroine. Miss L.M. Montgomery, the author of both stories, gives us in the latter book the picture of a glowing, fun-loving girl, endowed with much of her mother's enthusiasm, eagerness and lively spirit, yet with sharply outlined traits of her own. The World War broke out with Rilla sixteen years of age and the romantic thenceforth maiden finds herself plunged into the realities of life under its sternest conditions. As a background of the tale but not intruding disagreeably upon the current of events, the mighty struggle on the other side of the Atlantic has its heart-rending echoes in Rilla's[3] little community in Prince Edward Island. The boys off to fight German imperialism and the women folk at home engaged in Red Cross and similar work – Miss Montgomery paints it all in lively colors, with just enough of the shadows to bring out the bright spots and the final victory more vividly. Love too has its share in the progress of events.

In this romance we make delightful re-acquaintance with many old friends of the author's previous books. Susan has a big part to play and is more delightful than ever; Mary Vance is here; Miss Cornelia, and, of course, Anne's other children and their friends. Miss Montgomery will retain her host of "Anne" admirers and make many new friends with this novel. It is a story to appeal particularly to girls in their teens and the publishers have given it a dress suitable for gift purposes.

## [A Captivating, Sunny Story]
### *The New York Times Book Review and Magazine* (New York, NY)

Even those who never read *Anne of Green Gables* or *Rainbow Valley* will find agreeable entertainment in this new novel by the same author; while people already acquainted with Anne will doubtless experience exquisite pleasure in going through the volume with her impulsive, pretty, warm-hearted daughter. For Rilla is Anne Shirley's offspring, and she has been named Marilla, after her aunt at Green Gables, and she lives at Ingleside, on Prince Edward Island,[4] and is surrounded by the same kind of amiable, chatty folk as laughed and gossiped and sometimes suffered through the other books. Life at Ingleside is tranquil enough in itself, but the period of the story is during the great war, and the reaction of the European horror upon the even existence of Rilla and those about her makes it rumble subconsciously with the beat of drum and the roll and roar of machine gun and great cannon. Two of Rilla's brothers go to the war, and one is killed. Her lover, Kenneth Ford, also goes, but he, with her brother Jem, comes back. It is Walter, the brother who always was closest, who falls with a bullet in his brain as he goes "over the top" one morning.[5]

For the rest, the novel is mainly a pleasing recital of the doings, thoughts and aspirations of a very human young girl. We go with her to her first party, and peep over her shoulder while she reads her first love letter in a shady nook in Rainbow Valley, and we know that she has confided her most intimate conclusions and ambitions to her diary. Rilla is a charming girl, of the type which the author depicts so naturally and sympathetically, and the reader of either sex will love her. There is a cat of unusual propensities, and a good-natured, blundering dog of the most lovable kind, both of whom have several paragraphs to themselves here and there. The friends and acquaintances of Rilla are as attractive in their several ways as she is herself, and if some of them are inclined to be snippy and ill-natured, why, that is to be expected even in so Elysian a region as Ingleside where there are human beings. The author seldom touches a deep heart note, but it does not appear that she desires to do so. She writes a captivating, sunny story, and when one lays the book down after reaching the end, it is with the feeling that one has been in thoroughly wholesome company. The colored frontispiece by M.L. Kirk, showing Rilla in the woods with her love letter pressed to her bosom, is a dainty bit of work.

## An Island Heroine
### *The New York Tribune* (New York, NY)

#### Author of Famous Girl Story Writes a Sequel

The author of the popular novel *Anne of Green Gables* is in the field this fall with another story, in which one discovers little or no diminution in ability to create a lovable heroine. In fact, it is our conviction that *Rilla of Ingleside* is an improvement upon the well-known Anne of the book which gave Miss Montgomery her position as a novelist. There is a riper thought and a livelier humor in the later work that show growth. Its pages are rich in fun and pathos, with sentiment and philosophy of an unusual order.

Rilla, a daughter of Anne, is an impulsive, merry-hearted girl, whose faults, which emphasize her charms, are lost during the four hard years of wartime in the warmth and sweetness of her real nature. She finds herself at sixteen suddenly plunged into the stern actualities of 1914, and her unfoldment from the budding period of girlhood to the blossoming flower of womanhood forms the background of the story. The scene is laid in Prince Edward Island, the author's birthplace, and opens with Rilla's home life with her father and mother, her sisters and brothers and Susan, the housekeeper, whose delightful sayings run through the book, a never-failing stream of good sense and drollery. The thunderbolt of war scatters the household, the brothers going to the front and the older girls to attend the university in a distant city, leaving Rilla alone with her parents and Susan. She adopts a war baby, and her adventures in bringing him up form an amusing feature of the book. The sadness of her tender love for her brother, Walter, is in marked contrast to the happiness of her love for Kenneth, whom she marries.

There is a spine of continuity that runs through the pages of this human novel in the delicate manner in which Miss Montgomery maintains to the end the elements of personality that characterize her heroine. For instance, through the mere habit of a lisp she ties the final chapter to the earlier ones of the book in a way that differentiates it from the clumsy fiction of inexpert writers.

### [Perhaps Her Best Story]
*The Post Express* (Rochester, NY)

In her books Miss Montgomery gives us an interesting picture of people she seems to have known in Prince Edward Island. In *Anne of Green Gables*, she gave us a gentle, charming type of womanhood. But as in the course of nature Anne gets married, she has a daughter Rilla, who is the heroine of *Rilla of Ingleside*. With Miss Montgomery everybody that can marry gets married, and in the first chapter all the talk is either about match-making or cats. The cat talk is more original than the matrimonial talk. Thus a cat to which the name of "Dr. Jekyll-and-Mr. Hyde" has been given is endowed with the antithetic qualities dramatically, if absurdly, emphasized as belonging to the same individual in Stevenson's much overrated story.[6]

Rilla is an enthusiastic, impetuous girl. She longs for "beaux" – in the plural. She loves Walter who never calls her "Spider," as the others did, but "Rilla, my Rilla" – her name is an abbreviation of Marilla. Rilla herself hated the name – she had been named after her Aunt Marilla – her view being that it was a prim, old-fashioned name. At sixteen this girl was evidently what John Henry Newman called "viewy."[7] She tells her secrets to Gertrude Oliver, the teacher who boards at Ingleside.

Rilla thinks the nicest thing about days is their "unexpectedness."[8] But Miss Oliver – who is twenty-eight – knows that any day may bring something terrible.

The war breaks out over in Europe – and then things happen even in Prince Edward Island. But Rilla does not for a time realize what that means. She only thinks of how many boys will ask her to dance at her first party.

Miss Montgomery very naturally unlocks a young girl's heart. Really poor Rilla is only craving for love. Susan comes into the story and her fate is sealed, for she receives a proposal – and the sequel is, of course, the nuptial bond.

Several of the boys go to the front, and Walter has the courage to declare that he is a coward. It needs bravery to do this. Rilla has her troubles. One of them is Walter's outspokenness. There is a "war-baby" to be looked after, and Rilla hears that a baby can only be kissed on the forehead for fear of germs. At Christmas Ingleside is a little lonely. One fine boy, Jem – a boy with "fearless" eyes – is far away.[9] What is taking place in Flanders and in France has its reverberations in Ingleside. Letters arrive telling of "gassing," shell shock, and other things. The news of the war now makes itself felt day after day and month after month.

It is Kenneth, a young fellow wearing a lieutenant's uniform, who writes love letters from the front to Rilla. The affair reaches such a stage that Rilla is uncertain whether she is engaged to Kenneth or not.

The story travels through the years of the war until we come to the armistice. Walter, who had called himself a coward, proves to be the bravest man in his regiment. But Rilla has given her heart away – and the last chapter brings her wedlock and happiness.

This is perhaps Miss Montgomery's best story.

## [No Unpleasant Details]
### *Wisconsin Library Bulletin* (Madison, WI)

Rilla is the daughter of Anne of Green Gables. She is sixteen in 1914 and she grows to womanhood during the war. The war furnishes a romantic background. No unpleasant details and a happy ending.

## [A Faithful and Worthy Picture]
### *The Globe* (Toronto, ON)

The author of that Canadian classic, *Anne of Green Gables*, presents in *Rilla of Ingleside* a poignant picture of the sorrows, anxieties and emotions which the great war brought to the quiet countryside in Prince Edward Island, which has been made familiar to hosts of readers by the earlier "Anne" books and their successors. Rilla is a daughter of Anne herself, and her development into womanhood will be watched by many readers who followed the dashing career of Anne and her associates in the tranquil seaside village.

The present book is more a study of a period than a delineation of Rilla herself, for the time was so crowded with thrilling incidents that these overshadowed individuals. At the same time there is a variety of characters from the quiet Glen St. Mary. There are boys and girls, sorrowed prematurely by the partings and bereavements of the war, fathers and mothers bearing up as bravely as may be, and working actively in home service. Then there were the young men who heard the call to arms and responded willingly, going out to fight for the cause of civilization, some of them writing inspiring letters to home folk, others giving their lives, and some returning to parents or to sweethearts and to a life that will never be the same again. In fact, it is a story that might be written of a thousand communities in Canada, where the quiet life was suddenly upset by the European explosion which, at first, it was thought, could be ignored, but into which they were compelled to enter almost as fully as if they were a part of Europe.

As a record of the war years, as seen from Glen St. Mary, the author has presented a faithful and worthy picture, spiced by realistic conversation and records of sentiment, and often illuminated by poetic touches in describing the charm of life in that island garden. There is the love interest brought prettily to a culmination at the end; there is the trying time for Mrs. Dr. Blythe, the "Anne" of earlier day; the incidents of war weddings, the sympathetic care of a "war baby," and a host of incidents that will find their counterpart in other isolated communities.

There are some sage observations by Rilla, as she advanced to womanhood, her development hastened by the trials and emotions of the time, and there are experiences of idealism by other characters. As the story opens in the summer of 1914, Rilla at the age of 15 says: "I can't be sober and serious – everything looks so rosy and rainbowy to me."[10] It was a different girl who cried at the end of the war, when she heard of the enemy's suit for peace: "Oh, ... I have walked the floor for hours in despair and anxiety in these past four years. Now let me walk it in joy. It was worth living long dreary years for this minute, and it would be worth living them again just to look back to it. Susan, let's run up the flag – and we must 'phone the news to every one in the Glen."

"Can we have as much sugar as we want to now?" asked Jims, the war baby, eagerly.[11]

## [Not Too Much of the War]
### *San Francisco Bulletin* (San Francisco, CA)

The modern novelist doesn't write sequels – many readers shy at a story that is a sequel to something they have not read – instead he or she has characters that appear in several books, thus making them members of the author's romantic family. It helps the sales, and when well done is a source of additional pleasure.

Miss L.M. Montgomery brings the "Anne of Green Gables" folk into her latest, *Rilla of Ingleside*, a war-time story of a girl who was 16 in 1914, and therefore 21 at the signing of the armistice and the completion of the romance. Not too much of the war, and yet enough to follow up all its main incidents, from the first onslaught, through the impatient days when President Wilson was writing notes and on to America's participation and ultimate victory. "That man Simonds" is mentioned in the story, the same being Frank H., and the "that man" having reference to the pessimistic prophecies in which he sometimes indulged.[12] A happy ending to a wholesome romance.

## By the Author of *Anne of Green Gables*
### *The Family Herald and Weekly Star* (Montreal, QC)

Readers of the *Family Herald* have very pleasant recollections of Miss L.M. Montgomery's early writings, concerned largely with "Anne," a winsome Prince Edward Island Lassie. Most of those novels were introduced to thousands of Canadians through these columns, as were many other famous works.[13] Miss Montgomery is now Mrs. Macdonald and she left the Island with her clerical husband some years ago. But she still writes books which are in their way pleasing, although none of them preserve the flavor of the "Anne" books, nor are they greatly, if at all, out of the ordinary. Her latest book is *Rilla of Ingleside* and deals with the Great War as it affected a country village and especially as it touched the circle of friends about Rilla, daughter of Anne Blythe, formerly Anne Shirley, the original "Anne of Green Gables." The faithful Susan is encountered again, so is Mary Vance, Miss Cornelia and all the rest of them. But these war-time stories are all much alike and we have had rather a surfeit of them. Rilla's "war-baby," which she rescued and carried home in a soup-tureen, promised well at one time, but failed to develop individuality enough to save the book from becoming tedious.

## [Wholesome Fiction for Young People]
### *The Bookseller and Stationer* (New York, NY)

A sequel to the author's *Rainbow Valley*, in which the daughter of "Anne of Green Gables" is the central figure. It is wholesome fiction for young people from fifteen to twenty, of American small town family life and of the influence the Great War had on various of its members, particularly on the heroine, who, from a romping, frivolous selfish girl of fifteen, gradually develops into a fine capable woman, after all the boys she had "danced and moonlighted" with had gone off to play their parts in the big fight.[14] Some old favorites of earlier stories reappear and one of the joys of the book is that it has not appeared as a serial.

## [Deserves to Be Successful]
### *Boston Evening Transcript* (Boston, MA)

Again Miss Montgomery presents her readers with a story of the people who live in her native Prince Edward Island. But the first flush of the charm which captured her innumerable readers in *Anne of Green Gables* has vanished. *Rilla of Ingleside* is the story of Anne's six children, of whom Rilla is given the leading part, being endowed with a romance. It is a very vague romance, and though arriving at a happy conclusion, is as far as we are able to discern, a mere sentimental illusion. The story is set within the framework of the Great War, indeed, the war is more than a framework – it is the picture too.

Into the quiet and dreamy Prince Edward Island village reaches the bloody hand of the European conflict, snatching away the young men who leave behind heartaches and anxieties, hopes and yearnings, young hearts and old whose lives are tortured, week by week, as the battles flow in France and Flanders. Anne's sons go, one to return, and the other never. So does Rilla's sweetheart go, a young man whom Rilla rather hopes than positively knows is her sweetheart, but the hope makes all the difference to Rilla's career as a heroine. From a light, inconsequential young girl of fifteen the anxiety about the man whom her fancy paints as a sweetheart, Rilla grows, or so her creator would have us believe she grows, into quite a serious and responsible young lady. She takes an infant baby a few weeks old and assumes entire care of it; she does war work and she keeps a journal in which she jots down her thoughts and feelings about what goes on amongst her family and neighbors under the shadow of the war.

One character in the story both interests and amuses the reader – Susan, an excellent type of one-of-the-family "hired girls," whose patriotic comments on the war, international diplomacy and military strategy, saves the book from dulness. It is useless to say whether *Rilla of Ingleside* is a good story or not, because if it pleases the innumerable admirers of *Anne of Green Gables* it deserves to be successful.

## The Charming Daughter of Anne of Green Gables
### *The Boston Herald* (Boston, MA)
#### JOHN CLAIR MINOT

This time it is the war that gives Miss Montgomery the theme of her Prince Edward Island story, for many substantial echoes of the great conflict reached the peaceful region with which this author has made a multitude of readers familiar. Her heroine, christened Marilla, is the daughter of Anne of Green Gables fame, and the story is a sunny and wholesome narrative of her war-time reactions and experiences. Her lover and two of her brothers went overseas, and one of the brothers failed to return.

Not the least interesting of the characters are a cat and dog of unusual accomplishments and qualities. The droll philosophy of Susan, the housekeeper, brightens many pages. It was a bit daring for Miss Montgomery to give her heroine a lisp which is maintained even to the last line of the book, but lisp and all, the reader falls in love with Rilla and shares with undiluted sympathy the sorrows and happiness that the war era brought her.

## [Rilla and Her Destiny]
### *The Publishers' Weekly* (New York, NY)

Rilla is the daughter of "Anne of Green Gables," yet she is a person entirely different, being a product of these difficult, unsettled times that have upset the manners and customs of tradition. The story carries Rilla through many experiences as she works out her destiny, and it gives a chance for renewal of acquaintance with the characters of Miss Montgomery's earlier tales.

## [May Be Read by Others Than Girls]
### *Saturday Night* (Toronto, ON)

Although it is not to be expected that L.M. Montgomery could produce another such book as the original *Anne of Green Gables*, there is no denying the hold possessed by the galaxy of secondary Anne books upon their hosts of readers of all ages; and of these, *Rilla of Ingleside* is easily one of the best. To be frank, we were beginning to be a bit fed up with Anne. Marriage seemed to have dulled her intellect – and we never had very much use for that prize model of masculine perfection, her husband.

But in Rilla is reincarnated all the charm of the youthful Anne Shirley. She is not merely a rejuvenated Anne. Her temperament is different, and she is moulded into womanhood in a vastly different psychological environment.

The story is a gripping one in many ways. One after the other Anne's sons, Rilla's brothers, don khaki and march away to war. There are others, too, one of whom is of particular interest to Rilla. Yet he is hardly more so than the second of her three brothers, who hated war and wanted nothing so little as to go. But he went. Little comedies and big tragedies and a large amount of very human hopes and fears go to make up the narrative which traces its way through the fifty-odd painful months of war. Most Canadians lived and felt those months very much as did the Blythe family and their friends of Glen St. Mary. The events which then seemed so important, and which were the principal topics of conversation – the fall of Przemysl, Wilson's many notes, So-and-So's son who was reported "missing" – are all discussed by Rilla and her friends in a manner that makes the picture very real. There is a dog in it, too, who provides one of the best dog stories that has appeared in many a day – a bit unbelievable but good.

Altogether, it's a charming little story for girls, and one that may be read with a great deal of interest, and perhaps a slight moistening of the eyes, by others than girls.

## [Clean and Wholesome Romance]
### *Fort Worth Star–Telegram* (Fort Worth, TX)

To be 16 and to meet love and valor in the stirring days between 1914, when the World War broke over the nations, and 1918, when peace came again to the world – surely this is to experience that of which clean and wholesome romance is made. Mrs. Montgomery is one of the few writers whose clientele is to be found equally among young folks and grown-ups. Her "Anne" stories, which began with the delightful *Anne of Green Gables*, which classed as "juveniles," have quite as many lovers among the older generation as among the younger. And *Rilla of Ingleside*, her latest book, undoubtedly will please them all. For Rilla is Anne's daughter – she is, in fact, eternal youth, and Anne over again – and the period of the story is the same as the World War.

As in Mrs. Montgomery's other stories, the scenes are laid in Prince Edward Island,[15] and as Canada was in the war from the start, the war touches the life of Rilla and those whom she loves from the moment England declared war. The problems which this world disturbance brought into the life of this sweet young girl and how she faced them make satisfying reading. The wholesomeness and healthfulness of the story, together with the world character of the events forming the background of it, thereby making its appeal so in keeping with universal experience, as to make it just the book to place in the hands of one's daughter.

It is a worthy successor to Mrs. Montgomery's other books.

## [An American Girl at Home in War Time]
### *The Bookseller and Stationer* (New York, NY)

*Rilla of Ingleside*, by L.M. Montgomery,[16] introduces the daughter of "Anne of Green Gables," a fun-loving girl who, at sixteen, finds herself plunged into the realities of 1914. Old friends of earlier books reappear in the story which goes to show how an American girl at home in war time faced her problems. It is wholesome and interesting.

## Now Anne's Daughter Rilla
### *The Chicago Daily Tribune* (Chicago, IL)
#### FANNY BUTCHER

*Rilla of Ingleside*, by L.M. Montgomery, is ready for those who sit up and beg for another *Anne of Green Gables*. Rilla is the daughter of Anne and she is just as "nice" as her mamma.

## [A Canadian Girl in Love]
### *The Canadian Bookman* (Gardenvale, QC)

Rilla is the daughter of "Anne of Green Gables," and the scene of the love-declaration between her and her young Island soldier-boy with the implacable Susan looking on is one of the most idyllically beautiful things Mrs. Montgomery has ever given us. The rest of the book is mainly a series of comedy episodes, amusing enough but having little to do with the development of the characters, and chiefly showing life in a Prince Edward Island village during the war. Mrs. Montgomery has done more important work, but we should be sorry not to have had this pretty sketch of a proud and true and generous young Canadian girl in love.

## [Perhaps the Best Yet]
### *Farmers' Magazine* (Toronto, ON)

This is perhaps the best yet of the Anne books. It has all the author's whimsical imagination and humor and sympathy, with a pathos not touched in any of the previous Anne stories. The way the Piper came playing through the Glen in the August of 1914 calling the boys from the farms and the school and the university will be understood from experience in many a rural community. The romance of Rilla and the other Ingleside girls gives a color to the story, but it is the affection between Rilla and her poet-soldier brother that sets this book apart as one something unusually fine in Canadian fiction.

## [Useful to Historians]
### *Manitoba Free Press* (Winnipeg, MB)

Here they all are again, Jem and Walter, Rilla-my-Rilla, and all the others. But the Rainbow children are now no longer children, and when August, 1914, comes, Jem joins up and Ingleside is plunged into the dark shadows through which went so many Canadian homes. A hundred years hence, *Rilla of Ingleside* will be useful to historians for a picture of Canadian home life during the Great War. Every great event of the conflict is traced with its effects on Ingleside, and Walter, the shy, sensitive boy, the poet of the family, takes his leave – but, why spoil the story?

## [Domestic Canada during the War]
### *The Scotsman* (Edinburgh, UK)

The Ingleside in Miss L.M. Montgomery's bright and interesting novel, *Rilla of Ingleside*, is just the sort of place people used to think about as one where it was possible to get away from the war – a quiet house near the seaside in a glen somewhere in Canada, where most of the names of places and persons speak of Scottish origins, and where the domestic interest centres itself in the matrimonial prospects of young school teachers, masculine and feminine, under the somewhat Presbyterian supervision of thoroughly mature spinsters. But the story shows how the war turned the old maids into political controversialists, busy with Red Cross work; and also how the various matrimonial arrangements were modified by the loyalty and self-devotion of the young people both at home and in the battlefields far away.

## [A Wondrous Amount of Sentiment]
### *Western Mail* (Perth, Australia)

The book is a sequel to *Rainbow Valley*, and affiliated with *Anne of Green Gables*, in that it is the story of the daughter of that popular heroine of other of Miss Montgomery's novels. Indeed, the author introduces quite a number of the characters who have figured in her previous books into the present work. The story is of the war years and how they affect Rilla, who is 16 years old when the war breaks out. The tale harbours a wondrous amount of sentiment of a more or less amorous description, but Miss Montgomery's readers know by this time just what they have to expect, and in *Rilla of Ingleside* they will not be disappointed.

## [Quite Convincingly Idyllic]
### *Punch, or the London Charivari* (London, UK)

*Rilla of Ingleside* is one of those distillations of the soul of goodness in things evil which has come out rather more concentrated and sugary than most of us on this side of the Atlantic find palatable. However, Miss L.M. MONTGOMERY is quite convincingly idyllic in describing the pre-war home of her Canadian country doctor; and, though "Mrs. Dr., dear," as she is known to *Susan*, the help, is a thought too lavishly maternal, there is an admirably acidulated *Cousin Sophia*, with thin pale hands resignedly folded on a black calico lap, who makes a too brief appearance in the kitchen at Ingleside to comment on *Rilla's* first ball-dress. It is *Rilla* herself, as chastened by the War, whom I think you will find a trifle cloying. She was the feather-pate of the family and had set her heart on an idle and decorative existence; but, being impelled into the paths of domesticity and self-sacrifice, she achieved a striking success in these inevitably allied departments, adopted a singularly unprepossessing war-baby, and was lucky enough to hand it over to an excellent foster-mother before her own *Captain Kenneth* returned from France. Yet, crudely as she is handled, *Rilla* has a stray air of HAWTHORNE's *Phœbe Pyncheon*,[17] which suggests that the matter of the New World idyll is not lost, though the manner of it has been forgotten.

## [A Lesson for Every Family]
### *The Idaho Daily Statesman* (Boise, ID)

*Rilla of Ingleside*, by L.M. Montgomery, is a gem.

Everybody remembers Anne of Green Gables fame. This new book is the story of Anne's family, and what each member accomplished during the World war. "Rilla-my-Rilla," who impulsively brought home a war-baby, in a soup tureen, and proceeded to rear it "by book" with amazing success, is an inspiring little heroine. Her love for her poet brother Walter; her devotion to the war shaken mother; her faithful care of little Jims, endear her, while at the same time her "managing" ways and frequent "spunky spats" with girl friends, prove her not too angelic.

And Susan – too much cannot be said about Susan – the mother-servant philosopher friend of all the family – with her quaint speech, her hatred of Mr. Hyde, the cat, her fierce patriotism, her superstitions. It is hardly to be supposed that most women of sixty-three would chase the first man who proposed marriage to her out of the yard with a kettle of boiling dye, but that's what Susan does. She had no intention of marrying "Whiskers-on-the-Moon" and "that you may tie to."

Reading *Rilla of Ingleside*, you'll cry a little, and laugh a little, and you'll think a great deal: perhaps you'll wonder how your family compares with the kind, merry, clever family of Anne. I've heard so many folks say lately: "Large families of children aren't the comfort these days that they used to be." I think that's true. For the most part, large families don't exist, it "simply isn't being done." There's a lesson in *Rilla of Ingleside* for every family, large or small; the lesson of mutual helpfulness, love and understanding, that's a lesson we should learn everybody.

## [A Distinction of an Outstanding Kind]
### *Sunday School Chronicle* (London, UK)

With memories of *Anne of Green Gables* vivid in our mind, we greeted this writer's name on the title-page of a new book with expectant delight. We were not disappointed. And we had the added delight of meeting our old friend Anne again. For "Rilla" of this book is Anne's daughter. Anne is a matron now, and the mother of a large family. Readers of the earlier story and its sequel will remember that Anne was left half engaged to Gilbert Blythe. Years have passed since that early time, and Rilla is a worthy child of her mother, with as much imagination as Anne had in her own young days. The story is of war-time in a Canadian township – chiefly concerned with Anne's family, although many other inhabitants of Glen St. Mary are lovingly portrayed. How the war-call took away Rilla's brother – how another brother, highly strung, confessed himself afraid to go, but went at last and paid the supreme price – how Rilla's lover went with his love unspoken, though not unrevealed in other ways than speech – how days and weeks of agonising suspense weighed upon the house – how Susan (as delightful an old servant as fiction has ever given us) kept up her own courage and that of her mistress – how a pacifist met his Nemesis when he tried to turn a prayer-meeting into a pacifist lecture-room – these and many other homely and yet stirring things are told. The whole book is arresting in its very simplicity, and the authoress has undoubtedly scored another signal success. One of its great charms is that it chronicles moods and experiences which were common to thousands of homes during those awful years, and so goes straight to the heart. But over and above this, the authoress is a true artist. She gives just the one right touch. How we recognise ourselves as in a glass when we hear Susan trying to persuade herself that Antwerp and other places have "no military significance"![18] And the pathos of the last letter written home by Walter – the boy who hesitated but had gone – with its knowledge that the next day he must "go West" is almost unbearably poignant. Decidedly a book to read, and a book which has distinction of an outstanding kind.

## [Rilla the Empire-Builder]
### *The Queenslander* (Brisbane, Australia)

*Rilla of Ingleside*, by the author of *Anne of Green Gables*, L.M. Montgomery, is a book that one would have widely circulated in Australia. *Rilla of Ingleside* is the youngest daughter of Anne, a girl not out of school when the Great War began. And of her part and that of Canada, her country, the author writes with a sure touch on the little homely details, the tragedies and triumphs that will awake a responsive chord wherever the Empire holds its sway. "Rilla" would be more than astonished at hearing herself described as an Empire-builder, but, in bringing home to other parts of the Empire, "That we are members one of another" Rilla is "doing her bit."[19]

## NOTES

1  *St. Louis Globe–Democrat* (St. Louis, MO), review of *Rilla of Ingleside*,
   12 November 1921, in SR, 188; *The Brooklyn Daily Eagle* (Brooklyn,
   NY), "Daughter of 'Anne of Green Gables,'" review of *Rilla of Ingleside*, 24
   September 1921, in SR, 184; Helen Cody Baker, "A Real Testimonial for a
   Book," unidentified and undated clipping, in SR, 181.

2  *The Globe* (Toronto), ad for *Rilla of Ingleside* (17 December 1921), 16;
   ibid. (12 December 1921), 15; ibid. (15 December 1921), 8; ibid. (20
   December 1921), 10. See also *The Toronto Daily Star*, ad for *Rilla of
   Ingleside* (16 December 1921, 10); ibid. (20 December 1921), 31; ibid. (21
   December 1921), 22.

3  I have corrected the original, which reads "Rita's."

4  I have corrected the original, which reads "Prince Edward's Island."

5  *RI*, 246.

6  *Strange Case of Dr. Jekyll and Mr. Hyde* (1886), a novel by Robert Louis
   Stevenson.

7  John Henry Newman (1801–1890), initially a priest in the Church of
   England and later a Roman Catholic priest and cardinal, defined the term
   "viewy" as a dissatisfaction with things as they are and an eagerness to
   develop a new understanding, or a new view.

8  *RI*, 25.

9  *RI*, 118. I have corrected the original, which reads "Jan."

10 *RI*, 24.

11 *RI*, 337. I have corrected the original, which reads "Jim."

12 *RI*, 261. Frank H. Simonds (1878–1936), author of the five-volume work
   *History of the World War* (1919–20).

13 *Anne of Green Gables*, *Anne of Avonlea*, *Kilmeny of the Orchard*, and
   *Chronicles of Avonlea* were all serialized in *The Family Herald and Weekly
   Star* four to eighteen months after their initial publication in book form.

14 *RI*, 237.

15 I have corrected the original, which reads "Prince Edward's Island."

16 I have corrected the original, which reads "L.A. Montgomery."

17 Phoebe Pyncheon, a character in *The House of the Seven Gables* (1851), a
   Gothic novel by Nathaniel Hawthorne (1804–1864), American author.

18 *RI*, 302.

19 The phrase "we are members one of another" is from Ephesians 4:25
   (KJV). "Do Your Bit for America," a phrase from an address by U.S.
   President Woodrow Wilson (1856–1924) on 2 April 1917, four days before
   the United States declared war upon Germany.

# 13

## *Emily of New Moon*

—— 1923 ——

The relationship between this novel's publication in 1923 and its depiction of events at the turn of the twentieth century may be less evident to today's readers, but some reviews of the book noted that its setting sometime in the Victorian era highlighted the fact that it was meant to appeal nostalgically to adults of the 1920s, who would have remembered the time period in which the novel is set. Noting that the age of the protagonist might cause some people to categorize the book as a juvenile, the *Springfield Republican* of Massachusetts cautioned that "such classification would tend to damn it with faint praise. Emily is far older than the calendar allows, and while youngsters will enjoy her story, their elders will appreciate it more." An unidentified clipping elaborated on this notion: "This book is not written only for young people. Those more advanced in years will appreciate it more, if anything, as they will be able to perceive the literary qualities and recapture some of the thrills and heartaches of their own youth, which perhaps they have forgotten in the rush and hurry of the busy world. To read it is like recapturing a vision of spring, and to long for the days of youthful ambitions and lost ideals."[1]

This look back to a Victorian sensibility was perceived as a strength in other ways as well: as John Clair Minot noted in the *Boston Herald*, Montgomery "happily keeps away from Freud and all the new psychology when she portrays adolescent girlhood. That sort of thing is as far from her pages as it is from *Little Women*, and the result is not less an ideal story for girl readers than it is a story for those who look back on happy girlhood or who love it from any angle whatsoever." Indeed, for Minot, part of the appeal of the novel was its reliance on key characteristics of Montgomery's writing: "sweetness that never

gets cloying, and sentiment that never gets over the line into sentimentality."
For the *Oregonian*, the author "comes dangerously near slipping into sentimentality, once in a while, but she has a sense of humor that puts in those delectable
touches which leave the reader chuckling over something this startling little girl
has said or done." In contrast, the comments in the *Hartford Courant* were less
qualified: "Miss Montgomery's literary gift is genuine; she conveys to the reader
a delicious sense of leisure and space, there is, in her work, none of that effect
of breathless rush which characterizes so many of the books now offered for
the delectation of the rising generation; the author of *Emily of New Moon* is
blessed with a keen eye for character, an ample fund of kindly humor, and with
the power to hold her reader's interest from start to finish."[2]

Moreover, a review in the *Catholic Standard* of Philadelphia stated that, in
spite of Montgomery's gifts as "a born story-teller," "Emily's literary efforts
grow tiresome. One prefers her as just a little girl rather than a writer in the
making, and there is a surfeit of her early efforts. But one is interested in Emily,
and undoubtedly will look forward to a sequel with her 'House of Dreams' as
they did for Anne." Moreover, while the *New York Times Book Review and
Magazine* praised Emily as "a charmingly winsome character," its review added
that the novel "shows Miss Montgomery to be simply a pleasing story-teller.
There is little originality in either her plot or her characters. Her greatest charm
lies in a real understanding and sympathy for children, a sympathy which, even
though it may degenerate at times into the sentimental, nevertheless has a certain appealing quality and a depth of sincerity that is disarming."[3]

## A Child Poet Well Presented
### *The Chicago Evening Post Literary Review* (Chicago, IL)
RUTH M. SPONBERG

Because so many of childhood's evaluations have been upset, the reviewer began the chronicles of Emily with perturbation, altho she treasures
a recollection of her eighth-grade instructor's reading *Anne of Green
Gables*, an earlier book by Miss Montgomery. Happily the fear of disappointment has proved groundless, for Emily is a delightful little personage who lives and breathes. Rather, this amusing young girl would now
be a grandmother, for the story takes place during some undefined period
of the Victorian era. But in no way does this detract from the interest of
the tale. Had the author substituted electric lights for candles, automobiles for carriages and mentioned modern farming implements the story
would be as up to date as 1923. For it is not a reproduction of the time in

which it is laid, but a sympathetically humorous character study of Emily, an embryonic poetess.

When her journalist father dies, leaving Emily a penniless orphan, her mother's half-sisters, who have never forgiven her mother for her marriage, take her in at New Moon farm. Incapable of understanding the imaginative, beauty-loving nature of their niece, their treatment of her is inevitably harsh. She is especially forbidden to try to write. Unhappily, Emily secretly writes her father letters, in which she details all her wrongs, and whimsically summarizes her activities. Posting the letters under an old sofa in the attic, she immediately forgives and forgets her grievances.

The younger aunt tries to make life pleasant for the child, but since she is under the domination of the older aunt, her efforts are not very effectual. Unexpectedly the letters to her father serve Emily a good turn. The tyrannical aunt discovers the letters and learns what her niece really thinks of her. Angrily she endeavors to rebuke Emily, but the girl's scathing condemnation of her aunt for daring to meddle with private property forces the woman to realize that the child has a right to develop her own nature without undue interference. Thereafter, Emily is permitted to continue her writing openly, attempting novels as readily as short stories and poems.

The book is charmingly written with an honest understanding of the girl who loves the beautiful so much that she experiences a feeling of boundless joy, which she inarticulately terms a "flash," whenever she beholds a colorful sunset, a gay flower, hears the song of a bird or listens to the sound of the wind. As the story closes, Emily's teacher has just urged her to continue writing, in the hope that she may eventually create something of permanent value and beauty. This makes the reviewer wonder if Miss Montgomery intends to develop Emily's future in later books, as she earlier developed the career of Anne who came to the farm at Green Gables.

The story is of a potential esthete, there is no lack of action. With her playmates, Emily romps with their pets, stages plays, plays and quarrels and makes up. Unaided, Emily solves the mystery of the disappearance of her chum's mother.

This the reviewer deems insufficiently explained. However a child delirious with the measles could imagine a true solution passes her understanding.

But if you like stories of interesting children, tho you are grown up, read *Emily of New Moon*. If you're a parent or a teacher, read it to your children, or if you know a girl who likes to read buy her the book.

## [The Early Life of a Very Precocious Child]
*The Times Literary Supplement* (London, UK)

Both as a study of the early life of a very precocious child and for its original setting in Prince Edward Island, this story makes a considerable appeal. The little pictures of the island's coasts, with the pastures sloping up the valleys, and the long-settled homesteads and the quiet inland waters, are admirably done. No less interesting is the account of the life and peoples of the province, like us because essentially British in habits and feeling, yet unlike because here we have English, Scots, Irish, and French all living an intermixed and closely associated life.

In the story little Emily Byrd Starr, aged eleven, has been left an orphan. We are in time to see the death of her father, Douglas Starr, an unsuccessful journalist, and to learn that though he had never been forgiven for having eloped with Juliet Murray, yet the Murray pride is such that the family will certainly provide for Juliet's daughter. It is decided by the drawing of lots that she shall go to New Moon with two of her aunts. New Moon, called after the ship in which the Murrays sailed from the old country, had been built more than a century ago; the family had spread and prospered, its tentacles were deep down in the island soil, so that we may watch the founding of a new squirearchy as well as obtain glimpses of many aspects of an ordered colonial life.

## [The Dreamland Child]
*Edinburgh Evening News* (Edinburgh, UK)

Readers of L.M. Montgomery's *Emily of New Moon* will take the child heroine to their hearts, so winsome, so provocative, so lovable is she. Emily's principal handicap is that she is a genius, and when genius develops too early in life, it is apt to make things upsetting for the child's elders. This was what Emily found in the austere Prince Edward Island farmhouse whose doors were opened to her on the death of her indulgent father. An atmosphere of prohibition, especially in regard to novel reading and poetry-writing, was irksome to the dreamland child who lived in a fairy realm of her own sweet imaginings; but Emily conquers all, even Aunt Elizabeth, a grim type who is more readily submissive to the claims of duty than to those of affection. *Emily of New Moon* is a tender gracious study, and a further book telling of her later development would not be unwelcome.

# [A Few Years in the Life of a Little Girl]
## *The Globe* (Toronto, ON)

Here is another Canadian story by the author of *Anne of Green Gables*. The scenes are laid in Prince Edward Island, which Miss Montgomery knows so well, and the book is just a few years in the life of a little girl. The average reader will say that no little girl like Emily of New Moon ever lived – so wistful, so quaint, so knowing, so clever. But that does not matter. Little Emily's tragic surroundings gain one's sympathy in the first page or so, and whether she is naughty or impudent, or extremely good, she carries that same sympathy with her right to the end. The death of Emily's father, leaving her an orphan, sends her to the care of her mother's relatives – proud, unbending, frigid islanders with history behind them. Two aunts, who nurse the hallucination that their sister, Emily's mother, married far beneath her, take the child to their gloomy homestead. Of course, Emily suffers no physical discomfort, because physical poverty does not enter into the story, but the highly strung mite endures the mental poverty of the stubborn, fixed ideas of her guardians. "A little child shall lead them,"[4] and Miss Montgomery gradually, but skilfully, has her little heroine make lovable human beings of the maiden aunts, and by means of some phase of the occult bare the truth of the country doctor's tragedy, and bring him to his proper senses. But there never was a little girl like Emily, the reader will say – a little girl who wrote poetry and had such wonderful ambitions, and yet a little girl who got into all the mischief that the others do, and even told fibs and 'fessed up afterward. The child's written descriptions of some of these quaint islanders are really delightful. *Emily of New Moon* ought to be just as successful a volume as *Anne of Green Gables*. It is a pretty story and a restful story, so different from the many turbulent chapters being turned out these days. There is humor and tenderness in every chapter, and pictures of human nature which every person with "relatives" will not fail to comprehend and enjoy. Besides, there is a charming Prince Edward Island background which seems a place apart in this young nation.

# [The Eternal Child]
## *The Guardian* (London, UK)

Of late there have been not a few novels dealing with what may be called child-psychology, but we certainly have never met a more delightful imp than Emily of New Moon. The atmosphere of the book is Canadian, and the scene is laid in Prince Edward Island; but Emily belongs to all ages and to every clime, for she is the eternal child. Every single page in this charming work is pleasing and every single character attractive, but we give the palm, after some hesitation about the rival claims of Aunt Elizabeth, to great-Aunt Nancy,[5] whose vanity and native wickedness even her ninety years have failed to quench.

## [True as Far as It Goes]
### *The Canadian Bookman* (Toronto, ON)
RAYMOND KNISTER

One who has not read "the Green Gables" book since his interest in Anne was that of a contemporary, finds it difficult to say whether *Emily of New Moon* is an improvement or not. Emily is essentially Anne, in the same position in regard to staid guardian relatives. She is more volatile and more perceptive than Anne, as an embryo poet the reality of whose gift we are not allowed to doubt; and this, in allowing for an assortment of cute sayings and whimsical conceits whose arrangement calls for considerable tact, give the author more rope, with which, to put it bluntly, to hang herself. That she does nothing of the sort is owing to a real understanding of this type of child.

Yet there is a flatness, as though Emily were viewed always from the same angle, an underlying sentimentality which is so unobtrusively part and parcel of the matter that one wonders whether sentimentality is not excusable in regard to certain subjects, and which still weakens the book. The author is capable of describing a sunset as though it were a piece of confectionery; and since it is one attitude only to Emily which she is trying to define, the other characters conform, playing up to her with mechanical exactitude. Yet Aunts Elizabeth and Laura, Great-Aunt Nancy and Caroline, Doctor Burnley and Mr. Carpenter are "good," as one says of an art still less classic than that of the novel. They have intervals of life but they don't live; and Emily must have been as here pictured much of the time – only, where is the rest? One need not have swallowed whole the later revelations of "child psychology" to pose this. There is in fact no reason why this kind of book shouldn't be as good as *Peacock Pie* or *A Child's Garden of Verses*.[6] Possibly this one is a classic manque. At least Mrs. Macdonald's experienced deftness is not negligible, and it is honest work, true as far as it goes.

# [A Type of Colonial Life That Fascinates]
## *The Scotsman* (Edinburgh, UK)

*Emily of New Moon*, by L.M. Montgomery, was rather a precocious child. Left an orphan while yet quite young, she is adopted by two rather austere aunts. But Emily had inherited the itch for scribbling from her journalist father, and whenever the "flash" or inspiration came on, she put pencil to paper. The result did not always bring her happiness, for there were times when people read what they were not meant to see. There is humour in the story, and good character drawing, and pictures of a type of colonial life (Prince Edward Island) that fascinate.

# [Sweet without Being Sugary]
## *Punch, or the London Charivari* (London, UK)

I am afraid that some people who order Miss L.M. MONTGOMERY's latest book from the library under the impression that it is a novel in the ordinary acceptation of the term may be a little disappointed when they find that it is not. Therefore I would make a point at once of telling them that the heroine of *Emily of New Moon* is a little little girl when Miss MONTGOMERY begins to tell her story, and not a very big little girl when she stops telling it, and leaves me, for one, expecting and wishing for a sequel. *Emily* is a delightful young creature, original and racy. Though the principal incidents of her story include nothing more thrilling than her adoption, on her father's death, by stern *Aunt Elizabeth* of New Moon, a visit to a notable great-aunt and an attack of measles, in the delirium of which she solves the mystery of the disappearance of the doctor's wife, I found them quite sufficiently absorbing. Unlike many American stories it is sweet without being sugary. Looking back, I feel that Miss MONTGOMERY would have been well advised to tell a more moving tale; but while I was reading it the incidents by the way were much too good to leave me conscious that I was not being taken anywhere in particular.

## [Humor and Tenderness]
### *Manitoba Free Press* (Winnipeg, MB)

The author herself says: "I like this new book better than any I have written since *Green Gables*." Emily and the freckled-faced boy bring life and gaiety to New Moon, and change the stern and forbidding aunts into delightfully human people. This story is rich in humour and tenderness.

## [An Imaginative, Intelligent Child]
### *The New York Herald* (New York, NY)
#### HENRY WALKER

Here is a beautiful piece of literary workmanship of a rare order; fine in artistry, delicately accurate and subtle in its psychology which involves an understanding of childhood not often found in contemporary fiction. It falls into none of the traps that so often bring disaster to the adult who tries to think back, to reproduce the realities of early youth; it is never a travesty, and, above all, it is never oversentimentalized. There is nothing here of the mushy too muchness of pathos that led Don Marquis to sing of

> ... the stones that Dickens shied
> When he had treed a child,[7]

but there is more than one tear-starting passage, and others that move one to a just indignation, though the story, as a whole, is an uplifting, inspiring thing.

It is a record of three years or so in the life of a girl; from the moment of her father's death, just before her eleventh birthday, to the dawn of adolescence and the putting away of childish things. But Emily is no commonplace, stodgy child; it is the girlhood of a poetess and artist, one of the mysteriously elect, that is outlined here. And that is an extraordinarily difficult thing to portray, without slopping over.

The orphaned Emily, who has lived practically alone with her invalid father for several years before his death, naturally seems a wild, peculiar creature to her matter of fact, elderly aunts, the grim Aunt Elizabeth and the mild, ineffectual Aunt Laura, to whom she falls as a charge, as a result of the family council wherein she is disposed of by drawing lots. Aunt Elizabeth is a stern, narrow, but of course well-meaning person, no nonsense about her, but plenty of the "Murray pride." There is also the amiable Uncle Jimmy, who was supposed to be "not quite all there," and who sometimes drops into poetizing himself. The whole thing is dated some thirty years or more ago – at the age when the bustle was just disappearing – and the action all takes place on Prince Edward Island, which, by the way, is a corner neglected of the novelists.

The story is made up of a series of episodes, involving the clash of temperaments between Emily and her aunts, and also her progressive adjustment to the new environment of school, and the contacts with other children: the dreams and meditations and tribulations of a solitary, sensitive, misunderstood child, who is driven to find an outlet in writing letters to her dead father (to be hidden in the attic), and, later, in keeping a diary, wherein she sets down her impressions and also finds a release for her indignations. Some of these letters and entries may seem unchildlike to matter of fact readers, but no one who has been blessed with the confidence of a really imaginative, intelligent child will question the truth of any of them. Sometimes they might be called precocious – which is a compliment, if properly understood; sometimes they are the comic, naive comments, almost of a "Daisy Ashford,"[8] and sometimes they are bits of true poetic insight. Throughout, the narrative gives one the impression of having been lived, not merely imagined.

The character studies of the elders are all strikingly good; often humorous, and always understandingly clear. There is an abundance of action to carry the tale, in spite of its naturally episodic quality; plenty of story to hold the attention. But the rare thing of the book is its portrayal of the delicate, imaginative but always wholly normal and healthy minded child – a figure one will not forget.

## [Sweet with No Derogatory Implication]
### *The New York Tribune* (New York, NY)
ISABEL PATERSON

It is unfortunate that the word sweet has come to connote cloying; for here is a book that deserves the adjective with no derogatory implication. Neither sugary nor sickly, it has the fresh, honest sweetness of white clover honey. It is almost absolutely charming, unpretentious without apology, naive with the naivete of art.

This is a considered eulogy, for one does not dare to be enthusiastic by first intention nowadays. We are inclined to shy at sentiment, because that also has fallen into disrepute, being unjustly confused with sentimentality. The two are indeed separated only by a hairline; but if the genuine article were not priceless, imitations would not so abound, nor so easily pass current with the undiscriminating.

There is a really classic quality in *Emily of New Moon*,[9] a thread of pure gold, and the rest is not tinsel, but honest enough homespun, agreeable padding at which no sensible reader will cavil. For the "flash," as Emily herself called it, lights by reflection as well as instantly. I don't know precisely what Emily meant; but it may have been the same thing I mean. To all of us come moments of unreasoning delight in common things, running water, a flower, a butterfly in the sunshine, a solitary star. Or we come home weary to a room whose every corner we know by heart, and by good fortune find it set in order, with a fire lit on the hearth to welcome us; and heaven could not seem more desirable and dear. Miss Montgomery at moments has power to recapture and impart this sense of wonder, to present familiar objects in a kind of dawn light, as if they were shining new and marvelous.

Having such a rare gift, she has found her right medium and material, and wisely sticks to them. She writes exclusively of first youth, her heroines are always girls, whose story, so far as she is concerned, ends with their 'teens. She loves their awkward graces, their intuitive fumbling reactions to life, and the eternal comedy of their efforts to acquire and apply adult wisdom to their ingenuous difficulties. Her girls are nice girls always. The new psychology might sneer at them as too nice; but they are only normal products of average decent homes. Normal children cannot be anything but unsophisticated, and even precocity need not be morbid.

Miss Montgomery does not require much in the way of a plot to sustain the interest of her study of an unfolding personality. In fact, the story as such does not matter at all. What holds the reader's attention from page to page is the gentle humor, the airy fancies, the delicate and sure evocation of the atmosphere of youth. The finer essence of her talent cannot be isolated in any single paragraph. It consists in little touches, of which the effect is cumulative; so that she finally brings out on the canvas a complete and charming landscape, a whole neighborhood, grass and trees, sea and sky, houses furnished from cellar to attic; cats, dogs, cows and people; each with its own individuality, yet all shown mainly in their relation to and through the eyes of little Emily Starr, of New Moon Farm.

Emily is admittedly an unusual child; it is the novelist's prerogative to choose such. But Emily's difference is mainly an accentuation of normal girlish traits; she can express herself and hold her own at an age when children are mostly imitative in self-defense, taking on protective coloration. Emily is vivid and unsuppressed, because her father, who reared her to the age of eleven, knowing he must soon die, had but one thought in educating her – to enable her to stand alone and survive whatever pressure might later be put on her. Besides, she was a budding artist herself, determined to be "a famous *authoress*."[10] And it is easy to believe she did, ultimately. Her experiences might have been made utterly conventional, for the theme has been employed a thousand times in fiction; an orphan child left to the mercy of a queerly assorted and therefore perfectly credible raft of relatives, mainly uncles and aunts. But it all seems fresh and unhackneyed; the handling of old material is all there is to fiction writing.

Besides Emily there is another delightful child, Ilse Burnley, whose conversation was distinctly original, if not always strictly edifying. Their elders also are very well realized. Indeed, I cannot think, offhand, of a better story of this kind, except *Little Women*. It would take Emily herself to do it justice; she did review books, in her diary, which has all the graphic quality and unconscious humor of the immortal Pet Marjorie's.[11] Here it is possible to give a sample:

"A history of the reformation in France, very relijus and sad. A little fat book deskribing the months in England and the afoursaid Thompson's Seasons. I like to read them because they have so many pretty words in them, but I don't like the feel of them. The paper is so rough and thick it makes me creepy. Travels in Spain, very fassinating, with lovely smooth shiny paper, a missionary book on the Paciffic Islands, pictures very interesting because of the way the heathen chiefs arrange their hair. After they became Christians they cut it off which I think was a pity. Mrs. Hemans Poems. I am passhunately fond of poetry, also of stories about desert islands ... Reuben and Grace, a story but not a novel, because Reuben and Grace are brother and sister and there is no getting married ... Alice in Wonderland, which is perfectly lovely, and the Memoirs of Anzonetta B. Peters who was converted at seven and died at twelve. When anybody asked her a question she answered with a hym verse ... Before that she spoke English."[12]

Surely this is how reviews should be written.

## NOTES

1 *The Springfield Republican*, "Prince Edward Island," 16; "L.M.
  Montgomery Writes a Charming Study of Girlhood," review of *Emily of
  New Moon*, unidentified and undated clipping, in SR, 215.
2 Minot, "Another Montgomery Novel," 7; J.M.T., review of *Emily of New
  Moon*, 3; *The Hartford Courant*, review of *Emily of New Moon*, A12.
3 *The Catholic Standard* (Philadelphia, PA), review of *Emily of New Moon*,
  1 January 1924, in SR, 206; *The New York Times Book Review and
  Magazine*, review of *Emily of New Moon*, 24, 26.
4 This phrase, spoken by Dr. Burnley in *ENM*, 325, is from Isaiah 11:6.
5 I have corrected the original, which reads "great-Aunt Nan."
6 *Peacock Pie: A Book of Rhymes* (1913), by Walter de la Mare (1873–
  1956), English author; *A Child's Garden of Verses* (1885), by Robert Louis
  Stevenson.
7 The volume *Dreams and Dust* (1915) by Don Marquis (1878–1937),
  American author, includes a poem entitled "Dickens," but it does not
  include the two lines cited here.
8 Daisy Ashford (1881–1972), English writer whose novella *The Young
  Visiters*, written when she was nine years old, was published in 1919.
9 I have corrected the original, which reads "'Emily of Green Gables.'"
10 *ENM*, 38.
11 Marjorie Fleming (1803–1811), a Scottish child writer whose diary was
   published as *Pet Marjorie: A Story of Child Life Fifty Years Ago* beginning
   in 1864.
12 *ENM*, 99–100.

# 14

## Emily Climbs

—— 1925 ——

As with *Emily of New Moon*, reviews of *Emily Climbs* celebrated its depiction
of a highly appealing title protagonist, an engaging supporting cast of characters, and a story of adolescence that appealed to readers of all ages. In a review
in the *Boston Herald*, John Clair Minot declared that "Miss Montgomery
deserves her fast-growing audience for she tells her story with real artistry
and with a fine understanding of the things that count in young lives." The
*Pittsburgh Chronicle Telegraph* called the book "one of the most delightful
tales published by Mr. Montgomery," and while the *Philadelphia Inquirer*
was tepid in its praise – "The story is interestingly written. While it contains
no great literary qualities, it renders a worthwhile account of a simple life
raised above the level of the commonplace" – *The New Outlook* of Toronto
proclaimed that Emily "promises to become a Canadian tradition." To this
the *San Francisco Chronicle* added that "the mass of puppet characters who
parade the walks of the bulk of the new stories for girls become mere paper
dolls beside her."[1]

Additional reviews once again revealed much about reviewers' assumptions
about readerly expectations, the conventions of genre, and the author herself.
One clipping suggested that "readers interested in that high-hearted, dauntless,
and gifted heroine will not be satisfied to take leave of her on the threshold of
her literary career while somewhat in doubt concerning her young lover, Teddy,
who is beginning to win his way in art. For myself, I am curiously concerned
about a nobler lover, the deformed Dean Priest." According to the *Hartford
Courant* of Connecticut, "Miss Montgomery is a genuinely gifted writer of
books of this type, sensible, wholesome, old-fashioned stories suggesting the

tales of the lamented Louisa M. Alcott. It is interesting to note that there is still a vogue for such books, sophisticated and disillusioned as the oncoming generation is supposed to be." According to another clipping, "One is tempted to think L.M. Montgomery must have many 'Jimmy books' or diaries such as those in which Emily not only chronicled her life and gave vent to her poetic fancies, but recorded interesting tales she had heard." Yet another clipping commented that, "if the love story does not end quite as the reader wishes, the door is not finally closed and the reader is left speculating about the sequel ... There is nothing to regret in such a book as this, nothing for which to apologize. All is wholesome, simple, spontaneous and original, and the reader lays the book down with the determination to read it over again soon."[2]

Indeed, although many of the reviews identified *Emily Climbs* as somehow a "typical" Montgomery text, there was also the suggestion, once again, that Montgomery could never attain the same charm or popularity that she did with *Anne of Green Gables*. A clipping entitled "Second Story of Emily Typical of Its Author" elaborated on this notion: "When an authoress finds a pretty melody that she can play, and does it over and over again with variations, one always feels that it is losing something of its original charm in the process of repetition. Every time that a new book by L.M. Montgomery is published one thinks that she has never risen a second time to the level of *Anne of Green Gables*. Then the thought comes that perhaps 'Anne' stands out because that book had the added merit of freshness. Maybe if we had not read about the people at Green Gables, *Emily of New Moon* would take the same premiere position that the earlier book occupies."[3]

## [Emily of High School Age]
### *The Davenport Democrat and Leader* (Davenport, IA)

When Miss Montgomery wrote *Emily of New Moon* she created a character that was a worthy successor to *Anne of Green Gables*. In this story we have the developing Emily of High School age and at its close about to realize the career she had always dreamed of – who *wasn't* getting married. Yet here we have freckled-faced Perry, priggish Andrew and Teddy, whom she *might* have substituted for her career, trying to change her mind. The tale ends on a note that suggests Miss Montgomery's young readers will hear more about Emily and Teddy, and they will be quite eager to.

# [No Less Captivating]
## *The Advertiser–Journal* (Auburn, NY)

Brilliant and elfin little Emily of *Emily of New Moon* reappears this week, older and more mature but no less surprising, in L.M. Montgomery's follow up story *Emily Climbs*. It is a season when many important novels are being put forth but one can predict with safety that this new Emily story will not be submerged. For it has something to stand upon and can keep its head above the increasing autumn tide. Emily made her mark some seasons ago and Miss Montgomery goes ahead with her career in no less captivating a manner than before. Now we read of Emily in high school, a delightful miss who begins to dream and is prone to pranks. There is constant hubbub and interest where Emily and her new chums foregather, exciting happenings, good humor, wholesome atmosphere. Emily learns that love is nice but is eager to climb. A freckle-faced lad woos her and a bank-clerk would have her. Romantic fancies crowd the mind of this real girl. Her life is a whirl (without cesspool features that some modern writers would provide) and the reader's interest in Emily does not fall off for an instant. The climax of the pretty and brisk story comes when Emily is offered the chance which she has craved. Acceptance means cutting the ties at New Moon. Miss Montgomery narrates Emily's development with skill and the new book will afford much real pleasure. Readers who have not yet made Emily's acquaintance would do well to grasp this latest opportunity.

# *Emily Climbs*, Is New Book
## *St. Catharines Standard* (St. Catharines, ON)
### LILLIAN LEVERIDGE

A new book by L.M. Montgomery is something of an event in the Canadian literary world – at least, a multitude of readers feel that way about it. Miss Montgomery has a happy faculty of creating living, growing characters. We feel at the end of a book that we have not quite lost them, but only said goodbye for a while; and sure enough, they turn up again, even more winsome and alluring than before, beckoning us to follow them through a new series of whimsical or romantic adventures.

In *Emily of New Moon* the author introduced us to a new heroine and an entirely fresh set of characters and environment. Emily Starr brought her own love with her; and in the new book, *Emily Climbs*, we renew her acquaintance and live with her during the interesting High School period of young girlhood. All the old friends – the Aunts, Cousin Jimmy, Ilse, Perry, Teddy, Dean – as well as a number of new ones, are met with in these pages.

Emily is a typical Montgomery girl – sweet and innocent, piquant, dreamy, spontaneously original, and as lovable as she is lovely. This Emily is a budding literary genius, and one cannot but feel that the author has put a great deal of herself into this charming biography – not literal fact, perhaps, but soul truth, colored and tinctured with a romantic imagination. The young writer's inspiration, her sense of being the instrument of some mysterious, unseen Power – this is realism, but a realism that has nothing to do with sordidness, though some writers would have us believe that the words are synonymous. To quote Emily's own words: "When that line came into my mind it didn't seem to me that *I* composed it at all – it seemed as if *Something Else* were trying to speak through me – and it was the *Something Else* that made the line seem wonderful."[4] Who can doubt that this comes nearer to history than fiction?

It may be remembered that Emily had recorded a vow:

"I, Emily Byrd Starr, do solemnly vow this day that I will climb the Alpine Path and write my name on the scroll of fame."[5]

Even a genius could not more than begin that upward climb during the High School days, but Emily does make a very creditable beginning. She is not daunted, though often cast down, by the cold water cast by doubting relatives upon her ambitions, nor by any number of printed rejection slips; and when the coveted first cheque arrives, what reader does not share her ecstasy?

Emily's impulsive and daring spirit leads her into many a humorous predicament, as well as into some tensely dramatic situations. There is a touch of the psychic in her personality, and one episode in particular passes beyond the borders of explainable fact.

The rose light of love's young dream casts its glamour over her girlhood, but one does not look for anything very intense in a school girl of seventeen. The bewitching little heroine leaves the stage unclaimed, though not altogether heartwhole, and so we are reasonably confident of meeting her again some future day and following her maturer fortunes.

## [The Power of Imagery]
### *The Globe* (Toronto, ON)

"The wet dawn came up from the gulf in the wake of the spent storm and crept greyly into the little spare room of the whitewashed house on the hill. Emily woke with a start from a troubled dream of seeking – and finding – the lost boy. But where she had found him she could not now remember. Ilse was still asleep at the back of the bed, her pale-gold curls lying in a silken heap on the pillow. Emily, her thoughts still tangled in the cobweb meshes of her dream, looked around the room – and thought she must be dreaming still. By the tiny table, covered with its white, lace-trimmed cloth, a woman was sitting – a tall, stout, old woman, wearing over her thick grey hair a spotless white widow's cap, such as the old Highland Scotchwomen still wore in the early years of the century. She had on a dress of plum-coloured drugget with a large, snowy apron, and she wore it with the air of a queen. A neat blue shawl was folded over her breast. Her face was curiously white and deeply wrinkled ... The beautiful, clear blue eyes looked as if their owner had been dreadfully hurt sometime. This must be the old Mrs. McIntyre of whom Mrs. Hollinger had spoken. And if so, then old Mrs. McIntyre was a very dignified personage indeed."[6]

The passage is from Chapter XIV of L.M. Montgomery's new novel, *Emily Climbs*. Perhaps the strength of Miss Montgomery's (now Mrs. Ewan Macdonald) work lies chiefly in her power of imagery, of which the above paragraph is a vivid sample. In so many words has she not made the picture of that room complete? Note the sequence of her descriptive circles. The reader is taken from the atmosphere of the wet dawn – swiftly and without jar – into the room where Emily was sleeping and has just now awakened. The circle narrows to Emily and her room, and finally to this quaint old lady seated there. Note the ease with which the reader is transported from scene to scene in a paragraph of a little over one hundred words; yet the scene lies lucid before one, and the picture is complete. One becomes intensely interested in the old lady, and intensely curious to know more about her before the paragraph is completed.

This power of imagery with Miss Montgomery seems only second to her almost uncanny insight into the reactions of the mind of the growing girl. To write with the buoyancy and freshness that characterizes her work one must have to keep young in outlook and have an intense love of all things beautiful and good.

Perhaps these are the two great secrets of Miss Montgomery's books, for they certainly have some definite or indefinite charm that makes them popular. She is in the forefront of Canadian authors who have obtained a grip on the reading public outside the borders of their own country. Certainly there is little in the way of plot novelty to be found in her works. Things happen in them with the regularity of real life, and seldom bring about what might be called an exciting crisis. It is the bringing out of the true inward beauty of commonplace people and circumstances that lends continuous charm to her books.

The book at present under discussion is not a man's book – though fathers of growing daughters may read it with appreciation. It is essentially a woman's book – for the woman who likes to be taken a-back to the things dear to younger days, and for the young girl who yearns to glimpse the problems, the joys and the disappointments of another of her kind and live them with her. The stage of Emily's life that is herein taken up is that between the ages of fourteen and seventeen – the high school period. Readers of Miss Montgomery's previous books will recognize Emily as a typical Montgomery girl – unsophisticated but original: an idealist sometimes surprising one with her practical thoughts, and withal lovely and lovable. Like others of her chief characters, Emily has a flair of literature, and her curious and impulsive mind leads her into some odd predicaments and a few dramatic situations.

The novel concludes as though it undoubtedly would have a sequel in the life of Emily when she has grown to maturity.

## By L.M. Montgomery
### *The Gazette* (Montreal, QC)

Those who have read and enjoyed *Emily of New Moon* will better appreciate this continuation of Emily's career. The author has a pleasing faculty of depicting attractive young women. Emily was an orphan who was taken charge of by her aunts Elizabeth and Laura Murray, whose home was the New Moon farm. The first book, which read like a fine romance, brought Emily to the age of fourteen. In this new volume she climbs to the age of seventeen. The characters include those which helped to make her early story interesting, with some new ones she met at the high school. The meannesses and crankiness developed in a little community in Prince Edward Island, where the scene is laid, as well as the kindness and strength, are depicted in the characters, in a way to amuse or stir the better feelings of the reader. The book ranks well up among the good ones in an awful outpouring of fiction.

## [No Wavering of Interest]
### *Boston Evening Transcript* (Boston, MA)

There is always a question, when an author has created a really charming character, whether it is safe to carry on that character in another book. Apparently Miss Montgomery is one of the few persons who can do this safely. There is no wavering of the interest we felt in *Emily of New Moon* in this new story in which Emily grows up. She is literally growing up in the course of the story, for it finds Emily at fourteen, filled with her serious determination to be a writer and her more immediate ambition to go to Shrewsbury High School. And in spite of the love making which creeps into the story, it leaves Emily still a girl, still ambitious and with life just opening before her with no paths charted and the whole of happiness or achievement before her.

Miss Montgomery has an unusually successful way of establishing her heroines in the hearts of her readers. It is the definite and the recurrent charm of her books.

## [A Worthy Successor to the Beloved Anne]
### *The Montreal Daily Star* (Montreal, QC)

The numerous followers of L.M. Montgomery, who have already made the acquaintance of her new heroine in *Emily of New Moon*, will, of course, want to follow Emily's career just as closely as they followed that of Anne of Green Gables. The authoress obligingly provides them with the opportunity to do so in *Emily Climbs*, which carries Emily into and through the high school period from fourteen to seventeen. This high-spirited girl, whose impulsive character and love of adventure inevitably lead her into all sorts of situations, both humorous and embarrassing, is a genuinely attractive type, lovable, whimsical, full of romance, but never weak or maudlin. Emily is a happy and worthy successor of the beloved Anne.

## A Rosebud Garden of Girls
### *The New York Herald Tribune Books* (New York, NY)
ISABEL PATERSON

We left Emily Byrd Starr at New Moon Farm three years ago, by fiction time, when she had just turned fourteen. Her arduous but innocent climbing takes her three years further along; when we part with her this second time, no less regretfully, she'll be "seventeen come Sunday,"[7] but still the same sweet minx, at once prim and outrageous, bold and sensitive, naively ignorant and uncannily clever, with a suggestion of prunes and prisms and a dash of Puck. The charm of adolescence, which is something like the awkward grace of a very young colt, is a difficult thing to pin down on paper; so difficult that L.M. Montgomery has practically no rival in this field among contemporary writers. (Booth Tarkington is concerned rather with the humors of youth than with its fitful poetry.[8]) And while prophecy is rather an idle occupation, and it isn't likely I shall be revisiting these glimpses of the moon to verify the notion, still I shouldn't wonder if Emily took her place in due time among the immortal children of literature – with Meg and Jo and Amy, with Kim and the Brushwood Boy and the Marchioness and Huck Finn.[9]

This is a large claim, the larger because that happy band which inhabits the kingdom of perpetual youth is so small; but it doesn't really matter, for I'm not writing for posterity myself. All I mean to say is that here and now Emily is a joy for readers of any age. I didn't know, on reading *Emily of New Moon*, if it was what is known as a "girl's book" or not; so I gave it to a grandfather who likes Anatole France and Scott Fitzgerald, and so forth.[10] He read it with chuckles and serious appreciation.

Miss Montgomery's great gift is that she remembers the emotional values of youth and can depict the tragi-comedies of the 'teens without condescension or the untimely intrusion of an adult cynicism. She realizes with genuine sympathy that Emily could never, in after years, suffer more intensely from the greatest disappointment or humiliation life might bring than she did from appearing in class with a black moustache inked on her face by a spiteful schoolfellow. Nor would she ever come nearer touching the iridescent bubble of fame than when her first poem achieved print in a "real magazine" – even if they didn't pay cash, but only a subscription! No later achievement of a place among the Best Sellers could match that for a thrill.

Emily, as may be guessed, is going to be an authoress. But most of her activities are less dignified than scribbling. The events themselves are inconsequential, perhaps; Emily isn't. New Moon farm is no longer the main background. Emily had to go to Shrewsbury to complete her schooling, so she is out in the big world, as Prince Edward Island understands the term. But her companions are much the same – Ilse Burnley, of the high-explosive temper and vivid vocabulary, and Teddy Kent, who wanted to be an artist; and Perry Miller, the boy from Stovepipe Town, who fully intended to be Premier of Canada some day. Not that he ever said a word to that effect; nor does Miss Montgomery say so. She is really a highly skilled writer in the genre she has chosen; she knows what to leave out. The puppy loves of the four are quite delightfully indicated, though the only "love scene" has a touch of comedy and precipitates a terrific row. But one knows that Ilse will marry Perry – one knows it by her rages at him. A sentence in the last chapter clinches conviction:

"'He's such a cackling oaf,' said Ilse morosely."[11]

They might as well have been already married.

But Emily remains heart-free, though her fancy is a little touched by Teddy Kent; so her story breaks off: it does not end. This isn't a great book, nor an epoch-making one; but at the very least it is gay and charming and artfully artless and completely enjoyable.

## [Lack of Romance]
### *The Hamilton Herald* (Hamilton, ON)

There are a great number of women writers who write about girls, and most of their stuff reads like a sop to the religious welfare artists, but occasionally some gifted authoress can get beyond that, and write a book that is neither a flapper narrative of petting orgies, nor a treatise on duty and Christian living. This has been done by L.M. Montgomery, famed as the author of *Anne of Green Gables*, in her most recent work, *Emily Climbs*.

Taking the girl through her high school life, the authoress deserves much credit, for it is certainly not the most picturesque nor romantic part of a girl's life. And in assuming the task of portraying such a difficult age the authoress assumed much. We have a very vague idea indeed, of our great-grandfathers, but, on the other hand, we have a good idea of the physiognomy of granddad. The analogy can be drawn between our bewhiskered forebears and novels of child life. Our mature thoughts we know. We are men and women and can appreciate, to some degree, what is going on in the minds of our fellow creatures; but fleeting and childish impressions have gone the way of last winter's snow, and we can't conjure them up again, Faust fashion. So when L.M. Montgomery undertakes to portray the fourteen-to-seventeen age in a girl's life, she is assuming the task of crystallizing the whimsical thoughts of an immature, schoolgirlish mind. This means the love interest cannot be worked into the narrative fabric, and for some people, this lack of romance stales the book right away.

## Successor to Anne
### *The Chicago Evening Post Literary Review* (Chicago, IL)
LAURA HINKLEY

I apologize hereby to Emily and her author for having thought (without reading them) that all the "Anne of Green Gables" contingent must be a sort of lesser Pollyannity. This book is my first acquaintance with that exuberant clan; and I was wrong. Emily is delightful. Not that the book which presents her adolescence is without faults. It has, on the contrary, many faults, and the name of most of them is excess. Not that it isn't perilously poised between two stools: not exactly a "juvenile," and certainly not adult. Those old-fashioned people who can remember Louisa M. Alcott will have its nearest analog. But Emily is more exuberant and less proportioned than Meg and Jo. In fact, she is Meg, Jo and Amy all at once – but chiefly Jo – and not Beth at all.

To enumerate the faults of *Emily Climbs* in the hateful, nagging way reviewers have: The style, in spite of a sunny, singing sense of the beauty of common things, is too fluent, running on to unmeasured excesses of unselected detail. The plot is a thing of shreds and patches, held together only by the enlarging and interacting identities of the characters, which do not sufficiently enlarge and interact thereby to justify it. Particularly, I don't like Mrs. Montgomery's penchant for the non compos mentis.[12] This plot is rounded out by means of at least four persons who are not quite all there. The characters are just a little exaggerated, a little stereotyped. Even Emily is too charming. How could one girl combine all the allure of Emily? And the book has that quality which chiefly exasperates one in virtually all juveniles – the quality of being very nicely censored at the source.

In short, the very faults of this book are of the kind which will make a great many people like reading it all the better.

## Montgomery's Latest
### *The Toronto Daily Star* (Toronto, ON)

In a smaller and much more desirable way books by Lucy Montgomery occupy a place much akin to those of the Elsie and Pansy books of a generation ago. This author's Canadian stories are just as feminine, but they are written with vastly more knowledge of life and in far better literary style. It is no discredit to say this, because the stories of one B.P. Roe with an enormous vogue, had also the defects of their class, yet people still read them, and not long ago a Toronto newspaper published one as a serial.[13]

*Emily Climbs*[14] is a story of a girl who was born to better things than dishwashing, had a soul for poetry, and later a sale for it; left New Moon with its peculiarities, where she was half at home, and went to a boarding school; had her difficulties with the old aunt with whom she boarded – and in this old dame one detects the main spirit of the book, which seems to be a breaking out from the old life of the tansy tea, and the Murray traditions as grown on Canadian soil.

The story is much more robustious than most stories of that far back period; but it all grows out of the pensive girl on the cover, who wore nice prim dresses, and had three books on the grass, and looked away into the clouds for her dreams to come true – which of course was poetry. There was a scrimmage in a church at night, which in less delicate hands – say those of Sheila Kaye Smith – might have become very improper; there were walks at night which Ellen Glasgow would have made ten times more functional, and economic predicaments which Edna Ferber could have made much more vividly picturesque.[15] But none or all of these have quite the simple charm and lyric note of the Canadian novelist, who to her great credit has always had the courage to stick to her own sweet manner of writing, has no desire to become just dynamic, has a fine sense of expressed humor, and a great respect for the Canadian life, which she so eloquently and entertainingly depicts.

The life at boarding school is admirably depicted. The wry characters at New Moon are real and lifelike. Emily herself is real[16] – of that period, but not now, for no such girls exist any more – though girls were quite as real when men saw less of them at a time, in the days of long skirts, long hair, long sleeves, long letters, long courtships, long marriages – oh yes, quite as real.

## [The Beauty in All Things]
### *The New Outlook* (Toronto, ON)

Here is the sequel to *Emily of New Moon*, which introduced to us a new Montgomery character some time ago. Again the scene is laid in Prince Edward Island in the lovely old house, "New Moon," which is so vividly pictured for the reader that it is real indeed. Emily's aunts, who try so hard to discourage all attempts at writing because they are sure no good will come of it, are typical of a certain type of person, familiar to us all. Emily's happiest hours are those spent writing the stories and poems that are the product of her vivid imagination, into the books with which her uncle Jimmy provides her, and which she calls her "Jimmy Book."[17] Emily's experiences at high school, her friends there, the difficulties of her home life, as well as the beauty that she saw in all things, make up the story of the years in which *Emily Climbs*.

## Drawn on Old Lines
### *Regina Post* (Regina, SK)

Lucy Montgomery's books are hopelessly Victorian. Her Emilys and Annes are sweet and good and wholesome.[18] When Emily with a girl friend and two boy friends are caught out in a storm and have to stay in a deserted house all night, and Ilse gets drunk, there is no harm done although the tongue of scandal wags for a time. This is the story of a young girl, with love barely hinted at, for Emily is still heart-whole if not quite fancy free when we regretfully leave her.

The truth must out. Most of us are really Victorian in our taste, and the old fashioned heroine who is innocent and pure if she is pretty or witty, wears better in books as in real life than sophisticated ladies in green hats who think nothing of calling on a strange young man and staying a day or so with him if he is sufficiently emancipated from the restrictions of hum-drum morality.

Emily of New Moon was a fascinating child and as the girl is the mother of the woman, she grows up delightfully in the leisurely way of the Montgomery heroines so that we have only four years of school life, of dreams and hopes and beginnings, in this book. All the aunts and the cousins of *Emily of New Moon* are in this book. Aunt Ruth, the stern, fault-finding suspicious and unpleasant petty tyrant who made Emily's literary efforts so difficult, turns out a perfect darling in the end, and there are episodes like the story of "The Woman Who Spanked the King" which add spice to the quiet, pleasant story.

## [The Fine Philosophy of Youth]
### *The Scotsman* (Edinburgh, UK)

In *Emily Climbs*, Miss L.M. Montgomery enables us to renew acquaintance with an interesting character. Emily's diary is as natural and spontaneous as ever a schoolgirl kept,[19] full of joyous humour, little flashes of "cattishness," aspirations, and disappointments, the last borne with the fine philosophy of youth. The book has a Canadian atmosphere of much charm.

## [Every Bit as Irresistible]
### *The Bookman* (London, UK)

Every bit as irresistible as Anne in *Anne of Green Gables*,[21] Emily, whom we have already known as a child in *Emily of New Moon*, climbs in these pages into larger and wider adventures. The book is principally written in diary form and in her "Jimmy-book" (a present from the understanding Cousin Jimmy) delightful glimpses are gained of her fresh and refreshing views on many things. The narrow atmosphere created by the prim aunts with whom she lived would have crushed the spirit of many girls, but Emily was blessed with an absorbing passion for writing, and in her creative joy all else faded into nothingness. Her serenity was recovered immediately by a visit to the "Land of Uprightness" (a group of trees not far from the house). With a joyous nature and full of happy friendships she takes her literary successes and failures alike in a very game spirit and endears herself to all.

## [A Charming Delineation of Girlhood]
### *The Queenslander* (Brisbane, Australia)

L.M. Montgomery is the Louisa Alcott of Canada and the "Anne of Green Gable" books are almost as well known as the "Little Woman" series of that famous American. In *Emily Climbs*, Mrs. Montgomery has continued the history of Emily Byrd Starr (Emily of New Moon).

Emily has reached her 'teens and is consumed with literary ambitions, and the new story deals with the school life and gradual unfolding of the young girl's literary promise. Like all the Anne books, *Emily Climbs* is a wholesome and charming delineation of girlhood, and one is quite safe in predicting a successful future for Emily in the affections of Australian girls.

## [Sentimental Stuff]
### *Cape Times* (Cape Town, South Africa)

A story of American small-town girl-student life. Mrs. Montgomery's Emily has all the qualities we have learned to expect in the heroine of a novel of this sort. She is beautiful and virtuous, she excels in her class work, she has literary genius. She keeps the inevitable diary, of which we have extracts. She sees in the moon, in the wind, in the trees what no one else sees. She sweeps and dusts, and writes soulful poems. She has, in this case, in addition, the "Murray" pride, although just why the Murrays should be proud is difficult to see. She has the usual elderly admirer, waiting until her school days are finished to propose marriage. But the book is written in a simple and homely fashion, and, once away from the student atmosphere, there are some refreshing incidents and descriptions, such as the tale of "The Woman Who Spanked the King." *Emily Climbs* is sentimental stuff, but Mrs. Montgomery has descriptive qualities enough to keep her characters alive, and to paint them for us as she imagines them to be.

## [Not a Modern Type of Girl]
### *The Evening Post* (Wellington, New Zealand)

*Emily Climbs*, by L.M. Montgomery, is a good book for girls. It comes as a refreshing example of high literary art. Emily is a delightful girl, a lover of Nature in any shape or form; idealistic, a dreamer. Extracts from her diary show that she is not a modern type of girl. She lives in a world peopled with fairy folk, and the earthly joys of the modern "flapper" have no appeal for her. Stolid, critical grown-ups; selfish people of her own age; and dream folk all, have a hand in shaping the destiny of Emily of New Moon. The adventures of Emily are worth watching. Mrs. Montgomery has written many delightfully frank tales such as *Anne of Green Gables*,

*Chronicles of Avonlea, Kilmeny of the Orchard*, and *The Story Girl* with the same fragrance that characterises Emily's diary.

## [A Kick out of Emily's Climbs]
### *Manitoba Free Press* (Winnipeg, MB)

We didn't really intend to read this book – it looked, well, kind of mushy, but looking at the middle we found some interesting pages. Finally we arrived at the beginning and later on at the end. We got quite a "kick" out of Emily's climbs, out of her escapades and out of the satire which filled her "Jimmy Book." We say "we," advisedly, for probably the most important part of the "we" on this page would not subscribe to our sentiments. Anyhow it's an interesting story. It is Canadian and it shows pride in things Canadian. It has no beginning to speak of and no ending. It is clean all through and its only moral, determination to succeed, is the most essential element in success.

## *Cacoethes Scribendi*
### *The Englishman* (Calcutta, India)

*Emily Climbs*, by L.M. Montgomery, deals with the struggles of a would-be author to enter the hallowed circles of literature in spite of the efforts of her guardians to keep her at home engaged on ordinary feminine avocations. Miss Montgomery holds that the genius of a person cannot be suppressed by outward difficulties and the unsympathetic attitude of her friends. The difficulties and the trials of a freelance who by industry, persistence and an inherent capacity for writing rises to fame are cleverly portrayed.

## NOTES

1 Minot, review of *Emily Climbs*, 12; *Pittsburgh Chronicle Telegraph* (Pittsburgh, PA), review of *Emily Climbs*, 23 October 1925, in SR, 250; Mary F. Missett, "Simple Life Raised above the Commonplace," review of *Emily Climbs*, *The Philadelphia Inquirer* (Philadelphia, PA), 17 October 1925, in SR, 243; *The New Outlook*, review of *Emily Climbs*, 22; *San Francisco Chronicle*, "Younger Generation," B3.

2 Review of *Emily Climbs*, unidentified and undated clipping, in SR, 237; *The Hartford Courant* (Hartford, CT), "Well, Girls Still Read These Simple Stories!" 30 August 1925, in SR, 245; review of *Emily Climbs*, unidentified and undated clipping, in SR, 249; review of *Emily Climbs*, unidentified and undated clipping, in SR, 250.

3 "Second Story of Emily Typical of Its Author," unidentified and undated clipping, in SR, 250.

4 *EC*, 4.

5 *ENM*, 290.

6 *EC*, 191.

7 Title of a nineteenth-century British broadside ballad.

8 Booth Tarkington (1869–1946), American novelist best known for *The Magnificent Ambersons* (1918) and *Alice Adams* (1921), both of which won the Pulitzer Prize and were adapted for the screen multiple times.

9 These characters appeared in the following texts: *Little Women* (1868), by Louisa May Alcott; *Kim* (1901), a novel by Rudyard Kipling (1865–1936), English writer; "The Brushwood Boy," from Kipling's short story collection *The Day's Work* (1898); *Dear Little Marchioness: The Story of a Child's Faith and Love* (1895), published anonymously in the United States; *Adventures of Huckleberry Finn* (1885), by Mark Twain.

10 Anatole France (1844–1924), prolific and Nobel Prize–winning French author; F. Scott Fitzgerald (1896–1940), American novelist best known for *The Great Gatsby* (1925).

11 *EC*, 321.

12 A Latin phrase meaning "not of sound mind."

13 Possibly a reference to Edward Payson Roe (1838–1888), popular American writer of Evangelical literature known as E.P. Roe.

14 I have corrected the original, which reads "'Lucy Climbs.'"

15 Sheila Kaye-Smith (1887–1956), British author of novels with rural settings, whose book *The End of the House of Alard* (1923) had been a recent best-seller; Ellen Glasgow (1873–1945), American author of *Barren Ground* (1925); Edna Ferber (1885–1968), American author whose novel *So Big* (1924) had won the Pulitzer Prize.

16 I have corrected the original, which reads "The Emily herself is real."

17 Twice in this sentence, I have corrected the original, which reads "Jimmie." Jimmy Murray is in fact Emily's cousin.

18 I have corrected the original, which reads "Her Emilys and Annies."

19 I have corrected the original, which reads "ever schoolgirl kept."

20 I have corrected the original, which reads "Ann" when referring to both character and book title.

# 15

## *The Blue Castle*

—— 1926 ——

Reviews of *The Blue Castle* took the book seriously as a major departure for Montgomery, but some of them suggested that her concerns about straying too much from the expectations of her audience were not without foundation: As one unidentified clipping stated, "The name of L.M. Montgomery has long since become a by-word for a certain type of book in Canadian fiction. In fact the novelist from Abegweit has become nothing less than a Canadian institution." The *Daily Times* of Otago, New Zealand, even suggested that "it is a difficult matter ... for an author who has contracted the habit of writing for the young to attune her writing to the taste of the more mature reader." Fortunately, as stated in the *Calgary Herald*, "admirers of [*Anne of Green Gables*] have followed [Montgomery] loyally and patiently in the hope that one day she would give them a story which would equal or surpass Anne in theme and reader interest. That day has arrived, and *The Blue Castle* is the story." Yet as the *New York Times Book Review* noted, "although perhaps a little more mature in its spirit than the earlier books," this book "is unmistakably from first page to last an L.M. Montgomery novel, compact of sentiment, rosily trimmed with romance, peopled with beings drawn solely out of the imagination, but telling a well-made story with humor and pathos."[1]

This time, criticisms of the book were couched in largely positive comments. The *El Paso Times* of Texas referred to it as "another handful of mud slung at Main street people, but a good story," to which the *Boston Evening Transcript* added that Montgomery "has a strong vein of ironic humor which enlivens the somewhat unexciting settings of her stories." Bernice Clark, writing in the *Border Cities Star* of Windsor, Ontario, suggested that "the outcome of it all is rather obvious since one is so sure of a happy ending, but *The Blue Castle* is, nevertheless, a very interesting story and definitely in the field of adult fiction. It is written in Miss Montgomery's usual easy style, with sly bits of humor here and there and some really fine descriptions of the Muskoka woods and our Canadian seasons. Many of these descriptions verge almost on poetry." Indeed, *The New Outlook* in Toronto argued that "the chapters dealing with the four seasons as they are seen through the nature loving eyes of Valancy are by far the best in the whole book."[2]

The *Literary Review* of New York was more critical of the novel, referring to it as "a story that will cause impatience because it is implausible," adding that its protagonist "drugs herself with a saccharine confection, her Blue Castle in Spain, an imaginative creation suitable to the fancy and intelligence of pre-adolescence." Yet overall the reaction was positive, the Rochester *Democrat and Chronicle* even suggesting that the novel contains the "beauty of maturity. More than any of the others it is a real novel. [Montgomery] has progressed and gives promise of going far on a higher level than she has hitherto attained." The *Camden Evening Courier* of New Jersey noted that "there is a time in the life of almost every girl when she revels in slip-and-go-easy stories, romances in which the poor, unattractive, lonely girl marries an obscure man who turns out to be a prince in disguise or a millionaire recluse. *The Blue Castle* is this kind of a book." But this review then added, "It is better than many of its kind because the characterization is rather well done ... and the narrative moves so swiftly there is no time to question its probability." Commenting on Montgomery's success in breaking into "the field of adult literature" with this novel, the Charlottetown *Patriot* noted that "L.M. Montgomery definitely evades the problem novel, and writes, as she says, to provide fresh and sane entertainment, portraying the kind of people she knows, who have ideals of 'loyalty, upright dealing, kindness of heart, a sense of responsibility, a glint of humor and a little decent reserve.' This is a large order, but that she is capable of handling it, one need only to open her new book and fall under the spell of the heroine and the Blue Castle she builds of her dreams."[3]

But while reviewers were impressed with the departures found in this novel, some of them used language that suggested a somewhat different text. The *Times–Dispatch* of Virginia declared in its review that the book is "so full of tingles." Perhaps not surprisingly given this type of language, the *New York World* called it "the story of a girl who determines to have one last fling after being told she had only a year to live. A real romantic tale and one the flapper might well read." And a review in the *Springfield Sunday Union and Republican* of Massachusetts contains the following statement: "At 29 Heroine of *The Blue Castle* Transcends Repression."[4]

## [The Mouse Becomes the Lion]
### *The Argus* (Melbourne, Australia)

Known to all schoolgirls as the author of *Anne of Green Gables*,[5] Miss L.M. Montgomery has produced a novel for "grown ups" entitled *The Blue Castle*. As might be expected, Miss Montgomery's work is of no very great depth, and comes under that category that women readers describe as "sweet" or "pretty." The former is perhaps the better description, and "saccharine" would be better still. Valancy Stirling was a very much oppressed girl of no particular looks, and worst of all she was 29 years of age and no admirer had appeared on her horizon. This in itself was a tragedy to Valancy and a catastrophe to her family. The family were an appalling infliction for any girl, and had probably as much to do with the girl's absence of admirers as her lack of charm. They simply suffocated Valancy's youth. Then the girl suddenly finds she is smitten with heart disease that is incurable, and gives her but 12 months to live. She keeps her knowledge to herself, and the fact that she has no future gives her courage to defy the oppressors. If she must die, Valancy determines to make the remainder of her days a "welter." The mouse becomes the lion, and deals with the oppressors, family and relations, in a manner that is far more diverting than probable. She meets them either individually or in force as occasion offers, and routs them all. She decides that she will make the castle of her dreams come true, and after disclosing the brevity of her life to him she recklessly proposes marriage to a man who is regarded as the town's chiefest scallywag. Thereafter the readers must follow her fortunes for themselves. Valancy is an appealing figure, and very "sweet," but Miss Montgomery, though her methods are effective, displays some lack of ingenuity in working out her plot.

## [Natural, although Unusual]
### *The Auckland Star* (Auckland, New Zealand)

There are very few girls who would not be the better for reading Mrs. Montgomery's *The Blue Castle*, although parental strictness and the suppression by relatives which afflicted the heroine of this story are exceptional, if not unknown, in this country. A girl of twenty-nine, kept in domestic subjection all her life in a dull middle-class Canadian home, learns that she has no more than a year to live, and decides to kick over the traces of restraint, escape from her family, and get as much freedom and enjoyment as possible. The alarm of her relatives, her unselfish method of acquiring independence, and her adventures generally are most natural, although unusual. The conversations are as charming as they are witty, and the numerous related characters are each and all memorable, their failings being stressed in such a way by the authoress that the reader is constantly on the watch for faults of his own. As a book for girls, written by a woman, it is, of course, especially suitable for masculine amusement, and, speaking for ourselves, it is enjoyable throughout.

## [Sentiment and Humour]
### *The Australasian* (Melbourne, Australia)

As a writer of stories for girls, Miss L.M. Montgomery has a reputation which one imagines must be based rather on the tastes of a previous generation. Certain it is that her recent books, such as *Emily Climbs*, would make a limited appeal to the modern school girl. Her latest work, *The Blue Castle*, is described as a book, not for girls, but for their parents and older brothers and sisters. In spite of a certain tendency to saccharine sentiment, it would be a much more healthy story for girls than those of the Emily type, because the sentiment is leavened by a grateful proportion of humour. It tells of the revolt of a young woman of 29 years, who has been the victim of family tradition and family discipline in a small town where her family is regarded as among the elect. There are so many things that a Stirling must not do that Valancy gives up hope of finding anything that she might do without incurring family displeasure, and only the fact that her doctor tells her she has incurable heart disease gives her the courage to choose her own way for the rest of her life. A man comes into the story, and Valancy, who is regarded as hopelessly plain by her family, finds a new charm under the influence of her freedom. Eventually she marries the man. And one is not at all surprised when the supposed scallywag whom she marries turns out to be a famous writer and the son of a millionaire. But in spite of all this inevitableness there is a slight suggestion of originality in the working out of the climax. It is a book that any daughter might allow her mother to read without fear of shocking her sensibilities.

## [A Pleasant Tonic]
### *The Brisbane Courier* (Brisbane, Australia)

That famous Canadian writer, L.M. Montgomery, the creator of the "Anne of Green Gable" books, has broken new ground in her latest novel, *The Blue Castle*. *The Blue Castle* is a delightful love story, written with all the freshness and wholesome charm that made the "Green Gable" books so notable. Valancy Stirling[6] is told by her doctor that she has only a few months to live, and in the shock of realisation the girl discovers that she has never yet done just as she would like. So she decides to spend the remaining time in a delightful orgy of pleasing herself. Of this pursuit of happiness Miss Montgomery tells a romantic story that is a pleasant tonic.

## Cinderella Meets a Man
### *New Zealand Times* (Wellington, New Zealand)

*The Blue Castle*, L.M. Montgomery, tells the story of a young man whose father has made millions in Montreal by diligent advertising of a patent medicine. The heroine is the Cinderella daughter of an American suburban family. He finds life insupportable at school by the gibes of his school fellows, who are as cruel as boys can be, and after school by women after his money. She is soured by the neglect and suppression of years till at twenty-eight she can stand it no longer. Were it a matter of only the drab lines of the earlier period, the story would be unbelievably awful. But the relief that comes in the second period when these young people meet each other, might make any story a best seller. Their life is a charming idyll, strongly constructed, and worked out with literary and poetic grace, with a fine spice of sarcasm for the narrow people who do their best to make life hideous for all who come near them by their intolerance and snobbishness.

## One Year of Life
### *The Register* (Adelaide, Australia)

Like our own Jean Curlewis,[7] L.M. Montgomery has made such a name for children's books that the public has some difficulty in accepting her as a writer for grown-ups. However, as with *The Beach Beyond* and

*The Dawn Man*, this is a regulation novel; and the publishers do well to proclaim the fact boldly on the wrapper. It has still the engaging qualities that made *Anne of Green Gables* and the rest popular with younger readers. The fear of imminent death is one of the three great motives in fiction safe to attract every one; and Valancy, like other people in novels, is told that she has incurable heart disease and only a year to live. She has been almost incredibly bullied by her relatives, and resolves now to make the best of the time that is left. Breaking away ("I don't mean to hush ... I've hush-hushed all my life. I'll scream if I want to. Don't make me want to"[8]), she drifts somehow into romantic marriage and life in the Canadian woods with a comparative stranger. The family is rampant, with its usual incredibility, receiving news of the wedding with, "You are a shameless creature, lost to all sense of propriety and virtue"; or "I would rather ... see you dead before me than listen to what you have told me today." This frequent exaggeration – as where, again, the family "almost decided to erase Valancy's name from the family Bible" on hearing that she had cut her hair short – is the only blemish on a delightful book; for of course the doctor was quite wrong, and of course the stranger turned out to be a most desirable match. Many a girl who does not claim to be pretty will be glad to identify herself with this heroine, "of the type that looks its best in the woods."[9]

## Creator of "Anne" Sees Muskoka
### *The Globe* (Toronto, ON)

Prince Edward Island Author Pictures New Field in *The Blue Castle*

The creator of the immortal *Anne of Green Gables*, L.M. Montgomery, has sprung a surprise. Neither "Anne" nor "Anne's" descendants appear in the story of *The Blue Castle*, which is altogether grown-up, and with a setting that is quite remote from Prince Edward Island. A dash of originality in the plot creates an interest which holds the reader throughout, and it is with a protest that interruptions are incurred in the perusal of the story. The setting – the lovely Muskoka Lake region – provides many charming descriptive passages, while characterization portrays with delightful realism small-town folk, clannish in family and relations and ties.

It is the story and the romance of a girl, Valancy Stirling, who has grown into spinsterhood, never having experienced the thrill of a man declaring his love for her. The victim of unsympathetic, narrow-minded guardians at home, Valancy leads a monotonous, melancholy existence, enlivened only by mystical dreams of an entrancing "Blue Castle." On her twenty-ninth birthday Valancy discovers that she is suffering from a heart malady which will give her just one more year of life. She determines to make the most of the precious twelve months. She woos happiness, and finds it in thrilling abundance, but her leap for liberty overwhelms and prostrates her "clan" with dire consternation. Most of us have known Valancy's type of relative – domineering and prone to demand that the younger generation conform to older standards of conventionality.

But it is Valancy's marriage that "scandalizes" the proud-spirited Stirlings. A strange, impulsive marriage, with the girl in quest of happiness wedding a mysterious hermit, garbed in blue shirt and overalls, about whom wild and untrue tales were told. In the cabin-home of the isolated island, amid the rustic beauty of the Northern lake, Valancy discovers her dream, "Blue Castle." It would be unfair to the prospective reader to unfold the climax that features the daring little spinster's entertaining adventure. [* * *]10

## [Neither So Good nor So Bad]
### *The Press* (Christchurch, New Zealand)

Those who were afraid when they heard that Mrs. L.M. Montgomery (*Anne of Green Gables*) had written another book that they would either like it too well or not well enough – that they would surrender again to the old sentimental lure or not be able to surrender to it any more – need not disturb themselves. *The Blue Castle* is neither so good as *Anne* nor so bad. The plot is ordinary, very ordinary, but the telling is good enough to make it seem unusual. The sentimentalities, also, though you are very sharply aware of them when you are finished, you pass during the reading without a shudder – for the simple reason that the love-making is quite real and convincing, even if the hero is the type of strong silent man that the picture public adores.

## A Pleasant Tale
### *The New York World* (New York, NY)

She only had a year to live – that was what she was told – so she decided to live that year with as much interest and happiness as she possibly could.

The book does not lead up to any crowning tragedy but it is saved from obviousness by its simple spriteliness. The proposal scene is quite delightful, the potential husband so completely trampish – he is even unshaved. But they have both realized "the freedom to choose our prison,"[11] and the story continues its pleasant way, avoiding the mawkish puddles.

## [Exclusively for Feminine Readers]
### *The Pittsburgh Press* (Pittsburgh, PA)
#### BURT M'MURTRIE

L.M. Montgomery has used the well-worn theme of a chief character given, by a doctor, a year or less to live, and the consequent weighty problem of how to get the most out of the intervening time, in his book, *The Blue Castle*. Valancy Stirling, repressed, unattractive old maid of 29, is the chosen victim, and when she learns that her days are numbered, she seeks in all too familiar ways to gain one blissful hour. The imaginative reader may suspect that Valancy's malady will not prove fatal, that in revolt she will tardily ripen and thrive, win the man of her heart in belated mating and live happily ever after. But all these foregone eventualities are gracefully unfolded with not a little broad humor, and a merciful restraint. The story is, of course, exclusively for feminine readers.

## [Cinderella in Small-Town America]
### *The Times Literary Supplement* (London, UK)

Valancy Stirling was Cinderella, only she lived in a small town in America and instead of two ugly sisters she had a large and elderly family which spent its time in making life as unpleasant for her as it could. Her fairy godmother, or godfather rather, was a doctor who told her that her heart was so bad that she could not possibly live for a year, and would probably die in an even shorter time. This knowledge gave Valancy a freedom she had never known before. Seen in front of the dark background of death her mother, her aunts, and her uncles seemed stupid and petty people, and Valancy, usually so gentle and meek, electrified them by telling them all exactly what she thought of them. In the end, of course, it turns out that the doctor has made a mistake, and the disreputable Barney, whom she had startled the town by marrying, turns out to be not only the son of a man who made a fortune out of pills, but also the celebrated writer, John Foster, whose books Valancy had always adored.

## [A Sort of Cinderella]
### *The Canadian Bookman* (Toronto, ON)
#### T.D. RIMMER

*The Blue Castle* is a novel dealing with a girl who is a sort of Cinderella until a doctor informs her that she has only a year more to live. This results in the assertion of her personality that has lain dormant for twenty-nine years, and she finds emancipation from the sway of her relatives. The rest of the book is occupied with the sequel to her emancipation and the achievement of her desire to find a husband. The attitude taken up strikes a queer note in these days of sophistication and there is a certain pettiness that puts us out of sympathy with the character of Valancy,[12] the verbal lengths to which she goes in her rebellion seeming rather illogical. Within its limits, however, the novel is not below the ordinary fare.

## L.M. Montgomery Writes First Novel for Adults
### *The Mail and Empire* (Toronto, ON)

In her first attempt at an adult novel, *The Blue Castle*, L.M. Montgomery has used her method of writing juvenile fiction to unfold a plot that probably would not interest children. Miss Montgomery is, undoubtedly, the best writer of stories for girls now turning out books on this continent. She knows just the sort of sentiment and romantic improbabilities that they will like. You will find the same characteristics in *The Blue Castle*. It is a very pleasant little sentimental romance, only remotely related to actual life, but with a certain wholesome charm that will be much liked by persons who do not want strong meat in their fiction. Valancy Stirling is the bullied and thwarted member of an extremely unpleasant family, the other members of which rather fancy themselves. They are Anglicans, but among the other things that Valancy Stirling does when she breaks away from them, she joins another creed, so the author intimates. When Valancy is bordering upon what old-fashioned writers seem to regard as the reproachful stage of spinsterhood, she consults a doctor about her health. The medical man had two patients with practically the same name on the same day, both seeking a diagnosis. You might think that when a doctor was writing a diagnosis telling a patient that she was going to die inside of a year, he would use a little care to see that the right woman got it. Fortunately for Valancy, she received the wrong prediction. I say fortunately, because she immediately resolved to make the most of what remained of life. She put her relatives where they belonged, and did kindly acts to which they objected. To crown the joy that she had gathered for herself, Valancy married a mysterious and fascinating youth, who was just as romantic as the girl could wish. He turned out to be an author, and the son of a millionaire – as all Canadian authors ought to be – and everything ended happily, when she discovered that the lady who should have received the disheartening diagnosis had died, as the doctor called for. Altogether a pretty and happy story, which will be welcomed by the young girls who first enjoyed *Anne of Green Gables* and have since grown up.

## [A Dainty and Fragrant Concoction]
### *Philadelphia World* (Philadelphia, PA)

The author of *Anne of Green Gables* is at it again! Not that we think that we'll ever read another series as fascinating as seemed the story of the red-headed orphan Anne,[13] which in our childhood attained the heights of beauty. Wonder what our reaction would be upon a rereading at this late date. But we don't venture disillusion.

Having announced our bias at the very outset, we can go on to say that *The Blue Castle* fails to displace *Anne of Green Gables* of our youthful predilection.

At the same time *Blue Castle* is a charming love story far removed from modernism. Of course, it is highly flavored with romance, but at least its sentiment never cloys. Miss Montgomery's style is light, graceful, excellently adapted to the type of stories she writes.

And if you want to lose the world of reality and wander in the land of it might be so, here's your chance in *The Blue Castle*, with Valancy Stirling as your guide.[14]

In Valancy's world bachelor women were unknown, and so at twenty-nine she was simply an old maid who had never been kissed, and, what is worse, seemed doomed never to be kissed. A tired, meek little old maid, shriveled before she had bloomed, who had never done a single thing she wanted to do, completely subjugated by her mother and relatives.

Valancy's only release from the stifling, colorless aridity of her life was in day dreaming. But even day dreams were rudely shattered by officious relatives.

Then after twenty-nine years of submission – revolt! The explosive was a leaking heart. Told that she had but a single year to live, she determines to devote it to converting her dreams of romance into some semblance of reality.

Her first step is to throw off the shackles of relatives. Her second to become nurse to a young consumptive girl and a social outcast because she has trespassed conventional boundaries in love. There she meets Barney, whose careless appearance and complete disregard for the town's opinion has set up the persistent rumor that he is a law-breaker, disreputable, dangerous. And Valancy, daughter of the town's most righteous, and therefore most inspired mud-slingers, asks Barney to marry her! Horror of horrors!

To make matters worse, she goes off with him to find her blue castle in Spain on a little Canadian island. And blooms! Blooms! Old maidish Valancy flowers in the rare atmosphere of freedom, kindness and beauty.

Comes the storm, and with one single sweep sends low the whole beautiful structure!

But Miss Montgomery is too sympathetic a narrator to leave us the dregs of romance when she can send the cup brimming over. And so all's well ends well.

Swallow it or not – as you will, but you must agree that it is a dainty and fragrant concoction.


## [An Innocuous and Sentimental Tale]
### *Cape Times* (Cape Town, South Africa)

There was once a naturalist who remarked that even the worm will turn if unduly provoked, and so too the meekest of daughters under the continual oppression of maternal tyranny. This is precisely what happened in the case of Valancy Stirling. At an age which should have pointed to more discretion, Valancy ran away from home. Now all this is all very terrible, and the publishers are careful to announce on the wrapper that the book is "*not* for girls," lest the young apparently should read and be corrupted thereby. It is, however, the wrapper continues, "intended for fathers, mothers, brothers and elder sisters." Fearing that the censor should suspect the worst, we now hasten to add that this is an entirely innocuous and sentimental tale, and may quite safely be relegated to its place among Miss Montgomery's previous volumes in the school library.

## A Dream Castle
### *The Havana Post* (Havana, Cuba)

Valancy Stirling is twenty-nine and for just that number of years she has never dared to call her soul her own to say "boo" to the proverbial goose. She has been a good and dutiful daughter and as a result has lived a deadly dull and entirely virtuous life, surrounded in equally dull and equally virtuous relations who regard her either as an old maid or a little child – according to their respective viewpoints – and therefore not worth making any fuss about anyway.

Then, just on her twenty-ninth birthday, she gets two severe shocks. The first that she has, according to the family doctor, a year to live and the second that if she isn't actually in love with Barney Snaith, the town scandal, it wouldn't need a very big jolt to push her over the edge into his arms, provided he chose to hold them out to catch her.

The two shocks together wake up the little devil who has, apparently, been peacefully sleeping in her soul since her birth and having waked up he sets to work to make up for those lost years as completely and effectually as possible.

The result is L.M. Montgomery's *Blue Castle*, as delightfully fresh and spontaneous a story as one can hope to look for and still less expect to find. Her description of Valancy's first rebellion against the principles which have governed her entire life is one of those bits of fiction one hopes never to forget.

Released from the shackles of respectability and duty; housekeeper to disreputable old Roaring Abel and his fragile daughter; ultimately Barney Snaith's wife, Valancy is the freshest thing imaginable and there is, throughout the book, a wholesomeness and cleanness that makes it a very welcome addition to one's bookshelves.

## [Valancy's Revolt]
### *The Scotsman* (Edinburgh, UK)

Valancy Stirling had been too long the Cinderella of a smug Canadian household, her spirit only kept up by the castles in Spain that she carried in her mind and the gallant knights she had as lovers. Then came a time of revolt, and she said – "I've been trying to please other people all my life and failed ... After this I shall please myself. I shall never pretend anything again. I've breathed an atmosphere of fibs and pretences and evasions all my life. What a luxury it will be to tell the truth!"[15] How she set about this is told by Miss Montgomery in clever and amusing fashion. Valancy's revolt shocks her numerous relations, but she goes out into the world and fights her battles bravely, and soon a gallant knight comes riding past her castle wall. The castle wall may be only that of a shack, and the knight a reputed ne'er-do-well, but strange things happen in fiction. Valancy is happily married, and all her dreams come true, for the reputed ne'er-do-well was – but that is something the readers of the story should best find out for themselves.

## [Emerging from Her Dream-World]
### *The Montreal Daily Star* (Montreal, QC) ·

*The Blue Castle*, the latest story from the pen of L.M. Montgomery, the popular authoress of *Anne of Green Gables*, and a host of other tales for girls, but also read by many grown-up folk, is a delightful study of a young woman who has lived a repressed and secluded life to the age of twenty-nine, finding solace in a dream-world of her own creation – a world that holds a wondrous blue castle which is her residence and where she enjoys incredible happiness. Shaken out of her repression and her seclusion by a sudden discovery concerning herself that prompts her to take her fling in life, she emerges from her dream-world into the practical world of today, and finds in its manifold human interests and in the dawn of real romance a fascination and a beauty far exceeding any she had conceived in her dream-days. Mrs. Montgomery has lost none of her happy gift of word-painting, her penetrating comprehension of the feminine heart, and her broad and tolerant attitude towards life. This should find a very wide public both among young people and adults.

## [Essentially a Woman's Book]
### *The Canadian Churchman* (Toronto, ON)
#### FAITH SMITHSON

Unlike the leopard, Miss Montgomery has changed her spots. In her new

story, Nova Scotia has been discarded for Muskoka, and the young Anne
and Rilla type for Valancy, twenty-nine and not married yet. *The Blue
Castle* accordingly makes its appeal to a different class of readers or rather, it has widened her circle of admirers to admit the older woman, while
yet holding the interest of the school girl.

I am glad to review this book on the Women's Page because it is essentially a woman's book, and has to do with the eternal question with
us – the question as to how we should bring up our daughters – how far
fear and repression should be a part of their education. Valancy's mother
was a firm believer in the old adage, "A child should be seen and not
heard." On the other hand we are forced to admit this generation doesn't
know the meaning of repression, and that they would be the better if a
little more fear and respect had been forcibly instilled into them in their
youth. Just where to draw the line between repressing and encouraging
their personalities is a very weighty question. Miss Montgomery does not
try to answer it; she just tells us in her usual clever and humorous way
the evils of the nagging parent.

Valancy Stirling,[16] commonly called Doss, is the only child of a widowed mother, who believes in the old idea that widow's lot is not a happy one and that she must show her grief by making everyone around
her as miserable as possible. It is more by her constant sighing, whining
and sulking she completely crushes any natural cravings Doss may have
for a little fun, pretty clothes, young companions or even an attractive
bed-room.

I picked up a religious magazine of ancient date the other day and saw
this: "A woman who puts on Christ will not put on style?" Mrs. Stirling
would heartily agree with this. Flannel petticoats and unattractive brown
silk for best was the outward and visible sign of being respectable and a
perfect lady.

After twenty-nine years of this mouse-like existence in the bosom of
her dull and proper family she goes to see a doctor, unknown to her
mother, and finds she has heart trouble and has only one year to live. Her
dormant character shakes itself into action. She realizes she has never
been allowed to do, be or say anything she wanted to and for this one
year left to her she resolves to be selfishly happy.

"I've had nothing but a second-hand existence," she says to herself.
"All the great emotions of life have passed me by. I've never even had a
grief ... My life has been empty – empty ... I've been trying to please other people all my life and failed ... After this I shall please myself. I shall
never pretend anything again ... What a luxury it will be to tell the truth!

I may not be able to do much that I want to do but I won't do another thing that I don't want to do,"[17] and from this point the large respectable Stirling family, relatives and connections begin to sit up and take notice.

She not only threw away the jar of potpourri and the beaded pin cushion but O horror! she had her hair bobbed, and was seen eating a hot dog. Her family thought her mad and consulted the family physician. They finally threw her over entirely when she left home to nurse poor Cissy Gay,[18] who was dying alone of tuberculosis. Cissy had committed the unpardonable sin. She had "gone wrong." All Doss' relatives had lapped up the messy details in their usual unctuous way.

Valancy finds happiness for the first time and rather than return to her old monotonous life after Cissy's death, is swept into a hasty marriage with a mysterious young man living alone in the Canadian woods and thought to be a criminal because of his very secrecy.

I won't tell you the surprise at the end of the book because it has little to do with the development of Valancy's character. We go back to the question, "How much repression, how much spoiling?" And there now, I find I've forgotten to tell you about *The Blue Castle*. Well, you must read it yourself.

## [That Particular Quality of Naïve Zestfulness]
### *Punch, or the London Charivari* (London, UK)

*Valancy Stirling*, the heroine of *The Blue Castle*, comes out of the very same box as the Emilys and Annes of Miss L.M. MONTGOMERY's earlier novels. Like them, she finds a refuge in a dream-world of her own fashioning from the dull realities of life in a Canadian "small town," and, when the local doctor informs her that she has only a year to live, she proceeds to throw her bonnet over the church steeple and ask a young man to marry her – on the understanding, of course, that she is going to die according to schedule. Needless to say, if *Valancy* had received a proper grounding in the rules of sentimental fiction, she would have guessed – as the reader does – that the doctor's verdict would turn out a mistake, and that her temporary husband would have conveniently fallen in love with her during her allotted span; but one of the restrictions of her "small town" existence having been a ban on novels she cannot be expected to know this, and the requisite game of cross-purposes ensues until the time is ripe for a happy ending all round. The plot is as threadbare as could well be imagined; the odd thing is that in the telling it acquires a surprising semblance of freshness, thanks to that particular quality of naïve zestfulness which is the specialty of more than one popular Transatlantic novelist.

## NOTES

1 "Muskoka Romance," unidentified and undated clipping, in SR, 265; *The Daily Times* (Otago, New Zealand), "An American Love Story," review of *The Blue Castle*, 9 October 1926, in SR, 276; *The Calgary Herald*, review of *The Blue Castle*, 11; *The New York Times Book Review*, "Canadian Romance," 33.

2 *El Paso Times* (El Paso, TX), review of *The Blue Castle*, 6 March 1927, in SR, 297; *Boston Evening Transcript*, review of *The Blue Castle*, 5; Clark, review of *The Blue Castle*, 12; *The New Outlook*, review of *The Blue Castle*, 16–17.

3 Denison, review of *The Blue Castle*, 12; *Democrat and Chronicle* (Rochester, NY), "When a Dream Comes True," review of *The Blue Castle*, 19 September 1926, in SR, 260; *Camden Evening Courier* (Camden, NJ), "Death Sentence Leads to a New Lease on Life," review of *The Blue Castle*, 12 November 1926, in SR, 268; *The Patriot* (Charlottetown, PE), "An Idyl of the Cool Canadian Woods," review of *The Blue Castle*, 20 September 1928, in SR, 280. The quotation refers to L.M. Montgomery's article "'I Dwell among My Own People,'" which appears in Volume 1 of *The L.M. Montgomery Reader*.

4 *The Times–Dispatch* (Richmond, VA), "'The Blue Castle' Is Full of Tingles," 3 October 1926, in SR, 256; *The New York World* (New York, NY), review of *The Blue Castle*, 2 October 1926, in SR, 257; *The Springfield Sunday Union and Republican*, "The Spinster Makes Good," 7F.

5 I have corrected the original, which reads "'Anne of the Green Gables.'"

6 I have corrected the original, which reads "Valancy Sterling."

7 Jean Curlewis (1898–1930), Australian author of several novels, including *The Beach Beyond* (1923) and *The Dawn Man* (1924), also mentioned here.

8 *BC*, 64–65.

9 *BC*, 142, 143, 149, 150.

10 A lengthy extract of a description of November, "pictured with a touch of mastery," is omitted here. See *BC*, 159.

11 *BC*, 153.

12  I have corrected the original, which reads "Valency."
13  I have corrected the original, which reads "Annie." Harold Gray's comic strip "Little Orphan Annie," also featuring a red-headed protagonist, had begun in 1924.
14  I have corrected the original, which reads "Valancy Sterling."
15  *BC*, 45–46.
16  Here and throughout, I have corrected the original, which reads "Sterling."
17  *BC*, 45–46.
18  I have corrected the original, which reads "Cissy Gray."

# 16

## Emily's Quest

### —— 1927 ——

Montgomery may have had some serious misgivings about this final volume about Emily Byrd Starr, but for the most part her pessimism was not shared by reviewers. The *Boston Herald* declared that in the novel "the young heroine attains success as a writer, but finds that there is a greater goal. She reaches out for happiness – and four young people are swept on to the delightful climax." The *Natal Mercury* of South Africa commented that "there is no sickly sentiment or nauseous introspection about it. It is a clean, sprightly book, which everyone will enjoy." To this the *San Antonio Jewish Record* added that, "in spite of its title," the novel "is a clean, invigorating contribution to Mrs. Montgomery's literary family. It abounds in human interest and appeal and will be gratefully received by the many who still like to be refreshed by romances that show such a sympathetic understanding of young people who think and act rightly."[1]

Although the focus of the novel is as much on Emily's writing career as on her relationships with men, many reviewers concentrated solely on Emily's love story, as Montgomery had done when describing the book to Ephraim Weber. The *Aberdeen Press and Journal* saw "romance pure and simple" as the novel's theme, and according to the *Hull Daily Mail*, her success as an author is only "by the way. The real interest is in her love episodes." For its part, the *Grand Rapids Herald* of Michigan declared that "there are lots of beaux in it and a lost sweetheart, a lost diamond, and a lost letter, and all are eventually found. Girls will find *Emily's Quest* good reading, and there is no reason why it shouldn't provide pastime for older readers." The *Weekly Press* of Christchurch, New Zealand, called Emily "a young woman and a sufficiently attractive one to be sought by young men," whereas the *Utica Press* of New York expressed its hope that there would be "another book dealing with Emily's married life."[2] Two newspapers from India offered negative assessments – one calling it "light, inconsequential reading of the harmless, schoolgirl type," another noting that "even [Emily's] efforts after fame do not take hold of us. Perhaps we are to blame, for the struggling authoress has become very plentiful in fiction" – but these comments should not be construed as indicative of the reception of the book outside North America and the United Kingdom; included in Montgomery's scrapbook is a notice, published in the *Cape Argus*, indicating that *Emily's Quest* ranked fifth in the list of eleven best sellers in late September 1927 in Cape Town, South Africa. Moreover, a review in the *Manchester Leader* of New Hampshire offered unqualified praise: "As always, Miss Montgomery's young people are high class. Ambitious and with high ideals, they never offend with either their manners or their conduct, and yet they are spirited and gay. Sophisticated flappers will think them tame and prosy, but there is still a large reading public which will think them typically the best the 'younger generation' has to offer and which will read the story with a comforting sense that much of the world is after [all] sane and wholesome, and that is a distinct contribution to the present state of affairs."[3]

## Emily Now Grown Up
### *Trenton Evening Times* (Trenton, NJ)

Another "Emily" book has been written by L.M. Montgomery and will undoubtedly find as great favor as the earlier chronicling of the girl's doings in *Emily of New Moon* and *Emily Climbs*.

In the new volume, *Emily's Quest*, the Canadian girl is searching for happiness but passes through much of the uncertainty of mind of those who fall in and out of love. She is tortured in her friendship with Teddy through a series of misunderstandings. Each thinks the other prefers to remain aloof. Meanwhile, she becomes engaged to another man older than herself but she breaks the tie when she fully realizes there can be only one.

Earlier readers of Emily's affairs will probably regret that she has grown up, with half a dozen years of her life covered in a single book. Surely, L.M. Montgomery cannot be accused of giving "Emily's" followers small portions to reserve further doings for later publication. The same author will also be remembered for *Anne of Green Gables* which was produced some time back.

The book has a wholesome flavor that compensates for a rather desultory pace. It is well suited for girls who are growing up and will give parents who feel concerned about "what is daughter reading now?" little worry when they examine the book.

## Pine Woods and Pigsties
### *The Canadian Bookman* (Toronto, ON)
#### V.B. RHODENIZER

"The story is a charming one, charmingly told. The characters are skilfully depicted, the dialogue deftly handled, the descriptive passages surprisingly effective. The quiet humor is simply delightful."[4] The review of Emily's first published book applies here. L.M. Montgomery's novels are concrete examples of the philosophy of fiction expressed by Mr. Carpenter on his deathbed; "Remember – pine woods are just as real as – pigsties – and a darn sight pleasanter to be in ... And don't – tell the world – everything. That's what's the – matter – with our – literature. Lost the charm of mystery – and reserve."[5] The third Emily book is a worthy successor of the other two. If sequels as a general rule are not as good as their predecessors, our author knows how to write the exceptions. *Emily's Quest* shows how interest may be sustained and brought to a successful climax without recourse to improbably romantic incidents. It is the story of Emily's uneven climb from success in the short story to success in the novel, and of the entanglements in the love affairs of Perry Miller, Dean Priest, Teddy Kent, Ilse Burnley, and Emily Starr. There is the same logical interrelation of plot and character as in the preceding Emily books, and the characters are consistently drawn throughout the three volumes. There is perhaps even greater power in the handling of emotional situations, such as the scene in which Emily's "second sight" prevents Teddy Kent from sailing on the *Flavian* and that in which Ilse flees a few moments before her intended marriage. There is also increased skill in comic scenes, such as that in which Mark Delage Greaves proposes to Emily. As to the illusion of reality, Aunt Elizabeth's words are to the point: "Well, I never could have believed that a pack of lies could sound as much like the real truth as that book does."[6] The setting is painted with a brush perhaps more subtle than ever before, and one reads on for the expected in a state of delighted expectancy. L.M. Montgomery's happy endings are dictated not so much by the wishes of readers and publishers, as by her philosophy of life.

## A Charming Emily Book
### *The Gazette* (Montreal, QC)

L.M. Montgomery's host of readers will rejoice in this new Emily book, which is a charming story of a young girl's quest for happiness. Emily is a dreamer but very practical at the same time. She is engaged in writing short stories for magazines and has the budding writer's usual trials and successes. All the while there are suitors for her hand, but the one that should persist is discouraged by events over which he or Emily on occasion have no control. There is near disaster again and again, but Providence interferes in the right way in the end. It is pleasant reading, that takes the reader from the beauties of the beloved Island to Montreal and even over to Paris. For two of the principals are youths who have risen from humble rural surroundings to proud positions.

The author's characters are always interesting and true to nature. There are the usual circles with their eminently respectable members, most of whom are horrified at times over Emily's doings. Some of these people are noble at heart but descend to depths of meanness in striving to have their desires fulfilled. The impulses that prompt them are understandable by the discerning reader. Altogether, *Emily's Quest* is a happy addition to the library of Anne and Emily books.

## [Pretty Sure to Be Acceptable]
### *The Outlook* (New York, NY)

Having carried Anne (her of Green Gables) through a most successful series of girls' books, the Canadian author is now doing the same for Emily. A story that is quiet and gay in turn and that leads its young girl readers to the verge of love is pretty sure to be acceptable.

## A Book for Girls
### *The Evening Post* (Wellington, New Zealand)

Girl readers will revel in Mrs. Montgomery's delicate imagery of thought permeating each page of this novel. *Emily's Quest* completes the adventures of Emily of New Moon, and follows on *Emily Climbs*, with a nice regard for what has happened before. This latest story is of the awakening of a girl's fragile soul. It will be found a counterpart to the gradual development of very many young girls with some thought for the finer things of life, girls who delight in Nature and who thoroughly deserve a lover of the kind of Teddy, Emily's lover. She and this handsome friend come to their happiness through many vicissitudes, but she is a better woman, he a finer man for all the stormy journey. Mr. Carpenter, a friendly old schoolmaster, proved a great help to Emily in her writings. Perry Miller, who attains fame as a lawyer, and Ilse Burnley, fascinating mad-cap, are interesting characters. Ilse, being angry because she cannot have Perry, takes Teddy Kent as her second-best. She soon realises the folly of her selfishness. Dean Priest, lover of Emily Byrd Starr and almost her husband, and Emily's quaint relatives, are excellent character studies. This is a delightful tale of simple, homely, natural, loveable people who help to keep the world sane and sweet.

## [Begins to Wear Thin]
### *The Times Literary Supplement* (London, UK)

In this novel the author continues the story of Emily, her Prince Edward Island heroine, who makes her reappearance "with her high school days behind her and immortality before."[7] As often happens with sequels, the material in this book begins to wear somewhat thin, and the account of Emily's rather tepid love affairs and of her vicissitudes on "commencing author" is eked out by numerous excerpts from her diary, descriptions, for the most part, of "glamorous" landscapes and of romantic moods, which, however, fail to sound any hitherto unplumbed depths in the heroine's personality. Towards the end things move a trifle more briskly.

## [Bewildering and Unintelligible Emily]
### *The Pioneer* (Allahabad, India)

Emily is a bewildering and unintelligible character. The author has, however, tried to make the most of a feeble plot and the book closes with the usual happy ending. Emily, the dreamer, the "chaser of rainbows,"[8] is a prolific writer of short stories, keeps a diary and turns out a book in six weeks, and then consigns it to the flames after three rejections. She loves one man, has "an affection" for another, to whom she becomes engaged, and finally breaks the engagement and goes back to the man she loves.

## [Her Best Tale of Prince Edward Island]
*Manitoba Free Press* (Winnipeg, MB)

*Emily's Quest*, the last of a trilogy by L.M. Montgomery, is perhaps her best tale of Prince Edward Island, "the Garden of the Gulf." At all events, its nature descriptions are many and realistic, if one can use that word concerning the delicacy, the nuance in colors of day and night in our world. On "the Island," Nature's own compulsion of a willing mind – that is all Nature asks – has won the author of the Emily books. Nothing of beauty in natural phenomena escapes her sympathetic and understanding eyes. I cannot recall any contemporary novel known to me that has in it so much of the healing and sweet influences of earth and sky.

Emily is one of those lovable, human heroines that, without any contriving, or desire either for that matter, has proposals of marriage thrust upon her. There are certain young and elderly men, who seem necessary to her in friendship's way, but they all want to marry her. She is fond of compatible masculine pals, as we say, but she loves only one. The story is all about her love affairs and her ambitions and efforts in authorship. She wrote for the same reason that the linnets sing, as Tennyson's term is.[9] And she was prepared to take refusals in a sporting spirit. She was impervious to the pride of her ancestry and immediate family, the socially overbearing Murrays. For there is caste on "the Island." And she knew well that many despairing moods awaited her.

The death-bed scene has verisimilitude, I know. The old teacher, who loved the classics and hated clap-trap, and had been Emily's good counsellor, was dying. He was done with curiosity about life, but eager to know what was beyond death. The prating housekeeper is banished from the room and the last words are for Emily. Oh! but it will be good "to be young – *again*." Emily, who is young, cannot know the meaning of that longing to be young again. She is advised in broken sentences to hold hard by her own high ideals. "Never write – to please anybody – but yourself ... Promise." Emily promises. The old man cannot remember one other thing which is a warning; but in the end, with his last breath, it comes to him and he whispers – "Beware – of – italics."[10] There are here and there, in the tale, spontaneous literary touches. I liked reading this healthy, well-written story.

## By the Creator of "Anne"
### *The Globe* (Toronto, ON)

In these days of stressed "realism" – which, after all, is often not as realistic as it is sordid and crude – a healthy, wholesome story such as this comes as a pleasant stimulant. It is like meeting good, old, tried friends whom you understand and yearn for after wearying yourself with the superficialities of light acquaintances.

Like other books by this author, *Emily's Quest* is simple in its narrative, setting and characters, but profound in its everyday philosophy. There is no strained effort for grand effect, no creation of supermen and women, only an ordinary thread, as it were, but so well spun by the author of *Anne of Green Gables* that it gives the reader a lingering sense of pleasure and value.

Perhaps there are few experiences more common to humanity – particularly the ambitious element – than that of starting out in early life with a dream of one kind and discovering another part way along the road. Emily, in the zeal of her youth, is determined to be a writer. She meets with the bright hopes and the bitter disappointments that beset the path of most literary aspirants. When success comes, finally, she finds it is, after all, secondary to that great elemental thing in every woman, namely, love. The many lights and shadows that play upon both her writing and her affections belong to the reader, and must not be divulged here, but it may be said they quickly become real and interesting, like neighbors one has known for years.

There is another feature that applies to this, as to other L.M. Montgomery stories. It keeps its feet on the ground, and Canadian ground at that. The author writes about places she knows, not about imaginary things and places she does not know. She stays close to the ordinary, yeoman type of human beings, and for some strange reason which seems to be basic in all things, average men and women like to meet people of their own brand. Obviously there must be a lot of persons who are very near to the earth themselves, or books of this sort would not meet such generous popularity.

Those who have not read the previous books will find it none too pleasant, at times, trying to locate in their minds places and people to whom reference is made in retrospect, as though the whole world knew of them. It is doubtful whether an author, even one read as widely as L.M. Montgomery, should assume that a lot which has gone before in other stories may be taken for granted by every reader.

## More about Emily
### *Saturday Night* (Toronto, ON)

Emily is already a familiar and popular character with readers of Miss Montgomery's books. This novel, while a sequel to the two which told of her childhood and adolescence, *Emily of New Moon* and *Emily Climbs*, is complete in itself. Serious students of Miss Montgomery's art will not find it necessary to delve into Emily's innocent past if they missed reading the previously published novels, for this tale of her early twenties contains sufficient evidence of its blamelessness. On the verge of womanhood, Emily was like this: [* * *]11 More intimate details of the heroine's appearance are supplied by the frontispiece, which shows her in a Victorian nightgown, catching pneumonia beside an open window.

Emily achieves her girlhood ambition of becoming an author, and her experiences with editors and reviewers are probably drawn from the author's own encounters with that unsympathetic tribe. She also has some love affairs, marred by disappointments, but eventually working out to the triumphantly happy ending upon which Miss Montgomery's admirers can always rely.

## Love and a Career
### *Democrat and Chronicle* (Rochester, NY)

Miss Montgomery has compassed another success in her depiction of character and her description of life and conditions in Prince Edward Island. *Emily of New Moon* was the means of starting a series of novels as charming as those which recorded the doings of Anne in the books which first brought fame and fortune to the author. Emily is not a sugary sweet heroine. On the contrary she is very human; she actually lives as a normal and healthy and a bit headstrong girl and young woman under the magic of Miss Montgomery's pen.

Her quest, as set forth in this newest book, is double in its nature. Or rather she sets out in quest of fame as a writer and gets all mixed up in a combination of love affairs which develop into an unconscious quest for happiness in that direction. Everything turns out for the best in the end, and she is completely successful in both quests.

For those who enjoy clean love stories with a wealth of fine description and the recording of such a collection of startling incidents as impetuous Emily is bound to figure in, it would hardly be possible to find a more satisfactory book than *Emily's Quest*. It is wholesome and sparkling and contains a great amount of sentiment without degenerating into sentimentality. It is a striking bit of proof that there is no necessity of conflicting with any censor of morals in books to write a story that is well worth reading.

## [Dancing Off into Matrimony]
### *Punch, or the London Charivari* (London, UK)

If *Emily's Quest* had been the first novel by Miss L.M. MONTGOMERY dealing with *Emily Byrd Starr* and her friends that I had read I am not quite sure how much enjoyment I should have got out of it. As it was I found myself inclined to resent an occasional little figure inserted in the text with a note below referring me to *Emily of New Moon* or *Emily Climbs*. It seemed a little out of place in a pretty childish tale of a young American girl's essays in authorship and adventures in love. It would have cost Miss MONTGOMERY very little trouble to make each of the books in which *Emily* appears self-contained and they would have been much better bargains then for the railway-bookstall. I who knew simple-minded *Cousin Jimmy* and proud *Aunt Elizabeth* and wild *Ilse Burnley* and clever *Frederick Kent* and many more, of old, quite enjoyed this pleasant chronicle of how the younger folk of Blair Water set to partners and danced off into matrimony, told with a generous use of capital letters. Even a chapter devoted to contradictory reviews of *Emily's* first novel and her (and, I suppose, Miss MONTGOMERY's) opinion that "the favourable ones were written by morons" shall not persuade me to be less pleasant than that.[13] But if she is moved to write of *Emily* again I hope Miss MONTGOMERY will speed her story up a little – she has been very long in getting where this book leaves her. I also hope that she will use some more new exciting words, such as "kididoes." It seems to mean "capers" and it sounds much more like them.[14]

## [A Sense of Impatience]
### *Natal Advertiser* (Durban, South Africa)

This book, the third of the series composed of *Emily of New Moon* and *Emily Climbs*, carries on the story of Emily Byrd Starr after she has left school. She is now on the threshold of womanhood, and full of a great ambition to write. Gradually her stories gain popularity and her name appears frequently on magazine covers. But she hankers after the greater fame of having a novel to her credit. *Emily's Quest* is a prettily told story, and the author shows keen insight in his study of Emily's nature, a nature which is changing and developing from day to day. Many of the quaint, old-world inhabitants of New Moon are gems of character drawing, and the author's quiet humour is delightful. One sympathises with Emily – full of ideas and the love of freedom – in her environment of Victorian respectability and gentility, but at the same time one can't help liking these quaint old folks who so obviously love Emily and are so solicitous for her welfare. True, her somewhat unorthodox adventures in love exasperate and rather shock her uncles and aunts, but behind it all we sense a real and deep desire to protect the young girl from harm and to see her happily settled in life.

There is, however, a lack of action in the story which is scarcely compensated for by clever character drawing. The superstructure of psychological analysis is too heavy for that foundation of incident without which no novel can survive.

The effect on the reader is a sense of impatience that the tale does not move faster to its logical conclusion. Apart from this fault in construction, the novel is a delightful piece of character study and well calculated to pass a pleasant evening's reading.

## NOTES

1 *The Boston Herald*, review of *Emily's Quest*, 8; *Natal Mercury* (Natal, South Africa), "A Canadian Love Story," review of *Emily's Quest*, 24 September 1927, in SR, 285; *San Antonio Jewish Record* (San Antonio, TX), review of *Emily's Quest*, 23 December 1927, in SR, 288.

2 *Aberdeen Press and Journal* (Aberdeen, UK), review of *Emily's Quest*, 6 October 1927, in SR, 288; *Hull Daily Mail* (Hull, UK), "Emily Grows Up," review of *Emily's Quest*, 9 September 1927, in SR, 295; *Grand Rapids Herald* (Grand Rapids, MI), review of *Emily's Quest*, 28 August 1927, in SR, 293; *The Weekly Press* (Christchurch, New Zealand), review of *Emily's Quest*, 3 August 1927, in SR, 291–92; *The Utica Press* (Utica, NY), review of *Emily's Quest*, 28 September 1927, in SR, 295.

3 *Civil & Military Gazette* (Lahore, India), "A Tale for Schoolgirls," review of *Emily's Quest*, 29 October 1927, in SR, 292; *The Englishman* (Calcutta, India), "Four New Novels," review of *Emily's Quest*, 14 November 1927,

in SR, 290–91; *Cape Argus* (Cape Town, South Africa), "Best Sellers," 28 September 1927, in SR, 303; *Manchester Leader* (Manchester, NI I), "Emily Now Seeks Literary Fame," review of *Emily's Quest*, 17 September 1927, in SR, 290.

4  The source of this extract has not been located; it does not, for instance, appear in Raymond Knister's review of *Emily of New Moon*, originally published in *The Canadian Bookman*, reproduced above.

5  *EQ*, 24.

6  *EQ*, 182.

7  *EQ*, 1.

8  *EQ*, 5.

9  "I do but sing because I must, / And pipe but as the linnets sing." From "In Memoriam," by Alfred, Lord Tennyson (1809–1892), English poet.

10  *EQ*, 24, 25.

11  A lengthy extract describing Emily physically, appearing in the original review, is omitted here. See *EQ*, 4–5.

12  Montgomery dedicated *Emily's Quest* "to Stella Campbell Keller of the tribe of Joseph." For more on the significance of this phase, see Austin Bothwell's article "On Being of the Tribe of Joseph" in Volume 1 of *The L.M. Montgomery Reader*.

13  *EQ*, 179.

14  *The Lucy Maud Montgomery Album* defines "kididoes" to mean "shenanigans" ("Lucy Maud Words," 414).

15  I have corrected the original, which reads "ANNE OF GREEN CABLES."

16  I have corrected the original, which reads "Prince Edwards Island."

17  I have corrected the original, which reads "Tansey Patch."

# 17

## *Magic for Marigold*

—— 1929 ——

It may surprise today's readers, among whom *Magic for Marigold* is rarely a favourite Montgomery title, but reviews of the book after its first publication were quite strong, at times suggesting that Montgomery had not only maintained the high standard set with *Anne of Green Gables* but surpassed it. As the *Australian Christian World* noted, "This must be her sixteenth book, yet it is packed with the same whimsical charm, as her well-loved *Anne of Green Gables* which so delighted us almost twenty years ago." An unidentified clipping added that Montgomery was "getting better and better" and, moreover, that this "somewhat different heroine will rival the delightful Anne in popularity." Over in New Zealand, the *Evening Post* of Wellington claimed that "here is Anne back again almost, but a quainter child, more full of charming things, and quite as full of mischief." Indeed, Montgomery's depiction of child life received high praise, not only from the *Daily Northwestern* of Illinois, which commented on Montgomery's "almost uncanny insight" into "the feelings of a child," but also from the *Liverpool Daily Post*, which noted that "in some ways little New England Marigold is more precocious and capable than our own children of the same age." As the *Oregonian* observed, "Few writers have such a keen understanding of children and their mental processes as to enable them to write a full-size novel around such a simple subject, yet in the very simplicity of the nature of children lies the complexity of writing about them." Moreover, as the *Salt Lake City Telegram* suggested, "Prince Edward Island must be a place of incredible beauty. Either that, or it may be just the genius of the author in depicting nature that so enchants the reader."[1]

This praise for Montgomery's depiction of what the *San Francisco Chronicle* termed "a little girl's jolly times" led once again to questions of target audience. As Mary Hinkley noted in the *Chicago Evening Post*, "it would be too bad if anyone should think of this as a children's book and so miss it, for while it is that, it is much more. It has character analysis, accurate genetic psychology, poetic quality, and a style. Also it makes you laugh, makes you cry; the spirit of it is contagious." To this the *Boston Evening Transcript* added that "once in a great while someone writes a book which is about children, but so charming that older people like it just as well. Provided that children love it, too, this is a real accomplishment." Although Jean Graham's review of the novel in *Saturday Night* was entitled "A Book for Girls," she noted that "though [Marigold] may truthfully be called old-fashioned, she is neither pert nor smart, and is really the kind of youngster who would make a satisfactory companion on a long walk."[2]

This time, moreover, the suggestion that Montgomery's books offer an alternative to popular fiction resonated around the world: as one clipping suggested, "Those of you who are weary of the general run of modern novels, can turn to *Marigold* with a sigh of relief. For though it is essentially a story for children, the grown-up children will adore it too!" A review of the UK edition of the novel praised it as an example of "what ladies call a 'pretty' story, one which can be warmly recommended to all who like something out of the common, different from the thrillers which are being turned out by the thousand nowadays." Meanwhile, the *Natal Advertiser* of South Africa proclaimed it to be "outstandingly pleasant – a simple story, charmingly told, of human interest but without any of the love element so heavily emphasised in modern fiction. In telling the life of a child as a sort of fairy tale, the author introduces us to many characters a little aloof from the present generation." Although the Rockhampton *Morning Bulletin* of Australia noted that "surely the gifted authoress will write a sequel to Marigold, who must prove an attraction to the young men," evidently such an idea did not appeal to Montgomery, and so Marigold remained a child forever for readers of this novel.[3]

## [Another Little Girl]
### *The New York Telegram* (New York, NY)

Once upon a time – that's the way this book begins, so that is the way I shall begin telling about it – once upon a time, when our fathers and mothers were boys and girls, there was a book written about a little girl called *Anne of Green Gables*, which was very widely read. Now the author, L.M. Montgomery, who has written many other books, gives us another little girl, whom she tells about in *Magic for Marigold*.

It is a question whether this book is meant for children or grown ups. On the jacket it is called a "novel," but it certainly is not a novel. It is one of the stories about children, like *Rebecca of Sunnybrook Farm*, *Pollyanna*, and *Captain January*, which older people like to read, too.[4] The children in such books are never commonplace, but always full of imagination and pretty fancies, and they generally don't live in a perfectly normal family with brothers and sisters, but with aunts and uncles and other relatives. They appeal somehow to older readers, at the same time that many girls and boys find them the sort of children to make real friends of, going back time after time to read about them and become better acquainted with them.

This new story opens with a family conclave about what to name the baby. After they have all suggested all sorts of silly sounding names, the jolliest uncle of all says: "It's my opinion children shouldn't be named at all. They should be numbered until they're grown up, then choose their own names." The most entertaining member of the family is the sharp-tongued old grandmother who is always saying sharp things and can't be bothered with children. "Unspanked nuisances," as she calls them.[5]

Marigold, herself, although just the kind of a girl any one would like to play with, is no plaster saint. When asked why she is so bad, she answers: "It's more *int'resting* than being good."[6] And there is a good deal be said for her point.

One way to tell it is not a novel is the ending. Instead of Marigold meeting some young man she wants to marry, it closes with her discovering that the old magic of childhood has gone, and she is about to "grow up."

## In a Small World
### *Nottingham Journal* (Nottingham, UK)

Here is a story in the best tradition (and it is a fine tradition) of the "Anne" and "Emily" books. It is Marigold in this case who is the heroine and the charm of her nature has a background in the society of some very nice and other rather queer folk of older growth.

They all live in a world which is very circumscribed, but Mr. Montgomery makes their prejudices interesting and we like them, not excepting even Old Grandmother, who is 93 and is called old to distinguish her from Young Grandmother, a mere child of 60 odd.

A very hard nut to crack is the Old Grandmother; but perhaps people are apt to become irascible and impatient with the ways of youth at that age. On the whole, Marigold's grown-up friends and relatives are a very happy, pleasant and humorous company – nice people to write and to read about – and the book is a sheer delight for the lovers of light reading whose name is legion.

## [Child Life Once More]
### *The Northern Whig and Belfast Post* (Belfast, UK)

"Good wine needs no bush,"[7] and the writer who gave us *Anne of Green Gables* needs no recommendation when she sets her hand once more to the depicting of child life. In *Magic for Marigold* L.M. Montgomery has created, in the first place, a delightful little heroine with whom we journey through the first dozen years of her life, and, in the second, a family circle composed of clear-cut figures and instinct with genuine human emotions. Old Grandmother is a masterpiece of the creative art, and her last interview with her little great-grandchild is the real thing. As for Marigold herself we love her through everything, her brilliant impieties, her hot little loyalties, her progressive disillusionments, her very human adventures in search of affection. "Thank you, dear God," she prayed, "for 'ranging it so that nobody knows what I think." Then, when she learnt that her father's first wife, who had such beautiful hands, had really large feet, she ceased to be jealous of her (for her own mother's sake) and was sorry instead. And once when driven by the sudden arrival of company to try her prentice hand at baking she dealt honestly with the facts. "Oh, dear God," she said, folding floury hands over the cake-bowl, "I think I can manage the biscuits but You *must* help me with the cake."[8] Thank you for Marigold, Miss Montgomery!

## A Sensitive Girl
### *London Daily News* (London, UK)

It takes 40 pages to choose a name for Marigold, who nearly dies in the process; and no wonder, poor child, with a family like hers. The author shows a certain skill in depicting the reactions of Marigold to her various relations and friends, and her gradual desertion of the world of imagination for that of fact; but the book is spoilt by excessive sentimentality, which a rather obvious humour fails to relieve.

## [Another Fascinating Tale]
### *The Church of England Newspaper* (London, UK)

After a long interval, during which we have had to content ourselves with re-reading the *Emily* and *Anne of Green Gables* books, L.M. Montgomery has given us another fascinating tale in *Magic for Marigold*. There is indeed something magical about Marigold, the "child of the singing heart,"[9] who at the age of five and a half already found life intensely "int'resting." She has a setting as charming as herself – an old homestead on Prince Edward Island – and although she is fatherless, she is blessed with a wealth of relatives, who are all described with unerring ability and a fine sense of humour. When Marigold is twelve years old we bid her farewell, but not, we hope, for good; there will be many beside ourselves who, having read *Magic for Marigold*, will eagerly look forward to a sequel at a not very distant date.

## Make Believe
### *The Globe* (Toronto, ON)

L.M. Montgomery throws all her cheerful whimsicality into this story of a happy little girl. Marigold, youngest of the innumerable Lesley clan in Prince Edward Island, is a dreamer whose fancy builds magic about all things. Her life is filled with magic doors and green gates which open into faery lands. She is a nice youngster, and, like all Miss Montgomery's smaller heroines, has a streak of naughtiness that makes her all the more real and likable.

The author's pictures of Marigold's elders are delightfully done, in particular those of Old and Young Grandmothers Lesley. Miss Montgomery has a shrewd eye for character, but she is at her best when dealing with the very young and the very old. The reader will be charmed by the clan gatherings, with marked personalities in affectionate combat, and loyalties surmounting the inevitable tiffs between one branch and another.

*Magic for Marigold* can be recommended to those who seek a bright and thoroughly wholesome book.

## Anne Reborn
### *The Mail and Empire* (Toronto, ON)
ROBERT HAZLEMERE

To read a new book by L.M. Montgomery is just like paying a visit to the Island and renewing old acquaintances. Her books are friendly and, like herself, full of charm. It is not a matter for wonder that she holds high place in the hearts of thousands of girls, young and old. Everybody has read or heard of *Anne of Green Gables* and the delightful series that follows, ending with *Rilla of Ingleside*. The present writer prefers her *Emily of New Moon* to any of her books, as being a more mature, sensitive and poetical piece of writing. Her latest creation, *Magic for Marigold*, is a typical Montgomery book with its quaint adult characters, so much akin to those in the stories by Joseph C. Lincoln,[10] and the delightful bits of nature description so typical of the Maritime provinces.

One of the best characters in the book is old grandmother, who is really Marigold's great-grandmother, and, like one or two other grandmothers in recent novels, is 99 years old and trying to achieve the century. The description of old grandmother in the orchard of Cloud of Spruce on her last night on earth is splendidly told. It is the high spot of the book and was worth writing for itself alone.

## [Suffused with Whimsicality]
### *The Montreal Daily Star* (Montreal, QC)

L.M. Montgomery's latest definite contribution to Canadian fiction, *Magic for Marigold*, is suffused with whimsicality. This tale, by the author of *Anne of Green Gables*, holds in store a promise of delightful hours for all who make its acquaintance. Human beings from seven to seventy will be captivated by its spontaneous humor, its delicate pathos, and, most of all, by the quaint philosophy of Marigold who, at six years, finds life in all its phases very "int'resting." Only a thorough knowledge and sympathetic understanding of the intricate workings of a child's reasoning could produce a story of such unalloyed charm.

Marigold goes a-visiting, and the tragedy of her poignant loneliness during those first nights away from home and mother strikes deep chords of response. And each of her young experiences is caught in the passing to be recorded with true insight. This little person to whom the "tiny green folk of the forest" really exist is so vividly alive that only a master touch could have created her. For the adult this simple, stimulating story will recall the days when we were young and revelled in the land of make-believe. For the child it will prove an enrichment of its imagination.

## [The Mind of an Imaginative and Attractive Child]
### *Punch, or the London Charivari* (London, UK)

I cannot help thinking that the child of whom Miss L.M. MONTGOMERY gives a sympathetic study in *Magic for Marigold* was encumbered by too many relations. Generations before *Marigold* was born the *Lesleys* had migrated to Canada, and there they had multiplied so fruitfully that a whole tribe or clan of them existed. *Marigold* indeed was blessed, or the reverse, by an old and a young grandmother and by such a bevy of uncles, aunts and cousins that at times she seemed to me in danger of being swamped by the crowd. These *Lesleys* I must admit are admirably drawn, and my only grievance against them is that they impede Miss MONTGOMERY in her difficult task of revealing the mind of an imaginative and attractive child. Nevertheless, in spite of impediments, *Marigold* emerges from the ruck and takes the chief honours of a charming and original story.

## [Lovable Qualities and Healthy Naughtiness]
### *The Sunday Times* (Perth, Australia)

To record that this is a story for children, and elders probably, by L.M. Montgomery, author of so many delightful books of this nature, is sufficient to secure its hall-mark among readers of this pleasing type of fiction founded on human examples. Marigold has the lovable qualities and the healthy naughtiness that made *Anne of Green Gables* so popular.

## [A Glamour All Its Own]
### *The Canadian Bookman* (Toronto, ON)
#### JOHN W. GARVIN

It was in the Fall of 1908 that *Anne of Green Gables* was published.[11] The unknown author had difficulty in finding a publisher, as readers of publishing houses are too often stupid or lacking in confidence in their own critical judgment. But the L.C. Page Company, of Boston, accepted the manuscript in the year mentioned on most favorable terms for the publishers, and at last this very popular novel was printed. It is probable that over a million copies have sold to date. The great humorist, Mark Twain, was one of the first to appraise it highly. He sent a letter to Francis Wilson, the actor, in which he wrote: *"Anne of Green Gables" is the sweetest creation of child life yet written.*

*Magic for Marigold* is the fifteenth work of prose fiction to appear from the same pen, and while not as great a creation as the first and several others, it has a glamor all its own which will charm thousands of youthful readers. It gives the many experiences and adventures, tragic and humorous, of Marigold Lesley for the first twelve years of her life and the interest never flags. No writer known to me understands children, boys as well as girls, more intimately, sympathetically and lovingly, than Mrs. Macdonald; and it is because of this rare understanding that adults of mature years read her books with pleasure and commend them to others ... I was present on the lawn at Government House, Toronto, when this most popular novelist arrived to greet, not only the royal princes, but Rt. Hon. Stanley Baldwin, Prime Minister of Great Britain, who had cabled from 10 Downing Street, London, before embarking, requesting her to meet him, if possible in the Dominion, while he was journeying through. It was a thrilling moment and a proud day indeed for one of Canada's best loved authors.[12]

## Character Growths
### *Natal Mercury* (Durban, South Africa)

Mrs. Montgomery takes the keenest delight in describing the development of a child, and in all her novels we have this emergence from childhood to womanhood and the making of strong and admirable characters. This new novel maintains the tradition, and Marigold grows up a fine woman in spite of her dull upbringing. But she has the spirit and the pride of ancestors, for the Lesleys were a proud, strong race, and the old grandmother was typical of the satirical harsh old gentlewoman who ruled everybody with a rod of iron but who had been a bit of a gay spark in her youth. The canvas is crowded with characters, with the mother, the young grandmother and the old grandmother, all of whom have an influence on the child. Then the life is well described. The connections between the characters are fresh and wise, and Mrs. Montgomery knows how to get her views on life, men and matters introduced through the conversations. The aunts and uncles are legion in number, but each has a distinctive individuality which makes the novel singularly attractive.

## [Strange to Modern Girls]
### *The Auckland Star* (Auckland, New Zealand)

It was doubtful if Miss Montgomery could repeat her success in *Anne of Green Gables*, but in *Magic for Marigold* she makes the attempt. Here is a family of rather tiresome people who are no more than a background for Marigold, whose biography might well stand alone as an excellent study in character. Miss Montgomery cannot do anything carelessly, and if there is a fault in this story it is in an overplus of detail relating to persons not material to the main theme. Marigold is a dreamer, and finds real life an adventure not to her liking. Modern girls may think this strange.

## [Simple Story, but Fine Character Drawing]
### *The Pioneer* (Allahabad, India)

Here is another novel from the pen of the author of *Emily of New Moon* and the other books of that series – one that fully maintains the naivete of style of those former contributions to our store of good fiction, and in addition shows a remarkable development in fine character drawing. The story is simple, being that of Marigold Lesley – one of that clan of clans – from soon after her birth until she reaches the age of twelve. In those brief twelve years the little heroine captivates the reader with her search for those things in life that are "int'resting," and it is amazing how many she finds and how many she introduces us to. With the conservatism of the clan all round her, hedged in by its traditions, its old world customs and beliefs, she still retains a fanciful streak of her own that gets her into many escapades, fraught with all kinds of danger, but finally brings her safely through them all. The author has a remarkable insight into the youthful mind, and while this book can be read with real pleasure as a novel, it is also in some respects an object lesson to parents – almost a study in child psychology.

NOTES

1 *Australian Christian World* (Sydney, Australia), review of *Magic for Marigold*, 6 December 1929, in SR, 333; review of *Magic for Marigold*, unidentified and undated clipping, in SR, 345; *The Evening Post*, review of *Magic for Marigold*, 22; C.F.M., review of *Magic for Marigold*, 2; *The Liverpool Daily Post* (Liverpool, UK), review of *Magic for Marigold*, 13 January 1930, in SR, 332; *The Oregonian*, review of *Magic for Marigold*, 9; *Salt Lake City Telegram* (Salt Lake City, UT), "L.M. Montgomery Presents Another Charming Book," review of *Magic for Marigold*, 10 November 1929, in SR, 348.

2 *San Francisco Chronicle*, review of *Magic for Marigold*, D5; Hinkley, "Successor to Anne of Green Gables," 9; *Boston Evening Transcript*, review of *Magic for Marigold*, 2; Graham, "A Book for Girls," 10.

3 Clara Bernhardt, review of *Magic for Marigold*, unidentified and undated clipping, in SR, 333; review of *Magic for Marigold*, unidentified and undated clipping, in SR, 342; *Natal Advertiser* (Durban, South Africa), "A Welcome Change," review of *Magic for Marigold*, 18 January 1930, in SR, 347; *The Morning Bulletin*, review of *Magic for Marigold*, 5.

4 *Captain January* (1891), a novel by Laura E. Richards (1850–1943), American author, that was made twice into a Hollywood film, including one featuring Shirley Temple.

5 *MM*, 14, 40.

6 *MM*, 41.

7 An expression used in *As You Like It*, a play by William Shakespeare (1564–1616), that suggests that something of quality does not need any publicity.

8 *MM*, 27, 224.

9 *MM*, 26.

10 Joseph C. Lincoln (1870–1944), American author of numerous works set in a fictionalized Cape Cod.

11 *Anne of Green Gables* was actually published in June 1908. Garvin had previously made this error in his review of *Anne's House of Dreams*, reproduced above.

12 See the headnote for "About Canadian Writers: L.M. Montgomery, the Charming Author of 'Anne,'" by Katherine Hale, in Volume 1 of *The L.M. Montgomery Reader*. The ellipsis in this paragraph appears in the original review.

# 18

## A Tangled Web / Aunt Becky Began It

### —— 1931 ——

Montgomery was annoyed at the fact that this novel was available as *A Tangled Web* in Canada, the United States, and Australia and as *Aunt Becky Began It* in England, but regardless of what title reviewers called it, they were almost unanimous in their praise. The *Portland News* of Maine called it "one of those family stories, etched with the precision of an artist ... the story is woven, a wise understanding of human nature guiding the pen that writes the several histories of the Darks." Montgomery even underlined extracts from a review in her scrapbook appearing in the *Jacksonville Journal* of Illinois: "This novel ... is an excellent commentary on human nature; for its many characters are intensely human ... All the tragicomedy of real life is here in full measure. You feel all the time that you are reading about actual flesh and blood people ... It is a great comedy, and rich entertainment." The *Ames Daily Tribune Times* of Iowa also suggested that "Mrs. Montgomery's work is improving in quality the last few years, and her more recent titles are having a wider circle of readers," and the Toronto *Mail and Empire* even called it "the most vigorous story she has written for some time." The *Boston Evening Transcript*, calling it "a story for adults, and for those adults who like unlimited romance," noted that "the author of so many stories for the mildly young has discovered that the latest fad is old age," whereas the *Lethbridge Daily Herald* called it "a book for adults, primarily, but none of her younger friends will miss it."[1]

In Australia, reviewers also sang the praises of this new novel: as the *Sydney Mail* declared, "Miss L.M. Montgomery is a novelist who has written many a good story, both for young and old; but I doubt if in any of her previous work she has attained the standard of her latest novel ... Unquestionably Miss

Montgomery's forte is character-drawing, and in *A Tangled Web* she has revealed herself at her very best." Meanwhile, the *Sydney Church Standard* noted that Montgomery "gives ample play to her plot-contriving powers. The interest is magnetically held, and the reader is kept in a continual state of excitement; no sooner does she create a happy-ever-after atmosphere, than the premature conclusion is enigmatically dissolved, and the reader is left to guess again." Calling Aunt Becky "a woman of remarkable insight and a bitterly acid sense of humour," this reviewer added that "there are times when the reader wonders whether to be engaged in a farce, a tragedy, or a comedy." And in South Africa, the *Natal Mercury* called it "a real picture gallery of humans who are diverse and yet the same, and we see them drawn hither and thither by their petty likes and fears, and how their lives are influenced."[2]

Moreover, most of the criticisms were counterbalanced with praise: while the *New York Herald Tribune Books* called the novel "a long-winded tale woven of sentimentality and whimsy," the *News Chronicle* of London acknowledged that "its rather thick sentiment is leavened with some very tart humour." Meanwhile, the *New York Times Book Review* noted that "although the long arm of coincidence handles events a little neatly at times, and romance and sentiment bloom too lushly for the sophisticated reader's taste, there is much charm in the story." Still, the critical response to this novel was overwhelmingly positive, including a glowing review in the Philadelphia *Public Ledger*, which called the novel "an ambitious, humorous and fascinating piece of work" and complemented Montgomery on her ability to depict a cast of sixty "separate and individualistic" characters, "an achievement too dizzying for our feeble mentality to comprehend how it can be done."[3]

## A Montgomery Novel
### *The Globe* (Toronto, ON)

With that old magic of hers, so simple and yet so compelling, the creator of *Anne of Green Gables* has again put that something into the 300-odd pages of her latest novel which puts her books in a class by themselves, and which draws thousands of tourists annually to Prince Edward Island.

Those who have grown up with Anne Shirley, the Story Girl, Rilla of Ingleside, and have discovered the beauty and charm of the Island through Miss Montgomery's pen will welcome this engrossing and colorful story of the clan of Dark and Penhallow. Laid in the author's well-loved and thoroughly understood Prince Edward Island, the story centres around an old Georgian jug, an heirloom in the Dark and Penhallow families, and the strange will of old Aunt Becky.

With amazing skill and sound understanding of that uncertain quantity, human nature, the author weaves the tangled threads of the web in and out, through deaths, marriages, births, heartbreaks, until the characters stand out clearly etched against a background of sea-swept beaches, red roads, moonlit meadows, and homely cottages sheltered by lombardies and apple trees.

*A Tangled Web* is a mature novel, decidedly different from any of the author's previous books, but it is refreshingly wholesome, alive with wit and humor, and rich in the history of the early settlers on the Island. In gathering her wealth of local color, of quaint stories and phrases, the author must have spent many an hour chatting with the older folk in the little villages.

In addition to the interest of the story itself, *A Tangled Web* delights the reader with its musical names – Bay Silver, Little Friday Cove, Rose River, Treewoofe Hill – and by its poetic descriptions of nature. One charming illustration:

"It was on an October evening as warm as June. A frolicsome little wind was stripping all the gold from the maple trees. The western sky was like a great smoky chrysanthemum over hills that were soft violet and brown. A few early autumnal stars were burning over the misty, shorn harvest fields. A great orange moon was rising over Treewoofe Hill, bringing out a remote, austere quality in its beauty. There was a pleasant smell of damp mould from red ploughed fields."[4]

## L.M. Montgomery Writes Humoresque
*The Toronto Daily Star* (Toronto, ON)

*Tangled Web* Is Modernistic Yet Still Characteristic

In *Tangled Web*[5] by L.M. Montgomery the author runs far from her usual pretty romantic milieus with a breezy humoresque. The story is of old Aunt Becky who made her will conditional upon the good behavior of the claimants after she is dead. The real humor of the book comes in what happens after the year is up. The author skilfully colors what 20 years ago she might have written as a tenderish romance into a rather rollicking humoresque in which may be traced some subtle influence of a writer called Mazo de la Roche.[6] But the simple naturalness of the story is Lucy Montgomery's own, which no mere modernistic suggestions can ever kill.

## Another Montgomery Book
### *The Gazette* (Montreal, QC)

L.M. Montgomery does not lose any of her charm as a story-teller with the passing of the years. Her style is more mature now, but the freshness still lingers. Prince Edward Island is once more the ground which her characters work and play in, and there are many persons tangled in the web. Only one or two are very young this time, little Gay especially, and hearts throb over her experience with the grim world. A start is made with old Aunt Becky Dark, who calls the clan of the Darks and Penhallows to her last party, in which the Dark jug, a family heirloom coveted by one and all, figures prominently. Aunt Becky tells them what she thinks of them and puts them on their good behavior for a year, with the Dark jug as a prize for the one her trustee thinks fit. Here the story starts and the lives of all the persons concerned are passed in review. Some extraordinary acts of folly have been committed and there is much heartache before the principals are brought to reason by circumstances. Humor, pathos and tragedy run through the pages and the Moon Man appears and reappears with his uncanny sayings. In the end the web is untangled and the young and the middle-aged and the old receive their rewards, according as each deserves. *A Tangled Web* will please all readers of the Montgomery books, for it is a familiar locality they are enabled to visit and its people seem like old friends.

## [A Capital Tale]
### *The Church of England Newspaper* (London, UK)

There can be few authors who retain such a strong hold on their readers' affection as L.M. Montgomery, whose delightful tales of Prince Edward Island are so well known and so widely appreciated. Her tenderness, whimsical humour and good-natured shrewdness show to the best advantage in her latest tale, *Aunt Becky Began It*, which describes a huge family clan, almost exclusively composed of the Darks and the Penhallows. They are introduced to us *en bloc* at a levée held by Aunt Becky Dark, who ruled the clan in life through her biting tongue and devastatingly good memory, and in death set them all by the ears by reserving the ultimate destination of a coveted heirloom, the Dark Jug. The amazingly far-reaching results of Aunt Becky's stipulation provide Miss Montgomery with the theme for a capital tale, in which she sustains our curiosity and interest to the last page and finally rewards us with a skilfully-managed "happy ending."

## United Families
### Punch, or the London Charivari (London, UK)

*Aunt Becky Began It* suffers, as *Magic for Marigold* suffered, from an overcrowded stage, but Miss L.M. MONTGOMERY writes so pleasantly and intimately that her tales, despite their handicaps, are always easy to read. Here she relates the fortunes of two families in Prince Edward Island, the *Darks* and the *Penhallows*. These families were enough, and in a sense more than enough, in themselves; if you happened to be born a *Dark* you married either another *Dark* or a *Penhallow*, and if you were a girl and born a *Penhallow* you either remained one at your marriage or became a *Dark*. And over these exclusive people *Aunt Becky* ruled, and at her death left an inheritance that, for better or worse, assuredly perpetuated her memory. *Aunt Becky* is a creation to be proud of, and indeed I have no word to say against these very human *Darks* and *Penhallows* except that there seemed to me too many of them.

## [So Utterly Lacking in Kindliness]
### The Canadian Bookman (Toronto, ON)
#### A.S. MARQUIS

In her latest book the well-known Canadian author, L.M. Montgomery, departs somewhat from the ever-popular "Anne" and "Rilla" novels which made her famous. The central character in this recent tale is not a mischievous, fun-loving, lovable child, but rather a sharp-tongued, witty, and somewhat cynical old lady of eighty-five, the acknowledged head of the family clan of Dark and Penhallow. The two families had intermarried for three generations and to take the author's own words – "The resultant genealogical tangle baffled everybody except Uncle Pippin."[7]

A family heirloom – the old Dark Jug, a cumbersome, crudely-decorated, broken and mended curiosity of no intrinsic value – is the slender thread which holds the story together, though why any member of the family should covet the thing is not exactly clear. Just why should men fight, husbands and wives quarrel, mothers and daughters bicker, and jealous feuds grow apace over a homely old jug? Surely among all the numerous members of the clan there were some who would be above bickering over such a trifle!

Aunt Becky, whose characterization is well done, shortly before her death invited her relations to a final party at which she proceeded to rake up all the various family skeletons just for the pleasure of seeing her guests squirm under her insults and jibes. With a worn red sweater pulled around her stooped shoulders, the old lady sat proudly erect in the big old walnut bed and greeted her callers – some forty in all – with sharp, cutting remarks, a clever and witty document of her own composition, and then distributed her few remaining valuables in a manner that brought many gasps of dismay and disappointment. The disposal of the coveted jug itself, however, she postponed for another year, and watched with keen enjoyment the discomfiture of her numerous relatives. The excuse she made to herself for the gathering was that she wanted this last bit of amusement before she entered eternity.

The author has given us what might be termed a pathological study of a family group, narrow and petty, seemingly with few redeeming qualities. The sketch of the old lady is clever and, at times, witty; the two young girls, Gay and Nan, are convincingly characterized; but the lesser individuals do not stand out clearly, possibly for the simple reason that there are too many of them. The two who do succeed in winning the love and sympathy of the reader are the visionary Margaret and the motherless little Brian.

The scene of the story is supposed to be Prince Edward Island, but it could be located anywhere. The selfishness and narrowness of the Darks and the Penhallows could be found among many family groups, but it would be rare indeed to find a group of human beings so utterly lacking in kindliness and gentleness of heart as are those of *A Tangled Web*.[8]

## [No Little Skill]
### *The Times Literary Supplement* (London, UK)

Aunt Becky was the head of the large clan of the Dark and Penhallow families. She ruled them with a caustic tongue and a bitter knowledge of all those little peccadilloes of which each member of the tribe was most ashamed. With hierarchical dignity she conducted her death-bed levée, and she allotted her worldly goods among the relatives gathered around her with an impish perversity; but the one heirloom which every Dark and Penhallow coveted – the Dark jug – she gave to the keeping of Dandy Dark, together with a sealed envelope which was to be opened a year after her death and which contained the name of the person to whom the jug was next to descend. For a year after she had passed away her terrorizing memory impressed the clan, and anticipation of the contents of the sealed envelope ordered their individual lives for twelve months. Mr. Montgomery has taken all the ramifications of the clan in his province. With no little skill he has given satisfying portraits of all its members, has sorted many of their life-long difficulties so that the memory of Aunt Becky can straighten them out. In the twelve months he describes marriages are made and remade, reputations formed and broken, enmities sealed and dissolved; and at the end of the period Dandy Dark had lost the envelope in the pig-sty, where the pigs had eaten it.

## [A Robust and Versatile Clan Saga]
### *The Toronto Telegram* (Toronto, ON)

A Tangled Web[9] is a decided change from L.M. Montgomery's usual style of romance so much beloved by her large Canadian public. Though the action takes place in the usual delightful surroundings of small town life in lovely Prince Edward Island, the author has given us in flowing language a robust and versatile clan saga in which a vast number of Darks and Penhallows mingle in a kaleidoscopic mixture of colors and variety. The story is woven chiefly around the disposal of an old jug, heirloom in the Dark family for several generations and greatly desired by all the relatives. It is bequeathed in a strange and unusual way by wily old Aunt Becky Dark on her deathbed, and the characteristic reactions of the numerous relatives to her biting satire and crusty personal allusions make excellent reading.

Tragedies, romances, quarrels, comic incidents and ridiculous situations jostle thick and fast in the many pages of the book, and the author is to be congratulated on the skill with which she differentiates the individual characters. Prince Edward Island lies before us in all the beauty of color, sound and surging shores, and the wealth of local color and the quaint personalities of village life are a charm alike to sophisticated and simple readers. The book should prove a popular addition to every bookshelf.

NOTES

1 *Portland News* (Portland, ME), review of *A Tangled Web*, 23 October 1931, in SR, 357; *Jacksonville Journal* (Jacksonville, IL), "Hate and Love – Twins?" review of *A Tangled Web*, 8 October 1931, in SR, 358; *Ames Daily Tribune Times*, "Library Notes," 3; *The Mail and Empire*, "Just Off the Press," 16; *Boston Evening Transcript* (Boston, MA), review of *A Tangled Web*, 22 December 1931, in SR, 361; *The Lethbridge Daily Herald*, review of *A Tangled Web*, 11.

2 *The Sydney Mail*, "Humour and Romance," 19; *Sydney Church Standard* (Sydney, Australia), review of *A Tangled Web*, signed M.B., 8 January 1932, in SR, 363–64; *Natal Mercury* (Durban, South Africa), "Character Study," review of *Aunt Becky Began It*, 25 January 1932, in SR, 370.

3 *The New York Herald Tribune Books*, review of *A Tangled Web*, 23; *News Chronicle* (London, UK), "Family Forest," review of *Aunt Becky Began It*, 23 November 1931, in SR, 357; *The New York Times Book Review*, "A Homely Chronicle," 19; *Public Ledger* (Philadelphia, PA), review of *A Tangled Web*, 9 January 1932, in SR, 362.

4 *TW*, 172.

5 I have corrected the original, which reads "'Tangled Nets.'"

6 Mazo de la Roche (1879–1961), Canadian author of *Jalna* (1927), the first of sixteen novels about the Whiteoak family in rural Ontario. A Hollywood film version of *Jalna*, from RKO Radio Pictures, was released in 1935; its producer, Kenneth Macgowan, also produced the RKO film *Anne of Green Gables* (1934).

7 *TW*, 1.

8 I have corrected the original, which reads "'The Tangled Web.'"

9 I have corrected the original, which reads "'The Tangled Web.'"

# 19

## Pat of Silver Bush

—— 1933 ——

Although scholars have claimed that Montgomery's literary reputation had begun to wane in the 1930s, reviews of this later novel about a young girl growing up on a Prince Edward Island farm remained largely positive. The *Portland Journal* of Oregon noted that "a charming feature of Miss Montgomery's stories is that they are wholesome and inspiring rather than stickily sweet," whereas the *Morning Bulletin* of Australia called it "a wholesome story that youth will read with eagerness, and age with quiet introspection." Carl Tarbox, writing in the *Knickerbocker Press* of Albany, New York, noted that "this is one of the delightfully rare books that defies being classified as belonging to any particular age" and that "will be enjoyed by all but that peculiar species known as the 'back-yard' realists." In her scrapbook, Montgomery underlined comments made in a review in the *Worcester Telegram* of Massachusetts: "Rarely can an author do a combination of juvenile and adult narrative as happily as can the creator of *Anne of Green Gables*." Even the *Publisher's Circular* of London jumped on the bandwagon, calling it "clever, light and artistic; it is also thoroughly amusing and packed with really witty snippets. The story of a growing country girl is good psychology and altogether pleasing." *The Hartford Courant* of Connecticut, commenting on this "charmingly told story for growing girls," added that "no living writer does this sort of thing better than Miss Montgomery," whereas the *Pittsburgh Post–Gazette* went as far as to call it "a normal yarn for normal girls."[1]

In addition to this praise, however, were several comments about the evolving expectations of readers of popular fiction: "If there are any survivors of the once numerous class of fiction readers who considered that a novel did not 'end happily' if the heroine was not joined in holy matrimony to the man of her choice before the close of the last chapter," an unidentified clipping from a UK periodical stated, "it is to be feared that Miss L.M. Montgomery's story of Prince Edward Island life ... will not be altogether to their taste." Moreover, although most of Montgomery's previous novels about girls growing up were followed by sequels, the *Nashville Banner* noted that "the author has left for himself ample room for a second book, which somehow one doesn't desire. One would prefer to leave Pat just where she is, and as she is."[2]

## [An "Old-Fashioned" Story]
### *The Liverpool Daily Post* (Liverpool, UK)

*Pat of Silver Bush* is what is called an "old-fashioned" story and would have suited the taste of half a century ago, which demanded that fiction should take a rosy, if not a rose-watery, view of life. Miss L.M. Montgomery has laid the scene of her novel in Prince Edward Island, and makes it as idyllic as lush sentiment can contrive. Those who like this sort of thing will like it very much. Those who prefer a more realistic treatment of experience may be advised to pass it by.

## [A Tale of Youth and Magic]
### *The Canadian Bookman* (Toronto, ON)

All the charm of the books upon which rests the fame of this Canadian writer are found in her new book, the setting of which is an old woodland homestead in Prince Edward Island. It is a tale of youth and magic, of young girlhood experiencing its griefs and joys and awakening to first love.

Early in the tale we are introduced to Silver Bush, the farm home which got its name from the big grove of white birch on the hill behind the farm, and from a favorite window seat, we look at the fields of the farm through the eyes of brown-eyed Pat, the lovable heroine of the tale. [* * *][3]

The family traced its Island existence back to Great-great-grandfather Nehemiah Gardiner[4] who had settled in Prince Edward Island in 1780 and in the grave-yard beside the orchard were the graves of this old progenitor of the family, and his wife Marie Bonnet of French Huguenot ancestry, and of Great-grand-father Thomas Gardiner, with his Quaker wife Jane Wilson. They had been buried there when the nearest cemetery was across the Island at Charlottetown. Another occupant of the family grave-yard was great-uncle Richard, "Wild Dick Gardiner" who was reputed to have eaten human flesh!

In this way the book builds up reader-interest at the outset and it is maintained in such measure as to make *Pat of Silver Bush* one of L.M. Montgomery's outstanding achievements.

## [Entertaining Little Tale]
### *The Toronto Telegram* (Toronto, ON)

A charming little tale that will delight the younger girl and also hold the absorbed interest of her older sister is this latest book from the popular pen of L.M. Montgomery. Full of the beauty and fragrance of life in a quaint sea-shore community in Prince Edward Island which the author knows so well, love, comedy and romance in wholesome quantities give us the very essence and glamor of youth and adventure. Warm-hearted little Patricia Gardiner grows up at Silver Bush loving every stick and stone of the old-fashioned homestead. Comical old Irish Judy, who loves and befriends generations of the Gardiner family and especially Pat, is a remarkably life-like character, and Jingle, the neglected young neighbor, Bets, Winnie, and the rigid maiden aunts all pass before us in a lively chronicle of homely beauty and humor. Full of charming descriptive writing and romance, this entertaining and gay little tale should take a high place in the affections of Miss Montgomery's numerous readers.

## Another "Anne" Romance
### *The Gazette* (Montreal, QC)

L.M. Montgomery has again returned to her native Prince Edward Island for material for this pleasant story, and has found it in plenty. Furthermore, Pat is another Anne girl, and a very lovable one at that. Pat Gardiner, to give her her full name, is a dreamy youngster who does not want to grow up and who dislikes to see things change. She is an important member of a woodland homestead on the island and she loves every tree, bush and flower on the place. She is followed from the awkward, long-legged period right up to early young womanhood and a fine picture is furnished of the development of the mind of a child and the transition that comes with the passing of girlhood. If in parts the telling of the progress drags, because of the amount of detail, at others it is beautiful. The emotional scenes are most skilfully dealt with, just as in the earlier Anne books.

The author knows her island people and describes them faithfully. The reader is made acquainted with many diverse characters, uncles and aunts, fathers and mothers, brothers and sisters, cousins, and just friends. As the years pass Pat has many joys and some sorrows and she rebels against the latter. "Change and decay" is not to her liking until more understanding comes to the troubled little heart.[5] She is borne up in her childish trials and tribulations by old Judy Plum, who has the Irish gift of seeing the hands of the fairies playing with the affairs of men. Judy is a tower of strength to the growing girl when love comes, and takes the side of Jingle, or Hilary, in the several episodes. There are two little dogs in the story of Pat and they lend pathos as well as fun to the record of her doings. There is a promise in the conclusion of the tale of *Pat of Silver Bush* which carries a hint of a sequel to this typical Montgomery romance of childhood amid pleasant rural scenes. That is something for her many readers to look forward to.

### Fascinating Native Characters Enliven
### Mrs. Montgomery's Novel
#### *The Globe* (Toronto, ON)

The author of *Anne of Green Gables* has further endeared herself to a wide circle of readers in Canada and abroad with *Pat of Silver Bush*,[6] another of her quaint and intriguing stories, having the familiar background of Prince Edward Island.

In this novel, Mrs. Montgomery, in her inimitable way, pictures the life of Pat, the odd little child in the Gardiner family, and the amusing and serious incidents of her younger years. And there's Judy Plum, the old Irish nurse, a lovable soul, who helps Pat over many a rough spot, more or less precipitated by Pat's own impetuosity. Judy's fierce loyalty to the Gardiner family, and her caustic criticism of neighbors who do not happen to see eye to eye with her, provide plenty of humor to season the serious side of the tale. Then there is Jingle, the young orphan boy, who really understands Pat, and who proves his genuine affection for her as the years go by.

There were those who read *Anne of Green Gables* again and again through sheer enjoyment of its clean, healthy philosophy of life and its sterling characters. No doubt this latest effort from Mrs. Montgomery will find as great favor with the reading public.

## [A Full-Length Story of Contemporary Life]
### *The New York Herald Tribune Books* (New York, NY)

There is a type of book that growing girls need and want: the full-length story of contemporary life, with the technique of the popular contemporary novel and differing from it only in keeping within the range of interests of a well bred girl in a harmonious family and presenting only problems that might be expected to confront her. The purpose of all these novels, avowed or unconscious, is to make home appear beautiful and desirable, and families, in Louisa Alcott's phrase, "the loveliest thing in the world."[7] English-speaking girls have been provided with novels like this by not more than two or three American or English writers in each generation since the days of Mrs. A.D.T. Whitney.[8] There can be no doubt that the present head of this dynasty is L.M. Montgomery.[9] Her Anne of Green Gables and Emily of New Moon are cousins of Rebecca of Sunnybrook Farm.[10]

"Pat of Silver Bush" is a Canadian like her predecessors. She lives in a large and rundown homestead among the trees of Prince Edward Island. Her family are quality: the Binnies may sweat, but the Gardiners perspire. At least they are thus admonished by the Irish cook-housekeeper whose running commentary on events keeps up a continuous ripple of humor. She is a real person, not stage-comic relief. It takes comic relief like this in real life to keep a large family in its place and bring it up properly, and this book may give one cause to wonder whether the gradual disappearance of the species of which Judy Plum is a specimen may not have something to do with the large family's steady decline.

It has not noticeably declined on Mrs. Montgomery's island. Home is home there. It has been said that Canadians are more English than the English, and surely old families there are nearer Victoria than Ramsay Mac.[11] There is something deeply Victorian in Pat's determination that things shall be kept as they have been; she does not want her sister to marry or the piano to be moved. She is homesick when she goes away for a visit – and writes back five letters to as many people, giving just the same facts and producing five completely different compositions, as twelve-year-olds do when addressing best friends, mothers, boys-next-door or the cook. But the change does go on steadily from the chapter in which she is seven to the conflict of young love and the old house on the last page. The conflicts marking these changes may not seem tremendous to a grown-up, but neither may his to the eyes of the indifferent stars. A mother, however, might do well to notice how Judy meets the one that arises when Pat goes to her first party and discovers that she will never be pretty. The wise and warm-hearted fashion in which Judy lets her find out that when she is old enough she will have "charm" might help some one to deal with a like situation.

If ladies who insist that grown-up fiction should be always as clean as a girls' book would stick to girls' books as rich in nourishment as this, it would be better for them. They would have an honest food-product brewed entire for the consumer, not one from which the intoxicating element had been artificially removed.

## [The Magic and Joy of Real People]
### *Boston Evening Transcript* (Boston, MA)

In *Pat of Silver Bush*, we are given another charming and wholesome story of young girlhood by the author of *Anne of Green Gables*. Pat is a wholly unspoiled girl, living her first romance and adventure on a beautiful farm on Prince Edward Island. The hero, Jingle (his name is really Hilary), and his ugly dog are interwoven in a most natural fashion with the visits of the girl to her elderly great-aunts, and the details of these visits and their consequences make for much pleasurable reading.

It is a relief to read of Pat's sincere friendship for the daughter of an artist, rather than the erotic adventures that authors give their heroines today, for here is the magic and joy of real people, written into a story that rings true throughout its every page.

## A Sister to Anne
### *Saturday Night* (Toronto, ON)
#### JEAN GRAHAM

Once upon a time, a lady of the name of Lucy Maud Montgomery, living in the delightful town of Cavendish, Prince Edward Island, wrote a story called *Anne of Green Gables*, with a red-haired heroine, who straightway walked into the hearts of the girls of the Dominion of Canada. Anne has had many successors, but none quite so charming as the original. The latest production is a story of Pat, who might well be of the household of Anne. Silver Bush is a beautiful old house in that delectable eastern island which is well-named "The Garden of the Gulf." Pat is wilful, merry and lovable – just the kind of girl to spend a camp holiday with, and have for a lifelong friend. She loves her home and exults in its beauties. Most interesting of all are the glimpses of the island loveliness. Its flowers, its birches and even the cats of tansy patch are all delightful. We are sorry for Miss Montgomery, who is now hostess in an Ontario manse – so dull after that glorious island.

## [Made to Order]
### *The New Outlook* (Toronto, ON)

Prince Edward Island is again the setting for a story by the author of the famous *Anne of Green Gables*. However, Pat, unlike Anne, never emerges into reality, never becomes a personality, but remains throughout made-to-order. Jingle, the orphan, is much more real, and the outstanding character is Judy, the old Irish nurse who tells most marvellous tales. The joys and sorrows, the adventures of childhood and youth have a place in the story, through all of which shines Pat's love for the old home at Silver Bush.

## [Home and Canadian Girlhood]
### *The Auckland Star* (Auckland, New Zealand)

Miss Montgomery, of *Anne of Green Gables*, still draws with a faithful and loving hand her pictures of Canadian girlhood. "See no evil, hear no evil, speak no evil" is her teaching, and through the rapids of modern life the authoress steers her girls in safety, if not always in comfort. To English minds Canada seems young to have homes so long established that they hold the lasting love of several generations, but in *Pat of Silver Bush* the home dominates the story and most of the characters. The domestic servant who "sticks to her job" is herein exalted, and wins love only second to the home. "Judy" is one of the last of the old order of maids who never quit.

## A Child Life Picture
### *The Border Cities Star* (Windsor, ON)
H.M. MORDEN

From the pen which has given Canadian literature two of its best-loved heroines comes a third, who should rival her elder sisters in the hearts of those who love appealing stories of child life. Patricia Gardiner, the charming little daughter of Prince Edward Island, is just the sort of a girl to stand beside Anne of Green Gables and Emily of New Moon.

Mrs. Montgomery, somewhat unjustly, has been looked on as the writer of books for girls. There is, of course, no doubt that her works have a peculiar charm for young members of the fair sex, but there is no reason to look on the writer as being restricted in her field to child readers. *Pat of Silver Bush* is the kind of book that thousands of adults can read with keen delight.

Not all grown-ups will find it interesting or entertaining. There are, after all, people who have forgotten what it is like to be young, what it is like to believe in fairies, to love fields and trees and flowers even more dearly than if they were human beings. To these, Mrs. Montgomery has nothing to offer.

But to those more normal and understanding persons who have not let the glamor that is childhood escape them, such a book as *Pat of Silver Bush* should come as the most refreshing surcease from a world that has almost forgotten the really worth while things in the struggle for existence and success. They will find Pat not a mere character in fiction, but a very real little girl, who dreams her dreams, suffers the keen disillusionments of childhood, and looks at her elders with the disconcertingly keen insight which might be very embarrassing to the grown-ups should the natural reticence of childhood not prevent its more frequent expression.

Pat, it must be admitted, is not an ordinary little girl. She is looked on as "queer" by some of her elders and childhood friends. She has odd notions about fairies and ghosts and trees and flowers, but they have been implanted in her by a great influence in the person of Judy Plum. This old Irish "hired girl," with her weird tales of the "little people" and of witches, is just as much a central character of the story as is Pat herself.

Mrs. Montgomery has glorified a type here. Judy is the epitome of the old family retainers who, through generations of loving service, have become truly members of the families to which they give their devotion. In real life, Judy might be looked on as something of a bad influence on a growing girl with an imaginative mind; in fact, there are those in the book who do so look on her. But Judy's loving and understanding heart far overshadows her proclivities for filling up little minds with what many would look on as rubbish.

There is something rather glorious in Judy's career. With a divine self-sacrifice, which she would be the first to deny, she devotes a lifetime to the upbringing of a large family. There is for her no complaining at long hours, heavy work and lack of modern labor-saving devices. These are part and parcel of her existence, and she resents fiercely any suggestion of change, even change that might make her lot easier.

The reflection of this side of her character is found in Pat, her undoubted favorite among the five Gardiner children. Pat loves Silver Bush with an all-consuming adoration. The slightest changes, the cutting down of a tree, the hanging of new paper upon a wall, even the shaving of her father's moustache, strike her as tragedies. Even at an age when "ordinary girls" are having their first beaux and thinking largely of marriage, Pat is still making plans to stay throughout her life in a Silver Bush that shall always remain the same.

Changes, however, do come. Each one brings its burden of pain for Pat, though the writer delicately depicts the gradual development of the growing girl, who finds, in her teens, that disappointments and sorrows are less even than in her very early childhood. Aunt Hazel's marriage, when Pat is but a tot, is a major catastrophe, but when Winnie, the elder sister, also takes a husband when Pat has been away to school and has seen more of life, the pain is less severe. There is still the inward rebellion against change, but the new responsibilities brought upon her by Winnie's marriage and the invalidism of her mother bring a new and more proper gauging of values and soften the blow.

Throughout her whole childhood and girlhood, however, Pat remains a girl fated to love too much. The very intensity of her feeling for persons and inanimate things brings to her depths of suffering unknown to those more moderate in their emotions. The death of a kitten is a blow from which she takes weeks to recover, even though Silver Bush is constantly overrun with feline pets. The temporary loss of McGinty, the dog, reduces the whole family to deepest gloom because of Pat's reaction to it.

Like all those who lavish love on the things about them, Pat naturally finds little of really deep devotion to give to a great number of people. Her family, of course, is within her jealously guarded circle of adored ones, naturally with Judy, as one of the family. Aside from these, however, Pat clings only to two or three chums.

Most important of all is Jingle, the little boy from the neighboring farm, left fatherless and worse than motherless to the care of an unsympathetic aunt and uncle. Here is the picture of the deepest friendship and love ripening throughout childhood and adolescent life, with Pat steadfastly holding to her scorn of romance even to the time when the book leaves her, at eighteen, the mistress of her beloved home, with Jingle going out into the world to seek success in the profession which throughout life has captured his imagination.

Suspense is maintained throughout the whole story by the progress of this friendship. As the two grow up together, Jingle is so thoroughly in love with Pat, that it seems romance must eventually come. It is to him she always returns after her incipient teen-age love affairs. But in the end she sends him away, still refusing to admit the romantic affection for him which is apparent to everyone but herself.

Another great love exists for a few years, that which she feels for Bets, her sole girl chum. Beginning in childhood, this love ripens and develops until stark tragedy brings it to a close, tragedy which overnight brings womanhood to Pat and teaches her that even love cannot hold the dear things of life when they are fated to depart.

The book is not entirely about Pat. There is the Gardiner family, with its many connections throughout Prince Edward Island. One hears of these connections mainly through the lips of Judy, who is a walking chronological record of the family. Her delightfully whimsical anecdotes of the many uncles and aunts and cousins are a constant delight. She knows them all, their weaknesses and their qualities, and she tells of them with a lack of reticence which brings to Pat a sense of familiarity even with those who lie buried in the family cemetery beside the Silver Bush orchard.

Mrs. Montgomery usually follows her characters along in other books. Anne and Emily walked through a series of chronicles. One is constrained to hope that Pat may become another of these ever-living heroines. There is still much of her story to be told.

## [Idealistic Realism for the "Teen" Age]
### *The Sherbrooke Telegram* (Sherbrooke, QC)

Suitable books for girls of the "teen" age have a particular appeal at the holiday season and we could think of nothing more appropriate than L.M. Montgomery's latest book *Pat of Silver Bush*.

The author's deep, inherent love for the old homesteads of Prince Edward Island is transmitted to "Pat" who grows up in this picturesque country where generations of farmers have tilled the soil with a reasonable degree of success.

Commonplace incidents of daily life are wrapped in idealistic realism and their interpretation is expressed in such a delightful style that they appear as occurrences of major significance.

Even the naming of a baby sister, a privilege invariably sought by all members of the family, is made the occasion of a novel experience of charming simplicity. This one little incident serves to emphasize the fascinating appeal of Pat who, according to Judy, "was touched, the day she was born, by a leprachaun wid a liddle green rosethorn."[12] Hope, patience, exuberance, filial love and regret are all reproduced in this one little matter of naming the baby.

But Miss Montgomery will surely earn the undying love of girls of the "teen" age when she makes Judy the mouthpiece for her thought "That al*gebra* now, it's mesilf do be thinking it isn't fit for girls to be larning."[13]

Pat learned to love every nook and corner on the old homestead; every field had a name of its own and every animal was a friend. There are many homesteads in Prince Edward Island which might well be called "silver bush" and if the children find the element of romance to the same degree as did Pat, Sid and Jingle, they will be well advised to scorn the shallow attractions of the larger urban centres.

Pat enjoys one continuous series of adventures in which a very refreshing appreciation of nature is characteristic of Miss Montgomery's own love for the beauty of the country and of her sympathetic understanding of animals.

Hilary, better known as orphan Jingle, and his homely dog McGinty, share in Pat's great adventures and they have some stirring times together. As years roll by, Pat experiences the pleasures and disappointments of young girlhood and in time her soul awakens to the call of her first love.

Miss Montgomery has already captured the hearts of Canada's youth. Her previous books, among which are *Anne of Green Gables*, *Emily of*

*New Moon, Blue Castle* and many others, have endeared her to girls of the "teen" age. They encourage the wholesome life of the outdoors and offer stories of youth and love and laughter which must appeal to any redblooded girl.

To parents, considering appropriate books for their children, we can only offer the suggestion "If in doubt ask for a story by L.M. Montgomery." They will admire your selection and you will appreciate the splendid ideals which cannot fail to be reflected in the lives of your own children.

## NOTES

1 *Portland Journal*, review of *Pat of Silver Bush*, 27 August 1933, in SR, 348; *The Morning Bulletin*, review of *Pat of Silver Bush*, 11; Carl Tarbox, "*Pat of Silver Bush* Finely Drawn," *Knickerbocker Press* (Albany, NY), 10 September 1933, in SR, 352; H.B., "Family Life on Prince Edward Island," *Worcester Telegram* (Worcester, MA), 17 September 1933, in SR, 350 and 353; *Publisher's Circular* (London), notice for *Pat of Silver Bush*, 26 August 1933, in SR, 350; *The Hartford Courant*, review of *Pat of Silver Bush*, D6; *Pittsburgh Post–Gazette*, review of *Pat of Silver Bush*, 10.

2 "Short Notices," unidentified and undated clipping (UK periodical), in SR, 389; *The Nashville Banner* (Nashville, TN), review of *Pat of Silver* Bush, 27 August 1933, in SR, 350.

3 A three-paragraph quotation from the novel, appearing in the original publication, is omitted here.

4 I have corrected the original, which reads "Nehemiah Gardener."

5 See *PSB*, 253.

6 I have corrected the original, which reads "Pat of the Silver Bush."

7 This phrase actually appears in *The Birds' Christmas Carol* (1887), a novel by Kate Douglas Wiggin.

8 Adeline Dutton Train Whitney (1824–1906), American author for girls.

9 I have corrected the original, which reads "L.A. Montgomery."

10 I have corrected the original, which reads "Rebecca of Sunny Brook Farm."

11 Ramsay MacDonald (1855–1937), Prime Minister of the United Kingdom at the time this review was published.

12 Properly, "a leprachaun touched her the day she was born wid a liddle green rose-thorn" (*PSB*, 2).

13 *PSB*, 196.

# 20

## Courageous Women

—— 1934 ——

### WITH MARIAN KEITH AND MABEL BURNS McKINLEY

For this volume of biographies of fifteen women from all over the world, Montgomery collaborated with Marian Keith – pseudonym of Mary Esther MacGregor (1872–1961), best known for her novel *Duncan Polite* – and Mabel Burns McKinley (1881–1974), author of the biographies *Canadian Heroines of Pioneer Days* (1929) and *Canadian Heroes of Pioneer Days* (1930); Montgomery's three chapters appear in Volume 1 of *The L.M. Montgomery Reader*. The volume appeared in a *Toronto Daily Star* ad for "Christmas Books – For the Whole Family," under the category "Little Brothers and Sisters." Although the volume did not get widely reviewed and evidently went out of print soon after its publication, critics were positive in their assessment of it: a review in the Montreal *Gazette* commented on the sketches' "easy, natural style" and suggested that the book "may be classified still further as a book particularly for Canadian girls, as fifteen of the twenty-one sketches deal with Canadian women." Moreover, a review in the Toronto *Globe* noted that "perhaps they should not be called by so cut and dried a name as 'biographies,' for the writers have been more concerned with the color, personality and drama revealed in each career than with mere matters of time and place ... The stories of these great women make enthralling reading – far more fascinating than fiction." As for Montgomery's chapter on Mary Slessor, this review added, "Into scarcely more than half a dozen pages has been crowded the drama of a lifetime, but it has been done in a vivid way."[1]

## [Vitality and Inspiration]
### *The Canadian Churchman* (Toronto, ON)

A delightful book, full of vitality and inspiration. The unique thing about this book is it combines in one volume the lives of twenty-one women, all of whom have had, or have, the highest ideals and still are human, happy, heroic and natural.

Placing the stories of living women with those of long ago makes them all live and speak. In these busy times, short biographies are appreciated, and the inspiration gained from them will make the readers wish to emulate such personalities.

## [Portraits of Immortal Women]
### *The Canadian Bookman* (Toronto, ON)

Each of these co-authors has a splendid literary reputation of her own, and now they have joined forces in making a book recording the heroism, courage, endurance, resourcefulness and cheerful spirit of women who have been more than famous, some of them even laying down their lives for their faith in their country or their cause.

The immortal women portrayed are: Joan of Arc, Florence Nightingale, Mary Slessor of Calabar, Laura Secord, Catharine Parr Traill, Queen Victoria, Madeleine de Vercheres, Helen Keller, Ada May Courtice, Caroline MacDonald, Elizabeth Louise Mair, Anna J. Gaudin, Edith Cavell, Sadie Stringer, Madam Albani, Pauline Johnson, Aletta Elise Marty, Dr. Margaret MacKeller, Margaret Polson Murray, Lady Tilley, and Marshall Saunders.

A book for girls which will surely please.

### NOTES

1 *The Toronto Daily Star*, ad for Timothy Eaton Company, 54; M.H.P., "Vivid Collaboration," 8; *The Gazette*, "For Girl Readers," 16.

# 21

## *Mistress Pat: A Novel of Silver Bush*

—— 1935 ——

Reviews of this novel showed no awareness of any strain caused by the circumstances in Montgomery's life as she wrote this follow-up to *Pat of Silver Bush*; if anything, what they liked about it was that it duplicated all the appealing aspects of her earlier work. The *Washington Post* called it the story of "another sweet and simple girlhood on Prince Edward Island," whereas the Williamsburg *Journal–Tribune* of Iowa noted that "because the author writes of health and happiness and humor, her books are unfailing refreshment and a welcome relief from fiction of problems and complexes." At the same time, some reviews were more ambiguous in their praise: as an unidentified clipping noted, "As might be expected from a writer of such experience and technical competence, [this author] gives us a modern story focussed against a background sketched with calm assurance on the most orthodox lines, so that as we read we are charmed; and in a welter of charmless books the reader should be grateful." As this review continued, "The writing is virile and colorful, with a real sense of actuality and of the dramatic. The dialogue, whether in dialect or not, is simply and warmly written, often trivial, gossipy and, in the manner of hero-worship, uncritical. From such qualities as these – the commonplace rhythm and unimaginative words of everyday conversation in the Canadian middle-class home, used with an admirable sense of balance, – it derives much of its strength. *Mistress Pat* surely is on its way to become a best seller." Moreover, as the *New York Herald Tribune Books* suggested, "*Mistress Pat* is a tranquil and heart-warming narrative, and its charm is that it pretends to be nothing more." The ending of the book was likewise read ambiguously, such as Reverend John

McNab's comment, that "Mistress Pat is successfully married in this story and one wonders if Pat must now follow the way of Anne and disappear."[1]

## Pat, Charming Elf of Silver Bush, Becomes Despair of Matchmakers
### *The Globe* (Toronto, ON)

### But as "Mistress Pat" She Is More Lovable Than Ever

Mrs. Montgomery in *Mistress Pat* provides us with another of her enjoyable and now justly famous Nova Scotian stories. Readers of her popular "Anne" stories will feel that they are in old-time atmosphere and treading familiar ground when they have started to absorb the opening chapters of this light yet thoroughly charming novel concerning events at the mythical Silver Bush Farm.

*Mistress Pat* must be conceded as a sequel of *Pat of Silver Bush*; and the characters who came to life in the earlier book appear once more on these pages; somewhat riper of experience and bearing the marks of the years, but quite like old friends returning to greet the reader, but bringing with them new people of the author's creation.

As for Pat, she is a thoroughly loveable and lively young woman; but, after suitor after suitor fails to attract her and is turned down, her family and all her aunts and uncles become obsessed by a fear that she loves her home, Silver Bush, so dearly that she will live out her days a maiden lady rather than part with its magic atmosphere.

Pat, however, delightfully deceives them all and finally makes her choice as between two fine young swains – and in her own mind knows definitely she has made the right choice of a life's partner.

Admirers of this author's former novels in no wise will be disappointed in this, her latest effort.

## [A Good Book]
### *Quill and Quire* (Toronto, ON)

The latest novel by this popular Canadian author will doubtless be gobbled up by the vast host of her admirers who have enjoyed her type of light, fanciful and wholesome writing. If you get a request for "something for a girl between the ages of 14 and 17," fill it by presenting *Mistress*

*Pat*. For this purpose the book is ideal. There are plenty of people, in addition, who don't want to think of anything but the sweet simplicity of Prince Edward Island farm life and who are themselves a bit like the central figure in the story, Mistress Pat. They will enjoy the book.

The story concerns the everyday doings of Mistress Pat at Silver Bush farm, a girl who is completely and entirely wrapped up in the beauty of the place and the folk that surround her. She hates change. For a person who resents winter coming because it kills the flowers, and refuses to face the fact that her sister "Cuddles" is growing up, the author scourges her sensibilities unmercifully. After 200 pages of nothing more than grief over the passing of a tree, imagine the shock when in the last 100 pages she is faced with change on every side. Her brother marries May Binnie, a hated neighbour. The favoured hired man, Josiah Tillytuck departs. Her sister marries and goes off to China. The lovable old cook, Judy Plum dies. Finally, her beloved Silver Bush farm burns. The happy ending is provided by the return of Pat's childhood friend to carry her off to a new and beautiful place that has Silver Bush for its only rival.

The story itself is nothing unusual, charmingly written, devoid of plot, full of good description and lovable characters. It holds interest mainly through the banting of the two characters, Judy Plum and Tillytuck who provide merriment and good clean fun. For example Tillytuck: "I have my ups and downs. Escaped from the Titanic for one thing ... Yes, I escaped, by not sailing on her." And Judy Plum: "I did be thinking my stars we had the turkey but oh, oh, what happened whin yer dad cut a slice off the brist, maning to give all white mate to the lady visitor! ... yer Aunt Hazel had niver taken out the turkey's crop and whin yer dad carved off that slice kernels av whate and a bunch av oats fell down all over the plate."[2] It is a good book.

## [Handicapped by Previous Creations]
### *Saturday Night* (Toronto, ON)
#### T.G. MARQUIS

*Mistress Pat* is a novel of Prince Edward Island, purely local. Silver Bush farm, the home of the heroine, is picturesquely set forth in the opening chapters and throughout the story it plays a predominating part. It is the background for the entire action. The author is handicapped by her previous creations. She set a high standard in *Anne of Green Gables* and readers look for something of the charm of that masterpiece. There is little of that charm in *Mistress Pat*. Cuddles, Pat's young sister, has some of it, but it vanishes as the story proceeds. The book has one serious fault. The author means Mistress Pat to hold the centre of the stage, but her place is usurped by her Irish housekeeper, Judy Plum, and Josiah Tillytuck, the man of all work. These two are continually present and never cease matching stories. A little of that sort of thing goes a long way, but after pages of exaggerated tales and strained witticism the reader is apt to grow weary.

*Anne of Green Gables* was to Mark Twain: "The sweetest creation of child life yet written"; and Bliss Carman said of her: "Anne must always remain one of the immortal children of fiction."[3] High and deserved tributes that could not be called forth by any of the characters in *Mistress Pat*. However, the story is not without romantic interest, and the Island scenery is charmingly and sympathetically described and the love scenes are handled with tact and becoming Victorian modesty.


# [A Trifle Overdressed]
## *The Guardian* (Charlottetown, PE)

L.M. Montgomery's new book *Mistress Pat* continues the story of Silver Bush, the snug old-fashioned home which was to Pat more of a religion than a house. But one need not necessarily have read *Pat of Silver Bush* to understand and enjoy *Mistress Pat*. It is complete in itself and like all of L.M. Montgomery's books is characterized by wholesomeness, humour, original episodes and glowing descriptions of typical Island backgrounds.

Pat is a rather unusual type of modern girl, one who realizes and eagerly grasps the happiness that comes with each single day. She almost fears the future, for it may be accompanied with dreaded change and she wants to keep Silver Bush intact and perfect as it is. She is however forced by circumstances to look forward to a future in entirely different surroundings – one which to her surprise she is finally able to contemplate with joy and eagerness.

The style of this book is at times a trifle overdressed with similes for comfortable reading, and the repeated use of P.E. Island for Prince Edward Island becomes annoying, but these are only minor defects in a book which is filled with very human characters, and very fine cats, and is as suitable for girls of all ages as the well loved "Anne" books.

## Charming P.E.I. Story
### *The Toronto Daily Star* (Toronto, ON)

L.M. Montgomery, author of *Anne of Green Gables*, has given to the reading public another charming and delightful romance, *Mistress Pat*, published by McClelland and Stewart, a story of a Prince Edward Island family through all the transition stages, with "Pat," the leading character, with enough personality, beauty and grace to bring many admirers, but eventually finding her real love in the friend of her childhood. Judy, the beloved and faithful old Irish servant, is a character one likes to meet in fiction.

## [Readable and Entertaining Up to a Point]
### *University of Toronto Quarterly*
#### E.K. BROADUS

Miss L.M. Montgomery has written another book – *Mistress Pat*. The dust-cover calls it "bright, readable, wholesome and entertaining." The adjectives are chosen with rather more discrimination than is usually characteristic of dust-covers. Bright and wholesome it certainly is. Readable and entertaining it is, up to a point, but not enough to sustain the present reader through all its 338 pages. But for those who enjoy Miss Montgomery (of whom, I am sure, there must be very many), I quote the concluding sentence of the novel as a delectable bait: "The old graveyard heard the most charming sound in the world ... the low yielding laugh of a girl held prisoner by her lover."[4]

### NOTES

1  *The Washington Post*, review of *Mistress Pat*, B10; *Journal–Tribune*, review of *Mistress Pat*, 3; G.K., review of *Mistress Pat*, unidentified and undated clipping, in SR, 437; *The New York Herald Tribune Books*, review of *Mistress Pat*, 15; John McNab, review of *Mistress Pat*, unidentified and undated clipping, in SR, 471.
2  *MP*, 23, 33.
3  This quotation from Bliss Carman is from a letter that is reproduced in full in Volume 1 of *The L.M. Montgomery Reader*.
4  *MP*, 277.

# 22

## *Anne of Windy Poplars / Anne of Windy Willows*

— 1936 —

Although Montgomery had doubts about the literary quality of this novel and about her success in recapturing the appeal of the earlier Anne books, coverage of Anne Shirley's unexpected return to fiction, particularly so soon after the hit 1934 film, was highly positive. "At last a new story of Anne Shirley, beloved heroine of that modern classic, *Anne of Green Gables*!" announced an ad in the *Globe and Mail*. "A charming romance to delight Miss Montgomery's great audience of readers, young and old." According to the *Lewiston Daily Sun* of Maine, "The passing of time in no way dims the luster of the 'Anne' books' shining popularity. Their refreshing wholesomeness, vivid description and splendid characterization have so long held fickle public favor that newer authors desirous of basking in the sun of success might take a tip from L.M. Montgomery, dipping their pens in 'health and happiness' which combined with a touch of humor and an alluring bit of romance makes an unbeatable combination." The *ALA Booklist* included it in the category "Light Romances," whereas a review in the *Hartford Courant* of Connecticut noted that Montgomery "is an adept at the sort of thing in which innumerable readers revel – a carefully balanced mixture of gentle sentimentality, 'folksiness,' and simple, obvious rural humor." Over in the UK, where it appeared under the title *Anne of Windy Willows*, the book also received favourable treatment, including in the prestigious magazine *The Saturday Review*, which called it "a light but fascinating tale which shows considerable power of characterisation." An unidentified and undated clipping also noted that *Anne of Windy Willows* had been declared the "August Romantic Book of the Month" by the *Daily Mirror*:

It has been selected from hundreds of new books as a novel which will be enjoyed by all men and women who like fiction packed with incident, drama and romance.

You Will Like This Book Because—

It is shot through with the simple humour of country folk who can't see they're being funny.

It is really not one but half a dozen stories of characters who are more universal than Canadian.

Its sunshine and shadow are as natural as the deftly-described lights and shades of its picturesque setting.[1]


## [Tribulations and Triumphs]
### *The New York Herald Tribune Books* (New York, NY)
LISLE BELL

The author of *Anne of Green Gables* dedicates this current contribution in a sequence of sequels "to the friends of Anne everywhere" – and no doubt they will return the compliment by pouncing upon the book with willing hands and welcoming eyes. It sets forth the tribulations and triumphs of Anne Shirley as a school teacher, living with a pair of precious widows in a Prince Edward Island village. There she gradually breaks down the antagonism of crotchety school officials, corrals a negligent father for a lonely little girl, shatters resistance right and loggerheads left with the belaying-pin of sentiment and the sabre of sweetness. Our favorite character in the assemblage is Rebecca Dew, an old retainer worth retaining.


## Anne-est Anne
### *The Gazette* (Montreal, QC)

Now Miss Shirley of Green Gables is a B.A., and the Principal of Summerside High School, but she has by no means gone prim and schoolmarmish on her thousands of admirers. She lives in a romantic old tower room in a house called Windy Poplars, in a street known as Spook's Lane, and she is the "very Anne-est Anne."[2] A large part of the latest Anne story is in the form of letters to Gilbert Blythe, the medical student, while she puts in a couple of years before they are married. She has her downs, but her good sense and her charm sustain her, and Gilbert is waiting. The

Anne-fans will like *Windy Poplars*. It is full of Mrs. Montgomery's familiar happy romance, and the people are human – some of them, of course, and especially Rebecca Dew, quaint. Some of them are old friends, because this book is a cut-back to a period of Anne's life that was skipped.

## An Old Favourite Again
### *The Sydney Morning Herald* (Sydney, Australia)

Miss L.M. Montgomery has dedicated her new book, *Anne of Windy Willows*, to "The Friends of Anne Everywhere," and we feel sure it will find a wide circle of readers. Anne is now quite grown up outwardly, but still retains much of her childish exuberance of spirit and love of fun. She has been appointed headmistress of the Summerside High School, and we follow her through her three years of trials and disappointments, friendships, and enmities, joys and sorrows. The chronicle is carried forward by means of letters to her fiance interspersed with sections of narrative and dialogue. The book is full of the small incidents which make up the daily life of a village community.

Miss Montgomery has a definite flair for this type of novel, and her character studies are full of life and colour. Lovers of Anne and many others will enjoy this simple tale. It is entirely free from modern pseudo-sophistication and affectation, and a number of readers will find it a welcome oasis in the arid desert of present-day realism.

## Real Canadian Humor
### *The Toronto Daily Star* (Toronto, ON)

L.M. Montgomery's Latest Adds to Brilliant Reputation

Whether calceolasia is a flower or a disease is one of the hundreds of numerous dialogue sallies in *Anne of Windy Poplars*, by L.M. Montgomery, from McClelland and Stewart. This new novel of the Prince Edward Island school teacher and the funny old maids is one more best-seller example of native Canadian humor. Rebecca Dew, one of the numerous droll characters, says, "My poor dead sister never et a thing three days afore she was married, and after her husband died we was all afraid she was never going to eat again."[3] There must be several hundred such feminine dry-humor speeches in this entertaining novel of quaint, scin-tillating characters – among whom Anne of the Poplars shines out as unmistakably as the one of Green Gables did many years ago. This kind of character-humor is a perennial, and this prankish, whimsical novel is one of its rarest examples.

## [Humorous and Sentimental Adventures]
### *Winnipeg Free Press* (Winnipeg, MB)

Looking for a home in the Prince Edward Island village where she is to assume the important role of school teacher for the two years pending her marriage to Gilbert Blythe, Anne finds rooms with the widows "Miss" Chatty and Mrs. Kate, with their servant Rebecca. From the tower room in their old house, Windy Poplars, Anne looks out upon the life in the village of Summerside, and is soon in the middle of all sorts of humorous and sentimental adventures. But through them all she remains true to Gilbert. One of the best of the "grown-up" Anne books.

## [A Splendid Story]
### *Women's Magazine* (UK)

Then comes another firm favourite in the shape of one more "Anne" book by L.M. Montgomery. This latest adventure of the happy-spirited Anne of Green Gables is entitled *Anne of Windy Willows*, and has been assessed as *the* "romantic book of the month" by the *Daily Mirror*. It certainly is a delightful story, written in this author's inimitable style, and tells of Anne's struggles and exploits – some rather dismaying, others so gay – as the Principal of Summerside High School. Even as a revered Principal and the proud possessor of a well-earned B.A. degree, Anne is the same delightful and impulsive creature whose thirst for knowledge at Green Gables aggravated or interested others – according to their indi-vidual temperaments! A splendid story for your first cheerful evening-by-the-fire this autumn.

## [More Good Deeds Than a Boy Scout]
### *University of Toronto Quarterly*
#### J.R. MacGILLIVRAY

I have space to mention only a few of the books for children and adolescents. Girls will, no doubt, be delighted with L.M. Montgomery's new book, *Anne of Windy Poplars*. Anne retires chronologically from her marital House of Dreams to maidenhood, to become a high-school principal and a fine influence down on The Island. She does more good deeds than a Boy Scout, and spends her spare time writing whimsies to Gilbert Blythe about pixies, dryads, and the land of to-morrow. "And it will be moonlight in Lover's Lane and on the Lake of Shining Waters and the old Haunted Wood and Violet Vale. There should be fairy dances on the hills tonight."[4] With such an imagination Anne should be a great Canadian poetess.

## More about "Anne"
### *The Family Herald and Weekly Star* (Montreal, QC)
#### RODERICK KENNEDY

*Anne of Windy Poplars* is the latest of the famous series of books by L.M. Montgomery, which started with *Anne of Green Gables*, when I was at college. I loved that book, and while this, like most later books in a long series, is not the equal of the first, it will still be pleasant reading to all who like Anne, – and that means every reader of L.M. Montgomery, for whatever else happens in the Anne books, you can be sure that every reader, as well as every character in the books, whether friend or enemy at first, ends in the last chapter by loving Anne.

This book records an earlier period in Anne's life than some that have appeared previously, going back to pre-war days when she was still engaged to Gilbert Blythe. She is head mistress of Summerside High School, and "Windy Poplars" is the house where she boards. The story deals with the veiled antagonism of the most powerful family in the city against Anne, and her conquest of their goodwill by her natural sweetness of spirit. Some of the minor characters in the book are charmingly drawn, and it manages to keep the reader's interest in spite of the fact that it is largely presented in the form of Anne's letters to her fiance. That method does not seem well chosen for such a book as this, for the theme is Anne's lovableness, and her own testimony to that effect, indirect though it is, is not quite as convincing as that of an unbiased witness.

## NOTES

1 *The Globe and Mail*, "A New Anne Book," 21; R.W.L., review of *Anne of Windy Poplars*, 4; *ALA Booklist*, notice for *Anne of Windy Poplars*, 54; *The Hartford Daily Courant*, review of *Anne of Windy Poplars*, D6; *The Saturday Review*, "Revaluation of Samuel Butler," 341; "August Romantic Book of the Month," unidentified and undated clipping, in SR, 469.
2 *AWP*, 77.
3 *AWP*, 169. I have corrected the original, which reads "Rebecca Daw."
4 *AWP*, 215.

# 23

## *Jane of Lantern Hill*

—— 1937 ——

This late novel received fewer reviews than even *Anne of Ingleside* would, but the reviews it did receive were enthusiastic. The *Springfield Sunday Union and Republican* of Massachusetts called Jane "as versatile and fascinating a heroine as her predecessors" and echoed a statement made by this newspaper fifteen years earlier, about *Emily of New Moon*: "This book may rate as a juvenile, but older people will perhaps appreciate its sentiment more than their juniors." Indeed, although the *Athens Banner–Herald* of Georgia, commenting on the novel's break from fantasy and fancy so common in children's books, called it "realistic with a vengeance" and "as modern as the last edition of a metropolitan paper," an ad in the *Globe and Mail* pronounced it "The Perfect Gift Book for women and girls of all ages." The *Auckland Star* of New Zealand declared that "as in Miss Montgomery's other novels, there is a freshness, a naturalness and a charm about this that, with its humour, makes it delightful to read." And as the *Dudley Herald* noted in the United Kingdom, "it reveals a remarkable understanding of human emotions, joys and sorrows."[1]

### [A Generous Helping of Sentiment]
### *The New York Herald Tribune Books* (New York, NY)
#### LISLE BELL

The author of *Anne of Green Gables* deals with a very popular commodity in fiction – sentiment. There is a generous helping of it in *Jane of Lantern Hill*, and it is adroitly served. L.M. Montgomery knows how to touch the heart strings, she understands the capacity of a sensitive child to be hurt, the tragedy of youthful loneliness. These things she has put into the present story – about a girl whose parents are separated and whose natural buoyancy of spirit is crushed by a domineering, unsympathetic grandmother. The plot is simple. Jane escapes from the tyranny and is instrumental in bringing her father and mother together. Many people like L.M. Montgomery's stories, and they will like this one particularly.

## [The Hard Facts of Reality]
### *The Family Herald and Weekly Star* (Montreal, QC)
RODERICK KENNEDY

In *Jane of Lantern Hill* Lucy M. Montgomery adds a new character to her list of heroines, and one who is distinctly different from all previous ones. While the book opens in a gloomy old house in Toronto where Jane and her pretty young mother live with the dominating old Mrs. Kennedy, Jane's grandmother, it switches after seventy pages to the soft red earth of the author's beloved Prince Edward Island, and thenceforth shuttles between Toronto and "the Island" with more and more space being devoted to the latter. For on the Island lives that mysterious "dad" about whom there had hung a veil of mystery which was never lifted in the gloomy Toronto house, – the "dad" who could not be mentioned there without a storm from the fierce old grandmother. It is the existence of that mystery, the nature of it, and the author's almost realistic attitude towards it, that makes *Jane of Lantern Hill* better and more interesting than any Montgomery book of recent years.

Jane is as loveable as any Montgomery heroine but she is not impossibly so. Her love is powerful in its effects, but not miraculously so. It brings together her long estranged father and mother, but it never conquers her grandmother, and there are minor unpleasant characters in the book whom it never transforms, and who remain unpleasant to the end, just as they do in real life. It is this reasonable, if slight, intermixture of the hard facts of reality which gives this book a value to readers who want romance, who want sweetness and light, who want honest sentiment and a happy ending, but do not want them laid on too thick. There are some nice portraits in this book, – more than usual, although L.M. Montgomery has always had a knack of presenting lifelike if superficial people to her readers. But here she gives several not-so-sweet portraits which lend added value to the rest by contrast, and which show effectively the result of good intentions when motivated by selfishness or foolish ignorance. I congratulate Mrs. Macdonald (which is the real life name of "Lucy M. Montgomery") on this book.[2] She has been writing romances for twenty-five years or more, and yet this latest book shows a definite advance.

## Fine Woman's Story Has Toronto Setting
### *The Toronto Daily Star* (Toronto, ON)

*Jane of Lantern Hill* Is Alluringly Simple Character Novel

Which is Gay St. in Toronto?

The only way to find out is to ask L.M. Montgomery whose recent novel, *Jane of Lantern Hill*, from McClelland and Stewart, opens with it ... "the most melancholy street in Toronto," thought Jane who lived at 60 Gay in "a huge, castellated structure ... with a pillared entrance porch, high, arched Georgian windows, and towers and turrets."[3] Find that house – one of many – and you will be on Gay St.

The story of the folk who lived there is in this author's happiest transparent style. She has the knack of making the reader instantly at home with the characters and the places – all so affectionately described, in such vivid, simple atmosphere, with such apt descriptions and animated natural dialogue. Jane's escape from the repressive grandeur of 60 Gay St. and her adventures on the Island are the focus of the story; but the old grandmother is quite as fascinating as Jane.

We have had several grandmas in literature and on the screen since *Jalna* was born;[4] seldom a grandma in either screen or story so curiously attractive as this old lady who failed to understand Jane.

## Canadian Girl
### *Saturday Night* (Toronto, ON)

Mrs. Ewan Macdonald (L.M. Montgomery) has created another delightful little heroine. The greater part of the story belongs to Prince Edward Island and is as winsome as can be, healthy, happy and wise, with red sands, sparkling seas, delectable food, an interesting plot and lovable people. The opening in Toronto, one regrets to say is a trifle depressing as a portrait of one's native town. But the end makes up for that; the native town is shown as an agreeable place in which to live. *Jane of Lantern Hill* is to be counted as a certain favorite for girls the world over.

## [Delightful Jane]
### *The New Outlook* (Toronto, ON)

The charm of the earlier Anne books is again evident in this latest story of "The Island." Jane is delightful, a bit suppressed when in Ontario under her grandmother's domination, but eager and bubbling over with mirth when home at Lantern Hill. No one can portray more perfectly than L.M. Montgomery the quaint humor and sound common sense of the Island folk. Girls just entered into their teens will greatly enjoy sharing the adventures of Jane and Jody, and the whole boisterous Lantern Hill tribe.

## That Ecstasy of Youth!
### *The Montreal Daily Star* (Montreal, QC)

Mrs. Montgomery is still almost inarticulate about some parts of The Island (P.E.I. to the uninitiated), but describing the view from one of the windows in a house Jane's father was going to buy, she says: "Across the channel a white lighthouse stood up against the sky and on the other side of the harbour were the shadowy crests of purple hills that dreamed with their arms around each other. And over it all the indefinable charm of a Prince Edward Island landscape."[7] As a general rule fiction must tend from its very nature to emphasise in life the exceptional and abnormal. Mrs. Montgomery, however, continues to write of the pleasanter things – Jane and the humorous-sentimental oldster who was her father but whom she hadn't seen for years and years – what marvellous fun to go house-hunting, what a thrill when they found what suited them both, a cottage on a hill with a view of the Gulf – a cottage with "tons of magic in it," and Jane, who never had done an ounce of work in a kitchen, barging in to get ready their first meal at their own table!

## [An Entirely New Character]
### *The Canadian Bookman* (Toronto, ON)

L.M. Montgomery [* * *] is in her element in *Jane of Lantern Hill*, but it is by no means a repetition of Anne or Emily. Jane is an entirely new character and you will surely enjoy making her acquaintance. The story is told with all the verve of this Canadian author's other tales and with a piquancy of humor that flavors it to a turn.

## [Repeated Success]
### *The Church of England Newspaper* (London, UK)

L.M. Montgomery is one of the few writers who can repeat their successes; moreover, she can write about the same places and the same type of people with ever-varying freshness. *Anne of Green Gables* made Prince Edward Island a delightful reality to many people in this country, and this book and successors immortalised the best type of Canadian girlhood. Mrs. Montgomery's newest book, *Jane of Lantern Hill*, opens in Toronto, where the unhappy little heroine lives in a formidable house with a formidable grandmother and a lovely mother, who, alas, can never "stand up to" people. Then the scene shifts to the magic of the beloved Island, and, with Jane's introduction to another world of friendly people and real home, comes her emancipation from the blighting effect of "60 Gay." *Jane of Lantern Hill* is as charming a book as this authoress has ever given us, and that is saying a great deal.

### NOTES

1 *The Springfield Sunday Union and Republican*, "On Lantern Hill," 7E; *Athens Banner–Herald* (Athens, GA), review of *Jane of Lantern Hill*, 15 August 1937, in SR, loose pages; *The Globe and Mail*, "The Perfect Gift Book," 27; *The Auckland Star*, review of *Jane of Lantern Hill*, 12; *Dudley Herald* (Dudley, UK), "An Unwanted Child," review of *Jane of Lantern Hill*, 3 November 1937, in SR, loose pages.
2 I have corrected the original, which reads "Mrs. MacDonald."
3 *JLH*, 1.
4 See "*A Tangled Web / Aunt Becky Began It*," note 6, above.
5 *JLH*, 75.

# 24

## *Anne of Ingleside*

—— 1939 ——

While more recent scholars have paid closer attention to the more distressing aspects of this final novel – namely, the cracks appearing in the foundation of Anne and Gilbert's marriage and an episode involving the funeral of an abusive man in the community – reviewers in 1939 kept their focus on the depiction of idealized family life. "Hours of delightful reading lie between the covers of this book," declared Bill East in the *Winston–Salem Sentinel* of North Carolina. "Humor and pathos march side by side and Anne Blythe, through all the joyous adventures and the small misadventures, remains the same endearing, glamorous Anne Shirley thousands of readers knew at Green Gables." An ad in the *Globe and Mail* referred to Anne as the "young apostle of gaiety and cheer [who] is now a charming matron with her own small children growing up around her." In terms of target audience, the *Lethbridge Daily Herald* declared that "all lovers of the Anne books will enjoy this story ... but it will be especially appealing to young girls," whereas the *Salt Lake Tribune* called it "a book for the grown-ups who as children loved the earlier Anne books," adding, "Old admirers of Anne will close this book still ready to read more about her." Jane Spence Southron, writing in the *New York Times Book Review*, declared the novel to be "a village gossip book and an album of queer village personalities" in the tradition of Austen and Gaskell, while for the *San Diego Union*, Anne was not solely an appealing character but "an antidote for this dizzy age."[1] The reviews collected here are quite positive for the most part, and while there are a few barbs about the excessive sentiment that reviewers perceived in the book, overall the perception is that the adult Anne is just as appealing as the child who appeared in *Anne of Green Gables*.

## [Anne and Her Offspring]
### *The New York Herald Tribune Books* (New York, NY)
LISLE BELL

If *Anne of Green Gables* is still green in your memory, the chances are that you have kept it fresh during the years by spraying it with L.M. Montgomery's sequels. You know about her marriage to a doctor, and her first years of married life. You are now ready for *Anne of Ingleside*, with the heroine surrounded by children, an adoring husband, admiring neighbors and a maid-of-all-work named Susan, who addresses her mistress invariably as "Mrs. Dr. dear." Anne's offspring are, by and large, as filled with noble thoughts and kindly impulses as one would expect and no doubt they will grow up and marry and propagate a third generation with identical virtues.

## [Same Old Charm]
### *The Times Literary Supplement* (London, UK)

Mrs. L.M. Montgomery's readers will welcome the further adventures of Anne Shirley, married now and mother of a growing family. *Anne of Ingleside* retains all her old charm, and this new book is written in the characteristic vein that has made these stories so popular.

## [Always an Event]
### *The Guardian* (Charlottetown, PE)

Another "Anne" book is always an event. To Islanders and summer visitors to the Island it is something more, because there is the added pleasure of identifying local scenes which Lucy Maud Montgomery describes with unfailing freshness and interest in all her stories.

*Anne of Ingleside* is the title of the latest book from this gifted Island author's pen. The Anne Shirley we knew at Green Gables is now a mature young woman, the wife of Dr. Gilbert Blythe, with two adorable small children whose escapades enliven the pages and add a new richness to Anne's life and to the reader's experience. The tale, like those which preceded it, is filled with humour and pathos, with shrewd character sketches, delightful descriptions of birds and animals, scenes and adventures.

One of the choicest characters is old Susan, the maid-of-all-work, whose homely wisdom is replete with local idioms.

Not only throughout Canada, but in England, United States, Australia and other countries the "Anne" books have attained immense popularity, and have been the means, indirectly, of giving Prince Edward Island invaluable publicity. It will be recalled that in 1935, in recognition of her literary work Lucy Maud Montgomery had conferred upon her the decoration of Officer of the British Empire.

It is sufficient to say of *Anne of Ingleside* that it measures up to the high standard of the previous stories. The book is attractively published by McClelland & Stewart, Ltd., Toronto, and contains a frontispiece in color by Charles V. John.

## [Family Love in Its Perfection]
### *The Buxton Advertiser* (Buxton, UK)

A very delightful tale of home life, mother love, and married happiness which will make instant appeal to those of the fairer sex who can appreciate the warm sympathy of outlook towards life and its many problems, the happy disposition, the delightful imaginative fancy, and the beautiful love, which live in the heart of Mrs. Montgomery's heroine, Anne of Ingleside, beloved wife of Dr. Blythe and happy mother of a young and charming family. It is one of the most delightfully simple, sincere, and dainty tales that I have read. With its touches of humour, its revealment of human nature and youthful minds, its warm love and delicate fantasy, it touches chords which remain immobile beneath other hands.

The book has no definite plot: it is a picture of happy family life, with only one fly in the ointment in the perpetually grumbling figure of Aunt Mary Maria, who can see no good in anything or anybody. She is but a passing figure, however, and vanishes beyond our reach after her presence in the story has achieved the author's desired effect. From the time of Aunt Maria's departure to the end of the tale the plot consists of various incidents in the lives of first one and then another of Anne's children, showing, in every instance, the part which Anne herself has to play.

This is a tale for women. There is nothing outside the home atmosphere to intrigue and excite. It is a tale of happiness, a happiness which reveals family love in its perfection. A delightful tale for those who appreciate simplicity.

## Anne's Children
### *The Globe and Mail* (Toronto, ON)

Saying that she always read all the "Anne" books, an adolescent girl fastened upon *Anne of Ingleside* and consumed it avidly within twenty-four hours.[2] Examined for discovery, as the legal phrase is, the young lady said she had not read any of the "Emily" or "Pat" books – also by L.M. Montgomery – but had heard they were just as good.

In *Anne's House of Dreams* two children were born, a girl and a boy, of whom the girl died. *Anne of Ingleside* opens with four more children in existence – "a boy, twins, and another boy." A baby girl arrives in the new book, making seven: it is about "incidents that happen" to these juniors. "Anne's husband, Gilbert Blythe, is a doctor, and there are a few of his cases, not many. Anne gets pneumonia."

"Is it humorous?"

"No-o-o-o. There are funny sayings by the children. There is trouble with an old aunt, who comes for a week-end and stayed a year or half a year."

"What about the story? Is it good?"

"There isn't any story (plot), but it is a very good book. *Anne of Green Gables* might have been a little better; but I don't think so. They are all just the same."

The 'teen-age reader can't have too much of a good thing.

## [Mild Emotional Adventures]
### *Winnipeg Free Press* (Winnipeg, MB)

Mrs. Montgomery is hard to best when it comes to the production of saccharine romances about the illustrious Anne who dwelt under green gables. No doubt you will have followed her adventures from that far-off period to the present – will be well aware that Anne married a doctor after she moved from her childhood home, and that she has reared a troop of offspring that promise to propagate her own sweet virtues across their countryside. Then you will relish the mild emotional adventures in this the latest "Anne" story, with Anne in a slight mixup over the professional duties of her husband, which is not helped by the juvenile (and laughing) adventures of the twins et al. Nice.

## [Another Charming Instalment]
### *Sunday Times* (Johannesburg, South Africa)

Here we have another charming instalment of the story of Anne Shirley, heroine of the famous series which began many years ago with *Anne of Green Gables*. Anne is married by now, of course, the wife of a general practitioner, Dr. Gilbert Blythe, and she has a brood of attractive children. When the present novel opens she has been away from home for a week to attend the funeral of her husband's father. She enjoys her brief freedom from domestic worries, but is enchanted at the reception she gets from the children and their Nanny on her return to "Ingleside." The book abounds in delightful sketches of domestic life, and is full of the quaint sayings and doings of the children – particularly of little Jem.

## [A Worthy Successor]
### *Christian World* (London, UK)

*Anne of Green Gables* has won for its author the admiration of those readers who best enjoy a straightforward story about real people told in a simple manner. They will find this latest addition to the "Anne" series to be a worthy successor to those that have gone before. Anne Blythe, as the wife of a busy doctor in a small Canadian town, and the mother of a large family, is a delightful character whose humour, tact and wisdom make life at Ingleside as perfect as home life can be. The children's adventures, their joys and sorrows, are recounted with a rare sympathy and understanding, and the character of Susan Baker, friend and servant, will at once endear herself to the reader. The story follows no set form, but it holds the attention from start to finish by its concern with the simple things of life – the return of the seasons, birthdays and anniversaries, domestic ups and downs, and human friendship at its highest and best.

## [Confusing Genealogy]
### *University of Toronto Quarterly*
#### J.R. MacGILLIVRAY

L.M. Montgomery's *Anne of Ingleside* is at first rather confusing genealogically, for Anne who was a moon-struck maiden in the last book a couple of years ago is now the model mother of six children. The present work is mainly on the proper care and feeding of the young to prepare them for carrying on the trade in whimsy and a new cycle of novels.

## Canadian Idyll
### *Saturday Night* (Toronto, ON)
LAURA MASON

A heroine whose earlier chronicles have been translated into five languages, and Braille, needs no introduction to English-speaking readers. Anne of Ingleside is just Anne of Green Gables grown up. The scene is still Prince Edward Island of pre-war days, with Anne the wife of Dr. Blythe, and the mother of six little Blythes, whose reputation varies, with the speaker, from "among the most admirable children I have ever known" to "that pack of Ingleside demons."[3] Personally we think the Blythe stork showed excellent judgment.

L.M. Montgomery (Mrs. Ewan Macdonald in private life) has rare insight into the hidden recesses of childish hearts, good and bad. Poor wee Walter Blythe, stumbling six miles along a lonely country road, in terrifying darkness, to the mother whom youthful tormentors had declared dying, is a case in point.

In rearing her stirring brood, Anne had the valiant support of her retainer Susan, to whom she was always "Mrs. Dr. dear." To call Susan a maid-of-all-work would be a cloddish insult, though her activities included everything from bandaging little knees, to "manur[ing] Mrs. Aaron Ward[, who was not] blooming as she ought to";[4] and concocting meals so delicious that sorrowing feasters forgot the minor tragedies of life.

The Prince Edward Island scene has the rich flavor of Devon, which it so closely resembles:[5] lovely vistas of sea and hill and wood; leisurely ways of life; and bountiful standards of living. All this the author has gathered up, and salted with a sprinkling of those "characters" fostered by life remote from metropolitan centres: Aunt Mary Maria, after a shocked survey of Anne's beautiful little reproduction of Artemis of the Silver Bow, cleansing her mind by meditation on a grandmother who "never wore less than three petticoats, winter and summer"; Wallace Young shocking even the thriftiest by "let[ting] a firm paint ads on his cows."[6]

A jolly book heartily commended to Educational Authorities for Supplementary reading without tears.

## [As Delightful as Ever]
### *The Auckland Star* (Auckland, New Zealand)

Admirers of Miss L.M. Montgomery, who first attracted attention by her *Anne of Green Gables*, will be glad that she has returned to Anne in her latest novel, and to Prince Edward Island. In *Anne of Ingleside*, Anne is the mother of several small children with the oldest of them still in their early 'teens, and, though she has been the central figure in six of Miss Montgomery's previous novels, she is as fresh and natural and delightful as ever. It is her home, her social life as a doctor's wife, her children and her management of them, and the attractive and unattractive among her guests and visitors and neighbours that form the staple of the story. Miss Montgomery knows the Island, and the essential character of its people, whom she describes by laying bare their thoughts, feelings and foibles. She is particularly at home in telling us about the children, Mrs. Malaprops,[7] and guests who get on one's nerves, and does it with humour, and in a style all her own.

## [Mirrors in Which We See Ourselves]
### *The Calgary Herald* (Calgary, AB)

Of course this is the old familiar "Anne of Green Gables" in another setting, which means that all her old friends will be following along with her in her Ingleside experiences. And as this well-known Canadian author pictures them, they are well worth following. *Anne of Ingleside* is another of the Montgomery type of family stories that will never grow old or become stale so long as the Montgomery pen sees fit to write them. Which isn't to be wondered at, because they are the sort of family stories that grow out of actual experiences and are truly a part of almost every family life – mirrors in which, if we look closely, we see ourselves and the rest of the family folk.

### NOTES

1 Bill East, "'Green Gables' Author Puts Another Link in Novel Chain," *Winston–Salem Sentinel* (Winston–Salem, NC), 30 July 1939, in SR, loose pages; *The Globe and Mail*, ad for *Anne of Ingleside*, 9; *The Lethbridge Daily Herald*, review of *Anne of Ingleside*, 6; A.M.S., "Fiction's Most

Lovable Child," 6D; Southron, "After Green Gables," 7; M.R.M., "Anne, Antidote for Dizzy Age," 7C.

2 Although unsigned, this review appears under William Arthur Deacon's column "Saturday Book Review," with a photograph of Montgomery and the following caption: "It was from Prince Edward Island nearly thirty years ago that Mrs. MacDonald [*sic*], wife of a Presbyterian minister, and now of Toronto, sent out 'Anne of Green Gables,' that is still finding a widening circle of readers in many countries. Another addition to the popular series is noticed today." Although the inclusion of a review of *Anne of Ingleside* in the pages of the *Globe and Mail* is indicative of its perceived critical worth, it is also noteworthy that the reviewer, rather than read the book, passed it down to a teenage girl instead. For more on Deacon's treatment of Montgomery's work, see the introduction to Volume 1 of *The L.M. Montgomery Reader*.

3 *AIn*, 58, 154.

4 *AIn*, 24.

5 Devon, a country in southwest England.

6 *AIn*, 70, 157.

7 Mrs. Malaprop, a character in *The Rivals* (1775), a play by Irish playwright and poet Richard Brinsley Sheridan (1751–1816), frequently uses wrong but similarly sounding words, to comedic effect; also the origin of the term "malapropism."

# Epilogue: Posthumous Titles, 1960–2013

## BENJAMIN LEFEBVRE

L.M. Montgomery died at her home in Toronto on 24 April 1942, more than three and a half years after the publication of *Anne of Ingleside*. Although obituaries and tributes appeared in newspapers and magazines across North America – many of them reprinted in Volume 1 of *The L.M. Montgomery Reader* – far less attention was paid to a publishing event that coincided with her death: the first Canadian editions, by the Ryerson Press, of *Anne of Green Gables*, *Anne of Avonlea*, and *Anne of the Island*. As Sandra Campbell notes in her recent book *Both Hands: A Life of Lorne Pierce of the Ryerson Press* (2013), sometime in 1941 Ryerson publisher Lorne Pierce negotiated these editions with Montgomery rather than with the publisher who controlled the copyright to these texts, demonstrating that he was "willing to risk tangling with the litigious L.C. Page." Rejoicing that "at last a Canadian publisher has printed Canada's favorite book," an unsigned review of the first title in the *Winnipeg Free Press* noted that *Anne of Green Gables* "can now be rightfully acknowledged as an immortal classic for girls," one whose "story rates as many laughs and tears from the adult today as it did when she read it in her teens."[1] The Ryerson Press soon added to its list the remaining Montgomery books originally published by Page: *Chronicles of Avonlea* in September 1943; *Kilmeny of the Orchard*, *The Story Girl*, and *The Golden Road* in September 1944; and, finally, *Further Chronicles of Avonlea* in September 1953. Meanwhile, beginning around 1947, McClelland and Stewart reprinted or reissued fourteen of its Montgomery titles (omitting *The Watchman and Other*

*Poems* and *Courageous Women*) as the Cavendish Library, which the publisher referred to as "a new standard edition of the works of L.M. Montgomery," even though this new set did not include the novel for which Montgomery was primarily known.[2]

Although these two sets of Montgomery books sold sufficiently well to keep them in print in the decades to follow, neither reprints nor special new editions generated much media attention, except for Ryerson's "de luxe" edition of *Anne of Green Gables*, which received a rather unexpected review in *The Atlantic Advocate* after its publication in 1964. Noting the book's status as a novel for girls and its link to a tourism industry in PEI, the unsigned reviewer revealed having made "a discovery":

> A book for girls? Nonsense! Well, girls in their teens may well read it with enjoyment, they read all kinds of stuff, I am given to understand. But what I have found out is that this *Anne* thing is really a work of humorous fiction for the elderly. It is full of vividly real characters, it has an imaginative series of adventures for the pathetic orphan, and it has Anne's torrent of conversation. The rich humour of this chatter, shot through with glints of pathos as the finest humour so often is, puts the author on the level of Stephen Leacock. Lucy Maud Montgomery had genius.
>
> So here is my advice to the elderly (for those only middle-aged, for that matter, too). If so far you have failed to read *Anne of Green Gables*, don't let the tourist promotion divert your attention from the reality behind it. You just buy that book for your grand-daughter and try reading it first for yourself.[3]

Because most periodicals do not bother reviewing reprints or new editions of older titles, it is little surprise that Montgomery's books did not receive the media attention that they had throughout her lifetime; in fact, it is especially noteworthy that her books continued to sell so well without that notice. Yet similar attention to her work has persisted in newspapers, magazines, and academic journals in the seven decades since her death, not only in reports on stage and screen adaptations of her books, but also in reviews of posthumous volumes of her work. Between 1960 and 2013, twenty-four volumes of letters, journals, autobiography, short stories, and poems, as well as a rediscovered book-length typescript, supplemented the twenty-four volumes published in Montgomery's lifetime, and they played a significant role in the scholarly and popular reassessment of her literary reputation throughout this period.[4] In terms of their assumptions about Montgomery's primary work and their evaluations of these new books, this second generation of Montgomery reviewers would express the same surprise as did the unsigned reviewer in *The Atlantic Advocate* in 1964. Moreover, these posthumous texts would often shed new light on the primary work, which continued to be enjoyed by succeeding generations of readers.

### "A Fascinating Footnote": *The Green Gables Letters*, 1960

When the first posthumous Montgomery text, Wilfrid Eggleston's edited volume *The Green Gables Letters from L.M. Montgomery to Ephraim Weber, 1905–1909*, was published in January 1960, it was billed on both the front cover and the dust jacket as "a fascinating footnote to the history of Canadian letters." Yet its publisher – once again the Ryerson Press, which had also published Hilda M. Ridley's biography *The Story of L.M. Montgomery* in 1956 – seemed unsure of the book's sales potential, adding on the dust jacket that the volume "should prove an absorbing book, both to those adults who have nostalgic memories of 'Anne,' and to writers who need encouragement in their struggle for literary recognition." The decision to focus this slim volume on the years surrounding the writing and publication of *Anne of Green Gables* was not only practical – as Eggleston revealed in his introduction, the fifteen letters included in the volume are the only ones of Montgomery's Cavendish years that were still extant – but wise from a marketing point of view. By including "an important sequence of letters covering an influential and critical period in the rise of L.M. Montgomery as a famous author," a period that, as Eggleston noted, "converted her almost overnight from a struggling contributor to a host of magazines ... into one of the literary sensations of the era," he was able to get around the fact that while the letters capture the author during the period of her most famous novel's composition and publication, there is far less mention of the novel than the title of the volume would suggest. As was the case in her journals, Montgomery made no mention of the project in these letters until it had been accepted by L.C. Page and Company in 1907, and even then, despite stating that she was "blatantly pleased and proud and happy," she relied on a form of feminine modesty that was to become a key component of the public persona that was shown in Volume 1 of *The L.M. Montgomery Reader*: "Don't stick up your ears now, imagining that the great Canadian novel has been written at last," she warned Weber.[5] Indeed, although this book consists of the first behind-the-scenes glimpses of the writing, publication,

and reception of *Anne of Green Gables*, it is equally if not more valuable
for its revelation, for the first time, of the private Montgomery beneath
the recognizable public mask, particularly for her comments about literature, religion, gardening, periodical markets for fiction and poetry, the
politics of family and rural community, and even the weather.

Reviewers of Eggleston's book in a range of Canadian periodicals took
notice of it as an early example of the kind of attention to letters and
journals that had hitherto not been a major part of Canadian literary
studies, particularly compared to the vast array of such materials pertaining to authors in the United States and the United Kingdom. In the *Globe
and Mail*, noting that "the field of Belles Lettres has been neglected in
Canada," Dorothy Dumbrille celebrated *The Green Gables Letters* as
"one of the most important literary contributions of the year." Arthur S.
Bourinot, who had edited volumes of the letters of Archibald Lampman
and Duncan Campbell Scott as well as the magazine *The Canadian
Author and Bookman*, stated in the *Lethbridge Herald* that "this is the
type of work for which this reviewer for many years has been campaign-
ing for, praying for, hoping for and waiting for: namely, the letters of a
well known Canadian writer." As if emphasizing the need for life writing
to provide a new context for Canadian literary studies, Bourinot added
rather ominously, "May other writers follow suit before it is too late."
Meanwhile, for S. Ross Beharriell, writing in *The Canadian Forum*, one
of the appeals of this volume "of an unsatisfyingly few Montgomery letters" was that it "point[s] up the fact that there is still a great store of
Canadian literary material waiting to be called upon; there is still much
to be done."[6]

Reviewers were equally impressed with the new voice of the private
Montgomery, although some of them seemed to have difficulty reconcil-
ing what they perceived to be the volume's strengths with the pattern of
male dismissal of Montgomery's novels that was only too common during this period. For Reginald Watters, writing in one of the first issues
of the University of British Columbia journal *Canadian Literature*, the
letters "reveal the friendly and cheerful spirit of a hard-working woman
who faced success with the same tempered good humour as she had earlier faced many a frustration." One of the "virtues" of this volume, for
Beharriell, was that "it suggests that L.M. Montgomery had resources of
understanding and imagination that her journalistic type of writing never
really called upon." He also noted that "the author of *Anne of Green
Gables* must be afforded a permanent, if somewhat minor, niche in the
Canadian hall of literary fame; in spite of today's distaste for sentiment,

pathos, and slick journalism, her first novel must be recognized as a minor classic in the realm of juvenile fiction. These compliments may seem overly qualified; but to say less would be unjust; and to say more would be condescending or chauvinistic." Desmond Pacey, whose comments on Montgomery's work were discussed in the introduction to Volume 2 of *The L.M. Montgomery Reader*, vacillated between disparagement and praise in *The Dalhousie Review*, calling the volume "no literary masterpiece but ... a very moving human document," one that "deserves a place in every Canadian library" even though the letters were "certainly not the product of a great intelligence nor of a learned mind." For him, the "great interest" in the volume was the revelation of Montgomery as a struggling author who expressed unorthodox religious beliefs and who, in experiencing fame for the first time, "did not lose her humility." John M. Robson, reviewing the book in the annual "Letters in Canada" section of *University of Toronto Quarterly*, resisted this kind of denigration of Montgomery and her work but was nevertheless tepid in his assessment of the volume: as he noted, "The main topics – religious doubts, flowers and horses, literary dreams and successes – are never laboured, never dull, and always informative." Unlike D. Kermode Parr, who referred to the volume in *The Atlantic Advocate* as a "charming little book," Robson found that the publication of the volume was not "monumental in any but an archival sense."[7]

Yet it is important to stress that these forms of ambivalence were not shared by all reviewers of *The Green Gables Letters* in the early 1960s: while Beharriell characterized the letters with the ambiguous phrase "charming enough," Bourinot's praise for the volume, which he referred to as "autobiography in its most revealing form," was unqualified: "These letters make fascinating reading ... They were written by a woman with a fine and inquiring mind, broad interests in people, events, literature and books, to a man who aspired to be a writer and who was interested in everything from books to bronchos." As Bourinot declared in the conclusion to his review, "We recommend the book without reservation. It is a landmark in our literary history."[8] Still, in spite of the overall enthusiasm for the first posthumous Montgomery volume, it would remain for a long time an isolated title rather than the beginning of a systematic culling of her life writing. Montgomery's correspondence to George Boyd MacMillan and her journals would not be discovered until the 1970s or published until the 1980s, and even Montgomery's remaining letters to Weber, already housed at the National Archives (now Library and Archives Canada) by 1960, would not be published until nearly a half-century later. Moreover, when the first volumes of Montgomery's periodical pieces began to appear in the 1970s, the response from reviewers was altogether different.

### "Scraps from the Barrel": Periodical Pieces, 1974–1979

As I mentioned in the introduction to Volume 2 of *The L.M. Montgomery Reader*, the next two posthumous Montgomery titles, although released in 1974, were not part of an organized commemoration of the centenary of Montgomery's birth. The Ryerson Press had merged with the McGraw–Hill Book Company in 1971, and in May 1974, under its new name of McGraw–Hill Ryerson, it published *The Road to Yesterday*, a "recently discovered collection of fourteen stories." "Anne … is married and has grown-up children of her own," declares the dust jacket. "But she still recalls the strange and funny tales and bits of gossip she heard as a child." Although the unsigned "Publisher's Foreword" to the volume declares that the text "becomes an enlargement, a filling-out of the *Anne* stories and the backgrounds for all of Lucy Maud Montgomery's other books," its attempts to place this new text within that larger body of work come across as rather awkward: "internal evidence and interpretation of the author's persona, Mrs. Blythe, … seem[] to place this work into the immediate pre–World War II period." Moreover, "we meet once again the characters from the village and surrounding area who were once neighbors of the Blythes at 'Avonlea' … Many of the author's sympathies and preoccupations are drawn from her own experiences. Various tales and bits of gossip from her youth are resurrected." Noting that Montgomery's own title for the book was "The Blythes Are Quoted," the foreword adds that "the original manuscript was divided into two parts, each part composed of a narrative introduction describing an evening in the Blythe household when the family would sit around the fireside and listen to poems and stories. For the purposes of this book, … all but one of the poems have been deleted, and the sequence of the stories has been reorganized."9

Although the respect for Montgomery's legacy is clear, evoking Anne's and Montgomery's childhoods interchangeably as a source for this material seems to simplify and camouflage the particular circumstances under which this manuscript was first written by Montgomery and then re-edited for publication more than three decades after her death. Given that McGraw–Hill Ryerson's existing Montgomery library ended with *Anne of the Island* and *Further Chronicles of Avonlea*, and given that the existing texts featuring Anne as a married woman were in print with a competing publisher, the attempt to link this project to the texts of Avonlea is perhaps understandable. Moreover, this explanation of the differences between "The Blythes Are Quoted" and *The Road to Yesterday* would be taken at face value and repeated in a number of future sources describing Montgomery's final book, as would be the suggestion that her son, Stuart Macdonald, who found the typescript entitled "The Blythes Are Quoted" in his mother's papers, edited the manuscript himself.[10] A set of files pertaining to this project housed at the University of Guelph archives clarifies some of these misconceptions. These papers indicate that Stuart Macdonald did in fact approach McClelland and Stewart with this manuscript first, but while the project was undeniably his initiative, the manuscript was certainly condensed by an unidentified in-house editor at McGraw–Hill Ryerson. Macdonald's lack of involvement with the project is perhaps best indicated by the fact that his name appears twice as "MacDonald" in the publisher's foreword, and that in Montgomery's biographical note, her birth date is listed as 20 November rather than 30 November 1874.

The archival files at Guelph include a photocopy of Montgomery's typescript with a series of cuts and emendations in red ink – not all extracts missing in *The Road to Yesterday* are so marked, indicating that another round of cuts was made later – for a project that was first entitled "Fifteen Stories," then "A Commonplace Woman and Other Stories," before the final title was settled on. Yet the paratextual material downplayed the scope of the transformation from typescript to printed book: in contrast to the "narrative introduction" in each of its two parts mentioned in the foreword, the actual typescript upon which the volume was based included over thirty poems and accompanying dialogue; moreover, a line-by-line comparison between the typescript and the published text reveals that the stories themselves were condensed, some of them by as much as 10 per cent. Correspondence between Toivo Kiil, editor-in-chief at McGraw–Hill Ryerson's General Books Division, and Stuart Macdonald indicates that the first run of five thousand copies sold out within a few months of publication and that an additional five thousand copies had sold by early 1977.[11]

Although the book was widely reviewed in Canada and the United States, the reviews were almost entirely negative. Anne Montagnes's review in the *Globe and Mail* – entitled "So Feeble. Why Do It Now?" – was damning to the point of viciousness: "They are rotten stories. There isn't a real character in one of them." Calling Montgomery "a popular and usually vigorous writer for girls and the romantic young-at-heart," she added that the designation of the volume's readership as consisting of adults "prove[s] once more that adults are an audience Montgomery is too unrealistic to please." Montagnes found negative significance even in Montgomery's own title, "The Blythes Are Quoted," which in her view showed that Montgomery "was somewhat aware what prigs Anne and Gilbert had become as the god-like referents in all the doings of their neighbors." Complaining as well about the "many plain errors" in the published volume, Montagnes concluded that "it seems a great pity that this feeble volume … should have been dragged out, now or any other time, and made to limp into print." Louise Wyatt, writing in the *London Free Press*, was equally negative in her assessment of "this unrewarding uncomfortable pitifully anti-climactic postscript," calling it "work from which the Muse had departed." Wyatt added that "the writing itself has faded into weak little sentimental and melodramatic fabrications with a ghastly sense of unreality in their telling," and finally that "it would have been better for L.M. Montgomery and for her admirers to have let these faint hollow shells rest in oblivion." For George Woodcock, writing in *Maclean's*, this "rather pathetic production" resembled "a mere parody of *Anne of Green Gables*." For Woodcock, though, the blame lay not with the author but with those who "decided to drag out after her death what with good reason she had consigned to the drawers of her desk."[12]

The negativity did not end there, either. In her review published in *Quill and Quire*, Adele Ashby declared that the book "proves beyond any doubt that Lucy Maud Montgomery possessed only a mediocre talent, talent enough to produce only one book of any merit, her first, and that neither she nor her publisher had the good sense to know when to stop." Even reviews that began more charitably ended up dwindling into negativity, such as Shirley Lewis's assessment, for *In Review: Canadian Books for Children*, in which she started by claiming that "the publisher has done her fans a great favour in making this final evocation of Ingleside available," even though the stories themselves "epitomize the writing style of by-gone days." Then Lewis went on: "the plots depend on coincidence that should even have strained the credulity of an audience of the 1900's. In 1974 one can only respond with laughter." As for the decades-long debate about whether Montgomery's books are intended for adults or for children, Lewis concluded that "this book is not for children. Nor is it destined to have a wide readership among adults used to contemporary times and styles." For Helen FitzPatrick in *The Canadian Author and Bookman*, the book's lack of reality was somewhat of an attraction, rather than a drawback, in that the book offered "a nostalgic trip to the never-never land of Glen St. Mary, where youthful dreams come true. It's whimsical, and sentimental – but what's wrong with rosy colored glasses?" John Robert Sorfleet, discussing the volume in his introduction to an early issue of the journal *Canadian Children's Literature* devoted to L.M. Montgomery, was equally tepid in his remarks about the "some quite pleasant" and "reasonably enjoyable" stories, as was *Kirkus Reviews*, which suggested that the book could be "of possible interest where the Anne books are still read." Only *The Publishers' Weekly* offered unqualified praise for the book, calling it "a rare literary find," filled with stories that were "fresh, finely constructed and entrancing."[13]

Moreover, only a few responses attempted to offer a balanced assessment of the strengths and weaknesses of the volume. Frances M. Frazer, writing in *Canadian Literature*, noted that "one might expect a new book by Montgomery to be hailed as a literary event, the sort of thunderbolt, albeit of much smaller voltage, that we would recognize in the discovery of the concluding numbers of *Edwin Drood*." Although Frazer conceded that *The Road to Yesterday*, in spite of "its charms, some dated and some not, some specious and some valid," was "unlikely to appeal to a wide audience," she pointed out several strengths, including "touches of the old magic that flashed most frequently in *Anne* but also flickered intermittently in most of Montgomery's subsequent works" and the "several winning people" who appear in the book, particularly "the gallery of the nonheroic." In addition, the protagonist of the short story "The Reconciliation" prompted Frazer to state that "for all her saccharine maunderings about enchanted blue castles, white ways of delight, and latterday dryads by P.E.I. ponds, there is a streak of tough, humorous realism in L.M. Montgomery, and a broader conception of the capabilities and proclivities of human minds and spirits than she is normally given credit for." She noted further that "perhaps this need to mix realism with sugared romanticism, as much as her preoccupation with the past, accounts for the large number of late lovers' reunions in Montgomery's fiction." And in *The Dalhousie Review*, Rae Macdonald noted that the volume "contains just enough exceptions to predictable endings and perfect matings to keep the reader guessing and make him [or her] wonder what Montgomery knew that her time and upbringing would not permit her to say." Moreover, "though [Anne] and her family only hover in the background, they are a sure touchstone. In Montgomery's world, only misers, gossips, and hardened cads fail to acknowledge the charm of the Blythes. In fact, Montgomery repeats this point with such regularity that one becomes tired of it and of the Blythes who never achieve the vitality that they do in earlier books." Rather than vilify Montgomery for modes of writing that had become old-fashioned by the 1970s, as did some of the earlier reviewers, Macdonald again attempted to find a balance in her assessment: "The sustained lack of the 'real' may bother the reader whose tastes have been formed by a literature that commonly depicts grimmer scenes. Montgomery's vision was moulded in the first decades of the century, and her work reflects the sense of moral duty and the romantic idealisation of nature that prevailed in the popular fiction of the time." Although she hastened to add that "it would be deluded ... to try to make a case for Montgomery as an innovator," she conceded that "Montgomery seems to have taken some note of the changing times, and the reader wonders what else lies beneath the benignly smiling face of Anne Shirley's most picturesque of all possible worlds."[14]

The second posthumous Montgomery text released in 1974, *The Alpine Path: The Story of My Career*, also had an ambivalent reception. Originally published in five instalments in the Toronto periodical *Everywoman's World* in 1917, this 25,000-word memoir contains, as the dust jacket of the first edition rightly proclaims, "the most complete account [Montgomery] ever published of her childhood and early years as a writer," and it is still a valuable resource as a major example of Montgomery's public persona, especially when read alongside her journals and letters. It was published not by McGraw–Hill Ryerson but by Toronto publisher Fitzhenry and Whiteside, which would also publish Mollie Gillen's acclaimed biography *The Wheel of Things* in 1975. But reviewers of *The Alpine Path* were consistently damning in their assessments: in a *Vancouver Sun* review sporting the unambiguous headline "Scrap from the Barrel," Alan Dawe expressed difficulty in deciding if the publication of the volume marked "a significant literary event or merely an indication that Canadian publishers in their zeal to reproduce all possible Canadiana are beginning to scrape the bottom of the barrel." Referring to the original publication in *Everywoman's World* as "a frail piece of journalism," he added that the narrator comes across as "a mixture of two voices – the ironic and the sentimental. When it's ironic, it's rather good; when it's sentimental, it's embarrassing and dreary." Sandra Martin, writing in the *Toronto Star*, advised that the "dull plodding autobiography" would "destroy all your illusions" about Montgomery, whom she described here as a woman with an "inability to write about herself with any vigor, charm or intimacy." Elsie Morris, in the *Lethbridge Herald*, claimed that the book, written in Montgomery's "usual witty style," is "light and easy to read," a statement echoed by Callie Israel, who added that "the charm of the book lies in the lighthearted optimism and sincerity which prevails throughout." Still, Israel "found the style of writing rather pretentious, at times verging on the 'purple.' This was not evident in a recent re-reading of several of her novels perhaps because these books were written for children and therefore purposely less complex. In any case, this small book is worth adding to our meagre supply of biographical material on Canadian authors for children." And for Helen FitzPatrick, writing once again in *The Canadian Author and Bookman*, this book of "tantalizing glimpses of the real Lucy Maud" would hopefully lead to further information about the author: "Perhaps her diaries, soon to be published, will be even more revealing."[15]

Despite FitzPatrick's interest in more life writing, the next posthumous Montgomery text led to similar misgivings on the part of reviewers. Published in 1979, once again by McGraw–Hill Ryerson, *The Doctor's Sweetheart and Other Stories* consists of fourteen short stories that originally appeared in periodicals between 1899 and 1935. Compiled and organized by Catherine McLay, a professor of English at the University of Calgary (now retired), the volume also boasted paratexts that discussed, in detail for the first time, Montgomery's considerable side career as a frequent contributor of short stories and poems to North American periodicals between 1890 and 1940. Claiming that the stories were "written with the same charm, delicacy, wit, and perception that readers down the years have come to expect from L.M. Montgomery," the dust jacket speaks highly of "the pleasure to be reaped from meeting the characters who live on these pages." As McLay noted in her introduction to the volume about the sheer number of stories that remained at large, "The discovery of these stories will contribute greatly to our knowledge of Montgomery's early years as a writer and of the development of her talent." McLay noted, too, that while Montgomery chose romance over realism, her focus on the "private and social expectations" of marriage make her work continually relevant: "Within this framework she examines such central problems as the demands of the individual versus those of the community, the demands of family relationships versus those of love, and the nature of marriage as personal fulfillment as opposed to economic necessity or to the duty to the family and society." Noting that the fourteen stories included in the volume show a continued emphasis on courtship and marriage, she concluded that, while the stories "indicate Montgomery's concern with 'lives of girls and women,' ... they also suggest a wider range of themes and styles than is evident in her twenty novels for girls. In these days of new interest in women's themes and women writers, we may come to see Montgomery not merely as a teller of simple girl's stories, but as the conscious literary artist and craftsman that she strove all her life to be."[16]

Although *The Doctor's Sweetheart* received few reviews compared to *The Green Gables Letters* and *The Road to Yesterday*, they were consistent about two aspects of the work. First, reviewers enjoyed the short stories included in the volume: as Mary Ainslie Smith noted in *Books in Canada*, "Sentimental and dated as they may seem today, Montgomery's writings still matter a great deal to a great many people who can think of Prince Edward Island only in terms of her fictional creations. She was a talented story-teller who could create a wonderfully strong sense of place and time; *The Doctor's Sweetheart* provides another glimpse of this secure world." Valerie Ward, in the Montreal *Gazette*, added that "these delightful and perceptive tales not only provide a nostalgic portrait of rural Maritime life at the turn of the century, but also display Montgomery's considerable gifts as an author." Moreover, as Ward noted further, "Montgomery's adept handling of character, her poetic use of language and imagery, her wit and sensibility, frequently turn over-worked material into discerning commentary on human foibles and vulnerabilities." And in *Quill and Quire*, Mary Rubio suggested that "the stories are often contrived and sentimental, but are nonetheless quite readable."[17]

But these same reviewers took issue with McLay's suggestion that, in Smith's words, "Montgomery had a greater depth to her writing than has previously been suspected." As Smith declared, "McLay asks far too much of these stories ... Obviously many of these stories were written to conform to the conventions of the time, and, as such, are hardly more than historical curiosities." Categorizing all the stories as "women's magazine fiction," Smith added that "to treat them as anything more significant is inappropriate and, for this reason, McLay's introduction jars. She discusses theme, character, plot structure, setting, point of view, humour – laying it all out like the introduction to a high-school English textbook. Sometimes this serious treatment borders on the ridiculous, as when McLay tries to justify Montgomery's outrageous use of coincidence in some of her plots." Rubio echoed this assessment, calling the stories "much inferior to *Anne of Green Gables* and to the Emily trilogy, which, by all standards, are works of considerable literary achievement." Rubio noted further that the stories "reveal the literary tastes of an era," and that a comparison between Montgomery and her contemporaries "would reveal ... that the Montgomery stories, though written according

to a conventional formula, are nevertheless based on a far more perceptive knowledge of human psychology." Ultimately, Smith suggested that
"if these represent the best of her hundreds of still uncollected stories,
Montgomery fans probably won't have to make much room on their
bookshelves for future volumes." Ward's review, though, echoed the
kind of assessment that was frequently made in reviews of Montgomery's
books throughout her lifetime and that are peppered throughout this
present volume: "The innocence and stability that pervade [these stories]
are a welcome relief from the cheap glitter and careless egotism of the
1970s. Even their sentimentality has a kind of nostalgic appeal."[18]

Throughout the 1970s, then, these posthumous texts proved to be
at odds with the academic and popular reassessment of Montgomery's
legacy that, as I showed in Volume 2 of *The L.M. Montgomery Reader*,
began during that decade and continues to this day. At the same time,
though, the fact that many of these reviewers persisted in using *Anne of
Green Gables* as a benchmark for determining the value of all her books
is curious, given that even the most devoted Montgomery fan will admit
that her books are not uniformly even in terms of quality, interest, subject
matter, or tone. Taken together, these reviews from the 1970s implied a
slight rigidity in terms of Montgomery's books, what they meant, and to
whom they appealed. But that would change.

### "A More Multifaceted Montgomery": Life Writing, 1980–1992

The tepid response from critics to both *The Road to Yesterday* and *The
Doctor's Sweetheart and Other Stories* must have proven disappointing to McGraw–Hill Ryerson, which continued to reprint its eight main
Montgomery titles throughout the 1970s. For its next Montgomery offering, the publisher issued *My Dear Mr. M: Letters to G.B. MacMillan
from L.M. Montgomery*, in 1980, exactly two decades after the publication of *The Green Gables Letters*. The volume editors, Francis W.P.
Bolger and Elizabeth R. Epperly, were both located at the University
of Prince Edward Island and had already demonstrated their tremendous respect for Montgomery, her work, and her legacy: Bolger's *The
Years Before "Anne"* (1974) is a treasure trove of material pertaining to
Montgomery's life and career prior to the publication of *Anne of Green
Gables*, and Epperly, who had left her native Virginia in order to pur-
sue an undergraduate degree at the University of Prince Edward Island
because of Montgomery, had returned to teach at this institution and
would later found the L.M. Montgomery Institute in 1993, the year after

the publication of her major book-length study *The Fragrance of Sweet-Grass: L.M. Montgomery's Heroines and the Pursuit of Romance* (1992). Their fascination for Montgomery is made clear in the dust jacket copy for *My Dear Mr. M*, which promised that the letters "reveal the character of one [of] our best-known authors; charming, witty, sometimes gloomy and morbid, she was above all stimulating." Calling Montgomery's correspondence to MacMillan "intimate and revealing," Bolger and Epperly argued in their introduction to the volume that the letters "give insight into the character of one of Canada's best-known authors, revealing her personality and its changes as the thirty-nine-year friendship develops."[19]

Unlike the three posthumous Montgomery texts published in the 1970s, however, this one received an enthusiastic response from reviewers. Writing in *Canadian Literature*, Muriel Whitaker celebrated the volume as "the authentic voice of Lucy Maud Montgomery describing her life and views to a friend. The result is far more lively and intimate than that achieved by any of her biographers." Indeed, as Susannah Joyce-Jones declared in *Atlantis: A Women's Studies Journal / Journal d'études sur la femme*, "readers will discover a more sophisticated and multifaceted Montgomery than the one usually evident in her novels." In fact, for Whitaker, the Montgomery who emerged from the pages of this volume was also more complex than the woman depicted by Stuart Macdonald, who seemed to suggest, according to Whitaker, that Montgomery's "rigidity and sensitivity prevented any easy camaraderie in the family. Yet the letters reveal a woman who is charming, tolerant, curious, humorous, passionately devoted to friends, cats, and the land of Prince Edward Island, and not unwilling to confess her proneness to depression, her questioning of religious orthodoxy, and her awareness of her own shortcomings. It's as if the geographical distance between the correspondents, the lack of physical contact ..., make it possible for her to pour out her heart." As Jean Johnston suggested in her review in *Quill and Quire*, "we see [Montgomery's] gift for adept phrasing, her humour, her love of nature and her sense of drama. What is surprising is the absence of joy, though Montgomery was probably not as disconsolate a person as these letters make her seem." Indeed, Joyce-Jones put her finger on a narrative strategy that would become even more apparent in later volumes drawn from Montgomery's life writing: "There seems a conscious attempt to create a somewhat romantic image of herself as author and to preserve some degree of distance even among her close friends."[20]

The publication of *My Dear Mr. M* in 1980 anticipated several events that would build the momentum of posthumous Montgomery texts over the following two decades. In 1981, perhaps prompted by the success of *My Dear Mr. M*, Borealis Press of Ottawa reissued *The Green Gables Letters* with a new preface by Eggleston, first as a jacketed hardcover and eventually as a trade paperback. That same year, the University of Guelph archives purchased ten ledgers consisting of journals written by Montgomery between 1889 and 1942, as well as the copyright to their contents.[21] Along with additional items that were donated after Stuart Macdonald's death in 1982, the journals became the basis for an extensive L.M. Montgomery Collection at the University of Guelph archives. That collection now includes everything from photographs and handiwork to scrapbooks and volumes from Montgomery's personal library. Archival collections such as this one have allowed researchers to find answers to some of their questions about Montgomery's life and legacy, but as Vanessa Brown and I discuss in Volume 2 of *The L.M. Montgomery Reader*, they also point to further questions and gaps. McGraw–Hill Ryerson had let its Montgomery texts go out of print by the end of the 1980s, at which point all of Montgomery's novels were being reprinted as a standard set of mass-market paperbacks by Seal Books. Its three posthumous Montgomery titles also found new homes in the early 1990s: *My Dear Mr. M* with Oxford University Press in 1992, and *The Road to Yesterday* and *The Doctor's Sweetheart* with Seal Books in 1993. Valerie Compton reviewed *My Dear Mr. M* in the *Edmonton Journal* shortly after its 1992 republication, commenting that "mostly it is Montgomery's public face we see in these letters, herself as she wished to be seen."[22] By then, her published journals had made that all too clear.

As Mary Rubio outlines in her contribution to *Working in Women's Archives: Researching Women's Private Literature and Archival Documents* (2001), the editorial process of preparing Montgomery's journals for publication proved problem-free in terms of access – as she notes, "The contract of sale designated me as 'licensee,' with permission to publish and develop the materials however I judged suitable" – but she encountered a number of obstacles in her quest for funding from the Social Sciences and Humanities Research Council of Canada. Even though interest in women writers and popular authors was gaining credibility in English departments by the early 1980s, SSHRC assessors responded to Rubio's application with hostility and contempt – a residue of the ongoing pattern of male dismissal of Montgomery's work that has been traced throughout all three volumes of *The L.M. Montgomery Reader*. Even after the project was funded after a third SSHRC application, she and her collaborator Elizabeth Waterston were faced with the daunting task of having to shorten Montgomery's text by 50 per cent, at the request of their publisher, Oxford University Press, and with having to "create a text that would appeal to the average reader as well as to the scholar," in order to "maintain scholarly standards without *looking so scholarly* that the public would be scared off." William Toye, the in-house editor at Oxford, revealed "a subtle masculine bias" in his suggestions about the kinds of material that could be omitted, but, as Rubio recounts, Toye "acknowledged that the book was ours, and he simply gave us a fixed number of pages for the written text of the entire first volume. Then he left the selection up to us."[23]

Published in November 1985, Volume 1 of *The Selected Journals of L.M. Montgomery* contains not only representative selections from over twenty years of journal entries, but also a detailed introduction, maps of Cavendish and of Prince Edward Island, a family tree, over one hundred photographs (placed in clusters rather than within the running text, due to the technological limitations of the time), extensive notes, a list of entries deleted in whole or in part, and an index. The dust jacket declares that the journals are "unusual for their narrative interest: Montgomery's gifts as a storyteller are as much in evidence here as in her novels," and further, that they "compris[e] perhaps the most vivid and detailed memoir in Canadian letters." In their introduction to the volume, Rubio and Waterston added that "because the journals are so full and frank and cover such a long period, and because they are the work of a successful professional writer, they provide a degree of information, anecdote, and personal history that makes them unique in Canadian letters ... The complete journals of L.M. Montgomery provide a fund of engrossing social history covering more than half a century and draw the reader surprisingly far into the depths of one woman's life."[24]

This time, reviewers were unambiguous in their praise for the book: David Staines, in the Montreal *Gazette*, called it "one of the most haunting documents in Canadian literary history"; Carol Goodwin, in the Kitchener–Waterloo *Record*, referred to it as "the picture of an intensely passionate and sensitive woman of high intellect whose resilient spirit and keen sense of humor helped her overcome periods of emotional anguish"; Sherie Posesorski, in *Quill and Quire*, declared that "the diaries reveal a complex woman whose turbulent inner life belied the public's image of her as the cheerful Gibson-girl author"; Elizabeth R. Epperly, in *The Island Magazine*, claimed that the volume revealed "a sharper, more developed picture than we have had before of the paradoxical Maud Montgomery"; Janice Kulyk Keefer, in *The Antigonish Review*, noted that "for devotés of the later *Anne* books, the *Journals* will be both a shock and, it is to be hoped, a lasting illumination of the reality behind the house of dreams Montgomery's fiction so assiduously constructs"; and in the *London Free Press*, Nancy A. Schiefer declared that "from beginning to end, Montgomery's journals fascinate." These reviewers also, for the first time, used the journals as a basis for reconsidering a work of fiction that remained incredibly popular – a critical strategy that, as I noted in the introduction to Volume 2 of *The L.M. Montgomery Reader*, would become and remains a dominant critical paradigm for Montgomery Studies (and, indeed, such a paradigm certainly drives all three volumes of the current study). Marilyn Powell, in the *Globe and Mail*, interpreted Montgomery as "a lonely little girl [who] was presented with the enormous task of discovering how to love herself when no one else appeared to think it very much worthwhile"; for Powell, discussing recurring motifs in Montgomery's body of work, Montgomery "longed to remain a child forever." Moreover, she deduced that "the most serious repercussion of her painful upbringing" was that "she shied away from serious involvements perhaps because she was afraid she would be abandoned yet again," even though "in one of those peculiarly graceful bargains of fate, what starved her as a person fed her as a writer." Powell predicted that remaining volumes of *Selected Journals* would reveal "a complete and textured expression, a narrative pieced together in entries of great vitality and richness, presenting a character that is more complex, more appealing than perhaps the original ever understood." Robert Fulford, in the *Toronto Star*, was so taken by the unexpected self-portrait of the creator of Anne that he noted that "there's something quite miraculous about the emergence of Anne Shirley – the spirited, imaginative, never-defeated adolescent – from the mind of the gloomily Presbyterian young woman who wrote these journals. If Anne is a self-portrait, she's a self-portrait that captures only one side of the original."[25]

Reviewers were equally fascinated by Montgomery's narrative strategies and by her depiction not only of the mores of rural Prince Edward Island throughout this period but also of her own social and sexual frustrations. As Hilary Thompson argued in *Canadian Literature*, "The implied reader whom the writer creates is a mirror and analyst, a confidant for her soul and a student of social history ... The narrative voice of Anne in the early journals gives way in the later entries to the mature and sometimes self-conscious voice of a successful writer." Thompson was equally astute in her observations about the social pressures imposed on Montgomery as an adolescent girl and later as an adult woman: "The adolescent L.M. Montgomery struggles to gain maturity in a world bound by family and duty, which imposes upon her a rigorous standard of both behaviour and matrimonial hopes. Her innate common sense in seeking a partner is thwarted by an environment which exports intellectually compatible young men and leaves her to meet those physically attractive partners whom she considers to be unsuitable." As Clifford G. Holland suggested in *Queen's Quarterly*, referring to the interest Montgomery received from men and her eventual decision to marry someone she respected but did not love, "Had she followed the dictates of her heart rather than her head, one suspects she might have achieved the sort of happy ending enjoyed by the heroines of her novels." Indeed, for a number of reviewers, Montgomery's decision to marry Ewan Macdonald in this volume proved to be a fascinating and perplexing component of her life story. Schiefer, for example, noted that the volume ends with Montgomery "about to embark, with some misgiving, upon what was to become a passionless and baffling marriage," and J.M. Bumsted suggested in *The Atlantic Provinces Book Review* that "Ewan Macdonald was a desperate stab at escaping spinsterhood by a woman who sensed that she was running out of time."[26]

Montgomery's development as a writer was mentioned less frequently by these reviewers, which is not surprising, since she did not see her journal as a space in which to discuss her work in detail: as with *The Green Gables Letters*, published twenty-five years earlier, the journals are less valuable as a record of Montgomery's writing life than they are of the personal and societal contexts that produced and shaped her texts. Keefer, referring both to this volume and to the second volume of *Selected Journals*, published in 1987, mentioned that while she enjoyed discovering the woman who comes across in these volumes as "intelligent, sensual, witty and fiercely determined to keep up the formidable appearances demanded by her roles as self-sacrificing granddaughter, mother, minister's wife, and internationally popular author," ultimately the journals would "disappoint anyone interested in the art of writing ... Nowhere in these first two volumes does Montgomery ever discuss or explore the act of writing, or even set down her struggles with various manuscripts ... If for nothing else, her journals are invaluable for their revelations of how and why Montgomery deliberately refused to take the risks which would have made her an artist rather than an author." But while Montgomery may not have discussed writing in detail, it was through the act of writing itself that she was able to work out her problems and record the minutiae of her life. As Coral Ann Howells noted in *Canadian Children's*

*Literature / Littérature canadienne pour la jeunesse*, "One of the reader's keenest pleasures is to watch Montgomery finding a voice of her own, working through various stylistic mannerisms to find a more direct language to record her private life, so that the journals also become the place of creative ordering and self-discovery." Indeed, the sheer readability of this volume of journals became a refrain throughout these of reviews. Margaret Conrad, writing in *The Canadian Historical Review*, referred to the volume as "a *bildungsroman* of exceptional power," noting that "Montgomery's great literary talent and her eye to posterity guaranteed that her life story would make even more absorbing reading than her fiction." Indeed, as Thompson noted, "L.M. Montgomery's narrative skills in creating roles for her readers to fill, together with her change of style and voice, make the journals as readable as a novel, not because they are like her novels or because they reveal how she came to write them, but because they intrigue us with her personal development, achieved with perceptive self-analysis and anecdote, from a young and carefree, often callous, girl into a thoughtful writer." And Bumsted, referring to Montgomery as "one of Canada's best, if woefully neglected, social novelists," suggested that "she may well achieve with her private writings what she was never quite able to accomplish in her published work."[27]

As Carole Gerson reports in her contribution to *Anne's World: A New Century of Anne of Green Gables* (2010), sales of the first volume of *The Selected Journals of L.M. Montgomery* reached twenty-five thousand copies in hardcover by 2000, and as Rubio notes, after the critical success of the first volume she and Waterston were able to get funding for the next two "without a problem." But as they resumed work on entries depicting Montgomery's final year in Cavendish and her post-marriage life in Ontario, they faced another obstacle: Montgomery's negative comments about people whose immediate descendants were still living. In the end, the imperative "to get Montgomery's story of her life into ongoing discourse on how femininity had been constructed under patriarchy" trumped the risk of hurt feelings, according to Rubio; she and Waterston "decided that we simply could not delete certain sections that made negative comments about the *ancestors* of living people, for Montgomery's judgemental stance towards people was an essential part of her personality and character. We thought that in the final analysis her critical remarks about others said more about her than about them." This perception was not shared by all readers whose ancestors had unwillingly become supporting players in this multi-volume saga, however, as Rubio reports. "They blamed Montgomery less for writing what she did than they blamed us for publishing it. Elizabeth and I were seen as the ones who were telling tales beyond the grave."[28]

Oxford University Press also relaxed its requirement that Rubio and Waterston trim Montgomery's text by 50 per cent, so the subsequent two volumes contained a greater percentage of Montgomery's own text. Moreover, whereas the second half of Volume 1 depicts Montgomery's feelings of depression and stagnation throughout her years as primary caregiver for an aging grandmother, Volume 2 (released in 1987 and including entries from 1910 to 1921) and Volume 3 (released in 1992 and including entries from 1921 to 1929) show Montgomery's reactions to cataclysmic change – namely "the possibility, the actuality, and the aftermath of a world war." In their introduction to the second volume of *Selected Journals*, Rubio and Waterston made a crucial point about the discrepancies between the private and public Montgomerys: "Part of her complex psychological make-up required her to construct a public image of herself as someone who was always dignified, cheerful, and self-controlled ... Her journals, in their psychological function, often provided ... a place where she could risk showing a side of her personality she preferred to hide, even from herself." Indeed, the dust jacket for Volume 3 suggests that in this volume Montgomery "turns more and more to her journal to record insights and opinions not voiceable by 'the angel in the house.'" In their introduction to the latter volume, Rubio and Waterston even started to question Montgomery's reliability in the telling of her life story, pointing out that her depiction of her husband as suffering from religious melancholia did not match the ways in which his community remembered him: "Are we to regard the diarist as functioning like the 'untrustworthy narrator' in a modern novel?"[29]

Among the many threads from these two volumes discussed by reviewers were Montgomery's depiction of her two primary adult relationships: that with her husband, whom Michael Bliss, in *Canadian Children's Literature / Littérature canadienne pour la jeunesse*, referred to as "a soul-destroying burden to his wife," and that with her first cousin, Frederica Campbell, whom Epperly, once again in *The Island Magazine*, called "her best friend, virtually her only soul mate." As Bumsted noted in *The Atlantic Provinces Book Review* when discussing the second volume, "The nature of her intense relationship with Frederica (Frede) Campbell is left more than a bit mysterious, but the language Maud uses to describe her feeling towards Frede is little different than that employed by Virginia Woolf and Vita Sackville-West at about the same period. Whether or not it was overtly lesbian, Maud's love for Frede is the grand passion of this volume." When reviewing the third volume in *The Island Magazine*, Bumsted added, "One does not know quite what to make of Maud's passionate relationship with Frederica (Frede) Campbell, who had died literally in Montgomery's arms early in 1919, particularly in terms of its connection with the dynamics of her marriage." As for Ewan Macdonald, according to Bumsted, "It is almost as though Maud has written him out of her life, although he reappears towards the end in the role which has become Maud's favourite: the incompetent male." Indeed, Lalage Grauer noted in *University of Toronto Quarterly* that "marriage, a stable centre in Montgomery's life, is perhaps the main source of emotional turmoil."[30]

Reviewers of these two volumes made further inroads in their quest to re-evaluate Montgomery's private and public contributions to Canadian letters: Epperly referred to her as "always the story-teller, always the craftswoman controlling the language," and Powell in the *Globe and Mail* suggested that "in her writer's soul she knew that she was trapped in evasion and that she had arrested her prose in adolescence," whereas in the journals, Montgomery herself "construct[ed] a portrait of the artist at once candid and premeditated." Laurel Boone added in *Canadian Literature* that "like the best fiction, the journals lead us to an understanding of human nature that extends beyond the time, place and characters at hand. The novels, on the other hand, lead us to an understanding of Montgomery's ideals." Although Heather Avery, in *Resources for Feminist Research / Documentation sur la recherche féministe*, noted that "one suspects that Montgomery viewed these journals, which she clearly intended to be read, as providing the explanation for her failure to make that more extensive contribution to Canadian literature," Howells provided another view in the journal *English*, claiming that the journals reveal "how her regional idylls represent a form of personal mythmaking and are her strategies of discreet resistance against the stereotypes to which Canadian provincial society forced her to conform." Indeed, as Lorraine York suggested in *Canadian Children's Literature / Littérature canadienne pour la jeunesse*, "The long-speculated-about reluctance of Montgomery to provide her fictional heroines with the traditional novelistic orange-blossom and lace nuptial finale finds a parallel in her own reluctance to face marital 'closure.'" But reviewers were unambiguous about the literary and cultural value they saw in the published journals: as Bumsted claimed, "The greatest literary character this famed Canadian author ever created was herself, and the great literary achievement of her life was the production of her journal, a conscious effort if ever there was one," adding that the second volume "is almost overwhelming in its impact." For Howells, the value of the journals was historical as well, for they revealed "fascinating insights into Canadian regional and provincial culture around the time of the first World War," particularly Montgomery's "distinctively colonial voice from maritime Canada, that of an ambitious woman caught up as surely as Jane Austen was in the conventionalities of provincial life, aware of the doubleness of being both a proper lady and a woman writer."[31]

By the time the third volume of *The Selected Journals of L.M. Montgomery* appeared in 1992, the novelty of the unexpected "private" voice of L.M. Montgomery had faded somewhat, but interest in her continuing life story remained as strong as ever. Moreover, following the suggestions of Rubio and Waterston, reviewers no longer interpreted the journals as an unmediated form: while Bumsted suggested that "like any great writer, L.M. Montgomery knew how to apply imaginative techniques to the events of everyday life, and in the process turned her journals into major artistic statements," Bliss noted that "there is little doubt that L.M. Montgomery pre-edited her diaries for literary effect and, possibly, for personal aggrandizement (she sometimes comes across as the all-knowing innocent victim surrounded by boors and dolts)." As well, reviewers began to view Montgomery's life in terms of tragedy, a premonition of things to come: as Mark Abley suggested in the Montreal *Gazette*, "From a feminist perspective, Montgomery's journals offer a devastating picture of a bright woman trapped in a dull home and a closed society." Bliss painted an even bleaker picture, noting that "the central theme of Montgomery's journals, like that of most of her novels, is the interplay between an intensely creative imagination and a mundane, disappointing world. A world-famous novelist buries herself as a minister's wife in small-town Ontario and has intense difficulties coping with her predicament ... Future volumes of the journals, and/or the official biography, will reveal the degree to which Montgomery shortened her life as a result of drug dependency." Grauer responded differently to the feminist component of the journals: calling the third volume "essential reading for anyone interested in Montgomery, autobiography, Ontario history, or women's writing," she noted that Montgomery's "response to fame is pervaded by a consistent feminism – it is important to her that she is a woman being recognized, that she indeed prove women capable of doing something worthy of tribute; otherwise, she responds to the mixed blessing of public recognition with a sense of humour and genuine humility."[32]

And so, by 1992 – just as the Canadian copyright to her work was about to expire, fifty years after her death – the dominant perception of Montgomery as a woman and as a writer had been transformed completely thanks to these three volumes of *Selected Journals*. But as I discussed in the introduction to Volume 2 of *The L.M. Montgomery Reader*, this form of life writing competed with other Montgomery texts that were in circulation by this time. For Bliss, "The Anne of Green Gables industry on Prince Edward Island has reached such overblown proportions ... that it threatens to trivialize the works of a woman increasingly recognized as one of Canada's more significant twentieth-century writers."[33] By the early 1990s, the tourist industry in Prince Edward Island had been joined by a Montgomery publishing industry in southern Ontario. But while the success of the *Selected Journals* and of popular screen adaptations of Montgomery's primary work continued to nurture an audience with an apparently insatiable appetite for all things Montgomery, reviewers proved to be ambivalent about or unappreciative of the remaining courses of this Montgomery feast.

### Reassessment by Theme: Rediscovered Writings, 1987–1995

In October 1987, a few weeks before the publication of the second volume of *The Selected Journals of L.M. Montgomery*, Fitzhenry and Whiteside published its next Montgomery title, John Ferns and Kevin McCabe's *The Poetry of Lucy Maud Montgomery*, a collection of eighty-six poems from Montgomery's career, organized into two main sections, "Poems of Nature" and "Poems of Humanity" (each broken down into several subsections) and accompanied by McCabe's detailed introduction. As with the paratextual material included with *The Green Gables Letters* in 1960, however, the dust jacket reveals a hesitation about the quality of the work itself: although it promises that "the poems in this collection will reach as deeply into the heart of today's readers as they did in those who first read them half a century ago," it adds that "Maud Montgomery was well aware that greatness as a poet was beyond her reach, but her verses were capable of putting into words what ordinary people felt and often could not explain."[34] In a way, this assessment of Montgomery's poetry as good but not great, as culturally valuable yet accessible to "ordinary people," echoes the comments made by reviewers of *The Watchman and Other Poems* seven decades earlier.

Indeed, although this title was not reviewed nearly as widely as any of the volumes of *The Selected Journals of L.M. Montgomery*, those who did review the text picked up on these ambivalences and proved unable to resolve them. As Laura Groening observed in *The Atlantic Provinces Book Review*, "Montgomery's editors clearly suspect they have got their hands on something worthwhile but they are obviously not sure where the value of the poetry lies." Other reviewers proved equally unsure: Eileen Manion noted in the Montreal *Gazette* that "readers who have formed their taste on T.S. Eliot, Ezra Pound and the descendants of the modernists will probably not see the point of republishing Montgomery's poems ... Although she wrote poems meant for ordinary readers, not for other poets or literary scholars, today they will probably appeal only to hardcore Montgomery fans or those professionally interested in Canadian literary history." Muriel Whitaker went further in her review in *Canadian Literature*, calling the volume "useless as a scholarly resource, since it makes no attempt at completeness and it lacks the most basic information about dates, places of composition and publication, or sources," and describing the introduction as "unreliable as a guide to the poetry's literary, intellectual and social contexts." Yet Groening's later observations about the importance of the volume in terms of "the recovery of a female past" offer a crucial exception to this overall negative assessment: "The poems are, in fact, quite a moving representation of female life in Canada at the turn of the century." Following "a series of cloying, sentimental nature poems that are difficult to wade through in their entirety" are, in Groening's view, clusters of poems that achieve a completely different effect:

> the traditional equations of human female and mother nature, of girl and flower, are more and more often displaced by poems with a more vigorous language and rhythm, a more colloquial language, and a more active theme. These are all poems with male personae. In other words, when Montgomery writes from the perspective of a female, she creates the dainty word pictures that symbolize the suffocating reality of her own life. When she writes from the perspective of a male, she is free to depict a wider-ranging existence, an existence of action and even heroism.[35]

A challenge facing all of these volume editors – McLay, Bolger and Epperly, Rubio and Waterston, Ferns and McCabe, all of them university-affiliated researchers – was to maintain high scholarly standards while still producing trade-published books that would appeal and sell to a wide and diverse audience. They managed to do so by purposely reprinting selections of material and by using a variety of strategies: Bolger and Epperly kept explanatory materials, particularly footnotes, to a minimum, whereas Rubio and Waterston compressed theirs into the back matter of their three volumes, using a combination of text treatments that would make the notes available but less daunting to trade readers. So, while Whitaker claimed that the lack of chronology or even of original publication sources made *The Poetry of Lucy Maud Montgomery* "useless as a scholarly resource," it is worth emphasizing that it was not actually conceived or published as such: its goal was to provide trade readers with a representative sample of the five hundred poems that Montgomery published throughout her fifty-year writing career, and it achieved that goal in the sense that the volume remains in print more than a quarter of a century after its initial publication.

This disconnect between scholarly editorial standards and the economic demands of trade publishing returned in full force a year after Ferns and McCabe's book appeared, when Rea Wilmshurst's first edited collection of rediscovered Montgomery stories, *Akin to Anne: Tales of Other Orphans*, was published by McClelland and Stewart. The dust jacket for the original hardcover edition, which features a colourized photograph of Montgomery as a child on the cover, notes that only seven of the nineteen stories appearing in the volume feature children, whereas the balance are about "older men and women whose lives are empty of love and family. In keeping with her longing for a happier life for herself, Montgomery finds warm and loving homes for all her lonely characters." The nature of the edition made an editorial apparatus unnecessary, but the book does contain a detailed introduction as well as a list of sources for all nineteen stories. Noting that most of the stories were first published before *Anne of Green Gables*, Wilmshurst suggested that "we can look on *Anne* as the culmination of Montgomery's impulse to write about orphans and give their stories happy endings."[36]

Reviewers across Canada were ambivalent about the volume's organization and contents, however. According on Leslie MacLean, in *The Island Magazine*, "Wilmshurst has organized what must have been an inchoate mass of material by grouping the stories thematically," but doing so "accentuates their failings without illuminating their strengths," so that "the stories expand [Montgomery's] work in only the quantitative sense." For Hugh McKellar, in the *Toronto Star*, the thematic arrangement "risk[s] presenting Montgomery as a deft performer on one fiddle-string." Helen Porter, complimenting Wilmshurst on her "fine introduction" and expressing surprise at the stories' "element of preachiness" and the absence of Montgomery's signature sense of humour, wrote in the *Globe and Mail* that *Akin to Anne* proved to be "the only Montgomery book that I've ever found a chore to finish." For Eileen Manion, writing in the Montreal *Gazette*, although the stories contained "echoes or foreshadowings" of Anne, none of the characters – "dully virtuous boys, girls or young women" – had "Anne's ability to transform reality to suit her imagination, nor her talent for getting into and out of 'scrapes.'" Noting as well that the book's focus on orphans revealed forms of familial dissolution and child abuse that were far more common at the turn of the twentieth century, Manion added that "these stories give us a good idea of Canadian social history, but Montgomery lovers looking for lost literary masterpieces will not find them here." For Epperly, however, writing in *Canadian Literature*, the repetition imposed by the book's structure proved to be not an impediment but a strength: "Precisely because the stories in *Akin to Anne* use and reuse the same techniques and the same themes, we can conveniently examine in them Montgomery's play with formula. We are able to see here where the writer transcends the limitations of a chosen convention and where she succumbs to them." As such, according to Epperly, Montgomery was "often exploiting an archetype rather than merely manipulating a formula."[37]

The reviews of *Akin to Anne* were not nearly as negative as those of *The Road to Yesterday* had been a decade and a half earlier, but they likewise did not express nearly the same level of enthusiasm or fascination as did reviews of *The Selected Journals of L.M. Montgomery*. Nevertheless, the book was evidently deemed enough of a commercial success not only to proceed with the three follow-ups that were initially planned – *Along the Shore: Tales by the Sea* (1989), *Among the Shadows: Tales from the Darker Side* (1990), and *After Many Days: Tales of Time Passed* (1991) – but to add four additional volumes as well: *Against the Odds: Tales of Achievement* (1993), *At the Altar: Matrimonial Tales* (1994), *Across the Miles: Tales of Correspondence* (1995), and, finally, *Christmas with Anne and Other Holiday Stories* (1995), which included excerpts from *Anne of Green Gables* and *Anne of Windy Poplars* to strengthen the connection to Anne Shirley. In all, these eight volumes brought 142 of Montgomery's 530 short stories to a new reading public. Wilmshurst noted in her afterword to *Across the Miles* (included in Volume 2 of *The L.M. Montgomery Reader*) that she was still planning to compile at least two additional volumes at the time, but she was unable to proceed with these due to illness, and after her death in 1996, the project was discontinued.

The response of reviewers to Wilmshurst's later books was likewise uneven. The organization of each volume around a chosen theme was often cited as a weakness, whereas the stories themselves, although not always celebrated for their literary quality, were seen as evidence of a woman writer earning a living within the narrow constraints of her culture – similar to some of the responses to *The Selected Journals of L.M. Montgomery*. Michael O. Nowlan, in *The Atlantic Advocate*, called *Along the Shore* "as exciting as" *Akin to Anne*: "These tales have retained a freshness and simplicity that is hard to find in stories today." Marilyn Powell, in the *Globe and Mail*, disagreed with that assessment, calling the stories in *Along the Shore* "quaint, contrived and dated," but she added that the volume demonstrated the extent to which Montgomery was "writing for a market with predictable tastes" while still showing "detectable evolution in her technical skills." To this last point Cecelia Frey added, in *Canadian Literature*, that while most of the stories in *Along the Shore* were quite conventional, "it is when romance gives way to passion, sentimentality to emotion and stereotype to character, that the game turns exciting." In the *Vancouver Sun*, Linda Rogers praised *Among the Shadows* for "giv[ing] substance to Montgomery's characterization of Victorian womanhood, modeling the anguish inevitable in the sort of social role-playing that was required in a repressive society that showed favor to men and women whose physical appearance and economic position determined their social mobility." Peter de Niverville, in *The Atlantic Provinces Book Review*, called *Among the Shadows* "a refreshing look at one of Canada's most popular authors," while Dave Jenkinson, in *CM: A Reviewing Journal of Canadian Materials for Young People*, cautioned that "the subject matter and writing style ... disqualify it from being a candidate for the recreational reading collections of either school libraries or juvenile/young adult departments in public libraries."[38]

Reviews of the four later titles were equally filled with ambiguities and paradoxes. Although she noted that "in these jaded times, some of us would regard Montgomery's values as naive, bordering on moronic," Nora Abercrombie stated in the *Edmonton Journal* that *Against the Odds* contained "capsules of Lucy Maud at her creative best." Marie Campbell, writing in *Canadian Children's Literature / Littérature canadienne pour la jeunesse*, faulted "the editorial decision to lump 17 similar tales together" for drawing readers' attention "to the ways in which Montgomery lucratively recycled her ideas and plots," but added that "there are distinct advantages for the *student* of Montgomery's work to this type of arrangement." The organizational structure of *At the Altar* proved too much for Wendy Thatcher, who noted in the Montreal *Gazette* that "as one reads one story after another, any original elements are subsumed by the relentless drive toward the inevitable proposal." Although the fact that some of the stories in this last volume were "so predictable and undeveloped" led Epperly to wonder, in *University of Toronto Quarterly*, "how Montgomery would feel about having them unearthed," she insisted that the bulk of Wilmshurst's collections "may be one of the best sources readily available to scholars for studying (primarily women's) periodical publications and markets in the early years of the twentieth century." Moreover, while some reviewers faulted Wilmshurst for seeing too much in these stories, Sylvia Bryce, in *Canadian Children's Literature / Littérature canadienne pour la jeunesse*, found even more in *At the Altar* and *Christmas with Anne* than Wilmshurst herself seemed to, namely "the extent of Montgomery's subtle attacks on the social conventions and stereotypes that limited women's power in Montgomery's day." In her view, the stories in these two volumes "have more significance as studies in women's experiences of oppression than can be inferred from the innocent-sounding titles of the collections. The stories should therefore not be seen simply as charming little entertainments; Montgomery's criticisms of social convention and her explorations of the often harsh realities of women will make these tales invaluable to Montgomery fans and scholars alike."[39]

Ultimately, as with *The Poetry of Lucy Maud Montgomery*, Wilmshurst received qualified praise as the hunter and gatherer of this material but was faulted for her inability to do the impossible – namely, satisfy all readers: scholarly and trade, students and non-students, adults and children. Indeed, the sheer size and diversity of Montgomery's readership is often daunting to any editor wishing to repackage her work for a new audience. When that target audience is narrowed, such problems can be minimized. In 2005, Montreal publisher Lobster Press reissued Montgomery's 1916 poem "The Way to Slumbertown" as a lullaby picture book illustrated by Rachel Bédard. Rather than fault the book for the absence of a scholarly apparatus, reviewers appreciated both the suitability of the text for young children and the complementing illustrations. In *Quill and Quire*, Jessica Kelley called the poem "one we can imagine Anne Shirley herself reading to her own children," adding that "Montgomery's old-fashioned imagery may be a pleasant change for contemporary children … No matter what age they live in, children still need comfort and companionship when settling into bed, and this poem, written almost a hundred years ago, serves its purpose very well indeed."[40] In rather pointed contrast to the volumes of periodical pieces by Ferns and McCabe and by Wilmshurst, this poem repackaged as a lullaby was still appropriate for twenty-first-century children; indeed, its old-fashionedness was a strength rather than a drawback.

## Concerns and Crises: Ending a Life, 1998–2009

When the fourth and fifth volumes of *The Selected Journals of L.M. Montgomery* were published in 1998 and 2004, readers were faced with a form of self-representation that was increasingly bleak, increasingly frustrated, and increasingly desperate. Indeed, Lorraine York in *Canadian Children's Literature / Littérature canadienne pour la jeunesse* referred to the fourth volume, containing entries from 1929 to 1935, as "an autumnal world in these personal writings," one filled with "traumas borne in public smiling silence." Rubio and Waterston nevertheless cautioned in their introduction to the volume that "[Montgomery's] self-revelation is tempered by the social mores of the time in which she lived. This is the record of a mature, intelligent woman, coping with both professional necessities and family demands, against the backdrop of history." As they noted in the fifth volume, the "growing friction" between her and her adult sons led to "gaps and evasions" in the entries from the final years of her life. Bleak as it often was, Montgomery's life story proved to be just as addictive as her fiction: as Laura M. Robinson revealed in her review of the final volume, which "paints a devastating portrait of this woman's descent into despair," "I flipped to the final page of her journal entries the moment I received the volume. I had to know once and for all how the story ended." Indeed, as Greg Gatenby noted in *Books in Canada*, the final volume was "a compelling read in the same way a highway accident is morbidly absorbing."[41]

This complex fascination proved to be shared by many reviewers and readers. In her review of the fourth volume in the *Globe and Mail*, Carol Shields noted that "Montgomery's interweaving of grief and joy makes her a felt presence on the page" and expressed her gratitude to volume editors Rubio and Waterston: "Their sensitive and sympathetic editing of this complex material has given us a literary treasure. As social history it is extraordinary. As an excavation into the mind of a woman it is priceless." Clara Thomas was also unambiguous about the cultural value of these journals in her review in *Books in Canada*: "For wealth of detail and emotional frankness, there is nothing else in Canadian literature that even approaches these volumes," with the fourth volume "the sad story of the disintegration of a wonderfully gifted, creative, high-spirited, and successful woman." Thomas also pointed out a discernible shift in tone as Montgomery aged: "It is impossible for the reader not to notice that, from being a wittily judgmental woman, Montgomery was fast becoming a bitterly judgmental one ... Partly through circumstance and partly because of her own temperament, she had become a controlling woman." As for the journal's treatment of Montgomery's husband, she added, "The reader's compassion for Ewan is twinned with a growing conviction that Montgomery's own all-too-obvious neuroses must have played a major part in his condition." As Cecily Devereux noted in *Canadian Literature*, however, what had not changed in these autumnal years was the function that journal writing had for Montgomery: "Her journal, clearly, was for her a place to organize and make sense of things in her life by constructing them as story, connecting events, and by situating occurrences and people in relation to herself as the story's heroine."[42]

While the dust jacket for the fifth volume promised that "this volume offers the counterpoint of dark realism and tragic irony, as well as insight and humour," reviewers were unable to concentrate on anything but Montgomery's despair. Margaret Anne Doody, in the *Globe and Mail*, declared that "the life of Lucy Maud Montgomery, when seen as the life of Mrs. Ewan Macdonald, belongs to a genre she never attempted in fiction. The five volumes of Montgomery's *Selected Journals* comprise a true tragedy." Doody identified two main sources of anxiety: Ewan Macdonald, whom she referred to interchangeably as "what we call today a manic depressive" and "not totally sane," and their eldest son, Chester, who "is sinning against everything that Maud believes in," with an important qualifier: "Not in the terms of religion, for she is at heart unorthodox, but in the terms of the real religion of respectability, which she mocked in her books and served with maniacal devotion in her life." As Doody explained, "Maud served the god of respectability in marrying a Presbyterian minister in the first place, in masquerading as a true believer in Christian and even Calvinist tenets, and in propping up Ewan, excusing him, trying to cover the slips and gaffes brought on by his mania as well as the lacklustre indifference produced by the depression. This work of perpetually manufacturing a family story for public consumption was doubtless exhausting."[43]

For Clara Thomas, too, this final volume became "a final litany of almost unrelieved misery," yet one that "enables us to go back to Anne, Emily, Pat, Jane and all the rest with a new respect for Montgomery's transcendent talent and the timeless light it sheds." Irene Gammel, in *University of Toronto Quarterly*, called the five-volume *Selected Journals* Montgomery's "magnum opus," "a landmark in Canadian life and letters and the capstone of three decades of groundbreaking scholarship." And in *The Canadian Historical Review*, Heather Murray made a crucial connection between Montgomery's narrative strategies and the "gaps and evasions" in the final volume: "As with most journals, this book has a loosely episodic structure, but there is a common, twisting theme of loss. An armchair analyst might diagnose melancholia, in which the loss, because suffusive, finds odd places to fix: Montgomery's dead cat recalled, nightmarishly, over and over again. (Freud theorized melancholia as incomplete mourning or separation, and saw repetition as intrinsic to it, giving the melancholic a sense of control over what cannot otherwise be worked through.)" Noting the complex ways in which Montgomery was a "canny editor of her own work," crafting and editing her journal entries with an eye on posthumous publication, Murray suggested that "the journals may be less melancholic than (technically speaking) melodramatic, with the allegorized sufferings and flattened characterizations of that genre. In either case, the journals' misproportions, narrative gaps, and relentless rehearsals mean that they will provide reading for only the most chastened devotee."[44]

The fifth volume of *The Selected Journals of L.M. Montgomery* brought readers and reviewers to the end of Montgomery's life, but its publication in 2004 was followed by two additional endings. The first, *After Green Gables: L.M. Montgomery's Letters to Ephraim Weber, 1916–1941*, published in June 2006, became a sequel of sorts to Wilfrid Eggleston's volume *The Green Gables Letters*, published nearly half a century earlier. Its editors, Hildi Froese Tiessen of Conrad Grebel University College and Paul Gerard Tiessen of Wilfrid Laurier University, had already published a volume of Weber's own letters to Leslie Staebler, *Ephraim Weber's Letters Home, 1902–1955* (1996), as well as articles on Montgomery and Weber's epistolary relationship in *Journal of Mennonite Studies* and the collection of essays *The Intimate Life of L.M. Montgomery*. In their introduction, they suggested not only that these letters "extend and interact" with previously published volumes of life writing – published volumes of journals, published and unpublished letters to G.B. MacMillan, and *The Alpine Path* – but also that "there is ... a distinctive voice at work here, a voice prodded into expression by Weber, who serves as both stimulus and audience."[45] Their introduction provided contextual information about Weber himself, which is crucially important given that his voice is silenced by the fact that his letters to Montgomery have not survived.

Although this volume was not reviewed as extensively as even the later volumes of *Selected Journals*, existing reviews gave *After Green Gables* high praise. E. Holly Pike, in an omnibus review of six then-recent additions to Montgomery Studies in the final issue of *Canadian Children's Literature / Littérature canadienne pour la jeunesse,* noted the "strange combination of parallel and disjunction" between the letters in this volume and the journal entries from the same period. Pointing out that Montgomery drew on her journal for material for her letters but omitted most of her major worries, Pike added, "It is natural enough that Montgomery would not share her burdens with a correspondent with whom she has had little personal contact, but that fact adds to our understanding of Montgomery's methods of dividing her public and private worlds, with her letter writing being part of her public world." In my own review of the volume in *Canadian Literature*, I noted as well that the volume "complements and complicates the poetics of self-representation established in her published journals," and described some of the recurring topics in the quarter-century of letters: "They discuss modern fiction (most of which she hated), the evils of free verse, the gradual irrelevance of organized religion, changes in fashion and technology, universal education (which she opposed on the grounds that those who did not want an education were wasting their time), and the 'melting pot' – the model of Canadianness that she preferred." And in *University of Toronto Quarterly*, Gammel called the letters "a window into the life and personality of a busy, multi-tasking wife, mother, and writer" and complemented the volume editors on their "critical introduction and meticulous scholarly annotations."[46]

And finally, Penguin Canada published my edition of *The Blythes Are Quoted*, completed near the end of Montgomery's life and intended to be the final sequel to *Anne of Green Gables*. It appeared in October 2009, thirty-five years after its publication in abridged form as *The Road to Yesterday* and just one year after Montgomery's granddaughter Kate Macdonald Butler revealed in the *Globe and Mail* her family's belief that Montgomery's death in 1942 had been a suicide. In a sense, as I noted in my afterword to the volume, *The Blythes Are Quoted* can be seen as another missing piece to the puzzle of Montgomery's death, given that her obituary, also in the *Globe and Mail* and reprinted in Volume 1 of *The L.M. Montgomery Reader*, suggested that the typescript had been dropped off at the office of her Toronto publisher the very day of her death. As a marketing strategy, rather than attempt to camouflage the darker elements found in the volume, the dust jacket placed them front and centre: "Adultery, illegitimacy, revenge, murder, and death – these are not the first terms we associate with L.M. Montgomery. But in *The Blythes Are Quoted*, completed at the end of her life, the author brings topics such as these to the fore." Indeed, in an interview with me, Elizabeth Renzetti of the *Globe and Mail* referred to the volume as "a bubbling cauldron of dark matter."[47]

Ultimately, what surprised me most about the reviews of *The Blythes Are Quoted* was that they proved to be diametrically opposed to those of *The Road to Yesterday*. In *Literary Review of Canada*, Noreen Golfman noted that this "much anticipated" restored volume "is a curious hybrid of genres, dominated by 14 short stories set in the verdant landscape of Prince Edward Island, and interspersed with poems and fragments of dialogue and private reflections." Golfman added, "These are not sunshine sketches of little town life so much as darkening narratives in which humans are up against their own weaknesses and fears, anxieties and delusions. This fine and respectful collection will sustain and enhance the Montgomery legacy, deservedly so." Aritha van Herk declared in the *Globe and Mail* that "this re-acquaintance with the voice of L.M. Montgomery is marvellously satisfying," whereas the fourteen short stories, "while often resolved with predictably happy endings and mawkish proposals, demonstrate a darker subtext, surprising to those who assign to Montgomery a Victorian felicity. They take up the underside of social amiability: lies and secrets, grievances and deception, murder and madness. They are compelling because they recognize that humans are capable of perfidy, and that beneath the smooth surface of respectable piety lurks imperfection, even wickedness." For Kerry Clare in *Quill and Quire*, "the book's fragmented structure is complicated and fascinating," and "the rawness of the text offers insight into its author and her writing process."[48]

All of this continues to make me wonder: How to account for such a drastic change in the responses to *The Road to Yesterday* and to *The Blythes Are Quoted*, given that they are, in many ways, the same text? Why did reviewers respond so harshly to a version of the text that, as a collection of loosely related stories, was in a fairly conventional form, whereas they responded so enthusiastically to a more fragmented and experimental version of the work? Could it be that the insights about Anne and her family revealed in the vignettes satisfied readers' appetite for another Anne book in a way that *The Road to Yesterday* could not? Or is it perhaps that, after the publication of her journals and letters, and after the public news about Montgomery's apparent suicide, readers of 2009 were better equipped than those of 1974 to handle the disproportionate amount of sadness and despair in her final book? I can only speculate, but it seems apparent now, in these posthumous reviews, that reader perceptions of Montgomery, her life, and her work have evolved considerably since 1960. Although I will always wonder what led McClelland and Stewart to pass on this final manuscript when it was apparently submitted to them the day of her death, it may be that Montgomery's editors worried that her readers were not yet able to reconcile the final text with their understanding of Montgomery as a writer. Perhaps the seven-decade delay between the submission of the text to her publisher and its eventual publication in 2009 was not only unavoidable, but entirely necessary.

### Complete and Unabridged: Revisiting a Life, 2012–2013

Although the publication of *The Blythes Are Quoted* in 2009 signalled an ending of sorts as far as Montgomery texts were concerned, it also anticipated a new beginning: in June 2012, responding to the continued interest in Montgomery's journals, particularly the much-abridged first volume of *Selected Journals*, Mary Henley Rubio and Elizabeth Hillman Waterston published, again with Oxford University Press, *The Complete Journals of L.M. Montgomery: The PEI Years, 1889–1900*, appearing in June 2012, followed by *The Complete Journals of L.M. Montgomery: The PEI Years, 1901–1911*, in February 2013. As I noted in my review of the first of these titles in *The Globe and Mail*, the volume offered readers "an opportunity to revisit Montgomery's earliest self-portrait now that we know so much more about her life: her disastrous marriage, her often tense relationship with sons and other family members, the gap between her cheerful public persona and her private, proud self, the periods of profound depression." With this prior knowledge of Montgomery's later life, I wrote, "returning to Montgomery's self-portrait of the artist as a young woman is a fascinating reading experience." As indeed it was: although readers of 1985 would likely have been attracted to the Anne-like adolescent Maud Montgomery and been surprised by the rapid shift in tone "as she recovers from two disastrous relationships, four significant deaths and a falling-out with her closest girl friend from adolescence," when reading this volume in 2012 I found the reverse: given that I was so accustomed to the depressed and despairing older Montgomery, it was the voice of the merry adolescent that jarred.[49]

Nancy Schiefer had a similar reading experience, noting in her review of the first volume in the *London Free Press* that "the exuberance of the young diarist" seemed at odds with "what readers know of Montgomery's later life, a slant which gives this edition its remarkable savour." Material that had been left out of the corresponding volumes of *Selected Journals* were of especial interest: as Faye Hammill noted in *The Times Literary Supplement*, "Montgomery's repetitions reveal her obsessions." Commenting as well on the long silences in the second volume about the writing of *Anne of Green Gables* and the courtship of Ewan Macdonald, Hammill characterized the journal as "much less a record of daily experience than a record of moods and thoughts," adding that "her continual return to the past produces a melancholic atmosphere, which is intensified by her repeated rereading of earlier volumes of her journal." For Emily Aoife Somers, writing in *Canadian Literature*, one of the delights of these volumes was not only the unabridged text but the reproduction of the "captions, images, cutouts, and other found materials" as part of the running text, rather than in clusters due to the technological limitations of the 1980s, "with a satisfyingly intimate effect that, I add cheekily, precludes the look and feel of Facebook."[50]

Given the speed at which academic journals tend to review books, it is still too soon to assess fully the critical reception of these two volumes of unabridged journals. But my sense is that readers' interest in the narrative voice of someone so complex and complicated as Montgomery does not wane after a single reading. Instead, as with her fiction, readers continue to enjoy reading both forward and backward, gaining new insights in the life, culture, and psyche of this favourite author with every encounter with the text in question.

## NOTES

1  S. Campbell, *Both Hands*, 388; M.L., review of *Anne of Green Gables*, 10.
2  Quoted in Wood, "The Cavendish Library," 471.
3  *The Atlantic Advocate*, review of *Anne of Green Gables*, 94.
4  This overview does not include Francis W.P. Bolger's *The Years Before "Anne"* (1974) and Elizabeth Rollins Epperly's *Imagining Anne: The Island Scrapbooks of L.M. Montgomery* (2008), both of which contain Montgomery's work or reproduce pages from her scrapbooks, nor does it provide coverage of numerous exhibits or websites featuring her photographs. For sources relating to these endeavours as well as reviews of

biographies and secondary sources, see the website of L.M. Montgomery Online at http://lmmonline.org.

5 *GGL*, front cover and dust jacket; Eggleston, "General Introduction," 1, 2; Montgomery to Weber, 2 May 1907, in *GGL*, 51.

6 Dumbrille, "Early Novelist's Letters," 21; Bourinot, "First Contribution to 'Belles Lettres,'" 5; Beharriell, review of *GGL*, 142.

7 Watters, "Letters from Avonlea," 87; Beharriell, review of *GGL*, 142; Pacey, review of *GGL*, 431, 429, 431; Robson, review of *GGL*, 422; Parr, review of *GGL*, 97.

8 Beharriell, review of *GGL*, 142; Bourinot, "First Contribution to 'Belles Lettres,'" 5.

9 *RY*, dust jacket; "Publisher's Foreword," n.pag.

10 See Sorfleet, "Introduction," 6; Wiggins, *L.M. Montgomery*, 54; Rubio and Waterston, *Writing a Life*, 115; Ferns, "Toronto," 298; Russell, Russell, and Wilmshurst, *Lucy Maud Montgomery*, 61; Gerson, "'Dragged at Anne's Chariot Wheels,'" 59.

11 I undertook this comparative work for my MA thesis, which also provides a more detailed summary of these archival documents relating to the publication of *The Road to Yesterday*. See Lefebvre, "Notes toward Editing," 461–68, 472–78.

12 Montagnes, "So Feeble," 33; Wyatt, "Disservice to Creator," 61; Woodcock, "Bittersweets for the Short Story Buffs," 94.

13 Ashby, review of *RY*, 19; Lewis, review of *RY*, 43; FitzPatrick, review of *RY*, 26; Sorfleet, "Introduction," 6; *Kirkus Reviews*, review of *RY*, 1112; *The Publishers' Weekly*, review of *RY*, 62.

14 Frazer, "Scarcely an End," 89, 92, 90, 91; Macdonald, review of *RY*, 784, 783, 784.

15 *AP*, dust jacket; Dawe, "Scrap from the Barrel," 30A; Martin, "L.M. Montgomery," G7; Morris, review of *AP*, 5; Israel, review of *AP*, 36; FitzPatrick, review of *AP*, 28.

16 *DSOS*, dust jacket; McLay, Introduction, 9, 12, 25.

17 Smith, "New Tales for the Maud Squad," 22; Ward, "Green Fables," 37; Rubio, review of *DSOS*, 48.

18 Smith, "New Tales for the Maud Squad," 22; Rubio, review of *DSOS*, 49, 48–49; Ward, "Green Fables," 37.

19 *MDMM*, dust jacket; Bolger and Epperly, Introduction, vii, ix.

20 Whitaker, "Literary Pen-Pals," 143; Joyce-Jones, review of *MDMM*, 144; Whitaker, "Literary Pen-Pals," 142; Johnston, review of *MDMM*, 27; Joyce-Jones, review of *MDMM*, 145–46.

21 For more on this sale, see Rubio, "Why L.M. Montgomery's Journals."

22  Compton, "Lucy Maud's Letters."
23  Rubio, "'A Dusting Off,'" 52, 56.
24  *SJLMM*, 1: dust jacket; Rubio and Waterston, introduction to *SJLMM*, 1: xxiv.
25  Staines, "Diaries Reveal Shimmer," C2; Goodwin, "Lucy's Story," D1; Posesorski, "Shedding Light on the Creator," 22; Epperly, review of *SJLMM*, 1: 38; Keefer, review of *SJLMM*, 1 and 2: 88; Schiefer, "A Writer Even More Enchanting," A15; Powell, "The Ideals of a Lonely Little Girl," D21; Fulford, "Sad Soul Vainly Seeking Tenderness," M5.
26  Thompson, "Role-Maker," 205, 206, 205; Holland, review of *SJLMM*, 1: 668; Schiefer, "A Writer Even More Enchanting," A15; Bumsted, "Who's Afraid of Lucy Maud Montgomery?" 1.
27  Keefer, review of *SJLMM*, 1 and 2: 83, 84; Howells, "LMM," 79–80; Conrad, review of *SJLMM*, 1: 437; Thompson, "Role-Maker," 206; Bumsted, "Who's Afraid of Lucy Maud Montgomery?" 1.
28  Gerson, "Seven Milestones," 28; Rubio, "'A Dusting Off,'" 61, 62, 66–67.
29  *SJLMM*, 2: dust jacket; Rubio and Waterston, introduction to *SJLMM*, 2: x–xi; *SJLMM*, 3: dust jacket; Rubio and Waterston, introduction to *SJLMM*, 3: xii.
30  Bliss, "The Travails of the Creative Spirit," 85; Epperly, review of *SJLMM*, 2: 38; Bumsted, "Maud Montgomery's Finest Character Creation," 10; Bumsted, review of *SJLMM*, 3: 38; Grauer, review of *SJLMM*, 3: 218.
31  Epperly, review of *SJLMM*, 2: 38; Powell, "Unhappy Times," C15; Boone, "Montgomery," 164; Avery, review of *SJLMM*, 2: 61; Howells, "Pluralisms," 87; York, "Darkness and Ecstasy," 72; Bumsted, "Maud Montgomery's Finest Character Creation," 10; Howells, "Pluralisms," 83, 86–87.
32  Bumstad, review of *SJLMM*, 3: 37; Bliss, "The Travails of the Creative Spirit," 86; Abley, "Author's Life Was Far Cry," J1; Bliss, "The Travails of the Creative Spirit," 85, 86; Grauer, review of *SJLMM*, 3: 217, 219–20.
33  Bliss, "The Travails of the Creative Spirit," 85.
34  Montgomery, *The Poetry of Lucy Maud Montgomery*, dust jacket.
35  Groening, "The Poetry of Lucy Maud Montgomery," 7; Manion, "The Two Faces of 'Anne,'" J9; Whitaker, "Women Alone," 228; Groening, "The Poetry of Lucy Maud Montgomery," 7.
36  Montgomery, *Akin to Anne*, dust jacket; Wilmshurst, Introduction, 7.
37  MacLean, review of *Akin to Anne*, 44, 45; McKellar, "Dreams Come True," M8; Porter, "An Abundance of Happy Endings," C17; Manion, "L.M. Montgomery Had Orphans," K9; Epperly, "Love Story," 165, 166.

38  Nowlan, review of *Along the Shore*, 61; Powell, "Before Anne's Pigtails,"
    C17; Frey, "Ambition," 156; Rogers, "Women of Substance," D18; de
    Niverville, "The Other Side of Lucy Maud Montgomery," 14; Jenkinson,
    review of *Among the Shadows*, 226.

39  Abercrombie, "Montgomery Collection a Real Tonic," D6; M. Campbell,
    "Against the Odds," 62, 63; Thatcher, "Lucy Maud's Altar Ego,"
    I4; Epperly, review of *At the Altar*, 243, 244–45; Bryce, "The Subtle
    Subversions of L.M. Montgomery," 79.

40  Kelley, review of *The Way to Slumbertown*, 43, 44.

41  York, "Dark Days," 87, 88; Rubio and Waterston, introduction to *SJLMM*,
    4: xii; Rubio and Waterston, introduction to *SJLMM*, 5: xvi; Robinson,
    "Tragedy of Everyday Life," 146, 145; Gatenby, "From the Crow's Nest,"
    30.

42  Shields, "Loving Lucy," D18; Thomas, "A Self-Portrait of Anne's Author,"
    11, 12; Devereux, "The Continuing Story," 180.

43  *SJLMM*, 5: dust jacket; Doody, "Lucy Maud Arrives in Hell," D7, D6.

44  Thomas, "Completing the Journals of L.M. Montgomery," 18; Gammel,
    review of *SJLMM*, 5: 326; H. Murray, review of *SJLMM*, 5: 143–44.

45  See H.F. Tiessen and P.G. Tiessen, "Lucy Maud Montgomery's Ephraim
    Weber"; P. Tiessen and H.F. Tiessen, "Epistolary Performance"; H.F.
    Tiessen and P.G. Tiessen, Introduction, 4, 5.

46  Pike, "Who Do We Think You Are?" 116; Lefebvre, "The Performance
    Anxiety of L.M. Montgomery," 190, 191; Gammel, review of *AfGG*, 330.

47  Butler, "The Heartbreaking Truth about Anne's Creator"; Lefebvre,
    Afterword, 512–13; *BQ*, dust jacket; Renzetti, "A Different Shirley
    and Gilbert," R12. I have not been able to verify the statement made in
    Montgomery's *Globe and Mail* obituary about the submission of *The
    Blythes Are Quoted* on the day of her death, although I do note that
    copies of the final of three extant typescripts eventually turned up in the
    McClelland and Stewart archives at McMaster University.

48  Golfman, "Bleak Island," 25; van Herk, "Blythe Spirits," F12; Clare,
    review of *BQ*, 23.

49  Lefebvre, "Lucy Maud of Macneill Farm," R16.

50  Schiefer, "Journals Bursting with Life," F2; Hammill, "Something Wild and
    Sweet," 21; Somers, "A Diary's Promise," 183–84.

# Sources

The items included in this volume were originally published as follows:

Reviews of *Anne of Green Gables*, by L.M. Montgomery:
"A Heroine from an Asylum," *The New York Times Saturday Review* (New York, NY), 18 July 1908, 404.

"[Will Appeal to Every Reader]," *The Montreal Daily Herald* (Montreal, QC), 21 July 1908, 4.

"[An Imaginative, Eager Child]," *The Sun* (New York, NY), 25 July 1908, 5.

"[A Pathetic Little Tale]," *Saint John Globe* (Saint John, NB), 8 August 1908, 10.

"[Picture of Prince Edward Island Life and Character]," *The Gazette* (Montreal, QC), 14 August 1908, 8.

"[A Pleasant Book of the Hour]," *The Boston Journal* (Boston, MA), 15 August 1908, 9.

"[A Story So Pure and Sweet]," *The Globe* (Toronto, ON), 15 August 1908, Saturday Magazine Section, 5.

"[A Girl to Remember]," *The Living Age* (New York, NY), 15 August 1908, 446.

"[An 'Ugly Duckling' Story, After All]," *The Plain Dealer* (Cleveland, OH), 13 September 1908, Editorial and Dramatic Section, 3.

"*Anne of Green Gables* Is a Story for Girls," *The Evening News* (San Jose, CA), 8 October 1908, 3.

"[An Engaging Bit of Juvenilia]," *The New York Tribune* (New York, NY), 31 October 1908, 8.

"[Lively Story of an Orphan Girl]," *ALA Booklist* (Chicago, IL), November 1908, 274.

"[A Winner of Hearts]," *The Book News Monthly* (Philadelphia, PA), November 1908, 200–1. Also in *Fort Worth Telegram* (Fort Worth, TX), 29 November 1908, Section 3, 8.

"[A Charming Character Study]," *The Canadian Magazine* (Toronto, ON), November 1908, 87–89.

"[Fresh Tale of Country Life]," *Colorado Springs Gazette* (Colorado Springs, CO), 28 November 1908, 9.

"[Arcadian Purity and Simplicity]," *The National Magazine* (Boston, MA), December 1908, Books o' the Month Section, n.pag.

"[A Delightful Book]," *The New York Observer* (New York, NY), 3 December 1908, 736.

"[A Canadian Tale of Domestic Sentiment]," *The Times Literary Supplement* (London, UK), 21 January 1909, 27.

"[An Irrepressible Idealist and Optimist]," *Vogue* (New York, NY), 4 March 1909, 382.

"[An Alternative Entertainment]," *The Spectator* (London, UK), 13 March 1909, 426–27.

"[Straight to the Heart]," *Home Needlework Magazine* (Florence, MA), April 1909, 166.

"[Lifelike – Never]," *The Bookman* (London, UK), May 1909, 97.


Reviews of *Anne of Avonlea*, by L.M. Montgomery:

"[The Next Few Years of Anne's Life]," *The Nation* (New York, NY), 2 September 1909, 212.

"[A Pretty Story Prettily Told]," *The Boston Globe* (Boston, MA), 4 September 1909, 7.

"[Anne of the Bronze Tresses]," *The Evening Star* (Washington, DC), 18 September 1909, Part 3, 6.

"[A Prose Lyric of Rural Life]," *The Globe* (Toronto, ON), 18 September 1909, 14.

"[Quiet Days in a Country Village]," by Florence Bosard Lawrence, *Los Angeles Sunday Herald* (Los Angeles, CA), 19 September 1909, Junior Section, 5, 7.

"[Radiating Sunshine]," signed Anne, *The Lethbridge Daily Herald* (Lethbridge, AB), 25 September 1909, 7.

"['Let Well Enough Alone']," *The San Francisco Call* (San Francisco, CA), 26 September 1909, 7.

"[Not Quite as Bewitching]," by Margaret Merwin, *The Bookman* (New York, NY), October 1909, 152.

"[A Little More Sentimental]," *The Outlook* (New York, NY), 2 October 1909, 276.

"The Reappearance of Anne," *The Boston Herald* (Boston, MA), 9 October 1909, 8.

"[Studies in Canadian Village Life]," *The Scotsman* (Edinburgh, UK), 21 October 1909, 2.

"[An Ideal Heroine]," *The Bookman* (London, UK), November 1909, 102–3.

"[Sympathetic Prose Epic]," *Vogue* (New York, NY), 6 November 1909, 777.

"[A Pleasing Chapter in Canadian Fiction]," by Jean Graham, *The Canadian Courier* (Toronto, ON), 27 November 1909, 13.

"[A Separate Entity]," *The Canadian Magazine* (Toronto, ON), December 1909, 199.

"[An Exceedingly Pretty Story of Young Girlhood]," *The Living Age* (New York, NY), 11 December 1909, 702.

"Anne Grows Up," *The Salt Lake Tribune* (Salt Lake City, UT), 12 December 1909, 36.

"[A Somewhat Commonplace Story]," *The Independent* (New York, NY), 16 December 1909, 1355.

"[Commonplace, If Pretty]," signed Hal, *Saturday Night* (Toronto, ON), 1 January 1910, 15.


Reviews of *Kilmeny of the Orchard*, by L.M. Montgomery:

"[Perpetual Fitness for Romance]," *The Nation* (New York, NY), 9 June 1910, 587.

"[A Vision of Springtime]," *The Times–Dispatch* (Richmond, VA), 13 June 1910, 7.

"[An Idyll of Prince Edward Island]," *Saturday Night* (Toronto, ON), 18 June 1910, 7.

"[Some Delightful People]," *The Washington Herald* (Washington, DC), 23 June 1910, 6.

"[Happy in Setting and Plot]," *The Times Literary Supplement* (London, UK), 7 July 1910, 243.

"[Romantic as It Should Be]," *The Living Age* (New York, NY), 9 July 1910, 126–27.

"[Not So Good, but Good Enough]," *The Bookman* (London, UK), August 1910, 223.

"[The Charm of Naive Innocence]," *Vogue* (New York, NY), 15 August 1910, 43.

"[Wholesome as Bread and Milk]," *The Independent* (New York, NY), 18 August 1910, 362–63.

"[More for Sentimentalists Than Realists]," *The English Review* (London, UK), September 1910, 372–73.

Reviews of *The Story Girl*, by L.M. Montgomery:
"[Attractive Children]," *The Sun* (New York, NY), 3 June 1911, 7.

"[An Intuitive Knowledge of Child Nature]," *The Bookseller, Newsdealer and Stationer* (New York, NY), 15 June 1911, 465.

"[Romance, Vitality, and Barbarian Instinct]," *The Boston Herald* (Boston, MA), 17 June 1911, 4.

"[A Remarkably Vivid Little Personality]," *The Scotsman* (Edinburgh, UK), 29 June 1911, 2; also in SR, 17.

"[The Far, Fair Land of Youth]," *Chicago Record–Herald* (Chicago, IL), undated clipping (June 1911), in SR, 5.

"[A Magnetic Personality]," *Pittsburgh Chronicle Telegraph* (Pittsburgh, PA), undated clipping (June 1911), in SR, 5.

"[The Tender Sweetness of Childhood]," *The Globe* (Toronto, ON), 8 July 1911, 16; also in SR, 12.

"[A Far-Off Golden Age]," *The Christian Advocate* (New York, NY), 13 July 1911, 945.

"Charming Children," *The Register* (Adelaide, Australia), 15 July 1911, 4.

"Arcadia," *The Young Woman* (London, UK), August 1911, in SR, 29–30.

"[A Group of Merry Children]," *The Nation* (New York, NY), 10 August 1911, 122.

"Childhood Days," *The Springfield Union* (Springfield, MA), 20 August 1911, C5; also in SR, 14–15.

"'The Story Girl,' by the Creator of Kilmeny," *The Feilding Star* (Feilding, New Zealand), 2 September 1911, Supplement, 6.

"[Capital Reading]," *The Outlook* (New York, NY), 2 September 1911, 46–47; also in SR, 16.

"[A Far More Finished and Subtle Art]," *The Montreal Daily Star* (Montreal, QC), undated clipping (September 1911), in SR, 9.

"[The Essence of Girlhood and Boyhood]," *Westminster Gazette* (London, UK), undated clipping (September 1911), in SR, 8.

"[A Story of Children for Grown-Ups]," *The Catholic World* (New York, NY), October 1911, 116.

"[Simple Realism]," *Vogue* (New York, NY), 15 October 1911, 102.

"[An Entertainment for the Young]," *The Canadian Magazine* (Toronto, ON), November 1911, 92; also in SR, 5.

"[Simple Life in a Fascinating Land]," *The Christian Work and the Evangelist* (New York, NY), 11 November 1911, 636; also in SR, 3.

"[The Gift of Telling a Story]," *The Dallas Morning News* (Dallas, TX), 11 December 1911, 5; also in SR, 3.

"[Vivid and Real Children]," *The Lexington Herald* (Lexington, KY), 24 December 1911, 2; also in SR, 2.

"[A Dangerous Rival for Anne]," *The Republic* (Boston, MA), undated clipping (1911), in SR, 13.

"[An Irresistible Appeal]," *Southport Guardian* (Southport, UK), undated clipping (1911), in SR, 15.

"[A Story of Simple Sweetness]," *Simmons Magazine* (New York, NY), undated clipping, in SR, 6–7.

Reviews of *Chronicles of Avonlea*, by L.M. Montgomery:

"Book of Smiles and Tears," *The Boston Globe* (Boston, MA), 8 June 1912, 11.

"Down East Idyls," *The Boston Herald* (Boston, MA), 8 June 1912, 4; also in SR, 37.

"[An Intrinsic Worth of Their Own]," *Saint John Globe* (Saint John, NB), 22 June 1912, 9; also in SR, 35.

"[Gently Sentimental and Enjoyably Humorous]," *The Outlook* (New York, NY), 29 June 1912, 500.

"[Chronicles of Perfect Characters]," *The Lexington Herald* (Lexington, KY), 30 June 1912, 3.

"Re-enter Anne of Avonlea," *The San Francisco Call* (San Francisco, CA), 7 July 1912, Book Page; also in SR, 33.

"[Middle-Aged Love Stories of Unusual Type]," *Boston Evening Transcript* (Boston, MA), 17 July 1912, 18; also in SR, 34.

"[Each Tale a Gem]," *The Brooklyn Daily Eagle* (Brooklyn, NY), 20 July 1912, 5; also in SR, 33.

"[Romances of Middle Age]," *The Nation* (New York, NY), 22 August 1912, 171.

"[Happy Sentiment]," *Newport Daily News* (Newport, RI), 28 August 1912, 3.

"[Miss Montgomery's Best Work]," *The Canadian Magazine* (Toronto, ON), September 1912, 483–84; also in SR, 41–42.

"[Thoroughly Delightful Sketches]," *The Globe* (Toronto, ON), 7 September 1912, 18; also in SR, 42.

"Charming Stories," *The Register* (Adelaide, Australia), 21 September 1912, 4.

"[Clean, Sparkling Humor]," *The Catholic World* (New York, NY), October 1912, 103; also in SR, 40.

"[Leisurely Love-Making]," *The Scotsman* (Edinburgh, UK), 31 October 1912, 2.

"[Engaging 'Heart-Interest Stories']," *The Times Literary Supplement* (London, UK), 31 October 1912, 482.

"[A Little Disappointed]," *The Bookman* (London, UK), Christmas Supplement 1912, 148.

"[Delightful Summer Reading]," *The Boston Watchman* (Boston, MA), undated clipping (1912), in SR, 43.

"[Chronicles of Autumn Flowers]," *The Republic* (Boston, MA), undated clipping (1912), in SR, 45.

"[Stories of Real People]," *The Rochester Herald* (Rochester, NY), undated clipping (1912), in SR, 44.

"[Full of a True Human Nature]," *The Toronto News* (Toronto, ON), undated clipping (1912), in SR, 34.

"[The Concealment of Art]," *The Toronto World* (Toronto, ON), undated clipping (1912), in SR, 42–43.

"[Aroma of New England]," *Trenton Times–Advertiser* (Trenton, NJ), 23 February 1913, Part 3, 2.

"[The Simple Life of Homely People]," *Eastern Western Review* (Boston, MA), undated clipping (April 1913), in SR, 60.

"[Whether or Not an Anne Book]," *The Independent* (New York, NY), 10 July 1913, 100.

"[Plain Everyday Folk]," *Kansas City Post* (Kansas City, KS), undated clipping, in SR, 44.

"[Harmless and Easy Reading]," *The Louisville Post* (Louisville, KY), undated clipping, in SR, 32.


Reviews of *The Golden Road*, by L.M. Montgomery:

"[The Power to Charm]," *The Bookseller, Newsdealer and Stationer* (New York, NY), 15 September 1913, 264–65.

"[Merry, Bright Young People]," *Boston Evening Transcript* (Boston, MA), 20 September 1913, Part 3, 8; also in SR, 56.

"[An Arcadian Byway]," signed M.G.H., *The Globe* (Toronto, ON), 4 October 1913, 16; also in SR, 52–53.

"[A Wholesome, Out-of-Door Atmosphere]," by Doris Webb, *The Publishers' Weekly* (New York, NY), 18 October 1913, 1330–31.

Sources

"[Entertaining Family Chronicles]," *The Boston Herald* (Boston, MA), 25 October 1913, 6; also in SR, 54.

"[More or Less Delightful]," *The Book News Monthly* (Philadelphia, PA), November 1913, in SR, 63.

"[Excessively Commonplace Young People]," signed J.D.K., *The Mail and Empire* (Toronto, ON), 15 November 1913, 24; also in SR, 53.

"[Intelligent and Resourceful Children]," *Philadelphia Press* (Philadelphia, PA), 15 November 1913, in SR, 59.

"[A Genius for Understanding Youth]," excerpted from "Canadian Genius in Poetry, Humour and Fiction," by Marjory MacMurchy, *The Canadian Courier* (Toronto, ON), 29 November 1913, 12.

"[Chronicles of a Group]," *Grand Rapids Press* (Grand Rapids, MI), 5 December 1913, 19.

"Childhood Days," *The Los Angeles Times* (Los Angeles, CA), 7 December 1913, Part 6, 7; also in SR, 62.

"Youthful Memories," *The Register* (Adelaide, Australia), 10 January 1914, 4.

"[Bog of Shoddy Sentiment]," *Saturday Night* (Toronto, ON), 14 February 1914, 24–25; also in SR, 62.

"[A Merry Party of Young Folks]," *The Scotsman* (Edinburgh, UK), 26 February 1914, 2.

"[Transatlantic Young People]," *The Times Literary Supplement* (London, UK), 26 February 1914, 107.

"[The Simple Life of American Country Children]," *The Glasgow Herald* (Glasgow, UK), 13 March 1914, 13.

"[A Certain Homely Appeal]," *The Bookman* (London, UK), Spring 1914, 7–8.

"[Apt to Wear Thin]," *London Post* (London, UK), 13 April 1914, in SR, 65.

"[Transatlantic Farm Life]," *The Globe* (London, UK), 8 May 1914, in SR, 63.

"[At Times Wearisome]," *The Montreal Daily Star* (Montreal, QC), undated clipping, in SR, 57.

"[More of a 'Juvenile']," signed F., *The Toronto World* (Toronto, ON), undated clipping, in SR, 55.

Reviews of *Anne of the Island*, by L.M. Montgomery:

"A Trilogy Completed," *The Montreal Daily Herald* (Montreal, QC), 31 July 1915, in SR, 72.

"[Busy with Affairs of the Heart]," *The Sun* (New York, NY), 31 July 1915, 5.

"The New Page Book," *The Waterbury American* (Waterbury, CT), 4 August 1915, in SR, 73.

"[Ever Charming, Ever Heartsome]," *Pittsburgh Leader* (Pittsburgh, PA), 6 August 1915, in SR, 73.

"[The Same Old Anne]," *Boston Evening Transcript* (Boston, MA), 7 August 1915, 8; also in SR, 74.

"[Possibly the Last, Possibly the Best]," *Wilmington Every Evening* (Wilmington, DE), 7 August 1915, in SR, 73.

"[A Fluctuating Participant in Romance]," *The Springfield Republican* (Springfield, MA), 8 August 1915, 15; also in SR, 73.

"The Third Book of Anne," *The New York World* (New York, NY), 12 August 1915, in SR, 75. Also in *The Idaho Daily Statesman* (Boise, ID), 24 August 1915, 4.

"[A Perfunctory Fumbling with Obstacles]," excerpted from a joint review of *Anne of the Island* and of *Michael O'Halloran*, by Gene Stratton-Porter, *The Nation* (New York, NY), 26 August 1915, 263.

"More about Anne," *The Mail and Empire* (Toronto, ON), 28 August 1915, in SR, 80.

"[Presumably the Last]," *The Duluth News Tribune* (Duluth, MN), 5 September 1915, Section 3, 5.

"[Good Times at College]," *The Bookseller, Newsdealer and Stationer* (New York, NY), 15 September 1915, 325.

"[A Story of Young Life]," by Rebecca D. Moore, *The Publishers' Weekly* (New York, NY), 18 September 1915, 790; also in SR, 79.

"[A Sunny Young Woman]," *ALA Booklist* (Chicago, IL), October 1915, 35.

"[Anne Goes to College]," *Wisconsin Library Bulletin* (Madison, WI), October 1915, 298.

"'Anne of Green Gables' in a New Role," *Boston Advertiser* (Boston, MA), 2 October 1915, in SR, 86.

"[Plenty to Entertain]," *The New York Herald* (New York, NY), 4 October 1915, in SR, 77.

"[Sentiment and Fun]," *The Living Age* (New York, NY), 16 October 1915, 192.

"[The Simple but Sentimental Chronicle Continued]," *The Times Literary Supplement* (London, UK), 4 November 1915, 395.

"[Slips between the Cup and the Lip]," *The Scotsman* (Edinburgh, UK), 11 November 1915, 2; also in SR, 85.

"Irresistible Heroine of Green Gables and Avonlea," *North American* (Philadelphia, PA), 13 November 1915, in SR, 82–83.

"Anne Engaged," *The Daily Graphic* (London, UK), 17 November 1915, in SR, 76.

"[Anne's College Life and Engagement]," *The Spectator* (London, UK), 4 December 1915, 796.

"[Completed Trilogy]," *The Bookman* (London, UK), Christmas Book Supplement 1915, 82.

Reviews of *The Watchman and Other Poems*, by L.M. Montgomery:
"[A Volume Full of Charming Things]," *The Globe* (Toronto, ON), 22 November 1916, 6.

"[The Fancies of a Young Heart]," *The Toronto World* (Toronto, ON), 28 November 1916, 3.

"Canadian Verse," *The Christian Guardian* (Toronto, ON), 6 December 1916, 13; also in SR, 87.

"[This Gifted Canadian Writer]," *The Canadian Magazine* (Toronto, ON), January 1917, 293; also in SR, 93–94.

"Poems by Author of 'Anne of Green Gables,'" *The Family Herald and Weekly Star* (Montreal, QC), 31 January 1917, 3; also in SR, 90.

"[Breezy and Inspiriting Book of Poems]," *The Scotsman* (Edinburgh), 13 May 1920, 2; also in SR, 173.

Reviews of *Anne's House of Dreams*, by L.M. Montgomery:
"[Charm and Action]," *Saint John Globe* (Saint John, NB), 18 August 1917, 9.

"[A Love-Nook in the Hearts of Innumerable Readers]," by John W. Garvin, *The Globe* (Toronto, ON), 24 August 1917, 4; also in SR, 129.

"[Happenings and Vistas]," *The New York Times Book Review* (New York, NY), 26 August 1917, 318; also in SR, 115.

"Anne Shirley," *The Oakland Tribune* (Oakland, CA), 2 September 1917, 18.

"[All the Elements of 'Sixteen-ness']," by Carmelite Janvier, *The Times–Picayune* (New Orleans, LA), 2 September 1917, C4.

"Anne the Matron," *The New York Tribune* (New York, NY), 8 September 1917, 5; also in SR, 112.

"[The Puzzling Business of Being Married]," *The Evening Star* (Washington, DC), 16 September 1917, Part 4, 2; also in SR, 108.

"A Scotch-Canadian Village," *The Evening Post* (New York, NY), 22 September 1917, in SR, 109.

"A New Anne Book," *The Montreal Daily Herald* (Montreal, QC), 24 September 1917, in SR, 120.

# Sources

"[More or Less Exciting Events]," *The Hartford Courant* (Hartford, CT), 26 September 1917, 8; also in SR, 108.

"[Hard on the Shut-Outs]," *Life* (New York, NY), 27 September 1917, 514; also in SR, 107.

"[A Gem of a Love Story]," *Portland Express–Advertiser* (Portland, ME), 29 September 1917, in SR, 103.

"[Outside and Inside]," *Troy Record* (Troy, NY), 3 October 1917, in SR, 105.

"An Old Friend Again," *The Hartford Times* (Hartford, CT), 20 October 1917, in SR, 101.

"[A Simple and Pleasant Story]," *Everywoman's World* (Toronto, ON), November 1917, 53.

"[A Splendid Sequel]," *The Canadian Churchman* (Toronto, ON), 1 November 1917, 698; also in SR, 103.

"Anne of Green Gables in Her New House of Dreams," *North American* (Philadelphia, PA), 10 November 1917, in SR, 99.

"[Meeting with Real People]," *The Bookseller, Newsdealer and Stationer* (New York, NY), 15 November 1917, 696; also in SR, 97.

"With Many a Sparkle," *Chicago Continent* (Chicago, IL), 15 November 1917, in SR, 102 and 127.

"[Mr. Montgomery's New Book]," *Minneapolis Bellman* (Minneapolis, MN), 17 November 1917, in SR, 98.

"Montgomery Book Is Good Reading," *Spokane Chronicle* (Spokane, WA), 8 December 1917, in SR, 95.

"[Delightful and Womanly Novel]," *The Scotsman* (Edinburgh, UK), 7 March 1918, 2; also in SR, 124.

"[Fresh, Charming, but Sentimental Anne]," *The Times Literary Supplement* (London, UK), 7 March 1918, 118.

"An Island Heroine," *The Globe* (London, UK), 9 March 1918, in SR, 125.

"[The Story of Anne's Happy-Ever-After]," *Punch, or the London Charivari* (London, UK), 20 March 1918, 192.

"A Canadian Idyll," *The Saturday Review* (London, UK), 11 May 1918, 416; also in SR, 106.

Reviews of *Rainbow Valley*, by L.M. Montgomery:

"The Manse Children," by Christine McAllister, *The Publishers' Weekly* (New York, NY), 16 August 1919, 484–85; also in SR, 152.

"[A Story of Love and Life]," *The Philadelphia Inquirer* (Philadelphia, PA), 30 August 1919, 6.

Sources

"[Nothing Wild or Thrilling]," *The Chicago Daily Tribune* (Chicago, IL), 31 August 1919, Part 7, 7.

"Prince Edward Island Tale," *Trenton Times–Advertiser* (Trenton, NJ), 31 August 1919, Part 2, 3.

"[Another Story of Prince Edward Island]," by Constance Murray Greene, *The Sun* (New York, NY), 14 September 1919, Books and the Book World, 11.

"[More Distinctly a Novel]," *The Outlook* (New York, NY), 17 September 1919, 95.

"[A Homey Charm]," *The New York Times Book Review* (New York, NY), 21 September 1919, 484; also in SR, 160.

"[Clean and Healthy Country Life]," *Manitoba Free Press* (Winnipeg, MB), 25 September 1919, 13.

"Some Original Children," *The Post* (New York, NY), 27 September 1919, in SR, 154.

"Sure to Be Liked," *The New York Herald* (New York, NY), 28 September 1919, in SR, 154.

"[A Clever Woman Novelist]," excerpted from "Four Clever Women Novelists," review of *Rainbow Valley*, by L.M. Montgomery; *Mist of Morning*, by Isabel Ecclestone Mackay; *Janet of Kootenay*, by Evah McKowan; *Joan at Halfway*, by Grace McLeod Rogers, *The Canadian Bookman* (Ste. Anne de Bellevue, QC), October 1919, 59–60; also in SR, 161–62.

"[Between Sprightly and Pastoral]," *The Dial* (New York, NY), 4 October 1919, 324.

"[Human and Wholesome, with No Morbidity]," *The Post Express* (Rochester, NY), 11 October 1919, 17; also in SR, 166.

"Just Bubbling Over with Whimsical Humor," *The Boston Globe* (Boston, MA), 25 October 1919, 4; also in SR, 163.

"[An Infinite Charm All Its Own]," *The Oregonian* (Portland, OR), 26 October 1919, 9.

"Latest 'Anne of Green Gables' Story," *The Dallas Morning News* (Dallas, TX), 16 November 1919, Magazine Supplement, 6.

"[Back to the Old Ground]," *The Scotsman* (Edinburgh, UK), 25 May 1920, 6; also in SR, 168.

"[Still the Same Person]," *The Times Literary Supplement* (London, UK), 27 May 1920, 338; also in SR, 159.

"[Might Have Been Worse]," *The Outlook* (London, UK), 29 May 1920, in SR, 131.

"[The Relentless Logic of Childhood]," *The Glasgow Herald* (Glasgow, UK), 14 June 1920, 11; also in SR, 131.

"A Group of Children," *Glasgow News* (Glasgow, UK), 17 August 1920, in SR, 173.

"[A Story of Old World Days]," *The Times of India Illustrated Weekly* (Mumbai, India), 8 September 1920, in SR, 174.

"[An Absurd Review]," *The New Age* (London, UK), 18 November 1920, 35; also in SR, 173.

"[The Gift of Humour]," by Austin Bothwell, unidentified and undated clipping, in SR, 164–65.


Reviews of *Further Chronicles of Avonlea*, by L.M. Montgomery:

"In Avonlea," *The Boston Herald* (Boston, MA), 10 April 1920, 7.

"[Further Doings of Widely Popular People]," *The Bookseller, Newsdealer and Stationer* (New York), 15 April 1920, 388.

"More about Avonlea," *Evening Public Ledger* (Philadelphia, PA), 24 April 1920, 8; also in SR, 130.

"[Plain and Simple Lives]," *The Sunday Sentinel* (Milwaukee, WI), 23 May 1920, Music–Drama, Editorial, Motor News Section, 5; also in SR, 328.

"Chronicles of Avonlea," *The Evening Missourian* (Columbia, MO), 23 July 1920, 2.

"[Sentiment a Bit Thick]," *The Independent* (New York, NY), 13 November 1920, 247.

"Title of Book Warrants Interest," unidentified and undated clipping, in SR, 330.


Reviews of *Rilla of Ingleside*, by L.M. Montgomery:

"An Agreeable Romance," *Trenton Times–Advertiser* (Trenton, NJ), 4 September 1921, Part 1, 5.

"[A Captivating, Sunny Story]," *The New York Times Book Review and Magazine* (New York, NY), 11 September 1921, 23; also in SR, 179.

"An Island Heroine," *The New York Tribune* (New York, NY), 11 September 1921, Part 5, 9; also in SR, 182–83.

"[Perhaps Her Best Story]," *The Post Express* (Rochester, NY), 14 September 1921, 10; also in SR, 179.

"[No Unpleasant Details]," *Wisconsin Library Bulletin* (Madison, WI), October 1921, 157.

"[A Faithful and Worthy Picture]," *The Globe* (Toronto, ON), 1 October 1921, 19; also in SR, 183–84.

"[Not Too Much of the War]," *San Francisco Bulletin* (San Francisco, CA), 1 October 1921, in SR, 179.

# Sources

"By the Author of *Anne of Green Gables*," *The Family Herald and Weekly Star* (Montreal, QC), 5 October 1921, 17; also in SR, 184.

"[Wholesome Fiction for Young People]," *The Bookseller and Stationer* (New York, NY), 15 October 1921, 24.

"[Deserves to Be Successful]," *Boston Evening Transcript* (Boston, MA), 21 October 1921, in SR, 186.

"The Charming Daughter of Anne of Green Gables," by John Clair Minot, *The Boston Herald* (Boston, MA), 5 November 1921, 8.

"[Rilla and Her Destiny]," *The Publishers' Weekly* (New York, NY), 5 November 1921, 70.

"[May Be Read by Others Than Girls]," *Saturday Night* (Toronto, ON), 5 November 1921, 8–9; also in SR, 190.

"[Clean and Wholesome Romance]," *Fort Worth Star–Telegram* (Fort Worth, TX), 6 November 1921, 9.

"[An American Girl at Home in War Time]," *The Bookseller and Stationer* (New York, NY), 15 November 1921, 56.

"Now Anne's Daughter Rilla," by Fanny Butcher, *The Chicago Daily Tribune* (Chicago, IL), 20 November 1921, G1; also in SR, 187.

"[A Canadian Girl in Love]," excerpted from "Our Woman Novelists Are Busy," review of *Rilla of Ingleside*, by L.M. Montgomery; *Little Miss Melody*, by Marian Keith; *Miriam of Queen's*, by Lilian Vaux MacKinnon, *The Canadian Bookman* (Gardenvale, QC), December 1921, 20; also in SR, 192.

"[Perhaps the Best Yet]," *Farmers' Magazine* (Toronto, ON), 1 December 1921, 28.

"[Useful to Historians]," *Manitoba Free Press* (Winnipeg, MB), 3 December 1921, Christmas Books Section, 2; also in SR, 194.

"[Domestic Canada during the War]," *The Scotsman* (Edinburgh, UK), 3 December 1921, 13; also in SR, 197.

"[A Wondrous Amount of Sentiment]," *Western Mail* (Perth, Australia), 15 December 1921, 39.

"[Quite Convincingly Idyllic]," *Punch, or the London Charivari* (London, UK), 21 December 1921, 499; also in SR, 196.

"[A Lesson for Every Family]," signed F.W.T., *The Idaho Daily Statesman* (Boise, ID), 27 December 1921, 6.

"[A Distinction of an Outstanding Kind]," *Sunday School Chronicle* (London, UK), 29 December 1921, in SR, 185.

"[Rilla the Empire-Builder]," *The Queenslander* (Brisbane, Australia), 14 January 1922, 3.

Sources

Reviews of *Emily of New Moon*, by L.M. Montgomery:

"A Child Poet Well Presented," by Ruth M. Sponberg, *The Chicago Evening Post Literary Review* (Chicago, IL), 7 September 1923, 8; also in SR, 209.

"[The Early Life of a Very Precocious Child]," *The Times Literary Supplement* (London, UK), 13 September 1923, 605; also in SR, 224.

"[The Dreamland Child]," *Edinburgh Evening News* (Edinburgh, UK), 15 September 1923, in SR, 344.

"[A Few Years in the Life of a Little Girl]," *The Globe* (Toronto, ON), 15 September 1923, 21; also in SR, 208.

"[The Eternal Child]," *The Guardian* (London, UK), 27 September 1923, in SR, 218.

"[True as Far as It Goes]," excerpted from "A Sheaf of Canadiana," by Raymond Knister, review of *Emily of New Moon*, by L.M. Montgomery; *Stories of the Land of Evangeline*, by Grace McLeod Rodgers; *The Master Breed*, by Francis Dickie; *The Rosary of Pan*, by A.M. Stephen, *The Canadian Bookman* (Toronto, ON), October 1923, 264.

"[A Type of Colonial Life That Fascinates]," *The Scotsman* (Edinburgh, UK), 4 October 1923, 2.

"[Sweet without Being Sugary]," *Punch, or the London Charivari* (London, UK), 21 November 1923, 504.

"[Humor and Tenderness]," *Manitoba Free Press* (Winnipeg, MB), 8 December 1923, Christmas Book Supplement, 1.

"[An Imaginative, Intelligent Child]," by Henry Walker, *The New York Herald* (New York, NY), undated clipping, in SR, 214.

"[Sweet with No Derogatory Implication]," by Isabel Paterson, *The New York Tribune* (New York, NY), undated clipping, in SR, 220.


Reviews of *Emily Climbs*, by L.M. Montgomery:

"[Emily of High School Age]," *The Davenport Democrat and Leader* (Davenport, IA), 6 September 1925, 20.

"[No Less Captivating],". *The Advertiser–Journal* (Auburn, NY), 28 August 1925, in SR, 244.

"'Emily Climbs,' Is New Book," by Lillian Leveridge, *St. Catharines Standard* (St. Catharines, ON), 10 September 1925, in SR, 252. Also in unidentified clipping (Vancouver periodical), 13 September 1925, in SR, 246; also, unsigned, in unidentified clipping, in SR, 253.

"[The Power of Imagery]," *The Globe* (Toronto, ON), 12 September 1925, 21; also in SR, 243.

"By L.M. Montgomery," *The Gazette* (Montreal, QC), 19 September 1925, 14; also in SR, 247.

"[No Wavering of Interest]," *Boston Evening Transcript* (Boston, MA), 23 September 1925, in SR, 247.

"[A Worthy Successor to the Beloved Anne]," *The Montreal Daily Star* (Montreal, QC), 26 September 1925, 7.

"A Rosebud Garden of Girls," by Isabel Paterson, *The New York Herald Tribune Books* (New York, NY), 27 September 1925, 9; also in SR, 252–53.

"[Lack of Romance]," *The Hamilton Herald* (Hamilton, ON), 3 October 1925, in SR, 246.

"Successor to Anne," by Laura Hinkley, *The Chicago Evening Post Literary Review* (Chicago, IL), 6 November 1925, 7; also in SR, 254.

"Montgomery's Latest," *The Toronto Daily Star* (Toronto, ON), 7 November 1925, 7; also in SR, 248 and 251.

"[The Beauty in All Things]," *The New Outlook* (Toronto, ON), 11 November 1925, 15.

"Drawn on Old Lines," *Regina Post* (Regina, SK), 5 December 1925, in SR, 249.

"[The Fine Philosophy of Youth]," *The Scotsman* (Edinburgh, UK), 22 December 1925, 9.

"[Every Bit as Irresistible]," *The Bookman* (London, UK), January 1926, 234–35.

"[A Charming Delineation of Girlhood]," *The Queenslander* (Brisbane, Australia), 20 February 1926, 8.

"[Sentimental Stuff]," *Cape Times* (Cape Town, South Africa), 11 March 1926, in SR, 266.

"[Not a Modern Type of Girl]," *The Evening Post* (Wellington, New Zealand), 13 March 1926, 21.

"[A Kick out of Emily's Climbs]," *Manitoba Free Press* (Winnipeg, MB), 5 April 1926, 10; also in SR, 237.

"*Cacoethes Scribendi*," *The Englishman* (Calcutta, India), 17 May 1926, in SR, 265.


Reviews of *The Blue Castle*, by L.M. Montgomery:

"[The Mouse Becomes the Lion]," *The Argus* (Melbourne, Australia), 13 August 1926, in SR, 259.

"[Natural, although Unusual]," *The Auckland Star* (Auckland, New Zealand), 21 August 1926, 22.

"[Sentiment and Humour]," *The Australasian* (Melbourne, Australia), 21 August 1926, in SR, 259.

"[A Pleasant Tonic]," *The Brisbane Courier* (Brisbane, Australia), 21 August 1926, 18.

"Cinderella Meets a Man," *New Zealand Times* (Wellington, New Zealand), 28 August 1926, in SR, 259.

"One Year of Life," *The Register* (Adelaide, Australia), 11 September 1926, 4.

"Creator of 'Anne' Sees Muskoka," *The Globe* (Toronto, ON), 18 September 1926, 20; also in SR, 256–57 and 278.

"[Neither So Good nor So Bad]," *The Press* (Christchurch, New Zealand), 18 September 1926, in SR, 272.

"A Pleasant Tale," *The New York World* (New York, NY), 19 September 1926, 4M; also in SR, 239 and 256.

"[Exclusively for Feminine Readers]," by Burt M'Murtrie, *The Pittsburgh Press* (Pittsburgh, PA), 26 September 1926, Theatrical and Photoplay Section 6; also in SR, 255. An earlier version, unsigned, *The Saturday Review of Literature* (New York, NY), 18 September 1926, 122–23; also in SR, 239.

"[Cinderella in Small-Town America]," *The Times Literary Supplement* (London, UK), 30 September 1926, 657; also in SR, 259 and 266.

"[A Sort of Cinderella]," by T.D. Rimmer, *The Canadian Bookman* (Toronto, ON), October 1926, 307–8.

"L.M. Montgomery Writes First Novel for Adults," *The Mail and Empire* (Toronto, ON), 2 October 1926, 15; also in SR, 282.

"[A Dainty and Fragrant Concoction]," signed L.S., *Philadelphia World* (Philadelphia, PA), 5 October 1926, in SR, 256.

"[An Innocuous and Sentimental Tale]," *Cape Times* (Cape Town, South Africa), 14 October 1926, in SR, 259.

"A Dream Castle," *The Havana Post* (Havana, Cuba), 17 October 1926, in SR, 260.

"[Valancy's Revolt]," *The Scotsman* (Edinburgh, UK), 21 October 1926, 2.

"[Emerging from Her Dream-World]," *The Montreal Daily Star* (Montreal, QC), 23 October 1926, 23; also in SR, 266 and 269.

"[Essentially a Woman's Book]," by Faith Smithson, *The Canadian Churchman* (Toronto, ON), 4 November 1926, 733; also in SR, 271.

"[That Particular Quality of Naïve Zestfulness]," *Punch, or the London Charivari* (London, UK), 15 December 1926, 672; also in SR, 266.

Reviews of *Emily's Quest*, by L.M. Montgomery:

"Emily Now Grown Up," *Trenton Evening Times* (Trenton, NJ), 28 August 1927, 7.

"Pine Woods and Pigsties," by V.B. Rhodenizer, *The Canadian Bookman* (Toronto, ON), September 1927, 273.

"A Charming Emily Book," *The Gazette* (Montreal, QC), 3 September 1927, 6; also in SR, 291.

"[Pretty Sure to Be Acceptable]," *The Outlook* (New York, NY), 7 September 1927, 28.

"A Book for Girls," *The Evening Post* (Wellington, New Zealand), 17 September 1927, 21.

"[Begins to Wear Thin]," *The Times Literary Supplement* (London, UK), 6 October 1927, 696; also in SR, 292.

"[Bewildering and Unintelligible Emily]," *The Pioneer* (Allahabad, India), 9 October 1927, in SR, 288–89.

"[Her Best Tale of Prince Edward Island]," *Manitoba Free Press* (Winnipeg, MB), 13 October 1927, 15; also in SR, 294.

"By the Creator of 'Anne,'" *The Globe* (Toronto, ON), 22 October 1927, 25; also in SR, 289, 294, 295.

"More about Emily," *Saturday Night* (Toronto, ON), 22 October 1927, 11; also in SR, 290.

"Love and a Career," *Democrat and Chronicle* (Rochester, NY), 30 October 1927, in SR, 290.

"[Dancing Off into Matrimony]," *Punch, or the London Charivari* (London, UK), 23 November 1927, 587–88; also in SR, 293.

"[A Sense of Impatience]," *Natal Advertiser* (Durban, South Africa), 26 March 1928, in SR, 297.

Reviews of *Magic for Marigold*, by L.M. Montgomery:

"[Another Little Girl]," *The New York Telegram* (New York, NY), 29 September 1929, in SR, 331.

"In a Small World," *Nottingham Journal* (Nottingham, UK), 4 October 1929, in SR, 346.

"[Child Life Once More]," *The Northern Whig and Belfast Post* (Belfast, UK), 9 October 1929, in SR, 346.

"A Sensitive Girl," *London Daily News* (London, UK), 10 October 1929, in SR, 331.

"[Another Fascinating Tale]," *The Church of England Newspaper* (London, UK), 18 October 1929, in SR, 346.

"Make Believe," *The Globe* (Toronto, ON), 19 October 1929, 25; also in SR, 329, 332.

"Anne Reborn," signed R.H., *The Mail and Empire* (Toronto, ON), 19 October 1929, 25; also in SR, 334. Also, signed Robert Hazlemere, in *The Ottawa Citizen* (Ottawa, ON), 14 October 1929, in SR, 331.

"[Suffused with Whimsicality]," *The Montreal Daily Star* (Montreal, QC), 26 October 1929, 31; also in SR, 337 and 348.

"[The Mind of an Imaginative and Attractive Child]," *Punch, or the London Charivari* (London, UK), 6 November 1929, 532; also in SR, 334.

"[Lovable Qualities and Healthy Naughtiness]," *The Sunday Times* (Perth, Australia), 24 November 1929, 24.

"[A Glamour All Its Own]," by John W. Garvin, *The Canadian Bookman* (Toronto, ON), January 1930, 13.

"Character Growths," *Natal Mercury* (Durban, South Africa), 13 January 1930, in SR, 339.

"[Strange to Modern Girls]," *The Auckland Star* (Auckland, New Zealand), 25 January 1930, 2.

"[Simple Story, but Fine Character Drawing]," *The Pioneer* (Allahabad, India), 23 March 1930, in SR, 341.

Reviews of *A Tangled Web / Aunt Becky Began It*, by L.M. Montgomery:

"A Montgomery Novel," signed M.B. McC., *The Globe* (Toronto, ON), 10 October 1931, 8; also in SR, 359.

"L.M. Montgomery Writes Humoresque," *The Toronto Daily Star* (Toronto, ON), 24 October 1931, 4; also in SR, 360.

"Another Montgomery Book," *The Gazette* (Montreal, QC), 31 October 1931, 20; also in SR, 365.

"[A Capital Tale]," *The Church of England Newspaper* (London, UK), 4 December 1931, in SR, 362.

"United Families," *Punch, or the London Charivari* (London, UK), 9 December 1931, 644; also in SR, 366.

"[So Utterly Lacking in Kindliness]," by A.S. Marquis, *The Canadian Bookman* (Toronto, ON), January 1932, 8–9; also in SR, 396.

"[No Little Skill]," *The Times Literary Supplement* (London, UK), 14 January 1932, 30; also in SR, 362.

"[A Robust and Versatile Clan Saga]," *The Toronto Telegram* (Toronto, ON), 17 October 1931, 45; also in SR, 358.

Reviews of *Pat of Silver Bush*, by L.M. Montgomery:

"[An 'Old-Fashioned' Story]," *The Liverpool Daily Post* (Liverpool, UK), 19 August 1933, in SR, 354.

"[A Tale of Youth and Magic]," *The Canadian Bookman* (Toronto, ON), September 1933, 123; also in SR, 356.

"[Entertaining Little Tale]," signed G. Kr., *The Toronto Telegram* (Toronto, ON), 2 September 1933, 31; also in SR, 353.

"Another 'Anne' Romance," *The Gazette* (Montreal, QC), 16 September 1933, 13; also in SR, 351 and 355.

"Fascinating Native Characters Enliven Mrs. Montgomery's Novel," signed F.M.J., *The Globe* (Toronto, ON), 30 September 1933, 10; also in SR, 357.

"[A Full-Length Story of Contemporary Life]," *The New York Herald Tribune Books* (New York, NY), 1 October 1933, Section 7, 9; also in SR, 351.

"[The Magic and Joy of Real People]," *Boston Evening Transcript* (Boston, MA), 7 October 1933, Books Section, 2.

"A Sister to Anne," by Jean Graham, *Saturday Night* (Toronto, ON), 4 November 1933, 8; also in SR, 357.

"[Made to Order]," *The New Outlook* (Toronto, ON), 15 November 1933, 811.

"[Home and Canadian Girlhood]," *The Auckland Star* (Auckland, New Zealand), 18 November 1933, 2.

"A Child Life Picture," by H.M. Morden, *The Border Cities Star* (Windsor, ON), 4 December 1933, 4.

"[Idealistic Realism for the 'Teen' Age]," *The Sherbrooke Telegram* (Sherbrooke, QC), 7 December 1933, 5.

Reviews of *Courageous Women*, by L.M. Montgomery, Marian Keith, and Mabel Burns McKinley:

"[Vitality and Inspiration]," signed G.E.G., *The Canadian Churchman* (Toronto, ON), 29 November 1934, in SR, 456.

"[Portraits of Immortal Women]," *The Canadian Bookman* (Toronto, ON), December 1934, 168–69.

Reviews of *Mistress Pat: A Novel of Silver Bush*, by L.M. Montgomery:

"Pat, Charming Elf of Silver Bush, Becomes Despair of Matchmakers," signed F.M.N., *The Globe* (Toronto, ON), 28 September 1935, 6; also in SR, 437.

"[A Good Book]," *Quill and Quire* (Toronto, ON), October 1935, 27.

"[Handicapped by Previous Creations]," excerpted from "Canadian Books," by T.G. Marquis, review of *Clearing in the West*, by Nellie L. McClung; *Mistress Pat*; *My Pets*, by Marshall Saunders, *Saturday Night* (Toronto, ON), 12 October 1935, 8–9.

"[A Trifle Overdressed]," signed F.R.H., *The Guardian* (Charlottetown, PE), 19 October 1935, 8.

"Charming P.E.I. Story," *The Toronto Daily Star* (Toronto, ON), 2 November 1935, 3.

Sources

"[Readable and Entertaining Up to a Point]," excerpted from "Letters in Canada, 1935: Fiction (List III)," by E.K. Broadus, *University of Toronto Quarterly* 5, no. 3 (April 1936): 368–88.

Reviews of *Anne of Windy Poplars / Anne of Windy Willows*, by L.M. Montgomery:

"[Tribulations and Triumphs]," by Lisle Bell, *The New York Herald Tribune Books* (New York, NY), 9 August 1936, Section 7, 8.

"Anne-est Anne," *The Gazette* (Montreal, QC), 22 August 1936, 11.

"An Old Favourite Again," *The Sydney Morning Herald* (Sydney, Australia), 11 September 1936, 6.

"Real Canadian Humor," *The Toronto Daily Star* (Toronto, ON), 12 September 1936, 7.

"[Humorous and Sentimental Adventures]," *Winnipeg Free Press* (Winnipeg, MB), 10 October 1936, 18.

"[A Splendid Story]," *Women's Magazine* (UK), November 1936, in SR, loose pages.

"[More Good Deeds Than a Boy Scout]," excerpted from "Letters in Canada, 1936: Fiction (List IV)," by J.R. MacGillivray, *University of Toronto Quarterly* 6, no. 3 (April 1937): 347–68.

"More about 'Anne,'" by Roderick Kennedy, *The Family Herald and Weekly Star* (Montreal, QC), 5 May 1937, 38.

Reviews of *Jane of Lantern Hill*, by L.M. Montgomery:

"[A Generous Helping of Sentiment]," by Lisle Bell, *The New York Herald Tribune Books* (New York, NY), 8 August 1937, Section 10, 8.

"[The Hard Facts of Reality]," excerpted from "Blue Noses and Red Earth," by Roderick Kennedy, *The Family Herald and Weekly Star* (Montreal, QC), 13 October 1937, 39.

"Fine Woman's Story Has Toronto Setting," *The Toronto Daily Star* (Toronto, ON), 16 October 1937, 36.

"Canadian Girl," *Saturday Night* (Toronto, ON), 23 October 1937, 14.

"[Delightful Jane]," *The New Outlook* (Toronto, ON), 19 November 1937, 1064.

"That Ecstasy of Youth!" excerpted from a review of *Jane of Lantern Hill*; *Susannah of the Yukon*, by Muriel Denison; *Carmen of the Rancho*, by Frank H. Spearman; *The Bridge*, by Francis Stuart, *The Montreal Daily Star* (Montreal, QC), 20 November 1937, 17.

"[An Entirely New Character]," excerpted from the column "Analecta," signed Scrutator, *The Canadian Bookman* (Toronto, ON), December 1937, 11.

## Sources

"[Repeated Success]," *The Church of England Newspaper* (London, UK), 2 December 1937, in SR, loose pages.

Reviews of *Anne of Ingleside*, by L.M. Montgomery:
"[Anne and Her Offspring]," by Lisle Bell, *The New York Herald Tribune Books* (New York, NY), 30 July 1939, Section 9, 9.
"[Same Old Charm]," *The Times Literary Supplement* (London, UK), 12 August 1939, 477.
"[Always an Event]," *The Guardian* (Charlottetown, PE), 19 August 1939, 4.
"[Family Love in Its Perfection]," *The Buxton Advertiser* (Buxton, UK), 26 August 1939, in SR, loose pages.
"Anne's Children," *The Globe and Mail* (Toronto, ON), 26 August 1939, 27.
"[Mild Emotional Adventures]," *Winnipeg Free Press* (Winnipeg, MB), 2 September 1939, 6.
"[Another Charming Instalment]," *Sunday Times* (Johannesburg, South Africa), 10 September 1939, in SR, loose pages.
"[A Worthy Successor]," *Christian World* (London, UK), 28 September 1939, in SR, loose pages.
"[Confusing Genealogy]," excerpted from "Letters in Canada, 1939: Fiction," by J.R. MacGillivray, *University of Toronto Quarterly* 9, no. 3 (October 1939): 289–301.
"Canadian Idyll," by Laura Mason, *Saturday Night* (Toronto, ON), 11 November 1939, 8.
"[As Delightful as Ever]," *The Auckland Star* (Auckland, New Zealand), 18 November 1939, Colour Section, 3.
"[Mirrors in Which We See Ourselves]," signed J.E.W., *The Calgary Herald* (Calgary, AB), 10 February 1940, 26.

# Bibliography

Abercrombie, Nora. "Montgomery Collection a Real Tonic." Review of *Against the Odds: Tales of Achievement*, by L.M. Montgomery, edited by Rea Wilmshurst. *The Edmonton Journal* (Edmonton, AB), 31 July 1994, D6.

Abley, Mark. "Author's Life Was Far Cry from Sunny Green Gables." Review of *The Selected Journals of L.M. Montgomery*, Volume 3: *1921–1929*, edited by Mary Rubio and Elizabeth Waterston. *The Gazette* (Montreal, QC), 31 October 1992, J1.

"Agreement between L.M. Montgomery and Her Publisher, L.C. Page and Company." MG 30 D 342, v. 1, Library and Archives Canada.

*ALA Booklist* (Chicago, IL). Notice for *Anne of Windy Poplars*, by L.M. Montgomery. October 1936, 54.

———. Review of *Anne of Avonlea*, by L.M. Montgomery. December 1909, 134.

*The American Jewish Chronicle* (New York, NY). Review of *Anne's House of Dreams*, by L.M. Montgomery. 7 December 1917, 141.

*Ames Daily Tribune Times* (Ames, IA). "Library Notes." 13 February 1932, 3.

A.M.S. "Fiction's Most Lovable Child in Adulthood." Review of *Anne of Ingleside*, by L.M. Montgomery. *The Salt Lake Tribune* (Salt Lake City, UT), 3 September 1939, 6D.

Ashby, Adele. Review of *The Road to Yesterday*, by L.M. Montgomery. *Quill and Quire* (Toronto, ON), July 1974, 19.

*The Athenaeum* (London, UK). Ad for *Anne of Green Gables*, by L.M. Montgomery. 13 February 1909, 187.

———. "Autumn Announcements." October 1917, 535–40, 542, 544, 546.

———. "Literary Gossip." 16 January 1909, 76.

———. Notice for *Anne of Green Gables*, by L.M. Montgomery. 23 January 1909, 104.

———. "Ready Next Week." 21 February 1914, 285.

*The Atlantic Advocate* (Fredericton, NB). Review of *Anne of Green Gables* (de luxe edition), by L.M. Montgomery. August 1964, 94.

*The Auckland Star* (Auckland, New Zealand). Review of *Jane of Lantern Hill*, by L.M. Montgomery. 18 December 1937, Week-End Pictorial, 12.

Avery, Heather. Review of *The Selected Journals of L.M. Montgomery*, Volume 2: *1910–1921*, edited by Mary Rubio and Elizabeth Waterston. *Resources for Feminist Research / Documentation sur la recherche féministe* 18, no. 2 (June 1989): 60–61.

Beharriell, S. Ross. Review of *The Green Gables Letters from L.M. Montgomery to Ephraim Weber, 1905–1909*, edited by Wilfrid Eggleston. *The Canadian Forum* (Toronto, ON), September 1960, 142.

Bliss, Michael. "The Travails of the Creative Spirit." Review of *The Selected Journals of L.M. Montgomery*, Volume 3: *1921–1929*, edited by Mary Rubio and Elizabeth Waterston. *Canadian Children's Literature / Littérature canadienne pour la jeunesse* 72 (Winter 1993): 85–86.

Bolger, Francis W.P., and Elizabeth R. Epperly. Introduction to Montgomery, *My Dear Mr. M*, vii–x.

*The Bookman* (London, UK). Ad for Constable & Co. May 1918, ii.

———. "The Booksellers' Diary: List of Forthcoming Books, January 1 to February 1, 1909." January 1909, 166.

———. "Books of the Month: From September 15th to October 15th." November 1929, 154–56.

———. "A Selection of Newly Published Books from Sir Isaac Pitman & Sons' Spring List." April 1909, 21.

*The Bookman* (New York, NY). Ad for *Anne of Green Gables*, by L.M. Montgomery. August 1908, 757.

———. "The Book Mart." September 1908, 85–96; October 1908, 179–92; November 1908, 281–96; December 1908, 392–408; January 1909, 502–20; February 1909, 617–32; March 1909, 96–112; April 1909, 205–24; May 1909, 321–36; June 1909, 433–56; July 1909, 552–76; August 1909, 664–80.

———. "Chronicle and Comment." June 1909, 339–59.

———. "From Page's List." August 1910, 687; October 1910, 217; February 1911, 695; September 1913, inside front cover.

———. "The 'Irresistible' Anne of Green Gables." February 1909, 739.

———. "'Leaders' from L.C. Page & Company's Fall List." February 1910, 933.

———. "New Books of Importance: From Page's List." October 1913, 94.

———. "New Stokes Books Well Worth Reading." October 1926, inside front cover.

———. "Worth While Vacation Reading: From Page's List." February 1916, 67.

*The Bookseller and Stationer* (New York, NY). Ad for *Rilla of Ingleside*, by L.M. Montgomery. 1 September 1921, inside front cover.

———. "New Stokes Books." 1 October 1921, 3.

———. Notice for *Rilla of Ingleside*, by L.M. Montgomery. 15 October 1921, 24.

*The Bookseller, Newsdealer and Stationer* (New York, NY). Ad for *Anne's House of Dreams*, by L.M. Montgomery. 15 August 1917, 184.

———. "From Page's List." 15 January 1920, front cover; 1 February 1920, back cover; 15 February 1920, front cover; 1 April 1920, back cover; 1 May 1920, back cover.

———. "Items of Interest." 15 June 1908, 401–2; 15 January 1920, 66.

———. Notice for *Anne of Green Gables*, by L.M. Montgomery. 1 April 1908, 226.

———. Notice for *The Watchman and Other Poems*, by L.M. Montgomery. 1 April 1917, 379.

———. Review of *Anne's House of Dreams*, by L.M. Montgomery. 1 September 1917, 205.

———. Review of *The Golden Road*, by L.M. Montgomery. 1 October 1913, 320.

———. "Stokes Novels Ready August 25th." 15 August 1919, 118.

Boone, Laurel. "Montgomery." Review of *The Selected Journals of L.M. Montgomery*, Volume 2: *1910–1921*, edited by Mary Rubio and Elizabeth Waterston. *Canadian Literature* 122–23 (Autumn–Winter 1989): 163–64.

*Boston Evening Transcript* (Boston, MA). Review of *Magic for Marigold*, by L.M. Montgomery. 2 October 1929, 2.

———. Review of *The Blue Castle*, by L.M. Montgomery. 23 October 1926, 5.

*The Boston Globe* (Boston, MA). Ad for *Anne of Avonlea*, by L.M. Montgomery. 4 September 1909, 7.

———. Ad for *The Story Girl*, by L.M. Montgomery. 27 May 1911, 7.

———. "Bits from Bookland." 15 January 1910, 7.

———. "Ready This Day." Ad for *Kilmeny of the Orchard*, by L.M. Montgomery. 30 April 1910, 4.

———. "The Reputation of the Author Should Help You to Decide." 25 November 1923, 9.

———. "Shock Gave Her Speech." Review of *Kilmeny of the Orchard*, by L.M. Montgomery. 7 May 1910, 11.

————. "Very Engaging Novel." Review of *The Story Girl*, by L.M. Montgomery. 27 May 1911, 11.

*The Boston Herald* (Boston, MA). Ad for *The Blue Castle*, by L.M. Montgomery. 28 August 1926, 6.

————. Ad for *Emily Climbs*, by L.M. Montgomery. 29 August 1925, 11.

————. Ads for *Emily of New Moon*, by L.M. Montgomery. 8 December 1923, 8; 15 December 1923, 7.

————. Ad for Frederick A. Stokes Company. 21 September 1929, 19.

————. Ad for *The Story Girl*, by L.M. Montgomery. 27 May 1911, 8.

————. "Among Books and Authors." 3 May 1911, 7; 6 May 1912, 7.

————. "The Best Fall Fiction: From Page's List." 19 October 1912, 8.

————. "The Big New Novel: From Page's List." 28 September 1910, 7.

————. "A Girl in a Class All by Herself!" Ad for *Anne of Avonlea*, by L.M. Montgomery. 8 September 1909, 2.

————. "Have You Met Her Yet?" Ad for *Anne of Avonlea*, by L.M. Montgomery. 18 September 1909, 8.

————. "Indian Wars of New England." 8 February 1911, 8.

————. "Mid-Week Book Notes." 17 February 1909, 6.

————. "New Novel by the Author of 'Anne of Green Gables.'" 10 September 1921, 5.

————. Review of *Anne of Green Gables*, by L.M. Montgomery. 5 December 1908, 8.

————. Review of *Emily's Quest*, by L.M. Montgomery. 24 September 1927, 8.

————. Review of *Kilmeny of the Orchard*, by L.M. Montgomery. 4 June 1910, 8.

————. "Stokes Books for Christmas Giving." 4 December 1926, 21.

————. "Three Notable Books: From Page's List." 24 March 1909, 7.

————. "Weather Forecast." 11 December 1923, 5.

————. "Week-End Book Notes." 27 June 1908, 7.

Bourinot, Arthur S. "First Contribution to 'Belles Lettres' in Canada." Review of *The Green Gables Letters from L.M. Montgomery to Ephraim Weber, 1905–1909*, edited by Wilfrid Eggleston. *The Lethbridge Herald* (Lethbridge, AB), 9 April 1960, 5.

Bradford, Anne Henszey. Review of *Anne of Green Gables*, by L.M. Montgomery. *The Boston Budget and Beacon* (Boston, MA), 8 August 1908, 4.

Browne, Stephenson. "Boston Gossip of Latest Books." *The New York Times* (New York, NY), 20 February 1909, BR105.

————. "Ingenious Novel by Paul Bourget: Boston Announcements Include Volumes by Herbert Hopkins, Washington Gladden, and Miss

Montgomery." *The New York Times* (New York, NY), 14 March 1908, BR146.

Bryce, Sylvia. "The Subtle Subversions of L.M. Montgomery." Review of *At the Altar: Matrimonial Tales*, by L.M. Montgomery, edited by Rea Wilmshurst; *Christmas with Anne and Other Holiday Stories*, by L.M. Montgomery, edited by Rea Wilmshurst. *Canadian Children's Literature / Littérature canadienne pour la jeunesse* 87 (Fall 1997): 78–79.

Bumsted, J.M. "Maud Montgomery's Finest Character Creation." Review of *The Selected Journals of L.M. Montgomery*, Volume 2: *1910–1921*, edited by Mary Rubio and Elizabeth Waterston. *The Atlantic Provinces Book Review* 15, no. 1 (February–March 1988): 10.

———. Review of *The Selected Journals of L.M. Montgomery*, Volume 3: *1921–1929*, edited by Mary Rubio and Elizabeth Waterston. *The Island Magazine* 34 (Fall–Winter 1993): 37–40.

———. "Who's Afraid of Lucy Maud Montgomery?" Review of *The Selected Journals of L.M. Montgomery*, Volume 1: *1889–1910*, edited by Mary Rubio and Elizabeth Waterston. *The Atlantic Provinces Book Review* 13, no. 1 (February–March 1986): 1.

Butcher, Fanny. "Tabloid Book Review." *The Chicago Daily Tribune* (Chicago, IL), 13 June 1915, Section 7, 3.

Butler, Kate Macdonald. "The Heartbreaking Truth about Anne's Creator." *The Globe and Mail* (Toronto, ON), 20 September 2008, F1, F6.

*The Calgary Herald* (Calgary, AB). Review of *The Blue Castle*, by L.M. Montgomery. 23 October 1926, 11.

Campbell, Marie. "Against the Odds." Review of *Against the Odds: Tales of Achievement*, by L.M. Montgomery, edited by Rea Wilmshurst. *Canadian Children's Literature / Littérature canadienne pour la jeunesse* 81 (Spring 1996): 62–63.

Campbell, Sandra. *Both Hands: A Life of Lorne Pierce of Ryerson Press*. Montreal: McGill–Queen's University Press, 2013.

*The Canadian Courier* (Toronto, ON). "Literary Notes." 10 December 1910, 31.

*The Canadian Magazine* (Toronto, ON). Review of *The Golden Road*, by L.M. Montgomery. November 1913, 106.

C.D. "A Wise 12-Year-Old." Review of *Jane of Lantern Hill*, by L.M. Montgomery. *The New York Times Book Review* (New York, NY), 15 August 1937, 22.

C.F.M. Review of *Magic for Marigold*, by L.M. Montgomery. *The Daily Northwestern* (Evanston, IL), 23 October 1929, 2.

*Charlotte Daily Observer* (Charlotte, NC). Ad for *Kilmeny of the Orchard*, by L.M. Montgomery. 29 July 1910, 6.

*The Chicago Daily Tribune* (Chicago, IL). "Here Are Christmas Books for Relatives, Friends." 12 December 1931, 21.

———. Review of *Anne's House of Dreams*, by L.M. Montgomery. 15 September 1917, 7.

*The Christian Advocate* (New York, NY). "Have You Met Her Yet?" Ad for *Anne of Avonlea*, by L.M. Montgomery. 2 December 1909, 1952.

———. Review of *Anne of Avonlea*, by L.M. Montgomery. 16 December 1909, 2034.

*The Christian Science Monitor* (Boston, MA). Review of *Chronicles of Avonlea*, by L.M. Montgomery. 24 June 1912, 2.

———. Review of *The Story Girl*, by L.M. Montgomery. 29 May 1911, 5.

Clare, Kerry. Review of *The Blythes Are Quoted*, by L.M. Montgomery, edited by Benjamin Lefebvre; *L.M. Montgomery*, by Jane Urquhart. *Quill and Quire* (Toronto, ON), December 2009, 23–24.

Clark, Bernice. Review of *The Blue Castle*, by L.M. Montgomery. *The Border Cities Star* (Windsor, ON), 4 October 1926, 12.

Compton, Valerie. "Lucy Maud's Letters Dance Past Painful Aspects of Life." Review of *My Dear Mr. M: Letters to G.B. MacMillan from L.M. Montgomery*, edited by Francis W.P. Bolger and Elizabeth R. Epperly. *The Edmonton Journal* (Edmonton, AB), 5 April 1992, D7.

Conrad, Margaret. Review of *The Selected Journals of L.M. Montgomery*, Volume 1: *1889–1910*, edited by Mary Rubio and Elizabeth Waterston. *The Canadian Historical Review* 67, no. 3 (September 1986): 437–38.

*The Daily Picayune* (New Orleans, LA). Review of *The Golden Road*, by L.M. Montgomery. 5 October 1913, 5.

*The Dallas Morning News* (Dallas, TX). "Books Make the Best Presents." 27 November 1921, 6.

———. "Published Today: From Page's List." 2 August 1915, 4.

Dawe, Alan. "Scrap from the Barrel." Review of *The Alpine Path: The Story of My Career*, by L.M. Montgomery. *The Vancouver Sun* (Vancouver, BC), 27 December 1974, 30A.

Denison, Mary A. Review of *The Blue Castle*, by L.M. Montgomery. *The Literary Review* (New York, NY), 16 October 1926, 12.

de Niverville, Peter. "The Other Side of Lucy Maud Montgomery." Review of *Among the Shadows: Tales from the Darker Side*, by L.M. Montgomery, edited by Rea Wilmshurst. *The Atlantic Provinces Book Review* 17, no. 4 (November–December 1990): 14.

Devereux, Cecily. "The Continuing Story." Review of *The Selected Journals of L.M. Montgomery*, Volume 4: *1929–1935*, edited by Mary Rubio and Elizabeth Waterston. *Canadian Literature* 177 (Summer 2003): 180–81.

———. "'See My Journal for the Full Story': Fictions of Truth in *Anne of Green Gables* and L.M. Montgomery's Journals." In Gammel, *The Intimate Life of L.M. Montgomery*, 241–57.

*The Dial* (Chicago, IL). "Announcements of Spring Books." 16 March 1908, 183–89.

———. "Notes." 1 July 1913, 27–28.

Doody, Margaret Anne. "Lucy Maud Arrives in Hell." Review of *The Selected Journals of L.M. Montgomery*, Volume 5: *1935–1942*, edited by Mary Rubio and Elizabeth Waterston. *The Globe and Mail* (Toronto, ON), 16 October 2004, D6–D7.

Dumbrille, Dorothy. "Early Novelist's Letters." Review of *The Green Gables Letters from L.M. Montgomery to Ephraim Weber, 1905–1909*, edited by Wilfrid Eggleston. *The Globe and Mail* (Toronto, ON), 30 April 1960, 21.

Eggleston, Wilfrid. "General Introduction." In Montgomery, *The Green Gables Letters*, 1–22.

———. "Preface to Second Edition." In *The Green Gables Letters from L.M. Montgomery to Ephraim Weber, 1905–1909*, edited by Wilfrid Eggleston, v–ix. Ottawa: Borealis Press, 1981.

Epperly, Elizabeth Rollins. *Imagining Anne: The Island Scrapbooks of L.M. Montgomery*. Toronto: Penguin Canada, 2008. 100 Years of Anne.

———. "Love Story." Review of *Akin to Anne: Tales of Other Orphans*, by L.M. Montgomery, edited by Rea Wilmshurst. *Canadian Literature* 122–23 (Autumn–Winter 1989): 165–66.

———. Review of *At the Altar: Matrimonial Tales*, by L.M. Montgomery, edited by Rea Wilmshurst. *University of Toronto Quarterly* 65, no. 1 (Winter 1995–1996): 243–45.

———. Review of *The Selected Journals of L.M. Montgomery*, Volume 1: *1889–1910*, edited by Mary Rubio and Elizabeth Waterston. *The Island Magazine* 19 (Spring–Summer 1986): 38–39.

———. Review of *The Selected Journals of L.M. Montgomery*, Volume 2: *1910–1921*, edited by Mary Rubio and Elizabeth Waterston. *The Island Magazine* 23 (Spring–Summer 1988): 38–39.

*The Evening Post* (Wellington, New Zealand). Review of *Magic for Marigold*, by L.M. Montgomery. 30 November 1929, 22.

*Evening Public Ledger* (Philadelphia, PA). "Green Gabling with Anne." Review of *Rainbow Valley*, by L.M. Montgomery. 30 August 1919, 13.

*The Evening Star* (Washington, DC). Review of *The Golden Road*, by L.M. Montgomery. 18 October 1913, Part 2, 9.

*The Evening World* (New York, NY). "The Pleasant Land of Story Books." 13 November 1919, 15.

Ferns, John. "Toronto: 1935–42." In McCabe, *The Lucy Maud Montgomery Album*, 295–98.

FitzPatrick, Helen. Review of *The Alpine Path: The Story of My Career*, by L.M. Montgomery. *The Canadian Author and Bookman* 50, no. 3 (Spring 1975): 27–28.

———. Review of *The Road to Yesterday*, by L.M. Montgomery. *The Canadian Author and Bookman* 49, no. 4 (Summer 1974): 26.

Frazer, F.M. "Scarcely an End." Review of *The Road to Yesterday*, by L.M. Montgomery. *Canadian Literature* 63 (Winter 1975): 89–92.

Frey, Cecelia. "Ambition." Review of *Along the Shore: Tales by the Sea*, by L.M. Montgomery, edited by Rea Wilmshurst. *Canadian Literature* 128 (Spring 1991): 155–57.

"From L.C. Page & Company's Announcement List of New Fiction." In *The Dominant Chord*, by Edward Kimball, n.pag. Boston: L.C. Page and Company, 1912.

Fulford, Robert. "Sad Soul Vainly Seeking Tenderness." Review of *The Selected Journals of L.M. Montgomery*, Volume 1: *1889–1910*, edited by Mary Rubio and Elizabeth Waterston. *The Toronto Star* (Toronto, ON), 14 December 1985, M5.

F.W.T. Review of *Rilla of Ingleside*, by L.M. Montgomery. *The Idaho Daily Statesman* (Boise, ID), 23 October 1921, 4.

Gammel, Irene, ed. *The Intimate Life of L.M. Montgomery*. Toronto: University of Toronto Press, 2005.

———. Review of *After Green Gables: L.M. Montgomery's Letters to Ephraim Weber, 1916–1941*, edited by Hildi Froese Tiessen and Paul Gerard Tiessen. *University of Toronto Quarterly* 77, no. 1 (Winter 2008): 329–30.

———. Review of *The Selected Journals of L.M. Montgomery*, Volume 5: *1935–1942*, edited by Mary Rubio and Elizabeth Waterston; *Anne of Green Gables*, by L.M. Montgomery, edited by Cecily Devereux. *University of Toronto Quarterly* 75, no. 1 (Winter 2006): 325–27.

Gammel, Irene, and Benjamin Lefebvre, eds. *Anne's World: A New Century of Anne of Green Gables*. Toronto: University of Toronto Press, 2010.

Gatenby, Greg. "From the Crow's Nest." Review of *Widener: Biography of a Library*, by Matthew Battles; *Noble Rot: A Bordeaux Wine Revolution*, by William Echikson; *Posters of the Canadian Pacific*, by Mark H. Choko and David L. Jones; *A Modern Life: Art and Design in British Columbia 1945–1960*, by Alan C. Elder, Ian M. Thom, et al.; *India: The Definitive Images: 1858 to the Present*, by Prashant Panjiar; *The Selected Journals of L.M. Montgomery*, Volume 5: *1935–1942*, edited by Mary Rubio and Elizabeth Waterston. *Books in Canada* (Toronto, ON), December 2004, 30.

*The Gazette* (Montreal, QC). "For Girl Readers." Review of *Courageous Women*, by L.M. Montgomery, Marian Keith, and Mabel Burns McKinley. 8 December 1934, 16.

Gerson, Carole. "'Dragged at Anne's Chariot Wheels': The Triangle of Author, Publisher, and Fictional Character." In *L.M. Montgomery and Canadian Culture*, edited by Irene Gammel and Elizabeth Epperly, 49–63. Toronto: University of Toronto Press, 1999.

———. "Seven Milestones: How *Anne of Green Gables* Became a Canadian Icon." In Gammel and Lefebvre, *Anne's World*, 17–30.

*The Globe* (Toronto, ON). Ad for *Magic for Marigold*, by L.M. Montgomery. 30 November 1929, 22.

———. Ads for *Rilla of Ingleside*, by L.M. Montgomery. 24 September 1921, 20; 15 December 1921, 8; 17 December 1921, 16; 20 December 1921, 10.

———. Ad for *The Watchman and Other Poems*, by L.M. Montgomery. 22 November 1916, 2.

———. "The Brightest Book of the Year." Ad for *Anne of Green Gables*, by L.M. Montgomery. 22 August 1908, 2.

———. "Canadian Books for Christmas." 6 December 1919, 16.

———. Review of *Emily of New Moon*, by L.M. Montgomery. 10 December 1923, 22.

———. Review of *Kilmeny of the Orchard*, by L.M. Montgomery. 11 June 1910, 18.

———. Review of *Rainbow Valley*, by L.M. Montgomery. 6 December 1919, 17.

———. "Under the Lamp." 21 August 1909, 14.

*The Globe and Mail* (Toronto, ON). Ad for *Anne of Ingleside*, by L.M. Montgomery. 11 November 1939, 9.

———. "A New Anne Book." Ad for *Anne of Windy Poplars*, by L.M. Montgomery. 7 November 1936, 21.

———. "The Perfect Gift Book." Ad for *Jane of Lantern Hill*, by L.M. Montgomery. 11 December 1937, 27.

Golfman, Noreen. "Bleak Island." Review of *The Blythes Are Quoted*, by L.M. Montgomery, edited by Benjamin Lefebvre. *Literary Review of Canada* (Toronto, ON), November 2009, 25.

Goodwin, Carol. "Lucy's Story." Review of *The Selected Journals of L.M. Montgomery*, Volume 1: *1889–1910*, edited by Mary Rubio and Elizabeth Waterston. *The Record* (Kitchener–Waterloo, ON), 22 November 1985, D1–D2.

Graham, Jean. "A Book for Girls." Review of *Magic for Marigold*, by L.M. Montgomery. *Saturday Night* (Toronto, ON), 2 November 1929, 10.

*Grand Rapids Press* (Grand Rapids, MI). Review of *Anne of Green Gables*, by L.M. Montgomery. 14 November 1908, 10.

Grauer, Lalage. Review of *The Selected Journals of L.M. Montgomery*, Volume 3: *1921–1929*, edited by Mary Rubio and Elizabeth Waterston. *University of Toronto Quarterly* 63, no. 1 (Fall 1993): 217–20.

*Greensboro Daily News* (Greensboro, NC). "The Montgomery Books." Ad for Wills Book & Stationer Company. 4 August 1911, 4.

Groening, Laura. "The Poetry of Lucy Maud Montgomery." Review of *The Poetry of Lucy Maud Montgomery*, selected by John Ferns and Kevin McCabe. *The Atlantic Provinces Book Review* 15, no. 2 (May–June 1988): 7.

Hammill, Faye. "Something Wild and Sweet and Unutterable." Review of *The Complete Journals of L.M. Montgomery: The PEI Years, 1901–1911*, edited by Mary Henley Rubio and Elizabeth Hillman Waterston. *The Times Literary Supplement* (London, UK), 18 October 2013, 21.

*The Hartford Courant* (Hartford, CT). Review of *Anne of Windy Poplars*, by L.M. Montgomery. 9 August 1936, D6.

———. Review of *Emily of New Moon*, by L.M. Montgomery. 9 September 1923, A12.

———. Review of *Pat of Silver Bush*, by L.M. Montgomery. 27 August 1933, D6.

Hathaway, E.J. Headnote for L.M. Montgomery. In *Canadian Poets*, edited by John W. Garvin, 353. Toronto: McClelland, Goodchild, and Stewart, 1916.

Hinkley, Mary. "Successor to Anne of Green Gables." Review of *Magic for Marigold*, by L.M. Montgomery. *Chicago Evening Post* (Chicago, IL), 11 October 1929, 9.

Holland, Clifford G. Review of *The Selected Journals of L.M. Montgomery*, Volume 1: *1889–1910*, edited by Mary Rubio and Elizabeth Waterston. *Queen's Quarterly* 93, no. 3 (Autumn 1986): 667–68.

Hopkins, Mary Alden. Review of *Chronicles of Avonlea*, by L.M. Montgomery. *The Publishers' Weekly* (New York, NY), 21 September 1912, 814.

Howells, Coral Ann. "LMM: Finding a Voice." Review of *The Selected Journals of L.M. Montgomery*, Volume 1: *1889–1910*, edited by Mary Rubio and Elizabeth Waterston. *Canadian Children's Literature / Littérature canadienne pour la jeunesse* 45 (1987): 79–81.

———. "Pluralisms." Review of *A History of Canadian Literature*, by W.H. New; *The Oxford Book of Canadian Short Stories in English*, selected by Margaret Atwood and Robert Weaver; *The Selected Journals of L.M. Montgomery*, Volume 2: *1910–1921*, edited by Mary Rubio and Elizabeth Waterston. *English* 39, no. 163 (Spring 1990): 83–87.

*The Idaho Daily Statesman* (Boise, ID). Review of *Kilmeny of the Orchard*, by L.M. Montgomery. 12 May 1910, 4.

*The Independent* (New York, NY). "Folk Who Write." 19 April 1915, 123.

Israel, Callie. Review of *The Alpine Path: The Story of My Career*, by L.M. Montgomery. *In Review: Canadian Books for Children* 9, no. 3 (Summer 1975): 36.

Jenkinson, Dave. Review of *Among the Shadows: Tales from the Darker Side*, by L.M. Montgomery, edited by Rea Wilmshurst. *CM: A Reviewing Journal of Canadian Materials for Young People* 18, no. 5 (September 1990): 226–27.

J.M.T. Review of *Emily of New Moon*, by L.M. Montgomery. *The Oregonian* (Portland, OR), 30 October 1923, 3.

Johnston, Jean. Review of *My Dear Mr. M: Letters to G.B. MacMillan from L.M. Montgomery*, edited by Francis W.P. Bolger and Elizabeth R. Epperly. *Quill and Quire* (Toronto, ON), January 1981, 27.

*Journal–Tribune* (Williamsburg, IA). Review of *Mistress Pat*, by L.M. Montgomery. 16 September 1937, 3.

Joyce-Jones, Susannah. Review of *My Dear Mr. M: Letters to G.B. MacMillan from L.M. Montgomery*, edited by Francis W.P. Bolger and Elizabeth R. Epperly. *Atlantis: A Women's Studies Journal / Journal d'études sur la femme* 7, no. 1 (Fall 1981): 144–46.

*The Kansas City Star* (Kansas City, MI). "Published Today: From Page's List." 24 July 1915, 12.

Keefer, Janice Kulyk. Review of *The Selected Journals of L.M. Montgomery*, Volume 1: *1889–1910*, edited by Mary Rubio and Elizabeth Waterston; *The Selected Journals of L.M. Montgomery*, Volume 2: *1910–1921*, edited by Mary Rubio and Elizabeth Waterston. *The Antigonish Review* 73 (Spring 1988): 83–88.

Kelley, Jessica. Review of *The Way to Slumbertown*, by L.M. Montgomery. *Quill and Quire* (Toronto, ON), July 2005, 43–44.

Kerfoot, J.B. Review of *Anne of Avonlea*, by L.M. Montgomery. *Life* (New York, NY), 25 November 1909, 746.

*Kirkus Reviews* (New York, NY). Review of *The Road to Yesterday*, by L.M. Montgomery. 15 October 1974, 1112.

Lefebvre, Benjamin. Afterword to Montgomery, *The Blythes Are Quoted*, 511–20.

———. "Lucy Maud of Macneill Farm." Review of *The Complete Journals of L.M. Montgomery: The PEI Years, 1889–1900*, edited by Mary Henley Rubio and Elizabeth Hillman Waterston. *The Globe and Mail* (Toronto, ON), 21 July 2012, R16.

———. "Notes toward Editing L.M. Montgomery's *The Blythes Are Quoted*." MA thesis, University of Guelph, 2001.

———. "The Performance Anxiety of L.M. Montgomery." Review of *After Green Gables: L.M. Montgomery's Letters to Ephraim Weber, 1916–1941*, edited by Hildi Froese Tiessen and Paul Gerard Tiessen. *Canadian Literature* 197 (Summer 2008): 190–92.

———. "Pigsties and Sunsets: L.M. Montgomery, *A Tangled Web*, and a Modernism of Her Own." *English Studies in Canada* 31, no. 4 (December 2005): 123–46.

———. "What's in a Name? Towards a Theory of the Anne Brand." In Gammel and Lefebvre, *Anne's World*, 192–211.

*The Lethbridge Daily Herald* (Lethbridge, AB). Review of *Anne of Ingleside*, by L.M. Montgomery. 16 December 1939, 6.

———. Review of *A Tangled Web*, by L.M. Montgomery. 13 November 1931, 11.

Lewis, Shirley. Review of *The Road to Yesterday*, by L.M. Montgomery. *In Review: Canadian Books for Children* 8, no. 2 (Spring 1974): 43.

*The Lexington Herald* (Lexington, KY). Review of *Anne of the Island*, by L.M. Montgomery. 5 September 1915, Section 4, 3.

———. Review of *The Golden Road*, by L.M. Montgomery. 14 September 1913, 4.

*The Los Angeles Times* (Los Angeles, CA). "Books for Christmas." Ad for Bullock's department store. 13 December 1908, Part 8, 6.

———. "Departmentized Index of Desirable Holiday Books Obtainable in Los Angeles." 13 December 1908, Part 8, 1.

———. "Romance Opens Doors to Joy." 13 December 1931, Part 3, 14.

"Lucy Maud Words." In McCabe, *The Lucy Maud Montgomery Album*, 414–15.

Macdonald, Rae. Review of *The Road to Yesterday*, by L.M. Montgomery. *The Dalhousie Review* 54, no. 4 (Winter 1974–75): 783–84.

Mackey, Margaret. Review of *L.M. Montgomery*, by Jane Urquhart. *Resource Links* 16, no. 1 (October 2010): 62.

MacLean, Leslie. Review of *Akin to Anne: Tales of Other Orphans*, by L.M. Montgomery, edited by Rea Wilmshurst. *The Island Magazine* 24 (Fall–Winter 1988): 44–45.

MacMurchy, Marjory. "Retrospect of a Year's Books." *The Canadian Courier* (Toronto, ON), 30 November 1912, 7.

*The Mail and Empire* (Toronto, ON). "Canadian Writers and a Year's Work." 29 December 1917, 19.

———. "Just Off the Press." 17 October 1931, 16.

———. "Pleasant Little Tale though Very Light." Review of *Anne's House of Dreams*, by L.M. Montgomery. 6 October 1917, 19.

Manion, Eileen. "L.M. Montgomery Had Orphans Other Than Anne." Review of *Akin to Anne: Tales of Other Orphans*, by L.M. Montgomery, edited by Rea Wilmshurst. *The Gazette* (Montreal, QC), 9 July 1988, K9.

———. "The Two Faces of 'Anne.'" Review of *The Selected Journals of L.M. Montgomery*, Volume 2: *1910–1921*, edited by Mary Rubio and Elizabeth Waterston; *The Poetry of Lucy Maud Montgomery*, selected by John Ferns and Kevin McCabe. *The Gazette* (Montreal, QC), 13 February 1988, J9.

*Manitoba Free Press* (Winnipeg, MB). "Christmas Gifts for Particular People." 6 December 1919, Book Section, 2.

Martin, Sandra. "L.M. Montgomery – Illusions Lost." Review of *The Alpine Path: The Story of My Career*, by L.M. Montgomery. *The Toronto Star* (Toronto, ON), 1 February 1975, G7.

McCabe, Kevin, comp. *The Lucy Maud Montgomery Album*. Edited by Alexandra Heilbron. Toronto: Fitzhenry and Whiteside, 1999.

McKellar, Hugh D. "Dreams Come True in These 'Orphan' Tales." Review of *Akin to Anne: Tales of Other Orphans*, by L.M. Montgomery, edited by Rea Wilmshurst. *The Toronto Star* (Toronto, ON), 11 June 1988, M8.

McLay, Catherine. Introduction to Montgomery, *The Doctor's Sweetheart and Other Stories*, 8–25.

Minot, John Clair. "Another Montgomery Novel Vibrant with the Spirit of Youth." Review of *Emily of New Moon*, by L.M. Montgomery. 1 September 1923, 7.

———. "The Herald's Mid-Week Book Page." *The Boston Herald* (Boston, MA), 31 October 1923, 21.

———. Review of *Emily Climbs*, by L.M. Montgomery. *The Boston Herald* (Boston, MA), 26 August 1925, 12.

M.H.P. "Vivid Collaboration." Review of *Courageous Women*, by L.M. Montgomery, Marian Keith, and Mabel Burns McKinley. *The Globe* (Toronto, ON), 23 December 1934, 8.

M.L. Review of *Anne of Green Gables*, by L.M. Montgomery. *Winnipeg Free Press* (Winnipeg, MB), 18 July 1942, 10.

Moberly, Lucy Gertrude. *A Tangled Web*. London: J. Leng and Company, 1926. London: Ward, Lock and Company, 1931.

Moffatt, James. *A Tangled Web*. London: Hodder and Stoughton, 1929.

Montagnes, Anne. "So Feeble. Why Do It Now?" Review of *The Road to Yesterday*, by L.M. Montgomery. *The Globe and Mail* (Toronto, ON), 23 March 1974, 33.

Montgomery, L.M. *Across the Miles: Tales of Correspondence*. Edited by Rea Wilmshurst. Toronto: McClelland and Stewart, 1995.

———. *After Green Gables: L.M. Montgomery's Letters to Ephraim Weber, 1916–1941*. Edited by Hildi Froese Tiessen and Paul Gerard Tiessen. Toronto: University of Toronto Press, 2006.

———. *After Many Days: Tales of Time Passed*. Edited by Rea Wilmshurst. Toronto: McClelland and Stewart, 1991.

———. *Against the Odds: Tales of Achievement*. Edited by Rea Wilmshurst. Toronto: McClelland and Stewart, 1993.

———. *Akin to Anne: Tales of Other Orphans*. Edited by Rea Wilmshurst. Toronto: McClelland and Stewart, 1988.

———. *Along the Shore: Tales by the Sea*. Edited by Rea Wilmshurst. Toronto: McClelland and Stewart, 1989.

———. "The Alpine Path: The Story of My Career." *Everywoman's World* (Toronto, ON), June 1917, 38–39, 41; July 1917, 16, 32–33, 35; August 1917, 16, 32–33; September 1917, 8, 49; October 1917, 8, 58; November 1917, 25, 38, 40.

———. *The Alpine Path: The Story of My Career*. N.p.: Fitzhenry and Whiteside, n.d.

———. *Among the Shadows: Tales from the Darker Side*. Edited by Rea Wilmshurst. Toronto: McClelland and Stewart, 1990.

———. *Anne of Avonlea*. 1909. Toronto: Seal Books, 1996.

———. *Anne of Green Gables*. 1908. Toronto: Seal Books, 1996.

———. *Anne of Green Gables*. 1908. Edited by Cecily Devereux. Peterborough, ON: Broadview Editions, 2004.

———. *Anne of Green Gables*. 1908. Edited by Mary Henley Rubio and Elizabeth Waterston. New York: W.W. Norton and Company, 2007.

———. *Anne of Ingleside*. 1939. Toronto: Seal Books, 1996.

———. *Anne of the Island*. Boston: L.C. Page and Company, 1915.

———. *Anne of the Island*. 1915. Toronto: Seal Books, 1996.

———. *Anne of Windy Poplars*. 1936. Toronto: Seal Books, 1996.

———. *Anne's House of Dreams*. Toronto: McClelland, Goodchild and Stewart, 1917.

———. *Anne's House of Dreams*. 1917. Toronto: Seal Books, 1996.

———. *The Annotated Anne of Green Gables*. Edited by Wendy E. Barry, Margaret Anne Doody, and Mary E. Doody Jones. New York: Oxford University Press, 1997.

———. *At the Altar: Matrimonial Tales*. Edited by Rea Wilmshurst. Toronto: McClelland and Stewart, 1994.

———. *The Blue Castle*. London: Hodder and Stoughton, 1926.

———. *The Blue Castle*. 1926. Toronto: Seal Books, 1988.

———. "The Blue Castle." *The Canadian Countryman* (Toronto, ON), 27 August 1927, 11, 15–17; 3 September 1927, 11–14; 10 September 1927, 13–16; 17 September 1927, 12–16; 24 September 1927, 12–15; 1 October 1927, 14–18; 8 October 1927, 9, 15–16; 15 October 1927, 7, 12–13; 22 October 1927, 9, 13–14; 29 October 1927, 9, 14–15; 5 November 1927, 14–18; 12 November 1927, 14–18; 19 November 1927, 14–16; 26 November 1927, 9, 17–18; 3 December 1927, 9, 16; 10 December 1927, 19, 47; 17 December 1927, 9, 30–31; 24 December 1927, 13–14; 31 December 1927, 9, 13; 7 January 1928, 9, 21–22; 14 January 1928, 13–15.

———. "The Blue Castle." *The Plain Dealer* (Cleveland, OH), 3 April 1927, Magazine Section, 2–11, 14, 16, 18–23.

———. *The Blythes Are Quoted*. Edited by Benjamin Lefebvre. Toronto: Viking Canada, 2009.

———. "Bobbed Goldilocks." *The Delineator* (New York, NY), July 1926, 10, 70–71.

———. *Christmas with Anne and Other Holiday Stories*. Edited by Rea Wilmshurst. Toronto: McClelland and Stewart, 1995.

———. *Chronicles of Avonlea*. Boston: L.C. Page and Company, 1912.

———. *Chronicles of Avonlea*. 1912. Toronto: Seal Books, 1993.

———. "Chronicles of Ingleside." *Onward: A Paper for Young Canadians* (Toronto, ON), 10 September 1939, 577–79, 591; 17 September 1939, 596–97, 602–3; 24 September 1939, 612–13, 619, 623; 1 October 1939, 625–28, 638–39; 8 October 1939, 644–45, 655; 15 October 1939, 662–63; 22 October 1939, 674–75, 687; 29 October 1939, 698–99, 702–3.

———. *The Complete Journals of L.M. Montgomery: The PEI Years, 1889–1900*. Edited by Mary Henley Rubio and Elizabeth Hillman Waterston. Don Mills, ON: Oxford University Press, 2012.

———. *The Complete Journals of L.M. Montgomery: The PEI Years, 1901–1911*. Edited by Mary Henley Rubio and Elizabeth Hillman Waterston. Don Mills, ON: Oxford University Press, 2013.

———. "A Day Off." *The Family Herald and Weekly Star* (Montreal, QC), 1 July 1936, 20–21.

———. *The Doctor's Sweetheart and Other Stories*. Selected by Catherine McLay. Toronto: McGraw–Hill Ryerson, 1979.

———. "Each in His Own Tongue." *The Delineator* (New York, NY), October 1910, 247, 324–28.

———. *Emily Climbs*. 1925. Toronto: Seal Books, 1998.

———. *Emily of New Moon*. 1923. Toronto: Seal Books, 1998.

———. *Emily's Quest*. 1927. Toronto: Seal Books, 1998.

———. "Enter, Emily." *The Delineator* (New York, NY), January 1925, 10–11, 56–57.

———. "Everybody Is Different." *The Family Herald and Weekly Star* (Montreal, QC), 27 May 1936, 20–21.

———. *Further Chronicles of Avonlea*. Illustrated by John Goss. Boston: The Page Company, 1920.

———. *Further Chronicles of Avonlea*. 1920. Toronto: Seal Books, 1987.

———. "The Gift of a Day." *The Family Herald and Weekly Star* (Montreal, QC), 20 May 1936, 20–21, 30.

———. *The Golden Road*. Boston: L.C. Page and Company, 1913.

———. *The Golden Road*. 1913. Toronto: Seal Books, 1987.

———. *The Green Gables Letters from L.M. Montgomery to Ephraim Weber, 1905–1909*. Edited by Wilfrid Eggleston. Toronto: The Ryerson Press, 1960.

———. "Her Dog Day." *The Delineator* (New York, NY), April 1925, 10, 80–83.

———. "How I Became a Writer." *Manitoba Free Press* (Manitoba, MB), 3 December 1921, Christmas Book Section, 3.

———. "In Lovers' Lane." *The Delineator* (New York, NY), July 1903, 16.

———. "'It.'" *The Chatelaine* (Toronto, ON), April 1929, 21, 56, 58.

———. *Jane of Lantern Hill*. 1937. Toronto: Seal Books, 1993.

———. *Kilmeny of the Orchard*. 1910. Toronto: Seal Books, 1987.

———. "Lost – A Child's Laughter." *The Delineator* (New York, NY), June 1926, 15, 68, 70.

———. "Magic for Marigold." *The Delineator* (New York, NY), May 1926, 10–11, 82, 85.

———. *Magic for Marigold*. 1929. Toronto: Seal Books, 1988.

———. "The Man Who Wouldn't Talk." *The Family Herald and Weekly Star* (Montreal, QC), 6 May 1936, 22–23, 30.

———. "Miss Much-Afraid." *The Family Herald and Weekly Star* (Montreal, QC), 3 June 1936, 20–21.

———. *Mistress Pat*. 1935. Toronto: Seal Books, 1988.

———. *My Dear Mr. M: Letters to G.B. MacMillan from L.M. Montgomery*. Edited by Francis W.P. Bolger and Elizabeth R. Epperly. Toronto: McGraw–Hill Ryerson, 1980.

———. "Night Watch." *The Delineator* (New York, NY), March 1925, 10–11, 96–97.

———. "One Clear Call." Illustrated by Diana Thorne. *The Household Magazine* (Topeka, KS), August 1928, 6–7, 21.

——. "One of Us." Illustrated by Elsie Deane. *Canadian Home Journal* (Toronto, ON), February 1928, 8–9, 54.

——. "Playmate." *The Delineator* (New York, NY), August 1926, 15, 66.

——. *The Poetry of Lucy Maud Montgomery*. Selected by John Ferns and Kevin McCabe. Toronto: Fitzhenry and Whiteside, 1987.

——. "The Promise of Lucy Ellen." *The Delineator* (New York, NY), February 1904, 268–71.

——. "The Punishment of Billy." *Canadian Home Journal* (Toronto, ON), February 1929, 16–17, 77.

——. *Rainbow Valley*. Toronto: McClelland and Stewart; New York: Frederick A. Stokes, 1919.

——. *Rainbow Valley*. 1919. Toronto: Seal Books, 1996.

——. *Rilla of Ingleside*. 1921. Edited by Benjamin Lefebvre and Andrea McKenzie. Toronto: Viking Canada, 2010.

——. *The Road to Yesterday*. Toronto: McGraw–Hill Ryerson, 1974.

——. "Scrapbook of Reviews from around the World Which L.M. Montgomery's Clipping Service Sent to Her, 1910–1935." XZ5 MS A003, L.M. Montgomery Collection, University of Guelph archives.

——. *The Selected Journals of L.M. Montgomery*, Volume 1: *1889–1910*; Volume 2: *1910–1921*; Volume 3: *1921–1929*; Volume 4: *1929–1935*; Volume 5: *1935–1942*. Edited by Mary Rubio and Elizabeth Waterston. Toronto: Oxford University Press, 1985, 1987, 1992, 1998, 2004.

——. *The Story Girl*. Boston: L.C. Page and Company, 1911.

——. *The Story Girl*. 1911. Toronto: Seal Books, 1987.

——. *A Tangled Web*. 1931. Toronto: Seal Books, 1989.

——. "Too Few Cooks." *The Delineator* (New York, NY), February 1925, 10, 78, 81–82.

——. "A Tragic Evening." *The Family Herald and Weekly Star* (Montreal, QC), 24 June 1936, 20–21.

——. "Una of the Garden." *The Housekeeper* (Minneapolis, MN), December 1908, 7, 18; January 1909, 11–12; February 1909, 8–9, 16; March 1909, 7, 17; April 1909, 8–9, 32.

——. "The Way to Slumbertown." *Holland's Magazine* (Dallas, TX), April 1916, 56. Also in *Canadian Verse for Boys and Girls*, edited by John W. Garvin, 137–39. Toronto: Thomas Nelson and Sons, 1930.

——. "The Watchman." *Everybody's Magazine* (New York, NY), December 1910, 778–83.

——. *The Watchman and Other Poems*. Toronto: McClelland, Goodchild, and Stewart, 1916. New York: Frederick A. Stokes Company, n.d.

———. *The Way to Slumbertown*. Illustrated by Rachel Bédard. Montreal: Lobster Press, 2005.

———. "The Wedding at Poplar Point." *The Family Herald and Weekly Star* (Montreal, QC), 13 May 1936, 22–23, 30.

———. "The Westcott Elopement." *The Family Herald and Weekly Star* (Montreal, QC), 10 June 1936, 20–21.

*The Morning Bulletin* (Rockhampton, Australia). Review of *Magic for Marigold*, by L.M. Montgomery. 19 November 1929, 5.

———. Review of *Pat of Silver Bush*, by L.M. Montgomery. 1 November 1933, 11.

———. Review of *The Blue Castle*, by L.M. Montgomery. 14 August 1926, 12.

Morris, Elsie. Review of *The Alpine Path: The Story of My Career*, by L.M. Montgomery. *The Lethbridge Herald* (Lethbridge, AB), 14 December 1974, 5.

M.R.M. "Anne, Antidote for Dizzy Age." Review of *Anne of Ingleside*, by L.M. Montgomery. *The San Diego Union* (San Diego, CA), 6 August 1939, 7C.

Murray, George. Review of *Anne of Green Gables*, by L.M. Montgomery. *The Montreal Daily Star* (Montreal, QC), 8 August 1908, 2.

Murray, Heather. Review of *The Selected Journals of L.M. Montgomery*, Volume 5: *1935–1942*, edited by Mary Rubio and Elizabeth Waterston. *The Canadian Historical Review* 87, no. 1 (March 2006): 143–44.

*The National Magazine* (Boston, MA). Review of *The Story Girl*, by L.M. Montgomery. January 1912, 711.

———. "The Vacation Girl Reads." August 1912, 679–86.

*The New Orleans Item* (New Orleans, LA). "Holmes Store News." 16 September 1919, 4.

*The New Outlook* (Toronto, ON). Review of *Emily Climbs*, by L.M. Montgomery. 25 November 1925, 22.

———. Review of *The Blue Castle*, by L.M. Montgomery. 17 November 1926, 16–17.

*The New York Herald Tribune Books* (New York, NY). Review of *A Tangled Web*, by L.M. Montgomery. 1 November 1931, Section 11, 23.

———. Review of *Mistress Pat: A Novel of Silver Bush*, by L.M. Montgomery. 8 September 1935, Section 7, 15.

*The New York Observer* (New York, NY). "Best Books for Boys and Girls." 3 December 1908, 740.

———. Review of *The Story Girl*, by L.M. Montgomery. 21 September 1911, 373.

———. "Successful New Books." Ad for L.C. Page and Company. 18 May 1911, 635.

*The New York Times* (New York, NY). Ad for *Anne's House of Dreams*, by L.M. Montgomery. 26 August 1917, 64.

———. Ad for Frederick A. Stokes Company. 5 October 1919, 98.

———. Ads for *Rainbow Valley*, by L.M. Montgomery. 28 August 1919, 14; 5 October 1919, 98.

———. "Boston Gossip of Latest Books." 20 June 1908, 358; 8 May 1909, BR297.

———. "Christmas Books for Children." 6 December 1919, 5.

———. "Literary Boston: News and Notes about All Kinds of Books from the Hub." 19 May 1912, BR307.

———. "New Novel by the Author of 'Anne of Green Gables.'" Ad for *Rilla of Ingleside*, by L.M. Montgomery. 11 September 1921, 52.

———. "Some of L.C. Page & Company's Spring Books." 11 April 1908, 35.

*The New York Times Book Review* (New York, NY). "Canadian Romance." Review of *The Blue Castle*, by L.M. Montgomery. 26 September 1926, 33.

———. "A Homely Chronicle." Review of *A Tangled Web*, by L.M. Montgomery. 20 December 1931, 9, 19.

*The New York Times Book Review and Magazine* (New York, NY). Review of *Emily of New Moon*, by L.M. Montgomery. 26 August 1923, 24, 26.

*The New York Tribune* (New York, NY). Ad for *Anne's House of Dreams*, by L.M. Montgomery. 25 August 1917, 5.

———. Review of *Anne of Avonlea*, by L.M. Montgomery. 8 January 1910, 8.

Nowlan, Michael O. Review of *Along the Shore: Tales by the Sea*, by L.M. Montgomery, edited by Rea Wilmshurst. *The Atlantic Advocate* (Fredericton, NB), December 1989, 60–61.

*The Oakland Tribune* (Oakland, CA). Review of *Chronicles of Avonlea*, by L.M. Montgomery. 30 June 1912, 10.

*The Oregonian* (Portland, OR). Review of *Anne of Green Gables*, by L.M. Montgomery. 30 August 1908, 11.

———. Review of *Magic for Marigold*, by L.M. Montgomery. 29 December 1929, 9.

Pacey, Desmond. Review of *The Green Gables Letters from L.M. Montgomery to Ephraim Weber, 1905–1909*, edited by Wilfrid Eggleston. *The Dalhousie Review* 41, no. 3 (Autumn 1961): 429, 431.

Parr, D. Kermode. Review of *The Green Gables Letters from L.M. Montgomery to Ephraim Weber, 1905–1909*, edited by Wilfrid Eggleston. *The Atlantic Advocate* (Fredericton, NB), June 1960, 97.

*The Philadelphia Inquirer* (Philadelphia, PA). "A Sequel to *Anne of Green Gables*." Review of *Anne of Avonlea*, by L.M. Montgomery. 20 September 1909, 5.

Pike, E. Holly. "Who Do We Think You Are?" Review of *Imagining Anne: The Island Scrapbooks of L.M. Montgomery*, by Elizabeth Rollins Epperly; *Through Lover's Lane: L.M. Montgomery's Photography and Visual Imagination*, by Elizabeth Rollins Epperly; *The Intimate Life of L.M. Montgomery*, edited by Irene Gammel; *Lucy Maud Montgomery*, by Elizabeth MacLeod; *After Green Gables: L.M. Montgomery's Letters to Ephraim Weber, 1916–1941*, edited by Hildi Froese Tiessen and Paul Gerard Tiessen; *The Selected Journals of L.M. Montgomery*, Volume 5: *1935–1942*, edited by Mary Rubio and Elizabeth Waterston. *Canadian Children's Literature / Littérature canadienne pour la jeunesse* 34, no. 2 (Fall 2008): 112–23.

*Pittsburgh Post–Gazette* (Pittsburgh, PA). Review of *Pat of Silver Bush*, by L.M. Montgomery. 11 November 1933, 10.

*The Pittsburgh Press* (Pittsburgh, PA). "Chronicles of Avonlea." Review of *Further Chronicles of Avonlea*, by L.M. Montgomery. 17 April 1920, 10.

*The Plain Dealer* (Cleveland, OH). "She Married a Tramp." 27 March 1927, Magazine Section, 7.

Porter, Helen. "An Abundance of Happy Endings." Review of *Akin to Anne: Tales of Other Orphans*, by L.M. Montgomery, edited by Rea Wilmshurst. *The Globe and Mail* (Toronto, ON), 23 April 1988, C17.

Posesorski, Sherie. "Shedding Light on the Creator of a Children's Classic." Review of *The Selected Journals of L.M. Montgomery*, Volume 1: *1889–1910*, edited by Mary Rubio and Elizabeth Waterston. *Quill and Quire* (Toronto, ON), December 1985, 22.

Powell, Marilyn. "Before Anne's Pigtails, There Were Soggy Tales." Review of *Along the Shore: Tales by the Sea*, by L.M. Montgomery, edited by Rea Wilmshurst. *The Globe and Mail* (Toronto, ON), 1 July 1989, C17.

———. "The Ideals of a Lonely Little Girl." Review of *The Selected Journals of L.M. Montgomery*, Volume 1: *1889–1910*, edited by Mary Rubio and Elizabeth Waterston. *The Globe and Mail* (Toronto, ON), 2 November 1985, D21.

———. "Unhappy Times." Review of *The Selected Journals of L.M. Montgomery*, Volume 2: *1910–1921*, edited by Mary Rubio and Elizabeth Waterston. *The Globe and Mail* (Toronto, ON), 9 January 1988, C15.

"Publisher's Foreword." In Montgomery, *The Road to Yesterday*, n.pag.

*The Publishers' Weekly* (New York, NY). Ad for *Anne's House of Dreams*, by L.M. Montgomery. 11 August 1917, 476.

———. Ad for *Rainbow Valley*, by L.M. Montgomery. 16 August 1919, 462.

———. Ad for *Rilla of Ingleside*, by L.M. Montgomery. 27 August 1921, 620.

———. Ad for *The Golden Road*, by L.M. Montgomery. 30 August 1913, 74.

———. "The Best Sellers of 1912: The Publishers' Weekly's Consensus." 25 January 1913, 280–81.

———. "Canadian Notes." 18 December 1915, 2002–4.

———. "Educational Books in Demand: From Page's List." 26 July 1913, 312.

———. "From Page's List." 5 July 1913, 4.

———. "Literary and Trade Notes." 21 June 1913, 2156–58; 10 July 1915, 91–93; 11 August 1917, 490–93.

———. "New Fiction: From Page's List." 30 May 1908, 1705.

———. "New Stokes Books." 3 September 1921, 658.

———. "Nineteen Hundred and Eight: Spring Publications of L.C. Page & Company." 21 March 1908, 1156–57.

———. "Notes in Season." 14 March 1908, 1113; 13 June 1908, 1913.

———. "Notes on Travellers and Their Lines." 29 February 1908, 941–60.

———. Notice for *Anne of the Island*, by L.M. Montgomery. 31 July 1915, 349.

———. Notice for *Anne's House of Dreams*, by L.M. Montgomery. 25 August 1917, 608.

———. "Published To-day: From Page's List." Ad for *Anne of Green Gables*, by L.M. Montgomery. 13 June 1908, front cover.

———. "Ready at Once: From Page's List." 2 May 1908, 1479.

———. Review of *The Road to Yesterday*, by L.M. Montgomery. 7 October 1974, 62.

———. "The Season's Outstanding Work." 1 October 1921, 1144.

———. "Spring Lines of the Publishers and Some of the Men Who Will Show Them." 24 February 1912, 615–40; 22 February 1913, 645–72.

———. "Stokes' Autumn Fiction." 27 September 1919, 1005.

———. "Two of a Kind: From Page's List." 13 September 1913, 706.

*The Register* (Adelaide, Australia). "Peaceful, Helpful Lives." Review of *Anne of Avonlea*, by L.M. Montgomery. 8 January 1910, 4.

Renzetti, Elizabeth. "A Different Shirley [sic] and Gilbert." *The Globe and Mail* (Toronto, ON), 24 October 2009, R12.

Ridley, Hilda M. *The Story of L.M. Montgomery*. Toronto: The Ryerson Press, 1956.

Robertson, Carl T. "On the Book Shop Shelves." *The Plain Dealer* (Cleveland, OH), 14 May 1910, 6.

Robinson, Laura M. "Tragedy of Everyday Life." Review of *Marian Engel: Life in Letters*, edited by Christl Verduyn and Kathleen Garay; *The Selected Journals of L.M. Montgomery*, Volume 5: *1935–1942*, edited by Mary Rubio and Elizabeth Waterston. *Canadian Literature* 189 (Summer 2006): 145–46.

Robson, John M. Review of *The Green Gables Letters from L.M. Montgomery to Ephraim Weber, 1905–1909*, edited by Wilfrid Eggleston. *University of Toronto Quarterly* 30, no. 4 (July 1961): 422.

Rogers, Linda. "Women of Substance with the Intellect to Beat Ordinariness." Review of *Among the Shadows: Tales from the Darker Side*, by L.M. Montgomery, edited by Rea Wilmshurst. *The Vancouver Sun* (Vancouver, BC), 6 October 1990, D18.

Rubio, Mary. "'A Dusting Off': An Anecdotal Account of Editing the L.M. Montgomery Journals." In *Working in Women's Archives: Researching Women's Private Literature and Archival Documents*, edited by Helen M. Buss and Marlene Kadar, 51–78. Waterloo: Wilfrid Laurier University Press, 2001.

———. *Lucy Maud Montgomery: The Gift of Wings*. 2008. N.p.: Anchor Canada, 2010.

———. Review of *The Doctor's Sweetheart and Other Stories*, by L.M. Montgomery, selected by Catherine McLay. *Quill and Quire* (Toronto, ON), July 1979, 48–49.

———. "Uncertainties Surrounding the Death of L.M. Montgomery." In *Anne Around the World: L.M. Montgomery and Her Classic*, edited by Jane Ledwell and Jean Mitchell, 45–62. Montreal: McGill–Queen's University Press, 2013.

———. "Why L.M. Montgomery's Journals Came to Guelph." In McCabe, *The Lucy Maud Montgomery Album*, 473–78.

Rubio, Mary, and Elizabeth Waterston. Introduction to Montgomery, *The Selected Journals of L.M. Montgomery*, 1: xiii–xxiv.

———. Introduction to Montgomery, *The Selected Journals of L.M. Montgomery*, 2: ix–xx.

———. Introduction to Montgomery, *The Selected Journals of L.M. Montgomery*, 3: x–xxv.

———. Introduction to Montgomery, *The Selected Journals of L.M. Montgomery*, 4: xi–xxviii.

———. Introduction to Montgomery, *The Selected Journals of L.M. Montgomery*, 5: ix–xxvii.

———. *Writing a Life: L.M. Montgomery*. Toronto: ECW Press, 1995.

Russell, Ruth Weber, D.W. Russell, and Rea Wilmshurst. *Lucy Maud Montgomery: A Preliminary Bibliography*. Waterloo: University of Waterloo Library, 1986.

R.W.L. Review of *Anne of Windy Poplars*, by L.M. Montgomery. *The Lewiston Daily Sun* (Lewiston, ME), 14 August 1936, 4.

———. Review of *Jane of Lantern Hill*, by L.M. Montgomery. 27 August 1937, 4.

*The San Francisco Call* (San Francisco, CA). Review of *Kilmeny of the Orchard*, by L.M. Montgomery. 19 June 1910, 15.

*San Francisco Chronicle* (San Francisco, CA). Review of *Magic for Marigold*, by L.M. Montgomery. 8 September 1929, D5.

———. "Younger Generation Finds in 'Emily' a Successor to 'Anne.'" Review of *Emily Climbs*, by L.M. Montgomery. 6 December 1925, B3.

*San Jose Mercury Herald* (San Jose, CA). Review of *Anne's House of Dreams*, by L.M. Montgomery. 17 March 1918, 6.

———. Review of *Rainbow Valley*, by L.M. Montgomery. 5 October 1919, 6.

*The Saturday Review* (London, UK). "Revaluation of Samuel Butler." 12 September 1936, 341.

Schiefer, Nancy A. "Journals Bursting with Life." Review of *The Complete Journals of L.M. Montgomery: The PEI Years, 1889–1900*, edited by Mary Henley Rubio and Elizabeth Hillman Waterston. *The London Free Press* (London, ON), 13 October 2012, F2.

———. "A Writer Even More Enchanting Than Her Heroines." Review of *The Selected Journals of L.M. Montgomery*, Volume 1: *1889–1910*, edited by Mary Rubio and Elizabeth Waterston. *The London Free Press* (London, ON), 13 December 1985, A15.

*The Seattle Sunday Times* (Seattle, WA). Review of *Anne of Avonlea*, by L.M. Montgomery. 31 October 1909, 8.

Sherwood, Margaret. "Lying Like Truth." *The Atlantic Monthly* (Boston, MA), December 1910, 806–17.

Shields, Carol. "Loving Lucy." Review of *The Selected Journals of L.M. Montgomery*, Volume 4: *1929–1935*, edited by Mary Rubio and Elizabeth Waterston. *The Globe and Mail* (Toronto, ON), 3 October 1998, D18.

Smith, Mary Ainslie. "New Tales for the Maud Squad." Review of *The Doctor's Sweetheart and Other Stories*, by L.M. Montgomery, selected by Catherine McLay. *Books in Canada* (Toronto, ON), May 1979, 22.

Somers, Emily Aoife. "A Diary's Promise, Extended." Review of *The Complete Journals of L.M. Montgomery: The PEI Years, 1901–1911*, edited by Mary Henley Rubio and Elizabeth Hillman Waterston. *Canadian Literature* 217 (Summer 2013): 183–84.

Sorfleet, John R. "Introduction: L.M. Montgomery: Canadian Authoress." *Canadian Children's Literature* 1, no. 3 (Autumn 1975): 4–7. Also in *L.M. Montgomery: An Assessment*, edited by John Robert Sorfleet, 4–7. Guelph: Canadian Children's Press, 1976.

Southron, Jane Spence. "After Green Gables." Review of *Anne of Ingleside*, by L.M. Montgomery. *The New York Times Book Review* (New York, NY), 30 July 1939, 7.

*The Springfield Republican* (Springfield, MA). "Books for Young People: A Variety of Entertaining Holiday Reading for Girls and Boys." 1 November 1908, 23.

————. "Prince Edward Island." Review of *Emily of New Moon*, by L.M. Montgomery. 9 December 1923, 16.

*The Springfield Sunday Union and Republican* (Springfield, MA). "On Lantern Hill." Review of *Jane of Lantern Hill*, by L.M. Montgomery. 12 September 1937, 7E.

————. "The Spinster Makes Good." Review of *The Blue Castle*, by L.M. Montgomery. 5 September 1926, 7F.

*The Springfield Union* (Springfield, MA). "Another 'Story Girl' Book." Review of *The Golden Road*, by L.M. Montgomery. 27 September 1913, 3.

Staines, David. "Diaries Reveal Shimmer, Shadows of Anne Author." Review of *The Selected Journals of L.M. Montgomery*, Volume 1: *1889–1910*, edited by Mary Rubio and Elizabeth Waterston. *The Gazette* (Montreal, QC), 11 January 1986, C2.

*The Sun* (New York, NY). Ad for *The Story Girl*, by L.M. Montgomery. 27 May 1911, 8.

————. "Published Today: From Page's List." 24 July 1915, 10.

S.W. Review of *The Road to Castaly and Later Poems*, by Alice Brown; *The Watchman and Other Poems*, by L.M. Montgomery. *Chicago Evening Post* (Chicago, IL), 13 July 1917, 8.

*The Sydney Mail* (Sydney, Australia). "Humour and Romance." Review of *A Tangled Web*, by L.M. Montgomery. 20 January 1932, 19.

*The Syracuse Herald* (Syracuse, NY). "New Books for Girls." 13 April 1920, 9.

Thatcher, Wendy. "Lucy Maud's Altar Ego." Review of *At the Altar: Matrimonial Tales*, by L.M. Montgomery, edited by Rea Wilmshurst. *The Gazette* (Montreal, QC), 16 April 1994, I4.

Thomas, Clara. "Completing the Journals of L.M. Montgomery." Review of *The Selected Journals of L.M. Montgomery*, Volume 5: *1935–1942*, edited by Mary Rubio and Elizabeth Waterston. *Books in Canada* (Toronto, ON), December 2004, 18.

————. "A Self-Portrait of Anne's Author." Review of *The Selected Journals of L.M. Montgomery*, Volume 4: *1929–1935*, edited by Mary Rubio and Elizabeth Waterston. *Books in Canada* (Toronto, ON), November–December 1998, 11–12.

Thompson, Hilary. "Role-Maker." Review of *The Selected Journals of L.M. Montgomery*, Volume 1: *1889–1910*, edited by Mary Rubio and Elizabeth Waterston. *Canadian Literature* 111 (Winter 1986): 205–6.

Tiessen, Hildi Froese, and Paul Gerard Tiessen. Introduction to Montgomery, *After Green Gables*, 3–52.

———. "Lucy Maud Montgomery's Ephraim Weber (1870–1956): 'A Slight Degree of Literary Recognition.'" *Journal of Mennonite Studies* 11 (1993): 43–54.

Tiessen, Paul, and Hildi Froese Tiessen. "Epistolary Performance: Writing Mr. Weber." In Gammel, *The Intimate Life of L.M. Montgomery*, 222–38.

*The Times–Dispatch* (Richmond, VA). Ad for *The Story Girl*, by L.M. Montgomery. 10 July 1911, 2.

———. "'The Blue Castle' Is Full of Tingles." Review of *The Blue Castle*, by L.M. Montgomery. 3 October 1926, 16.

*The Times Literary Supplement* (London, UK). Review of *Anne of Avonlea*, by L.M. Montgomery. 14 October 1909, 379.

*The Toronto Daily Star* (Toronto, ON). Ad for *Mistress Pat*, by L.M. Montgomery. 11 December 1935, 28.

———. Ads for *Rilla of Ingleside*, by L.M. Montgomery. 12 December 1921, 15; 16 December 1921, 10; 20 December 1921, 31; 21 December 1921, 22.

———. Ad for the Robert Simpson Company Limited. 16 May 1910, 9.

———. Ad for Timothy Eaton Company. 20 December 1934, 54.

———. "Creator of 'Anne' Addresses Women." 8 January 1936, 25.

Turner, Robert A. Review of *Anne of Avonlea*, by L.M. Montgomery. *The Des Moines News* (Des Moines, IA), 12 March 1910, 5.

van Herk, Aritha. "Blythe Spirits." Review of *The Blythes Are Quoted*, by L.M. Montgomery, edited by Benjamin Lefebvre. *The Globe and Mail* (Toronto, ON), 14 November 2009, F12.

Ward, Valerie. "Green Fables." Review of *The Doctor's Sweetheart and Other Stories*, by L.M. Montgomery, selected by Catherine McLay. *The Gazette* (Montreal, QC), 5 May 1979, 37.

*The Washington Post* (Washington, DC). Review of *Mistress Pat*, by L.M. Montgomery. 24 November 1935, B10.

Watters, R.E. "Letters from Avonlea." Review of *The Green Gables Letters from L.M. Montgomery to Ephraim Weber, 1905–1909*, edited by Wilfrid Eggleston. *Canadian Literature* 5 (Summer 1960): 87–88.

Weber, Ephraim. *Ephraim Weber's Letters Home, 1902–1955: Letters from Ephraim Weber to Leslie Staebler of Waterloo County*. Edited by Hildi

Froese Tiessen and Paul Gerard Tiessen. Waterloo, ON: MLR Editions Canada, 1996.

Whitaker, Muriel. "Literary Pen-Pals." Review of *My Dear Mr. M: Letters to G.B. MacMillan from L.M. Montgomery*, edited by Francis W.P. Bolger and Elizabeth R. Epperly. *Canadian Literature* 90 (Autumn 1981): 141–43.

———. "Women Alone." Review of *The Poetry of Lucy Maud Montgomery*, selected by John Ferns and Kevin McCabe; *Proper Deafinitions: Collected Theograms*, by Betsy Warland; *People You'd Trust Your Life To*, by Bronwen Wallace. *Canadian Literature* 132 (Spring 1992): 228–30.

Wiggins, Genevieve. *L.M. Montgomery*. New York: Twayne Publishers, 1992. Twayne's World Authors Series 834.

Williams, Sidney. Review of *Rainbow Valley*, by L.M. Montgomery. *The Boston Herald* (Boston, MA), 30 August 1919, 4.

Wilmshurst, Rea. Introduction to Montgomery, *Akin to Anne*, 6–12.

Wood, Joanne E. "The Cavendish Library." In McCabe, *The Lucy Maud Montgomery Album*, 471–72.

Woodcock, George. "Bittersweets for the Short Story Buffs." *Maclean's* (Toronto, ON), June 1974, 94.

Wyatt, Louise. "Disservice to Creator of Anne of Green Gables." Review of *The Road to Yesterday*, by L.M. Montgomery. *The London Free Press* (London, ON), 20 April 1974, 61.

York, Lorraine. "Dark Days." Review of *The Selected Journals of L.M. Montgomery*, Volume 4: *1929–1935*, edited by Mary Rubio and Elizabeth Waterston. *Canadian Children's Literature / Littérature canadienne pour la jeunesse* 99 (Fall 2000): 87–89.

———. "Darkness and Ecstasy." Review of *The Selected Journals of L.M. Montgomery*, Volume 2: *1910–1921*, edited by Mary Rubio and Elizabeth Waterston. *Canadian Children's Literature / Littérature canadienne pour la jeunesse* 55 (1989): 71–73.

Young, Gordon Ray. "Trials of a Publisher." *The Los Angeles Times* (Los Angeles, CA), 8 August 1915, Part 3, 27.

# Index

Index

- critical editions, 4, 5
- "de luxe" edition, 354
- endorsements, 12, 98, 103, 122, 156, 182, 215, 304, 332
- illustrations, 27
- origins, 42n19, 355–56, 387
- sales, 11, 12, 15, 16, 20, 21, 41n15, 156, 166
- screen adaptations, 37, 314n6, 334
- serialization, 240
- target audience, 9, 11, 12–13, 52, 53, 57, 58, 59, 64, 67, 76, 80, 89, 107, 152, 234, 354
*Anne of Ingleside* (Montgomery), 6, 38, 39, 340, 345–51, 352n2, 353; ads and notices, 345; cover art, 38; serialization, 38, 48n79; target audience, 345, 347
*Anne of the Island* (Montgomery), 8, 20–22, 23, 24, 26, 37, 155–70, 353, 358; ads and notices, 21–22; dedication, 21, 163, 167; target audience, 163
*Anne of Windy Poplars* (Montgomery), 37, 38, 39, 334–39, 378; ads and notices, 334; dedication, 335; target audience, 338
*Anne of Windy Willows* (Montgomery). See *Anne of Windy Poplars*
*Anne's House of Dreams* (Montgomery), 8, 24–25, 37, 38, 180–98, 215, 306n11, 348; ads and notices, 24–25; contract, 23; epigraph, 197, 199n24; frontispiece, 183, 188; target audience, 190, 191
*Antigonish Review, The*, 368–69
*Argus, The* (Melbourne, Australia), 271
Ashby, Adele, 360
Ashford, Daisy, 249, 252n8
*Athenaeum, The* (London, UK), 13, 20, 25
*Athens Banner–Herald* (Athens, GA), 340
*Atlanta Christian Index* (Atlanta, GA), 155
*Atlantic Advocate, The* (Fredericton, NB), 354, 355, 357, 379
*Atlantic Monthly, The* (Boston, MA/New York, NY), 85

*Atlantic Provinces Book Review, The*, 370, 372–73, 376, 379
*Atlantis: A Women's Studies Journal*, 366
*At the Altar: Matrimonial Tales* (Montgomery), 378, 380
*Auckland Star, The* (Auckland, New Zealand), 271–72, 305, 321, 340, 351
*Aunt Becky Began It* (Montgomery). See *A Tangled Web*
Austen, Jane, 26, 77, 83n13, 133, 138n27, 374, 375; *Pride and Prejudice*, 138n27
Austin, Alfred, 52, 68n6
*Australasian, The* (Melbourne, Australia), 272
Australia. See *The Argus*; *The Australasian*; *Australian Christian World*; *The Brisbane Courier*; *The Morning Bulletin*; *The Queenslander*; *The Register*; *The Sunday Times*; *Sydney Church Standard*; *The Sydney Mail*; *The Sydney Morning Herald*; *The Week*; *Western Mail*
*Australian Christian World* (Sydney, Australia), 297
Avery, Heather, 373

Baker, Helen Cody, 224
Baldwin, Stanley, 304
Barrie, J.M., 117–18, 127, 137n4; *Peter Pan*, 179n13
Barry, Wendy E., 5
Bédard, Rachel, 380
Beharriell, S. Ross, 356–57
Bell, Lisle, 335, 340–41, 346
Bliss, Michael, 372, 374, 375
*Blue Castle, The* (Montgomery), 31–33, 35, 269–84; ads and notices, 32; dedication, 33; serialization, 32; target audience, 32, 270, 276, 277–78, 279–80, 282
*Blythes Are Quoted, The* (Montgomery), 39, 48n81, 358, 359, 360, 384–86, 390n47
Bolger, Francis W.P., 365, 366, 376–77, 387n4
*Book News Monthly, The* (Philadelphia, PA), 59, 93, 144

440

# Index

# Index

Index